LINGUISTIC
ANALYSIS
OF
CHILDREN'S
SPEECH:

Readings

Edited by

Thomas M. Longhurst
Kansas State University

MSS Information Corporation
655 Madison Avenue, New York, N.Y. 10021

This is a custom-made book of readings prepared for the courses taught by the editor, as well as for related courses and for college and university libraries. For information about our program, please write to:

MSS INFORMATION CORPORATION
655 Madison Avenue
New York, New York 10021

MSS wishes to express its appreciation to the authors of the articles in the collection for their cooperation in making their work available in this format.

Library of Congress Cataloging in Publication Data

Longhurst, Thomas M   comp.
    Linguistic analysis of children's speech.

    A collection of articles previously published in
various journals.
    1. Children—Language—Addresses, essays, lectures.
2. Linguistic analysis (Linguistics)—Addresses, essays,
lectures. I. Title. [DNLM: 1. Language development
—Collected works. 2. Linguistics—Collected works.
3. Speech—In infancy and childhood—Collected works.
LB1139.L3   L854L   1974]
P136.L6   410   74-6104
ISBN 0-8422-5173-1
ISBN 0-8422-0404-0 (pbk.)

CONTENTS

PREFACE.

A child's speech is probably the most important single factor by which his or her development is assessed. For the child with disordered speech it is important that as accurate an assessment as possible be made. This assessment must be reliable and valid and should produce data that are representative of the child's everyday speech.

Speech pathologists, child developmentalists and educators concerned with children's linguistic development have traditionally relied heavily on standardized language tests. The reliability and validity of many of these tests have been seriously questioned. Specialists charged with improving the delayed or deviant speech of children express doubt about the relevance and usefulness of the results of many of these standardized language tests.

Linguists have developed procedures that have proven effective in describing language behavior. These procedures usually require that the linguist collect a sample, or corpus, of the informant's speech. This sample is then analyzed in systematic ways. The informant may be questioned further or additional data collected until the linguist can write a relatively complete description of the informant's behaviors.

This linguistic method is being applied to the disordered speech of children. The child is usually shown some pictures or toys that are designed to elicit speech. The examiner tape records the speech and prepares a written protocol which is then analyzed. Traditionally, relatively simple analysis methods such as mean length of response or type-token ratios have been computed. Recently, a number of authors have published more comprehensive analysis procedures.

This book presents some of the traditional analysis procedures as well as more recent procedures. Readings that relate to standardized language tests and methods of probing the child's competence and comprehension are not presented. These procedures can aid the assessment process but they are not the focus of this book.

We were unable to reprint the pioneering work of Mrs. Laura Lee. Her methods are available, however, in her book, *Developmental Sentence Analysis*, published by the Northwestern University Press, 1974.

SECTION I. Topography of Deviant Language

WHAT IS DEVIANT LANGUAGE?

Laurence B. Leonard

This paper presents a detailed description of deviant language, employing the transformational model. In addition to a review of existing work in the area, new information based on a comparison of data obtained from matched groups of normal and deviant language users is presented.

Most speech pathologists are able to describe in detail a language-handicapped child's ability in tasks ranging from rail walking to finishing incomplete sentences with appropriate grammatical forms. To be sure, such tasks often provide useful diagnostic information. But it is ironic that the speech pathologist is probably least proficient in describing the very behavior of the child that probably led to his presence at the speech clinic in the first place, namely, how he speaks. There may be a good reason for our lack of proficiency in describing a child's language; for many years, we had no clinical tool with which to describe in detail a child's language. In recent years, however, the search for more detailed measures has led into the field of linguistics at a time when Chomsky's (1957) transformational grammar was revolutionizing current linguistic thought. Although transformational grammar is based on a theoretical model, its specificity in describing language has been very appealing.

The transformational model of grammar proposes that, rather than memorizing every sentence he has been exposed to, a speaker uses a set of rules to understand and generate both sentences he has been exposed to and sentences he has never heard before. Each of the speaker's grammatical rules, according to this theoretical model, may be applied on one of three levels. Phrase-structure rules are applied at the first level. These rules permit the stringing together of parts of speech to form simple-active-declarative (kernel) sentences such as "The man play the violin." The second level consists of transformational rules which can act upon the kernel sentences to form more complex sentence types. For instance, the adjective transformation can be applied to the kernel sentences "The man play the violin" and "The man is dysarthric" to form the sentence "The dysarthric man play the violin." More precisely, the surface structure of the sentence (the actual form of the sentence

JOURNAL OF SPEECH AND HEARING DISORDERS, 1972, vol. 37, no. 4, pp. 427-446.

as we produce or hear it) "The dysarthric man play(s) the violin," was derived by applying the adjective transformation rule to the deep structure (an abstract representation dealing with the semantic interpretation of a sentence) kernel forms "The man play the violin" and "The man is dysarthric." The third level consists of morphological rules which permit inflections to be added to certain morphemes in the sentence. The sentence "The dysarthric man play the violin" becomes "The dysarthric man plays the violin" after application of the morphological rule for verb agreement.

The purpose of this paper is to present a detailed description of deviant language, employing the transformational model of grammar from a clinical perspective.

DEVIANT VERSUS NORMAL LANGUAGE

Several works have employed the transformational model in studying children's acquisition of syntax and morphology (Brown, Cazden, and Bellugi, 1968; McNeill, 1970; Menyuk, 1963, 1969). These endeavors have apparently uncovered developmental correlates to the Chomsky (1957) model. More recently, Lee and Canter (1971) have introduced a most useful measure of syntactic development in that it comes equipped with an abundance of empirical support (Koenigsknecht and Lee, 1971).[1] According to Lee and Canter (1971), their Developmental Sentence Scoring procedure represents "a developmental scale of syntax acquisition, showing the general order in which normal children achieve particular syntactic structures." While the Developmental Sentence Scoring data is useful in comparing the syntax of a child with the syntax of other children of his age group, Lee and Canter indicate that the procedure is probably not quite ready to be considered a "determining factor in recommending a child's enrollment in or dismissal from clinical teaching."

The syntactic structures analyzed by the Lee and Canter (1971) method are (1) indefinite pronouns or noun modifiers, (2) personal pronouns, (3) main verbs, (4) secondary verbs, (5) negatives, (6) conjunctions, (7) interrogative reversals, and (8) wh-questions. Not included in the analysis are such structures as adjectives, possessive markers, articles, and plurals. Within each syntactic classification employed, specific words or structures have been grouped into what is believed to be a general developmental order. Those words or structures developed at an early age earn fewer points; those developed later earn a greater number of points. Data collected on 200 children from ages two to six years, 11 months by Koenigsknecht and Lee (1971) suggest that, for the most part, the Lee and Canter (1971) ordering of structures in each syntactic category was quite accurate. In addition, the Developmental Sentence Scoring method shows good interclinician agreement (Lee and Canter, 1971; Koenigsknecht and Lee,

---

[1]Another measure of language development, the Length-Complexity Index developed by Shriner (1967) and presented in detail by Miner (1969), appears to be a potential measure for clinical use. At this point, however, no normative data have been acquired nor any comparisons made between the language of normal and deviant speakers using this measure.

1971) and good reliability over time (Koenigsknecht and Lee, 1971).

The children Lee and Canter (1971) studied were drawn from a general population. That those children they diagnosed as using deviant language should fall at the "younger" end of the developmental continuum is a subject of some controversy. After examining her data, Menyuk (1964) indicated that to term the speech of deviant language users as infantile is a misnomer. In the words of Menyuk:

> To say, for example, that a five-year-old child with infantile speech uses the grammar of a normal speaking child at age four or three or two is incorrect. His grammatical usage is not simply more infantile than normal for his age or delayed in time.

Lee (1966), herself, has also maintained that "children who may have been called 'language-delayed' are not merely following the natural pattern of development at a slower rate." Rather, Lee suggests that these children "are failing to make some of the linguistic generalizations upon which syntactic development depends."

It seems that to provide a useful clinical tool designed to assess a child's use of syntactic and morphological structures, the best approach would be to compare the language of deviant speakers with that of a matched group of normals. Such a comparison should include information regarding which syntactic and morphological structures serve to differentiate the two types of language users as well as which structures seem most related to the diagnostic label ascribed to the child.

The studies that have compared normal and deviant speakers on specific structures have been preliminary in nature. Lee (1966) compared the language of a normal three-year-old boy with that of a four-and-a-half-year-old boy diagnosed as using deviant language. Whether the two children discussed in the Lee paper differed greatly in their syntax or were less different but subject to differences in sampling procedures (see Bloom, 1967) is open to some question. The fact that only one of the two children was diagnosed as language-impaired, however, suggests that some differences in the language of the two children probably existed. The results indicated that the normal child used designative and predicative constructions from the two-word level ("There ducks"; "Really hungry") through the sentence level ("Here's a tractor"; "Now we're all through"), whereas the deviant child used no such utterances. Lee suggested that the absence of such constructions in the speech of the deviant language user at the two-word level may have prevented the child from using them in sentences. The lack of such sentences, in turn, may have prevented the child from transforming them into interrogatives and wh-questions (Lee, 1966).

Menyuk (1964) compared the language of a group of 10 normals, ages three to five years, 10 months, with the language of a matched group of 10 deviant language users, employing Chomsky's (1957) tripartite (phrase structure, transformational, and morphological) system. This system appears to adequately describe the adult system. Deviant forms are described in terms of whether they

11

represent a substitution, redundancy, or omission of the adult form at any of the three levels. For example, the utterance "Jeanette pretty" represents a verb-phrase omission at the phrase-structure level because the verb phrase is deleted from the kernel (phrase structure) sentence "Jeanette is pretty." The utterance "Herbie hopping" is an omission of the auxiliary (or contraction) at the trans-formational level, because the auxiliary is deleted from a structure derived from the auxiliary *be* transformation rule ("Herbie is hopping"). The utterance "Ricky ride the bike" is an omission of a verb form at the morphological level, for the morphological structure -*s* is deleted from the sentence "Ricky rides the bike."

After analyzing her data, Menyuk (1964) indicated that the normal and deviant groups differed in their use of many syntactic and morphological structures. Transformations were generally associated with the normal children whereas deviant forms, particularly omissions, were associated with the deviant speakers. Differences between normals and deviants were measured in terms of the number of children using each structure. Using this measure, the two groups of children significantly differed in their use of only one of 33 structures at the conventional 0.05 level of confidence. Instead, however, Menyuk treated any difference above the level of chance (0.50) between the two groups' use of a structure to indicate "real" differences. It is clear, however, that this cutoff point (0.50) was not intended to be nor should be used as a cutoff point in diagnosing children's language. If a child uses a particular deviant form that is known to be used by five out of 10 deviant speakers and three out of 10 normals, few clinicians would recommend therapeutic intervention, although the probability of such a finding is only 0.34.

Also employing Chomsky's (1957) model for analysis, Adams (1968) com-pared language samples of 15 deviant language users, ages four and a half years to five years, 11 months, with those of a matched group of 15 normal chil-dren. The deviant group did not differ significantly from the normal group in the total number of different structures produced at the phrase structure, trans-formational, or morphological levels. Such results, unfortunately, provide the clinician with little information. First, significant differences between groups in the use of specific structures may have been hidden. Second, even if the devi-ant group did differ significantly from the normal group in the total number of different structures used, the clinician still would have to determine which specific structures required clinical attention. Finally, Adams (1968) combined deviant structures with standard structures in her analysis of the total number of different structures each group produced. Out of 39 different transformations, for example, 16 represented deviant structures. The Adams finding that the deviant speakers used 31 different transformations while the normal used 35 is somewhat deceptive if, for example, we note that the deviants used all 16 of the deviant forms while the normals used only 12.

It is quite clear that the clinician responsible for assessing a child's language usage needs more information than has been provided thus far. Identifying a deviant language user does not appear to be the major problem; the people

12

responsible for referring these children to our clinics have performed this task adequately, on the whole. The clinician's major responsibility rests in determining which specific aspects of the child's language behavior make his language different from that of his peers, for it is these aspects that warrant clinical attention.

To determine more precisely which syntactic and morphological structures are used differently, we compared nine children diagnosed by their speech clinician as using "defective" language to nine children cleared by a speech clinician as using "normal" language. All the children attend kindergarten in Allegheny County, Pennsylvania. The mean chronological age of both groups was five years, three months. The children in the two groups were matched according to age, Peabody Picture Vocabulary Test score, and socioeconomic status. A 50-utterance language sample was obtained from each child in the following manner. After a brief conversation with the child, the examiner gave the instructions:

> I'd like you to tell me some stories. I'm going to show you some pictures and I'd like you to make up a story for each picture.

The Children's Apperception Test cards were then presented. To insure consistency in the method of obtaining the language sample, as well as to insure that each child emitted 50 utterances, five "directions" were given to each child for each of the 10 picture cards. After the first direction, each subsequent direction was given only when the child ended his utterance with a period of silence. If the child emitted a response such as "I don't know," a second direction was given. These directions are presented below. Segments of the script in parentheses were optional and were intended for occasional variation in order to preserve the sanity of both child and clinician.

> [(Now) (Here's one)] What do you think is happening in this picture? SECOND—Just tell me anything.

> [(Well) (Let's)] Look real hard all over the picture and tell me something else about it. SECOND—Tell me anything else.

> (Hey) What do you think was happening just before this picture was taken? SECOND—How do you think he/they got there?

> (Let's) Look at the picture again. (Why don't you) make up a story about what's going to happen next. SECOND—What do you think will happen in just a little while?

> If this were you, what do you think you'd say? SECOND—If this were you and this/these was/were your friend/friends, what would you say?

Only the first utterance in response to each direction was included in the analysis. Because five directions were given for each of the 10 picture cards, a sample of 50 utterances from each child was assured. Further, because utterance 12 from Child A, for example, was necessarily a response to the same direction and picture card as utterance 12 from Child B (because only the first utterance

13

in response to each direction was included), the obtained utterances were directly comparable between children.

The children's use of syntactic and morphological structures were analyzed according to the three levels (phrase structure, transformational, and morphological) of grammar as formulated by Chomsky (1957). Menyuk (1964) provides examples of some of these structures. In addition, the structures Lee and Canter (1971) analyzed were also analyzed in this study.

The percentage of intraexaminer agreement in the classification of these structures ranged from 93 to 100, with a mean of 98, while the percentage of agreement between the examiner and a clinician who analyzed the children's language from tape recordings of the sampling sessions ranged from 87 to 100, with a mean of 97. The reliability of the structures over time was computed by comparing data obtained in the first language samples with data obtained from these children one week later using the same sampling method. These correlations ranged from 0.29 to 0.96, with a mean of 0.70 when analyzed for the frequency with which a structure was used, and from 0.13 to 1.00, with a mean of 0.64 when analyzed for whether a structure was present or absent in the child's speech in each of the two language samples.[2] Apparently, temporal reliability varies considerably between structures.

The comparison between the normal and deviant sp'akers in the use of each syntactic and morphological structure was handled in two ways: in terms of the frequency with which each structure was used and in terms of the number of children using each structure. The results are presented in Table 1. While the use of each structure was tabulated, only the data for (1) those structures used by at least half of the normal or deviant speakers—that is, those structures "characteristic" of one or both groups—and (2) those structures revealing significant (0.05 level) differences between the two groups in the frequency of usage or the number of children using each structure are presented.

Clearly, then, the measure used to compare the normal and deviant language users is very important. We observed no significant differences between the normals and deviants in the use of any of the structures when the number of children using each structure was the comparative measure. When frequency of usage was the measure employed, however, we observed significant differences in the use of 14 structures.

Because of our somewhat limited sampling, it is quite possible that normal and deviant language users typically differ in their frequency of use of still other (perhaps less frequently occurring) structures. Morehead (in press) observed some of these less obvious differences when he matched a group of 15 normals and a group of 15 deviant language users according to mean number of morphemes per utterance. Such a method of matching probably minimized any differences between the two groups in the frequency of deviant forms such as noun-phrase omissions, verb-phrase omissions, article omissions, and other forms that result in fewer morphemes than the standard version. Morehead did,

---

[2] The percentage of intraexaminer and interexaminer agreement as well as the temporal reliability correlations for each of the structures are available from the author.

14

TABLE 1. Comparison between the normal and deviant language users in terms of the number of children using each structure and the frequency with which each structure was used. N = normal speakers; D = deviant speakers.

Structure	Number of Children Using Structures			Mean Frequency		Standard Deviation		
	N	D	p	N	D	N	D	p
Negation (He is *not* smiling.)	7	2	ns	2.44	0.67	1.59	1.66	0.05
Contraction (She's happy.)	9	8	ns	17.67	8.78	6.33	6.34	0.01
Auxiliary *be* (The lion *is* jump*ing* up.)	9	8	ns	22.00	7.78	6.48	5.83	0.001
Adjective (The *big* bear likes her.)	9	5	ns	6.78	1.44	4.21	1.59	0.01
Infinitival Complement (I want *to* sing.)	9	9	ns	14.56	5.89	6.88	6.47	0.05
Indefinite Pronoun (*It* was gone.)	9	8	ns	15.11	7.00	8.30	5.79	0.05
Personal Pronoun (The ghost saw *them*.)	9	9	ns	30.56	16.00	12.70	10.09	0.05
Main Verb (The plane *flies* funny.)	9	9	ns	51.00	22.89	7.25	11.01	0.001
Secondary Verb (He wants the boy *to sing*.)	9	8	ns	18.00	5.44	6.78	6.62	0.01
Conjunction* (I want it *but* I won't get it.)	9	6	ns	7.00	2.44	5.17	2.46	0.05
Verb-Phrase Omission (That funny.)	5	9	ns	1.00	11.78	1.32	8.60	0.01
Noun-Phrase Omission (Wanna go.)	3	9	ns	0.44	5.22	0.73	4.55	0.01
Article Omission (Ghost is gonna scare us.)	4	9	ns	0.78	3.22	0.97	2.39	0.05
Inversion Verb Number (There's the bears!)	8	5	ns	2.22	0.56	1.09	0.53	0.01

*Lee and Canter (1971) conjunction classification.

however, observe that the normal children still used many less frequently occurring transformations consistently and significantly more often than did the deviant group.

Normal and deviant speakers may also differ in their use of wh-questions. In our work, none of the directions presented to the child, (for example, "Make up a story about what's going to happen next") required a wh-question as part of the child's response. However, Menyuk (1969) noted a tendency for deviant speakers to use wh-questions of the deviant form Q + NP + VP ("Where hang it"). Clearly, more data in this area would be helpful. Another possibility, also not observed in our own work, is that the use of some structures may represent diagnostic "danger" signals, although they are used by only a small percentage of deviant speakers. Menyuk (1969) observed some such structures. These included "No ride feet" (I ride without using feet), "He'm put" (He's putting), and "Big the dog" (The dog is big). Menyuk noted that when a child used such utterances, he used them consistently. Although such structures may be used by a small percentage of the deviant-speaking population, they do appear to be very reliable entities in the language of those deviants who use them. The diagnostic significance of such utterances may be great. According to Menyuk (1969):

> These structures not only represent different hypotheses about language, but these hypotheses may be a deterrent to further grammatical development. They may not only lead to incorrect conclusions but may also be blind alleys which do not form the basis for further expansion and deepening of grammatical analysis.

Finally, Morehead and Ingram (1970) observed that even when certain deviant children use most of the same syntactic structures as normals, they differ from their normal peers in the mean number of lexical categories (noun$_{obj}$) used per syntactic (construction) type. That is, the deviant children did not use major linguistic categories in as many different syntactic contexts as did the normal children.

At this point, a discussion of the differences between the syntax and morphology of normal and deviant language users seems in order. That differences in syntactic and morphological functioning exist between the two groups of children is fairly obvious. However, care should be taken in describing the exact nature of these differences. With the possible exception of a few infrequently used structures used by one and not the other group, no qualitative differences between the normal and deviant speakers are apparent. For instance, by combining both samples obtained from each child in our work, every structure used by any or all of the normals was also used by at least two of the nine deviant children. Every structure used by any or all of the deviant speakers was used by at least three of the nine normal children. Therefore, any blanket statement that a particular structure is used by "normal" children and not by deviant language users (or vice versa) is quite inaccurate. Such a statement can be made somewhat more agreeable (to some) by stating that the use of certain structures is more characteristic of one group than the other. If we can agree that a structure is characteristic of a certain group when it is used by at least 50% of the children in that group, we can say from our data that question, possessive, and relative clause transformations are characteristic of the normals and not of the deviant speakers and that the noun-phrase and verb-form omissions are characteristic of the deviant group and not of the normal children. If one is interested in generalizing to all normals and deviants, however, even these statements may be invalid, for Menyuk (1964) found that at least 50% of her normal speakers used the deviant forms characterized by noun-phrase and verb-form omissions. It may be, then, that all of the transformations and restricted forms used with any regularity by either group are characteristic of both normal and deviant language users.

One might then turn to a comparison of the number of normal versus the number of deviant children using a particular structure, as Menyuk (1964) did. Even this measure, however, yielded differences between normals and deviants that are too close to the level of chance for a clinician to be confident in. In

16

our work, none of the normal-deviant comparisons using this measure reached significance at the 0.05 level, and only one out of 33 reached this level in Menyuk's (1964) work. Unless a large number of both normal and deviant-speaking children are sampled, this form of comparison does not appear to give the clinician enough to work with. For example, assume that we sample a five-year-old's language and find no use of the negation transformation. From Table 1, it can be seen that seven of the nine normals and only two of the nine deviant speakers used this form. Does the child's failure to use this transformation warrant clinical attention?

I propose that the differences in the use of each syntactic and morphological structure between normal and deviant speakers are probably best described in terms of frequency of usage. In addition to yielding many significant differences between normal and deviant speakers, frequency data provides useful clinical information. Assume that from a language sample it is observed that a five-year-old child uses the auxiliary *be* transformation 22.00 times on the average. It is probably valid to say that if the child used this transformation between 15.52 and 28.48 times ($\pm$ 1 standard deviation from the mean frequency of use of auxiliary *be* by the normals), his use of the auxiliary *be* transformation is characteristic of the normal speakers (see Table 1). On the other hand, if the child used this transformation between 1.95 and 13.61 times ($\pm$ 1 standard deviation from the mean frequency of use by the deviants), his use of the auxiliary *be* transformation is probably characteristic of the deviant language users. Clinical decisions can also be made when the standard deviations for the normal and deviant speakers yield overlapping frequencies. For example, in the use of the deviant form characterized by noun-phrase omissions, $\pm$ 1 standard deviation from the mean for the deviant language users represents use of noun-phrase omissions between 0.93 and 9.51 times, while for the normal language users $\pm$ 1 standard deviation from the mean equals between 0 and 1.23 noun-phrase omissions. If one wishes to avoid error, he may wish to treat only the child who omits noun phrases at least two times in the 50-sentence language sample.

The argument for examining syntactic and morphological performance in terms of the frequency with which a structure is used is made even stronger from the analysis of the structures used in the Developmental Sentence Scoring procedure. The differences in frequency between the normal and deviant language users were as evident in the use of the Lee and Canter (1971) structures as they were with the Menyuk (1964) structures. These differences were also not observed when the number of children using each structure was compared.

Providing that the language samples are obtained using specific procedures, it seems that the reliability of frequency of usage data over time is generally higher than for data measured according to whether or not the child used a given structure in each sample. Fifteen of the 23 structures studied in our work showed higher coefficients when frequency of usage was the measure. This finding suggests that a child is, in most cases, even more likely to use a structure in a second sample that he did not use in the first sample (or vice versa) than to show a disproportionate change from one sample to another in the frequency with which he used the structure.

The move towards implementing frequency of usage data requires an important change in the usual manner of obtaining language samples. If the difference between using the auxiliary *be* transformation 16 times or 12 times can mean the difference between "normal" or "deviant," it is mandatory that more specific and replicable procedures be employed.

Just as measures such as mean length of response have been occasionally dismissed as mere counting exercises (Tikofsky, 1968), the present support for a quantitative measure of grammatical functioning runs the same risk. But through such quantification, we feel that a new dimension may be added to the evaluation of children's grammar. Just as a t/k substitution may vary in its consistency and stuttering in its severity, so too might the adequacy or inadequacy in the use of a particular syntactic or morphological structure be a matter of degree. This is not to imply that a child's use of a particular structure is less frequent than normal, for example, because the child "occasionally" uses a deviant version of that structure in his speech. According to Muma (in press), the omission, redundancy, or substitution of a standard structure in a given sentence may be due to its "co-occurrence" with a particular structure in that sentence. This notion forms the framework of the "co-occurring and restricted structures procedure" (Muma, in press). An example of the speech of a child who omits verb inflections (verb-form omissions) "on occasion" is presented below.

"That man over there run fast."
"Jimmy eats like a pig."
"That clown makes funny faces."
"The monkey who fell jump back up."
"Mommy, a doggie walked home with me!"

The structures that co-occur with the verbs with omitted inflections appear to be embedded clauses ("over there"; "who fell") which are located between the verbs and the subjects they must agree with. Thus, a child may not be using a standard structure inconsistently, but rather may be using it consistently when it co-occurs with a particular grammatical structure. On the other hand, the child may never use the standard structure when it co-occurs with still some other structure.

CLINICAL VERSUS NONCLINICAL LANGUAGE DIFFERENCES

Once a clinician has isolated syntactic and morphological deviations which appear to be characteristic of deviant language users but not normal language users, his job of evaluating is by no means completed. He must have some evidence that the observed language behavior characteristic of deviants played some role in the child's being singled out as a child with a problem. This is a question of validity. For example, a child may rarely use adjectives and may frequently omit verb phrases. However, his infrequent use of adjective transformations such as "The green door opened" may not have been noticed by a clinician and thus may have played no role in his diagnosis, whereas the child's frequent omissions of verb phrases (for example, "Doggie sick") may have prompted a clinician (as well as those who referred him to the clinician) to suspect trouble.

In order to gain some possible answers to this question of validity, we borrowed the services of three speech pathologists with experience in the diagnosis and treatment of language disorders. The first divided protocols of the normal and deviant language users (having access only to the children's age) into those showing "deviant" syntactic and morphological usage, if any, and those showing "normal" syntactic and morphological usage, if any.

The speech pathologist placed all nine of the deviant language users into the "deviant" category and all nine of the normal language users into the "normal" category. This categorization suggested that whatever behaviors the children demonstrated which led to their original diagnosis were also displayed in the language samples we obtained. The other two speech pathologists ranked the protocols according to syntactic and morphological performance. It seemed that a rough estimate of the validity of each syntactic and morphological structure could be provided by examining the relationship between the frequency with which children use the structure and the speech pathologists' rankings of the children's syntactic and morphological performance. These correlations appear in Table 2. Only those structures used differently by the normal and deviant speakers are presented. Table 2 shows that frequent use of some structures may be quite characteristic of one group (deviant or normal) and not the other, yet may not be related to judgments regarding relative syntactic and morphological performance.

TABLE 2. Correlations between the frequency with which a structure is used by the children and the speech pathologist's ranking of the children according to syntactic and morphological performance.

| | Speech Pathologist | |
Structure	I	II
Negation	0.62	0.51
Contraction	0.59	0.61
Auxiliary be	0.69	0.71
Adjective	0.54	0.49
Personal Pronoun	0.70	0.43
Main Verb	0.88	0.87
Conjunction*	0.70	0.66
Verb-Phrase Omission	−0.82	−0.87
Noun-Phrase Omission	−0.79	−0.86
Article Omission	−0.45	−0.46

*Lee and Canter (1971) conjunction classification.

From the preceding discussion, it is apparent that a syntactic or morpho-logical structure requiring clinical attention should meet several criteria. One of these is that the structure should be a dependable member of the child's linguistic repertoire. A reasonable estimate of this dependability is the reliability of the structure over time. A high temporal reliability correlation, then, should be required. Another criterion is that the structure should be used differently by deviant and normal language users. The use of that structure should preferably be characteristic of one group (normal or deviant) and not the other. Last, the frequency with which the child uses the structure should be related to judgments about the child's relative syntactic and morpho-logical performance. Two structures best meet these criteria: verb-phrase omissions and noun-phrase omissions.[3] These two structures yielded temporal reliability coefficients of 0.94 and 0.72, respectively. Both types of omissions were used by all of the deviant language users (although noun-phrase omissions were used by only 90% of Menyuk's [1964] deviant language users). Both structures were used significantly more frequently by the deviant speakers than by the normals. In addition, an analysis of data received from Menyuk revealed that both verb-phrase and noun-phrase omissions were used significantly more frequently by her (1964) deviants than by her normals. Finally, the more frequently a child used these two types of omissions, the lower he was ranked in syntactic and morphological performance. The correlations between verb-phrase-omission frequency and the two speech pathologists' rankings were −0.82 and −0.87; for the frequency of noun-phrase omissions, these correlations were −0.79 and −0.86. Clearly, the speech clinician should closely examine a child's use of these two deviant structures.

DIFFERENT VERSUS DELAYED LANGUAGE

Many clinicians, particularly those working in the schools, have such large case loads that their services are unavailable, either temporarily or permanently, to many children requiring them. Decisions, therefore, must be made concerning whether or not to enroll a child in therapy. One of the factors that should enter into this decision is whether or not the child is likely to develop more appropriate language without clinical attention, albeit at a slow rate. That is, the clinician must determine whether or not the child's language is delayed.

Preliminary studies have suggested that the sooner the term *delayed language* ceases to be a catchall label for deviant language, the better. Such a term is probably inappropriate in most cases because (1) deviant language users use more standard English transformations than do younger normal children (Menyuk, 1964) and (2) after deviant language users reach a certain stage of syntactic and morphological development during early years of life, they often

---

[3] One of the Lee and Canter (1971) structures, main verbs, also met these criteria. Because a large number of verb-phrase omissions leads to a smaller number of main-verb occurrences, the evaluation of one structure's use adequately predicts the use of the other.

remain at this stage with little change for some time (Menyuk, 1964). It appears, then, that these children's language may plateau. The term *language delay* may be inappropriate because it implies a "stretching out in time of the normal sequence of development" (Menyuk, 1972).

The first indication to me that deviant language users were not necessarily "slower" than normals occurred when I compared the Pennsylvania normal and deviant speakers on the mean developmental score for each of the Lee and Canter (1971) structures. Koenigsknecht and Lee (1971) observed that the older the children, the higher the mean developmental score for most of the structures used. Unlike children differing merely in age, however, the Pennsylvania normal and deviant speakers did not differ significantly in their mean developmental scores for any of the structures. Although the normals used most of the Lee and Canter (1971) structures more frequently than did the deviant speakers, when a deviant speaker used a structure its weighted score was no lower than that of normals. Any differences in the total Developmental Sentence Score between these normal and deviant children, then, would be due solely to the frequency with which point-earning structures were used.

To more accurately determine whether deviant language users were speaking like younger children, we obtained language samples, using the previously described sampling method, from nine children ranging in age from three years, four months to four years, four months. A speech clinician cleared the children as demonstrating "normal" syntax and morphology. These children also resided in Allegheny County, Pennsylvania, and were matched with the deviant children according to socioeconomic status and IQ as measured by the Peabody Picture Vocabulary Test. A comparison between the five-year-old deviant speakers and the younger normal children on the mean developmental score for each structure revealed that the deviant speakers, on the average, used significantly (0.05 level) later-developing indefinite pronouns and main verbs. The mean developmental scores for indefinite pronouns were 2.19 and 1.45 for the deviant speakers and younger normals, respectively. For main verbs, these mean scores were 2.41 and 2.01. Deviant speakers did not differ from normal children of the same age on the mean developmental score for any of the Lee and Canter (1971) structures. At least for some structures, Menyuk's (1964) contention that deviant language users are not speaking like younger children appears to be quite accurate.

Although the younger normals used earlier-developing forms when using the Lee and Canter (1971) structures, the frequency with which they used these structures did not differ significantly (0.05 level) from that of the five-year-old Pennsylvania normals, except on secondary verbs. Secondary verbs generally represent transformations (for example, infinitival complements), however, and this finding should not be surprising. As will be seen below, the frequency with which a child uses the Lee and Canter (1971) structures may prove valuable in assessing whether the child requires therapy.

It appears that many deviant speakers (1) use indefinite pronouns, personal pronouns, main verbs, and secondary verbs with a lower frequency than their

21

normal peers, (2) use as many later-developing forms of these structures as their peers, (3) use negation, contraction, auxiliary *be,* and adjective transformations less frequently than their peers, and (4) more often use deviant forms characterized by verb-phrase omissions, noun-phrase omissions, and article omissions. This pattern may hold true for any deviant speaker using utterances more than two words in length. Because the language behavior of deviant language users does not seem to change much with age, immediate therapy for these children is imperative. Menyuk's (1969) observation that utterances of deviant speakers revealed no significant change in grammatical complexity when utterances produced at age six were compared to those produced at age three, provides a warning against postponing therapy for such children. Because cross-sectional designs have been chiefly employed when studying the nature of deviant language, however, we cannot be certain that all deviant children's language shows a plateau. Morehead's (in press) work provides a good example. After matching deviant and normal language users according to mean number of morphemes per utterance, Morehead observed that the deviant child was up to three and a half years older than his matched normal. What can not be determined from this study is whether some or all of the deviant children reached a certain grammatical level at the normal age but remained at this level for a long period of time, as Menyuk (1964) suggested, or whether some or all of them merely took longer to reach the level in the first place. It is quite possible that many children who acquire certain structures at a later age also use these or other structures in a deviant manner. Mentally retarded children who do, in fact, begin using language at a later age (due, presumably, to their intellectual deficit) were found by Newfield and Schlanger (1968) to show grammatical errors (morphological errors of plural nouns, possessives, and third person singular verbs) that could not be attributed merely to intellectual maturity. Even when the retarded children's performances were mathematically adjusted for "slowness," differences were still apparent between the retarded children's language and the language of normal children.

It is, of course, possible that some children demonstrate "delayed language" in some pure form. The pattern that these children display would probably vary, depending upon how slowly a particular child is developing. A five-year-old child who is approximately two years behind in language should reveal a pattern quite similar to that of three-year-old normals. Transformations such as auxiliary *be,* questions, and infinitival complements (as well as secondary verbs which usually represent transformations) would be used less frequently (as noted in our work and also by Brannon [1963]). Indefinite pronouns, personal pronouns, and main verbs would be used as frequently as by normals; however, the mean developmental scores for these structures would reveal fewer later-developing forms for these structures (Koenigsknecht and Lee, 1971). Third, verb form substitutions ("She throwed the ball"), preposition omissions ("I walk school"), noun-phrase redundancies ("I saw him the boy"), as well as article omissions would be the deviant structures most likely to be used (Menyuk, 1963). There is little reason to believe that such a child won't develop normal language without clinical intervention.

EARLY IDENTIFICATION OF DEVIANT LANGUAGE

It is quite possible that the Developmental Sentence Scoring method of Lee and Canter (1971) will provide the most effective means of distinguishing between deviant language users requiring treatment and "slow" language developers who may not require clinical attention. If indefinite pronouns, personal pronouns, and main verbs are used less frequently while the mean developmental score for each of these structures appears normal, the child may be a deviant speaker. If, on the other hand, a child uses these three structures with adequate frequency but reveals lower than normal mean developmental scores for these structures, a child may "catch up" in that he closely resembles a normal three-year-old.

The real problem arises when a child rarely, if ever, uses even kernel (phrase structure level) sentences. Certainly if the structures in a child's restricted utterances represent later developing forms such as "Several there" or "Might come home," we have reason to suspect that his restricted utterances are part of a deviant linguistic system. Such children probably make up a small percentage of the deviant speaking population, however. It is the future linguistic behavior of children who use restricted utterances made up of early-developing structures that proves difficult to predict. If such a child is three or older, it is not worth the risk of waiting to see whether his language develops further, for the social and educational developments in his near future will demand a more sophisticated linguistic system. And if the child is not yet three years of age? Many of us may not treat such a child because he may be a "late developer." A few of us may recommend some sort of language intervention, but all of us are only guessing.

It may yet be possible to accurately determine at the presentence level whether or not a child will acquire standard syntactic or morphological usage, regardless of his age. I propose that such a way may be through an analysis of a child's two-word utterances. By the age of 18 to 24 months, most children are producing many two-word utterances. Recent work by Bloom (1970, 1971), taking semantic intent of utterances based on referential and situational clues into account, has indicated that the two-word utterances occurring most often in different situations with different words (with the possible exception of utterances with initial /ə/) were "those which, in the adult model, express the basic grammatical relations: subject-object, subject-verb, and verb-object strings."[4] Similarly, McNeill (1966) observed young normals using many sub-

---

[4]In the style of Bever (1970), we could say that children's utterances must include any two of the semantic elements agent, action, and object. An analysis of the normal two-word utterances reported in Braine (1963), Miller and Ervin (1964), and Brown and Fraser (1964), however, reveals still other subject-predicate constructions ("That pretty"; "There dollie") that suggest the need for additional semantic elements in describing children's language. Such additional elements may be provided by case grammar, a system which describes a set of

ject-object and verb-object strings. Thus, children "appear to learn the expressions 'throw block' or 'Baby (subject) block (object)' before the expressions 'big block,' 'red block,' or 'blocks'" (Bloom, 1971).

What may be an important difference between the two-word utterances of the younger normal child (as well as of the "slow developer" who may eventually develop standard language usage) and those of the deviant language user is the frequency of subject-verb utterances such as "Shoe fall." While these two-word utterances appear fairly often in the speech of young normals (Menyuk, 1969; Bloom, 1970), they do not appear to be reliable entities in the speech of deviant language users. We do, of course, have some reason to believe this. A comparison of the percentage of two-word utterances representing subject-verb relationships used by the five-year-old deviant speakers and three-year-old normal speakers in our work revealed percentages of 3 and 80, respectively. (The data are presented in percentages rather than frequencies because data will be presented that were obtained using different sampling methods. In all cases, however, the group that used a structure a higher percentage of times also used it more frequently.) These data may not be representative, however, for two reasons. First, normal three-year-olds are in most cases using structures that approximate the adult grammar. The few two-word utterances that are used by these children may not necessarily reflect the same form of the two-word utterances used by one-and-one-half to two-year-old children. Second, the deviant language users were using some structures at the phrase-structure and transformational levels and therefore may not use the same form of two-word utterances that a deviant speaker who only uses two-word utterances might use. To determine the percentage of subject-verb utterances used by normals and deviants when the above conditions have been met, I compared the percentage of two-word utterances representing subject-verb relationships of two two-year-old normal children who used numerous two-word utterances with that of a six-year-old with deviant language restricted almost totally to two-word utterances. The samples for all of the children were obtained in a play situation where both a speech clinician and the child's mother were present, though not necessarily involved in the child's activities. Because there were some differences in the sampling method, however, the obtained results must be regarded as preliminary. For both of the two-year-old normals, subject-verb utterances represented 23% of the two-word utterances used. The deviant language user's subject-verb utterances represented only 4% of his two-word utterances.

Another important difference between younger normal (as well as slow developers) and deviant language users may be the regularity with which each group uses single-word verb utterances ("Eat"; "Sleeping") and two-word verb + particle utterances ("Sitting down"; "Fall down"). A comparison of the

---

universal, presumably innate, concepts which identify certain types of judgments human beings are capable of making about the events that are going on around them (Fillmore, 1968). Case grammar should prove useful in that it apparently provides adequate descriptions of child language (compare Ingram, 1971) and seems to account for the pivot-open constructions ("All gone egg") reported by Braine (1963), as well as the topic-comment constructions (for example, "All broken wheels") noted by Gruber (1967).

total percentage of these utterances (verb and verb + particle combined) revealed that they made up 22% of the five-year-old deviant speakers' one- and two-word utterances (combined) and 0% of the three-year-old normals' combined one- and two-word utterances. The percentage of the combined one- and two-word verb utterances of the two two-year-old normal children whose language was sampled in the play situation represented 6% (6% and 6% for each child, respectively) of their total combined one- and two-word utterances. These verb utterances made up 16% of the combined one- and two-word utterances of the six-year-old deviant speaker sampled in the play situation.

The possible diagnostic significance of these findings runs as follows. Deviants tend to differ from their normal peers on the basis of the frequency with which they use certain deviant forms and transformations—not on the number of different deviant forms and transformations used and not on the developmental level of the structure used. We may therefore guess (and at this point it is only a guess) that two-word utterances representing subject-object, subject-verb, and verb-object strings are necessary in order to develop adult forms (compare Menyuk, 1971), whereas two-word noun-phrase utterances (used by both normals and deviants fairly frequently) and one- and two-word verb utterances expand into adult (noun phrase plus verb phrase) forms less readily. Therefore, as the child develops, the frequency of subject-object, subject-verb, and verb-object utterances decreases with a corresponding increase in adult forms. Because the deviants used far fewer subject-verb utterances, fewer adult forms could develop. I am not implying that a two-word subject-verb utterance is itself literally expanded and that if an adult sentence such as "The boy runs" wasn't first used as "Boy runs" it could never be used in the adult manner. Rather, the more practice a child has in using such two-word utterances as subject-verb, the more routinely (and thus the more frequently) he will be able to use adult sentences that include a subject and verb. The high frequency of verb phrase omissions observed in the speech of deviants in both the Menyuk (1964) study and the present work may possibly be a reflection of the deviant child's lack of proficiency in combining verbs with subjects.

The relatively high frequency of verb and verb + particle utterances used by the deviant language users may, unfortunately, give the deviant child opportunity to use verbs independently of nouns and to treat verbs in utterances such as "Sitting" and "Eating lunch" as complete verb phrases. In the first case, utterances such as "Eat" or "Move truck" require no morphological structure, because the absence of a subject precludes the necessity of verb agreement and therefore the more frequently a child uses such utterances, the more likely he will omit morphological structures (for example, "Mommy move truck") when he begins to combine noun phrases and verb phrases more frequently. From an analysis of data provided by Menyuk, it appears that the deviants used in Menyuk's (1964) study omitted such verb forms at the sentence level significantly more frequently than the normals employed. This difference was not observed in the present study. In the second case, verbs such as "Sitting" and "Eating lunch" do not require an auxiliary verb, and therefore frequent use of such utterances will give the child little practice in combining auxiliaries with such verbs, making it less likely that he will add auxiliaries when he begins combining noun phrases with verb phrases. That is, the child may use utterances such as "Mommy sitting" rather than utterances such as "Mommy is sitting." The finding that deviant language users omitted the auxiliary *be* significantly more frequently than normals in Menyuk's (1964) work as well as our work is consistent with this viewpoint. Menyuk's (1969) observation that deviant children tend to omit modals also might comply with this notion. It is possible that if a child frequently uses utterances such as "Swing high" for "I can swing high," he will be more likely to use sentences such as "I swing high" when he begins combining noun phrases and verb phrases more frequently. Clearly, our profession needs to obtain more information regarding normal and deviant two-word utterances.

LIMITATIONS IN THE CLINICAL APPLICATION OF TRANSFORMATIONAL GRAMMAR

Since the advent of transformational grammar, we have acquired considerable insight into what a deviant speaker does to earn the label "language-handicapped." A fact perhaps easily overlooked, however, is that Chomsky's (1957) transformational grammar is based on a theoretical model. That correlates to this model have been frequently noted in the syntactic and morphological behavior of children is fortunate for those interested in describing children's deviant and normal language usage. However, a review of these data indicates that the transformational system should not necessarily be accepted as a total package in the clinical assessment of children's grammar. Many of the theoretically more complex structures that require the application of transformational rules (for example, infinitival complements) are used by as many deviant language users as normals. Some of these supposedly more complex structures (contractions) are used at an earlier age than their theoretically simpler forms which do not require additional rules, and one of the structures that theoretically represents a deviant form (inversion of verb number) is used more by normals who generally adhere most to the adult grammatical system. Even when viewed in terms of frequency of usage, some of the theoretically more complex structures such as conjunctions were used no more often by the normal speakers. It seems, then, that the clinical value of transformational grammar is that it informs us as to which may be the most important aspects of language in assessing differences between normal and deviant language users. From here, it is our role to determine through observation and analysis which of these aspects actually are clinically significant. I hope that this paper will make this task somewhat easier.

ACKNOWLEDGMENT

The author is grateful to Ruth Levine for her valuable assistance during the study. Appreciation is also expressed to Jean Buffardi, Donald Egolf, Audrey Holland, Karen Kaslon,

Barbara Kozbelt, Jeanette Leonard, Charles Perfetti, Herbert Rubin, Beverly Seitz, Michael Seitz, and George Shames for their aid during various phases of the author's work. Thanks also to Roy Koenigsknecht, Laura Lee, Paula Menyuk, Donald Morehead, and John Muma for providing the author with the answers, unpublished papers, and raw data requested of them. Requests for reprints should be addressed to the author at 1117 C. L., University of Pittsburgh, Audiology/Speech Pathology, Pittsburgh, Pennsylvania 15224.

REFERENCES

ADAMS, S. M. D., A descriptive linguistic investigation of language problems in preschool children. Doctoral dissertation, Southern Ill. Univ. (1968).

BEVER, T. G., The cognitive basis for linguistic structures. In J. H. Hayes (Ed.), *Cognition and the Development of Language*. New York: Wiley (1970).

BLOOM, L., A comment on Lee's "developmental sentence types: a method for comparing normal and deviant syntactic development." *J. Speech Hearing Dis.*, 32, 293-296 (1967).

BLOOM, L., *Language Development: Form and Function in Emerging Grammar*. Cambridge, Mass.: MIT Press (1970).

BLOOM, L., Why not pivot grammar? *J. Speech Hearing Dis.*, 36, 40-50 (1971).

BRAINE, M. D. S., The ontogeny of English phrase structure: The first phase. *Language*, 39, 1-13 (1963).

BRANNON, J. B., A comparison of syntactic structures in the speech of three- and four-year old children. *Lang. Speech*, 11, 171-181 (1968).

BROWN, R., CAZDEN, C. B., and BELLUGI, U., The child's grammar from I to III. Paper presented at Minnesota Symposium on Child Psychology, Minneapolis (1968).

BROWN, R., and FRASER, C., The acquisition of syntax. In U. Bellugi and R. Brown (Eds.), *The Acquisition of Language*. Child Development Monogr. 29. Chicago: Chicago Press (1964).

CHOMSKY, N., *Syntactic Structures*. The Hague, Netherlands: Mouton (1957).

FILLMORE, C. J., The case for case. In E. Bach and R. T. Harms (Eds.), *Universals in Linguistic Theory*. New York: Holt, Rinehart, and Winston (1968).

GRUBER, J. S., Topicalization in child language. *Foundat. Lang.*, 3, 37-65 (1967).

INGRAM, D., Transitivity in child language. *Language*, 47, 888-910 (1971).

KOENIGSKNECHT, R. A., and LEE, L. L., Validity and reliability of developmental sentence scoring: A method for measuring syntactic development in children's spontaneous speech. Paper presented at the Annual Convention of the American Speech and Hearing Association, Chicago (1971).

LEE, L. L., Developmental sentence types: A method for comparing normal and deviant syntactic development. *J. Speech Hearing Dis.*, 31, 311-330 (1966).

LEE, L. L., and CANTER, S. M., Developmental sentence scoring: A clinical procedure for estimating syntactic development in children's spontaneous speech. *J. Speech Hearing Dis.*, 36, 315-340 (1971).

MCNEILL, D., Developmental psycholinguistics. In F. Smith and G. Miller (Eds.), *The Genesis of Language*. Cambridge, Mass.: MIT Press (1966).

MCNEILL, D., *The Acquisition of Language: The Study of Developmental Psycholinguistics*. New York: Harper and Row (1970).

MENYUK, P., Syntactic structures in the language of children. *Child Develpm.*, 34, 407-422 (1963).

MENYUK, P., Comparison of grammar of children with functionally deviant and normal speech. *J. Speech Hearing Res.*, 7, 109-121 (1964).

MENYUK, P., *Sentences Children Use*. Cambridge, Mass.: MIT Press (1969).

MENYUK, P., *The Development of Speech*. New York: Bobbs-Merrill (1972).

MILLER, W., and ERVIN, S., The development of grammar in child language. In U. Bellugi and R. Brown (Eds.), *The Acquisition of Language*. Child Development Monogr. 29. Chicago: Chicago Press (1964).

MINER, L. E., Scoring procedures for the length complexity index: A preliminary report. *J. Comm. Dis.*, 2, 224-240 (1969).

MOREHEAD, D. M., Early grammatical and semantic relations: Some implications for a general representational deficit in linguistically deviant children. *J. Speech Hearing Res.* (in press).

MOREHEAD, D., and INGRAM, D., The development of base syntax in normal and linguistically deviant children. In *Papers and Reports on Child Language Development*. Stanford, Calif.: Stanford University, Committee on Linguistics (1970).

MUMA, J., Language assessment: The co-occurrence and restricted structures procedure. *J. psycholing. Res.* (in press).

NEWFIELD, M. U., and SCHLANGER, B. B., The acquisition of English morphology by normal and educable mentally retarded children. *J. Speech Hearing Res.*, 11, 693-706 (1968).

SHRINER, T. H., A comparison of selected measures with psychological scale values of language development. *J. Speech Hearing Res.*, 10, 828-835 (1967).

TIKOFSKY, R. S., Discussion of Menyuk's "theories of language acquisition and practices in therapy." *Asha*, 10, 201-202 (1968).

THE DEVELOPMENT OF BASE SYNTAX IN NORMAL AND LINGUISTICALLY DEVIANT CHILDREN

DONALD M. MOREHEAD *and* DAVID INGRAM

Language samples of 15 young normal children actively engaged in learning base syntax were compared with samples of 15 linguistically deviant children of a comparable linguistic level. Mean number of morphemes per utterance was used to determine linguistic level. The two groups were matched according to five linguistic levels previously established and grammars were written for the language sample of each child. Five aspects of syntactic development were chosen as the basis of comparison between the two groups: phrase structure rules, transformations, construction (or sentence) types, inflectional morphology, and minor lexical categories. While few significant differences were found for the more general aspects of syntax, such as phrase structure rules, frequently occurring transformations, inflectional morphology, and the development of minor lexical categories, significant differences were found for the less general aspects of syntax. For example, significant differences were found between the two groups for infrequently occurring transformations and the number of major syntactic categories per construction type. In addition, the deviant group also showed a marked delay in the onset and acquisition time for learning base syntax. These results are discussed according to transformational and cognitive developmental theory.

Recent evidence suggests that early stages in first language acquisition are difficult to impede, save extensive brain dysfunction. Even with serious brain dysfunction, the prognosis for acquiring a base linguistic system is good due to the plasticity of the developing brain (Lenneberg, 1967). Despite this apparent strong biological component for language development, some children (including those without any detectable brain dysfunction) experience extreme difficulty in acquiring language. Children with language learning deficits are generally felt to demonstrate a linguistic system which is, in certain significant aspects, quite different from that of the normal child. Recently this "qualitative" difference has become the central focus for studying linguistically deviant children (Menyuk, 1964; Lee, 1966).

Menyuk's (1964) early work represents the first systematic attempt to compare normal and deviant children using descriptive techniques based on Chomsky's early transformational grammar. She matched both groups according to the criteria of age, IQ, and socioeconomic level and found that the utterances sampled from linguistically deviant children were qualitatively different from those of normal children. The deviant group used fewer transformations and

JOURNAL OF SPEECH AND HEARING RESEARCH, Sept. 1973, vol. 16, no. 3, pp. 330-352.

produced more restricted or ungrammatical forms than did the normal group. More forms were also omitted by the deviant group in constructions representing the phrase structure, transformational, and morphological levels of the grammar. Since few statistically significant differences were found, these results were projected to indicate possible trends of differences between normal and deviant children. Menyuk (1964) did include a comparison between a normal two-year-old child and a deviant three-year-old child. The dissimilarities were again found to be more predominant than the similarities. Unfortunately, only two subjects were compared and they were not matched on any specific criteria.

Lee (1966) has designed four levels of developmental sentence types for comparing syntactic progress in normal and deviant children. In constructing the sentence types which postulate different linguistic levels, she followed closely the review of early work in syntactic development by McNeill (1966). As a pilot test of the utility of the sentence types and lingustic levels, a language sample of a normal three year old was compared with that of a deviant four and one-half year old. The normal child's utterances more closely approximated the sentence types at all four levels than did the utterances of the deviant child. The deviant child also omitted constructions that were not omitted by the normal child. From these findings, Lee concluded that there were qualitative differences between the two children.

The research involving rule-based behavior indicates that all level or stage changes appear to be qualitative (Piaget, 1970; Kohlberg, 1968). Therefore, unless subjects are matched according to criteria which reflect a specific level or stage of development, qualitative differences can be predicted on the basis that each level or stage of development is radically different from the preceding or following stage of development. Moreover, recent work in language acquisition suggests that finding qualitative differences may not be unique to deviant and normal subjects but may reflect linguistic level differences indicating individual differences in cognitive function and linguistic experience (Bloom, 1970; Brown, Cazden, and Bellugi, 1968).

During the past decade, research on language acquisition has focused primarily on the development of syntax. It appears that the most active period for learning base syntax is between 18 months and four years and that this period reflects distinct levels of linguistic development (McNeill, 1970; Brown, 1973). Thus, it is of considerable heuristic value to compare linguistically deviant children with normal children actively engaged in acquiring base syntax at a similar level of linguistic development.

In addition, recent methods for writing children's grammars vary considerably from the early notions of "pivot" grammars which do not include the important distinction between deep (semantic) and surface (phonetic) structure (Bloom, 1970; Brown, 1973). Morover, if deep and surface structure relations are to be adequately described, it is necessary to collect contextual information for each utterance in a language sample. For example, noun + noun constructions, such as *Daddy bike*, may require two or more deep or semantic interpretations to separate the possessive form from such forms as the subject-object. Grammar writing for young children now includes analysis of both aspects of grammatical relations (Bloom, 1970; Brown, 1973).

This study compared language samples that included contextual information of young normal children (18-36 months of age) actively engaged in learning syntax with those of deviant children of a comparable level of linguistic development.

METHOD

Subjects. The subjects were 15 normal and 15 linguistically deviant children, selected to represent as nearly as possible the five linguistic levels previously determined by Brown (1973), (Table 1). Mean morpheme per utterance

TABLE 1. Description of normal and deviant language-development groups in terms of mean number of morphemes per utterance (MM/U), mean sample size (number of relational utterances), and mean age (months). For comparison, the five levels of linguistic development defined by Brown (see Footnote 1) are presented. The ranges on which the mean for each group was based are given immediately below the MM/U in parentheses.

Linguistic Level	Brown MM/U	Normal MM/U	Sample Size	Age	Deviant MM/U	Sample Size	Age
I	2.00 (1.75-2.25)	2.23 (2.11-2.26)	76.7	20.0	2.33 (2.10-2.43)	79.7	62.3
II	2.50 (2.26-2.75)	2.72 (2.51-2.66)	100.7	21.0	2.83 (2.69-2.98)	155.3	71.3
III	3.13 (2.76-3.50)	3.70 (3.41-3.92)	223.3	33.0	3.80 (3.31-4.05)	161.0	70.0
IV	3.75 (3.51-4.00)	4.67 (4.62-4.86)	242.7	34.3	4.53 (4.33-4.73)	200.0	88.0
V	4.63 (4.01-5.25)	5.61 (5.36-5.88)	234.0	33.7	5.83 (5.21-6.50)	147.7	104.6

was used as the criterion for establishing linguistic level and, thus, for matching the two groups. This measure appears to be a more reliable indicator of linguistic development than is chronological age up to three years of age (Menyuk, 1969; Bloom, 1970; Brown, 1973). The normal group, representing the age when children acquire a base syntactic system, was selected from the population of the Bing Nursery School at Stanford University and within the Stanford community. The deviant group was selected from the deviant population of children currently seen at the Institute for Childhood Aphasia, Stanford University School of Medicine.

Three children from each group were assigned to each of Brown's five linguistic levels of development on the basis of the mean number of morphemes per utterance. Level I utterances were slightly over two morphemes in length while Level V utterances had slightly under six morphemes per utterance (Table 1). The age range for the normal group was one year, seven months to three years, one month, with a mean age of two years, four months. The deviant group had an age range of three years, six months to nine years, six months, with a mean age of six years, seven months (Table 1). The normal group was screened for speech and hearing pathologies. The linguistically deviant group was restricted to children who lacked sufficient intellectual or physiological impairment to account for their difficulties in acquiring language.

An adaptation of Chomsky's (1965) transformational grammar by Rosenbaum (1967) was modified (Ingram, 1970) and grammars were written for the language sample of each child. Rosenbaum's (1967) system was selected because it incorporates many of the recent advances on Chomsky's (1965) transformational grammar. The grammars accounted for all but 8 to 10% of the utterances in the samples of both groups. The two groups representing five linguistic levels of development were compared according to (1) phrase structure rules, (2) transformations, (3) construction types or surface realization of major syntactic categories and their relations, (4) inflectional morphology, and (5) select lexical items representing minor syntactic categories.

The five linguistic aspects were chosen because they reflect a broad assessment of base syntactic development. Phrase structure and transformational analysis presumably characterize some important aspects of the child's knowledge about sentence organization. From the characterization of the child's grammars, certain criterion measures were developed for comparing type and occurrence of phrase structures and transformations. In addition, construction types, inflectional morphology, and minor lexical items were selected to represent important aspects of the realization of the child's knowledge of sentences. However, the grammars were written from production data and therefore, in any strict sense, assess only language performance.

Language Samples. The language samples were collected under three conditions: free play with the experimenter or parent, elicitation while playing with toys, and elicitation while viewing a standard children's book. It was generally possible to collect samples under all three conditions, except for the younger normal children and the lower-level deviant children. In cases where it was not possible to collect the samples under all three conditions, samples were collected only under the first two conditions. The utterances of each sample were divided into spontaneous and response utterances to determine whether the conditions under which the samples were collected had differential effects for the two groups. The proportion of spontaneous to response utterances was nearly identical in both groups. In addition, separate grammars were written for the two types of utterances in each sample to determine any differences which might be attributed to performance variables or to the conditions used in collecting the samples. Since few differences were found, the spontaneous and response utterances were pooled for group comparison.

A high-fidelity tape recorder was used to record the linguistic interaction between the adult and the child. In addition, an observer recorded the initial adult utterance, if any, the child's utterance, and the adult expansion of the child's utterance. The expansion of the child's utterance was determined by the contextual information collected when the language sample was taken. In this way, the child's intended grammatical and semantic relations were more closely approximated than by tape recordings or by observational records alone. The utterances were then transcribed, generally on the same day, and compared with the observer's records before a final decision was made.

The mean number of utterances for the normal group was 175.5, while the mean number of utterances for the deviant group was 148.7. One-word utterances were not included in the samples of either group so that each utterance would involve base syntactic relations. In addition, each linguistic structure had to occur two or more times in order to be considered part of the child's productive system.

Established criteria do not exist for determining what is an adequate sample size for linguistic analysis. The number of utterances used in analysis varies considerably from less than 100 (Menyuk, 1964) to over 1500 utterances (Bloom, 1970). Brown (1973) collected nearly 700 utterances, including one-word utterances, for each time sample. We attempted to collect 100 relational utterances for the two lower levels of linguistic development and 200 relational utterances for the three upper levels of linguistic development (Table 1).

RESULTS

The phrase structure grammars necessary to account for the utterances of the normal and deviant groups were nearly identical for each of the five linguistic levels. Minor differences did appear in the grammars for the two groups at each of the five levels, but these differences were no greater than the differences between subjects within the same group at a given linguistic level. Two examples of the phrase structure grammars taken from one normal and one deviant child are presented in the list below. (A detailed description of the grammars is available in Ingram [in press].) In the list, S = sentence, NP = noun phrase, VP = verb phrase, N = noun, VB = verb, ( ) = optional element, # = sentence boundary, and → = "is rewritten as."

Normal—MM/U-2.66
S → # (NP) (VP) #
VP → VB (NP)
NP → N (S)

Conditions:
1. (S) is either an
   adjective or possessive
2. (S) only occurs
   when S → NP

Deviant—MM/U-2.69
S → # (NP) (VP) #
VP → VB (NP)
NP → N (S)

Conditions:
1. (S) is a possessive

2. (S) only occurs
   when S → NP

The two grammars are equally capable of generating or accounting for the utterances of either the deviant or the normal child, with the single restriction that the deviant child does not include adjective modifiers in constructions taking the form N(S).

The two groups also did not differ significantly in the proportion of utterances reflecting only phrase structure relations across the five linguistic levels. The proportion of phrase structure utterances, however, decreased with linguistic level for both the normal and the deviant groups. Nearly half the utterances at Level II were without transformations, while fewer than 10% of the utterances were without transformations at Level III. This rather dramatic change in phrase-structure-transformations ratio between Levels II and III held for both groups. Despite these similarities, when chronological age rather than linguistic level was considered, the deviant group showed a marked delay as compared to normals in both onset and acquisition time. The age disparity between the two groups, although the data is cross-sectional, suggests that the onset time for base syntax or two-word utterances may be delayed as much as three and one-half years in the deviant child. Moreover, acquisition time, or the time required to go from Level I to V, is nearly two and one-half years longer for the deviant children. This delay in onset and acquisition time also holds for transformations, construction types, inflections, and minor lexical categories. Given that normal children initiate and acquire base syntax between approximately 18 and 40 months, it appears that deviant children take on the average three times as long to initiate and to acquire base syntax.

Forty different transformations were identified in the language samples of both groups. The transformations of each group were assigned absolute ranks based on their frequency of occurrence. Listed in Appendix A are the transformations in order of their frequency of occurrence and examples of each. The examples provide the base form and its corresponding transformation. A Spearman rank order correlation was significant ($r = 0.96$, $t = 21.30$, $p < 0.01$), indicating a high degree of similarity between the two groups (Figure 1). In addition, the 40 transformations were compared individually for the two groups using the Mann-Whitney U Test (Siegel, 1956). Four of the 40 transformations showed significantly greater occurrence for the normal group (question *do* segment, locative segment, demonstrative segment, and noun deletion), while two showed significantly greater occurrence for the deviant group (progressive affix segment and plural affix segment).

To determine any differences between the two groups on infrequently occurring transformations, the 40 transformations were divided into frequently occurring and infrequently occurring transformations. Figure 1 shows that a convenient boundary exists between the frequent and infrequent transformations near the twentieth transformation for both groups. In order that an equal number of transformations could be compared, they were divided between the 20 most frequent and the 20 least frequent transformations. A sign test (Siegel, 1956) revealed no significant difference for the frequent trans-

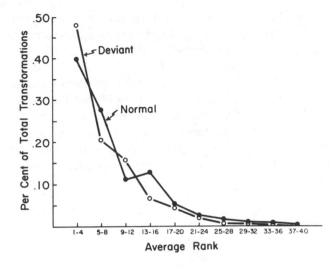

FIGURE 1. The average rank of the 40 transformations and their frequency of occurrence for the normal and deviant groups.

formations, while the infrequent transformations revealed a significant difference ($p < 0.06$). This finding suggests that while no overall significance exists between the two groups on the frequency of transformation types, the least frequent transformations, and those presumably more difficult as a group, were used significantly less by the deviant group. The infrequent transformations occurred 5% or less of the time (Figure 2).

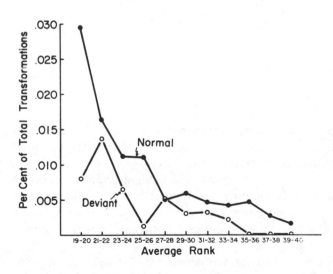

FIGURE 2. The average rank of the infrequently occurring transformations and their frequency of occurrence for the normal and deviant groups.

An additional check was made to determine if more specific differential use of the transformations could be found between the two groups. The 40 transformations were divided into four general categories: (1) sentence transformations, (2) noun transformations, (3) verb transformations, and (4)

35

question transformations. Significant linguistic level effects were found for sentence transformations ($F = 8.70$; $df = 4{,}20$; $p < 0.01$), noun transformations ($F = 48.62$; $df = 4{,}20$; $p < 0.01$), verb transformations ($F = 10.90$; $df = 4{,}20$; $p < 0.01$), and question transformations ($F = 9.32$; $df = 4{,}20$; $p < 0.01$). However, significant group differences were only found for question transformations ($F = 27.17$; $df = 1{,}20$; $p < 0.01$). In addition, a significant interaction was found between linguistic level and the two groups ($F = 5.53$; $df = 4{,}20$; $p < 0.01$) as a result of one deviant child having more questions marked at Level I, namely, marking questions by wh forms. The normal group had significantly more question transformations at the four remaining linguistic levels (Figure 3).

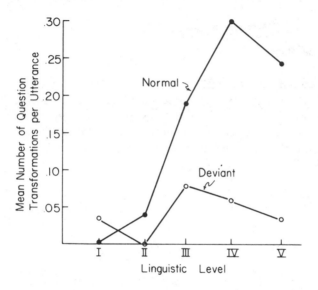

FIGURE 3. The mean number of question transformations per utterance plotted across five linguistic levels for the normal and deviant groups.

As noted previously, significant level differences were found for the transformation types across the five linguistic levels of development. Appendixes B and C present the transformations showing their frequency of occurrence at each of the five linguistic levels for the normal and deviant groups, respectively. The lists indicate that both the number and type of transformations change with each advancing level of development, and that there is considerable similarity in the transformational development of both groups across the five levels of linguistic development.

Finally, the mean number of transformations used per utterance was compared across the five linguistic levels for the normal and the deviant groups. No significant group differences were found; however, a significant level effect was found ($F = 66.12$; $df = 4{,}20$; $p < 0.001$), and the differences were significant for both groups across all five levels (Figure 4). When the mean number of transformations per utterance was correlated with age, the normal group had high positive correlation ($r = 0.905$; $p < 0.01$), while the deviant group

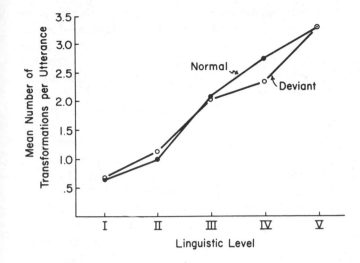

FIGURE 4. The mean number of transformations per utterance plotted across five linguistic levels for the normal and deviant groups.

did not ($r = 0.161$). Again, a major finding is the marked delay in onset time and acquisition period for acquiring transformations.

The construction types depict major lexical categories (that is, noun, verb, and noun$_{object}$) and their syntactic frames or possible relations (noun-verb and noun-verb-noun). Appendix D provides a list of the construction types and their corresponding examples. Two measures were derived from the construction types and compared for the two groups. The mean number of major lexical categories per construction type was used to determine the occurrence of major categories in a variety of contexts for the language samples of both groups. Significant differences were obtained between the two groups ($F = 5.51$; $df = 1,20$; $p < 0.05$) and across the five linguistic levels ($F = 23.81$; $df = 4,20$; $p < 0.01$) (Figure 5). In addition, each syntactic

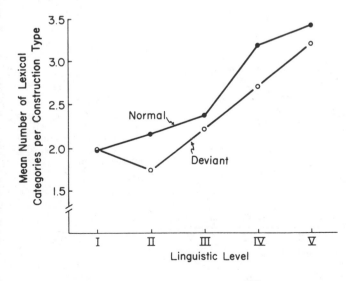

FIGURE 5. The mean number of lexical categories per construction type plotted across five linguistic levels for the normal and deviant groups.

37

relation or construction type was compared for the two groups on the basis of their frequency of occurrence. A low positive correlation was found when the construction types of the two groups were compared ($r = 0.435$). When age was correlated with mean number of lexical categories per construction type, the normals showed a high correlation with age ($r = 0.762$; $p < 0.01$), while the deviant group showed a low correlation with age ($r = 0.136$). The deviant group again manifested the marked delay in onset and acquisition time.

Linguistic level was found to be significant for both groups on the number of lexical categories per construction type. Appendixes E and F provide a list of the construction types in order of their frequency of occurrence for both groups at each of the five linguistic levels. The tables show that the type and number of constructions change for both groups with advancing levels of linguistic development. However, as the tables clearly indicate, the deviant group did not use major linguistic categories in as many different contexts or syntactic frames as did the normal group.

To determine the relative increase in the occurrence of inflections such as plurals, past tense, and possessives across the five linguistic levels, word-morpheme ratios were computed for the two groups. Utterances had either no inflections (that is, two words, two morphemes) or two inflections (that is, five words, seven morphemes). The findings were not significant for the two groups, although a significant level effect was again found ($F = 71.81$; $df = 4,20$, $p < 0.01$). The deviant group did, however, have more inflections at the first three linguistic levels than did the normal group (Figure 6).

Select lexical items that represent minor lexical categories were also compared for the two groups. The lexical items used for comparison were pronouns, demonstratives, wh forms, prepositions, and modals. The primary concern in this comparison was to determine at what level and in what order

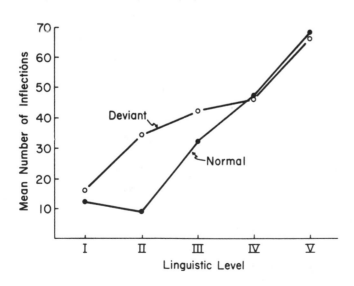

FIGURE 6. The mean number of inflections plotted across five linguistic levels for normal and deviant groups.

the various items appeared for the two groups. Thus, two or more children at each linguistic level had to use a given lexical category two or more times in order for that category to be included. With the exception of pronouns, only minor variance was found in the level or order of appearance of the lexical items. The deviant group by Level III had 16 pronouns, while the normal group had nine pronouns (Tables 2 and 3).

TABLE 2. Linguistic level and order of appearance of minor lexical categories for the normal group.

Linguistic Category Level	Normal				
	I	II	III	IV	V
Pronouns	I	my	you	we	her
		it	your	he	its
		it	she	they	her
		me	them	us	our
				you	
				him	
				his	
Demonstratives	that	this	these	those	
Wh forms		where	what	why	when
Prepositions		in	to	up	down
		on	with	at	of
				for	off
					like
					through
					over
					by
					under
					near
Modals`	want		gonna	can	won't
			hafta	will	don't
				could	can't
				shall	gotta
					would
					may
					might
					should
					better

DISCUSSION

Clearly, the major differences between normal and linguistically deviant children of comparable linguistic level were not in the organization or occurrence of specific subcomponents of their base syntactic systems. Rather, the significant differences were found in the onset and acquisition time necessary for learning base syntax and the use of aspects of that system, once acquired, for producing major lexical items in a variety of utterances.

Phrase structure development showed similar rule systems as well as similar

TABLE 3. Linguistic level and order of appearance of minor lexical categories for the deviant group.

Linguistic Category Level	I	II	Deviant III	IV	V
Pronouns	it I my	him	you it he them they she we you us your his	her their	its our her
Demonstratives	that	these	this	those	
Wh forms		what		where why	how when who
Prepositions	in		on at to down	with like	up of off out of for over by after into about except
Modals			gonna	can't can want	don't won't gotta would hadda will could didn't hafta

occurrences of phrase structure utterances for both groups across five distinct levels of linguistic development. No overall differences were found in the frequency or type of transformational rules produced in the language samples of the two groups. Of the 40 transformations compared, only six were significantly different in their frequency of occurrence. Four occurred more frequently in the normal group (question *do* segment, locative, demonstrative, and noun deletion), while two occurred more frequently in the deviant group (progressive affix and plural affix). Moreover, the mean number of transformations per utterance used by the two groups across the five levels was not significantly different, indicating no severe limitation in the deviant group in the number of transformations used in a particular utterance.

The two groups were also compared on frequently occurring and infrequently occurring transformations and four general categories of transformations. Significant differences were found between the two groups on infrequently occurring transformations and the general category of questions. The findings for differences in infrequently occurring transformations are similar to those of Menyuk (1964). Of the 28 transformations compared according to the number of subjects using a given transformation, she found that 16 were used less often by the deviant group. However, only one of the 16 transformations was used significantly less often by the deviant group. The relative absence of questions in the language samples of our deviant group could reflect either a general sampling problem inherent to children with productive liabilities or a general sociolinguistic posture which is antithetical to seeking information by linguistic code. It would be difficult to assume that question transformations are psychologically more difficult than many of the transformations acquired by the deviant group.

The development of inflections and minor lexical items (pronouns, demonstratives, wh forms, prepositions, and modals) was also compared in the two groups. In the case of minor lexical items only minor variance was found in the level or the order of appearance of these items, save pronouns. The deviant group at Level III had 16 pronouns as compared to nine for the normal group at the same level. The amount of time the deviant group spent between Levels II and III seemed to allow them to make more distinctions between self and others and for those distinctions to be linguistically marked.

There were no significant differences in the development of inflections as determined by word-morpheme ratio. The deviant group, however, did have more inflections at the first three levels of linguistic development than did the normal group. This difference was also reflected in the comparison of transformation types where both the progressive and plural affix were used significantly more often by the deviant group. These differences may reflect both the increased time the deviant group spends at each linguistic level and the fact that since inflections are not introduced by major transformations, they are easily detected in the surface structure. Where cognitive distinctions such as number are easily marked linguistically, as in the case of plural forms, deviant children appear to be somewhat less delayed in acquiring these forms.

Though few differences were found in phrase structure or transformational development, save infrequently occurring transformations and questions and including the mean number of transformations used per utterance, significant differences were found in the number of major lexical categories per construction type. Since the two groups were matched on essentially mean number of major lexical categories per utterance, the finding suggests a specific restriction in the variety of construction types produced by the deviant group. This finding is further supported by the low correlation found when types of constructions were compared between the two groups. Transformations also affect

41

the variety of construction types produced, and a significant difference was found between the two groups on the infrequently occurring transformations.

These results suggest that deviant children, when studied at their particular level of linguistic development, are not seriously deficient in the organization of phrase structure rules, types of transformations, number of transformations used in a given utterance, minor lexical items, or inflectional morphology. However, deviant children appear to be significantly restricted in their ability to develop and select grammatical and semantic features which allow existent and new major lexical categories to be assigned to larger sets of syntactic frames. To clarify the specific deficit these results indicate, it is useful to discuss the findings in terms of Chomsky's transformational grammar.

In Chomsky's (1965) linguistic system, the base component of transformational grammar is composed of a categorical component and a lexicon. The categorical component handles general properties of the deep structure, such as defining grammatical relations and determining base syntactic order. The lexicon handles less general properties, including (1) properties relevant to the function of transformational rules, (2) information regarding the varied placement of lexical items in a sentence, and (3) properties relevant to semantic interpretation. Thus, grammatical relations and order are determined by the categorical component, while contextual restrictions are determined by the lexicon.

The utterances produced by the deviant group manifested grammatical relations and base syntactic order not unlike that of the normal group. The finding of similar phrase structure rules indicates that the two groups were not different in their base organization for the categorical component. However, the members of the deviant group were restricted in their ability to handle less general properties specified by the lexicon as indicated by the finding of differences on infrequently occurring transformations and major lexical categories per construction type. When compared with normals they also showed a low correlation on types of constructions. Specifically, these restrictions would involve the function of transformational rules and information regarding varied placement of lexical items in a sentence. In addition, the delay in both onset and acquisition time for base syntax is, no doubt, closely related to the deviant group's ability to assign an adequate semantic interpretation to an utterance in comprehension as well as production. The properties of the lexicon are also closely related to how well formed an utterance is. Our observations of the language samples and those of Menyuk (1969) suggest that the utterances produced by deviant children are on the whole less well formed than those of normal children.

Other research has also found that linguistically deviant children have a specific deficit that is quantitatively different from normal children rather than a general qualitative deficit. Studies in both language and cognitive development have reported similar findings on the nature of the difference between normal and deviant children. Lackner (1968) reported that retarded children of different mental ages do not develop language behavior differently from normal children, but rather reflect a delayed developmental sequence with lower terminal development.

Inhelder (1966) and de Ajuriaguerra (1966) have studied the cognitive development of linguistically deviant children. Using Piagetion-type tasks, they found that children with a slow rate of linguistic development frequently had normal operative or base intellectual development. However, the deviant children did show a specific deficit in the figurative or representational aspect of cognition. According to Piaget's (1970) cognitive developmental theory, the child develops a general capacity for representation which includes aspects of perception, deferred imitation, imagery, symbolic play, drawing, and dreaming, as well as language.

The importance of these findings is that they suggest a possible relationship between delayed language acquisition and an underlying aspect of cognitive development. For example, perceptual deficiencies, which in Piaget's theory are related to general representational development, have long been suspect in children who fail to develop language at a normal rate. Such deficits have been demonstrated in both vision and audition (Mackworth, Grandstaff, and Pribram, in press; Rosenthal and Eisenson[1]). Moreover, Grandstaff et al.[2] have shown that the performance of linguistically deviant children on a simple match to sample task is not different from that of normal children in terms of the number of matching errors. However, the deviant children take nearly twice as long, once the correct symbol is located, to indicate their choice. These findings are consistent with those of Inhelder (1966) and de Ajuriaguerra (1966), who also found that deviant children are deficient in their ability to evoke reproductive images necessary for solving simple matching tasks. Lovell, Hoyle, and Siddal (1968) report a significant correlation between mean morpheme per utterance length and the amount of time spent in symbolic play by linguistically deviant children, that is, the fewer the number of morphemes per utterance, the less time spent in symbolic play.

In summary, linguistically deviant children do not develop bizarre linguistic systems that are qualitatively different from normal children. Rather, they develop quite similar linguistic systems with a marked delay in the onset and acquisition time. Moreover, once the linguistic systems are developed, deviant children do not use them as creatively as normal children for producing highly varied utterances. Other research suggests that these children may have a specific cognitive deficit in all aspects of representational behavior which, according to Piaget, includes language.

---

[1] W. Rosenthal and J. Eisenson, unpublished study on auditory temporal order in aphasic children as a function of selected stimulus features, personal communication.

[2] N. Grandstaff, N. Mackworth, A. de la Pena, and K. Pribram, unpublished study on model formation and use by aphasic and normal children during visual matching to sample, personal communication.

ACKNOWLEDGMENT

This research was supported by the National Institute of Neurological Diseases and Stroke Research Grant NS-07514 to the Institute for Childhood Aphasia, Stanford University School of Medicine. We want to express our appreciation to Jon Eisenson, project director, and to Dorothy Tyack, Judith Johnston, and Geoffrey Loftus for their assistance in the collection and analysis of the data. The authors also wish to extend special gratitude to Mark Solomon whose general competencies were invaluable to the study.

REFERENCES

AJURIAGUERRA, J. DE., Speech disorders in childhood. In C. Carterette (Ed.), *Brain Function: Speech, Language, and Communication.* (Vol. III) Los Angeles, Cal.: Univ. of California Press (1966).

BLOOM, L., *Language Development: Form and Function in Emerging Grammars.* Cambridge, Mass.: MIT Press (1970).

BROWN, R., *A First Language.* Cambridge, Mass.: Harvard Univ. Press (1973).

BROWN, R., CAZDEN, C., and BELLUGI, U., The child's grammar from I to III. In S. P. Hill (Ed.), *The 1967 Minnesota Symposium on Child Psychology.* Minneapolis: Univ. of Minnesota Press (1968).

CHOMSKY, N., *Aspects of the Theory of Syntax.* Cambridge, Mass.: MIT Press (1965).

INGRAM, D., IBM Grammar II: An adaptation for child language. In *Papers and Reports on Child Language Development.* Stanford University, December (1970).

INGRAM, D., The development of phrase structure rules. *Lang. Learn.,* 22, 23-33 (1972).

INHELDER, B., Cognitive development and its contribution to the diagnosis of some phenomena of mental deficiency. *Merrill-Palmer Quart.,* 12, 299-319 (1966).

KOHLBERG, L., Early education: A cognitive developmental view. *Child Devel.,* 39, 1013-1062 (1968).

LACKNER, J., A developmental study of language behavior in retarded children. *Neuropsychol.,* 6, 301-320 (1968).

LEE, L., Developmental sentence types: A method for comparing normal and deviant syntactic development. *J. Speech Hearing Dis.,* 31, 311-330 (1966).

LENNEBERG, E. H., *Biological Foundations of Language.* New York: John Wiley (1967).

LOVELL, K., HOYLE, H., and SIDDALL, M., A study of some aspects of the play and language of young children with delayed speech. *J. Child Psychol. Psychiat.,* 9, 41-50 (1968).

MACKWORTH, N., GRANDSTAFF, N., and PRIBRAM, K., Prolonged orientation to pictorial novelty in severely speech-disordered children. *Neuropsychol.* (in press).

MCNEILL, D., Developmental psycholinguistics. In F. Smith and G. A. Miller (Eds.), *The Genesis of Language: A Psycholinguistic Approach.* Cambridge, Mass.: MIT Press (1966).

MCNEILL, D., *The Acquisition of Language: The Study of Developmental Psycholinguistics.* New York: Harper and Row (1970).

MENYUK, P., Comparison of grammar of children with functionally deviant and normal speech. *J. Speech Hearing Res.,* 7, 109-121 (1964).

MENYUK, P., *Sentences Children Use.* Cambridge, Mass.: MIT Press (1969).

PIAGET, J., Piaget's theory. In P. H. Mussen (Ed.), *Carmichael's Manual of Child Psychology.* (Vol. I) New York: John Wiley (1970).

ROSENBAUM, P., *IBM Grammar II, IBM Research Report.* (1967).

SIEGEL, S., *Non-parametic Statistics.* New York: McGraw-Hill (1956).

Forty transformations listed in order of their combined frequency of occurrence for the normal and deviant groups. The examples provide the base form and its corresponding transformation.

Frequent Types	Examples
Pronoun segment	Ball . . . it
Article segment	Ball . . . a ball
Demonstrative segment	Ball . . . that ball
Preposition segment	Table . . . on table
Adjective genitive placement	Ball red . . . red ball
Verb particle segment	I go . . . I go up
Type placement	Not I go . . . I not go
Locative segment	Table . . . there
Plural affix segment	Ball . . . balls
Progressive affix segment	He go . . . he going
Copula contraction	It is red . . . it's red
Number segment	Ball . . . two ball
Wh question	That ball . . . what ball
Noun deletion	That ball . . . that
	John's ball . . . John's
Progressive auxiliary segment	He running . . . he is running
Present affix segment	He run . . . he runs
Conjunction segment	Boy girl . . . boy and girl
Question tone	Ball . . . ball?
Infinitive segment	I want go . . . I want to go
Question *do* segment	I go . . . do I go?

Infrequent Types	Examples
Copula segment	It red . . . I make it red
Negative *do* segment	I not go . . . I do not go
Tag question	I go . . . don't I?
Past affix segment	I bat . . . I batted
Question copula shift	He is going . . . is he going?
Pronoun number segment	Them . . . two of them
Complete all segment	It gone . . . it all gone
Genitive affix segment	John ball . . . John's ball
Vocative segment	I go home . . . Daddy, I go home
Verb deletion	I pick up ball . . . I up ball
Verb qualifier statement	I run . . . I (really) run
	(just)
Inchoative segment	It red . . . it got red
Particle intensive segment	I go up . . . I go (way) up
	(back)
	(right)
Verb particle shift	I pick ball up . . . I pick up ball
Question modal shift	He will go . . . will he go?
Noun object shift	Hit ball . . . ball hit
Stative verb particle shift	Ball up . . . up ball
Object noun retention	Hit ball . . . hit it ball
Repetition segment	I go . . . I go again
Demonstrative copula	That there . . . that's there

Appendix B

Transformation types pooled in order of their frequency of occurrence across five linguistic levels of development for the normal group.

Linguistic Level I

Locative segment
Pronoun number segment
Adjective genitive placement
Complete all segment
Pronoun segment
Vocative segment
Preposition segment
Stative verb particle shift
Demonstrative segment
Verb qualifier segment
Plural affix segment

Linguistic Level II

Adjective genitive placement
Article segment
Verb particle segment
Plural affix segment
Demonstrative segment
Pronoun segment
Locative segment
Noun object shift
Question tone
Noun deletion
Wh question
Pronoun number segment
Verb deletion
Object noun retention
Noun retention

Linguistic Level III

Demonstrative segment
Verb particle segment
Pronoun segment
Preposition segment
Article segment
Locative segment
Noun deletion
Pronoun number segment
Adjective genitive placement
Wh question
Type placement
Present affix segment
Question tone
Progressive affix segment
Plural affix segment
Infinitive segment
Copula contraction
Progressive auxiliary segment
Conjunction segment
Question *do* segment
Inchoative segment
Tag question
Question copula shift
Copula segment

Linguistic Level III

Past affix segment
Verb particle shift
Verb deletion

Linguistic Level IV

Pronoun segment
Demonstrative segment
Type placement
Preposition segment
Adjective genitive placement
Article segment
Wh question
Verb particle segment
Copula contraction
Pronoun number segment
Locative segment
Noun deletion
Progressive affix segment
Plural affix segment
Question *do* segment
Progressive auxiliary segment
Present affix segment
Question tone
Conjunction segment
Tag question
Copula segment
Infinitive segment
Genitive affix segment
Question copula shift
Negative *do* segment
Question modal shift
Verb particle shift
Past affix segment

Linguistic Level V

Demonstrative segment
Pronoun segment
Article segment
Preposition segment
Type placement
Adjective genitive placement
Verb particle segment
Locative segment
Present affix segment
Copula contraction
Wh question
Noun deletion
Pronoun number segment
Plural affix segment
Question *do* segment
Infinitive segment
Conjunction segment
Negative *do* segment

46

Appendix B (Cont.)

Linguistic Level V

Copula segment
Past affix segment
Question copula shift
Pronoun number segment
Progressive affix segment
Question tone

Linguistic Level V

Tag question
Progressive auxiliary segment
Question modal shift
Verb qualifier segment
Repetition segment
Genitive affix segment

Appendix C

Transformation types pooled in order of their frequency of occurrence across five linguistic levels of development for the deviant group.

Linguistic Level I

Adjective genitive placement
Plural affix segment
Number segment
Locative segment
Wh question
Verb particle segment
Pronoun segment
Progressive affix segment
Demonstrative segment
Preposition segment
Copula contraction
Noun object shift

Linguistic Level II

Article segment
Preposition segment
Progressive affix segment
Adjective genitive placement
Verb particle segment
Pronoun segment
Demonstrative segment
Plural affix segment
Verb deletion
Genitive affix segment
Locative segment
Number segment
Noun deletion
Demonstrative copula

Linguistic Level III

Article segment
Pronoun segment
Preposition segment
Demonstrative segment
Progressive affix segment
Plural affix segment
Adjective genitive placement
Locative segment
Verb particle segment
Type placement
Wh question
Noun deletion

Linguistic Level III

Conjunction segment
Copula contraction
Number segment
Question tone
Progressive auxiliary segment
Copula segment
Demonstrative copula
Pronoun number segment
Past affix segment
Verb particle shift
Present affix segment

Linguistic Level IV

Article segment
Pronoun segment
Preposition segment
Adjective genitive placement
Verb particle segment
Demonstrative segment
Plural affix segment
Progressive affix segment
Progressive auxiliary segment
Type placement
Question tone
Locative segment
Wh question
Conjunction segment
Number segment
Noun deletion
Infinitive segment
Copula contraction
Negative *do* segment
Past affix segment
Copula segment
Inchoative segment
Present affix segment
Demonstrative copula

Linguistic Level V

Pronoun segment
Article segment
Preposition segment

Appendix C

Linguistic Level V

Adjective genitive placement
Type placement
Progressive auxiliary segment
Progressive affix segment
Copula contraction
Plural affix segment
Demonstrative segment
Verb particle segment
Conjunction segment
Number segment
Present affix segment

Linguistic Level V

Infinitive segment
Past affix segment
Negative *do* segment
Locative segment
Wh question
Genitive affix segment
Verb qualifier segment
Copula segment
Question *do* segment
Question tone
Complete all segment

Appendix D

Construction types listed in order of their combined frequency of occurrence for the normal and deviant groups. Key: N = noun, VB = verb, V = copula, T = type, N_o = object noun (used only with copula), N_{loc} = locative noun, Q = question, S = sentence, and Tag_Q = tag question.

Construction Types	Examples
N-VB-N	Me find a hotdog
VB-N	Open the gate
N-VB	Ducks are quacking
N	Another hamburger
$N-V-N_o$	That's a ladder
N-T-VB-N	We will take this out
$N-V-N_{loc}$	Here's an owl
VB	Go up
N-S	Pretty shoe
Q-N-VB-N	Do you got a hurt?
N-T-VB	I hafta go
$Q-N-V-N_{loc}$	Where the dolls?
$Q-N-V-N_o$	Is this a hot dog?
N-VB-N-N	We have the bear for dinner
$N-V-N_o-S$	Here's my knee
Q-N-VB	Are you going?
VB-N-N	Put truck in garage
N-VB-N-S	I have blue box
Q-N-T-VB-N	Would you do this?
N-T-VB-N-N	I'm gonna put playdough on it
T-VB-N	Gonna take this
Q-N-T-VB	Why doesn't this stay up?
VB-N-VB-N	Let's take this off
VB-N-S	Fix Jim's car
N-VB-VB-N	He went to fix the baby
T-VB	Gonna go
N-T	It isn't
$N-S-V-N_{loc}$	Round balls in there
Q-N-T-VB-N-N	Where the people gon drive on it?
$Q-N-S-V-N_{loc}$	Where's his dinner?
VB-N-VB	Make this one stand up
Q-VB-N	Go here?
$Q-N-S-V-N_o$	What is the name of this color?
VB-N-VB-N-N	Let's put these back in here
N-T-VB-N-S	I can't ride a big bike

48

Appendix D

Construction Types	Examples
$N\text{-}VB\text{-}N\text{-}Tag_Q$	You put these back, okay?
Greeting N	Hi daddy
N-S-VB-N	My mommy put them on
N-S-VB	Poor snail cry
Q-N	Right here?
$N\text{-}T\text{-}VB\text{-}N\text{-}Tag_Q$	I have to put this away, okay?
Q-N-VB-N-N	What do you put in there?
$N\text{-}T\text{-}V\text{-}N_o$	There's no water
N-VB-S	I think it is
Q-N-T	It can?
$Q\text{-}N\text{-}V\text{-}N_o\text{-}N_{loc}$	What's that in there?
$Q\text{-}N\text{-}V\text{-}N_o\text{-}S$	That mommy's bear?
Adverb-S-S	When you have your mask on, it scares you
$N\text{-}V\text{-}N_{loc}\text{-}Tag_Q$	It was in here, wasn't it?
S-what-S	Look what he taked from you
VB-VB	Want go
N-S-S	A big big bear
VB-VB-N	Gonna put these away
VB-N-VB	Make this one stand up
$N\text{-}V\text{-}N_o\text{-}Tag_Q$	There a train, right?
Q-N-VB-N-S	When do we had the marble game?
Q-N-VB-VB	Who mommy want hit?
N-VB-N-VB	You make it stand up
N-VB-N-VB-N	I want you stay there
N-VB-VB	I want talk
S-because-S	This doesn't open because it's too little
N-VB-N-N-S	I have this in my program
$N\text{-}V\text{-}N_o\text{-}N$	There's more in it
N-N	Elephants and giraffes
T-VB-N-N	Gonna take this one home
N-say-S	My mom said I can't go
N-VB-VB-N-S	I want to go to the marble game
$N\text{-}S\text{-}V\text{-}N_o$	Dog name's Jippy
N-VB-N-S-N	It's got my thumb in this
N-T-VB-N-N-S	He will throw ball in his eyes

Appendix E

Construction types pooled in order of their frequency of occurrence across five linguistic levels of development for the normal group.

Linguistic Level I	Linguistic Level II	Linguistic Level II
N-VB	VB-N	N-S-S
VB-N	N-VB-N	
N	N-S	**Linguistic Level III**
VB	N-VB	VB-N
$N\text{-}V\text{-}N_{loc}$	VB	N-VB-N
$N\text{-}V\text{-}N_o$	N	N-VB
N-S	$N\text{-}V\text{-}N_{loc}$	VB
T-VB	VB-N-S	N
N-VB-N	VB-N-N	$N\text{-}V\text{-}N_o$
N-T	Q-N-VB	$N\text{-}V\text{-}N_{loc}$
Greeting-N	N-S-VB	$Q\text{-}N\text{-}V\text{-}N_{loc}$
$N\text{-}S\text{-}V\text{-}N_{loc}$	N-VB-N-S	VB-N-N
VB-N-S	Greeting-N	N-S
$Q\text{-}N\text{-}V\text{-}N_o$	VB-VB	N-T-VB-N

Linguistic Level III	*Linguistic Level IV*	*Linguistic Level V*
N-VB-N-N	T-VB-N	Q-N-VB-N
Q-N-VB-N	Q-N-T-VB-N	N-VB-N-N
T-VB-N	VB-N-VB-N	$N-V-N_o-S$
N-T-VB	VB	$N-V-N_o$
Q-N-VB	Q-VB-N	$Q-N-V-N_o$
$Q-N-V-N_o$	N-VB-N-S	N
$N-V-N_o-S$	N-V-N-N	N-T-VB-N-N
N-VB-VB-N	N-VB-VB-N	N-VB-N-S
N-VB-VB	N-T-VB-N-N	Adverb + S + S
N-S-VB-N	$Q-N-S-V-N_{loc}$	Q-N-V-N
N-VB-S	$Q-N-V-N_{loc}$	VB-N-VB-N
Q-N-T-VB-N	Q-N	N-T-VB-N-S
VB-N-S	VB-N-VB	$N-S-V-N_{loc}$
VB-VB-N	$Q-N-S-V-N_o$	Q-N-T-VB-N
T-VB	Q-N-T	Q-N-T-VB-N-N
VB-N-VB	N-T	$N-T-V-N_o$
N-T	$Q-N-VB-N_o-N_{loc}$	VB-N-VB-N-N
N-VB-N-S-N	$Q-N-VB-N_o-S$	Q-N-VB
	VB-N-S	$N-V-N_{loc}$-Tag Q
	Q-N-T-VB-N-N	N-VB-N-Tag Q
Linguistic Level IV	N-S-VB	S-what-S
	VB-N-VB-N-N	$Q-N-S-V-N_{loc}$
N-VB-N	N-T-VB-N-Tag Q	Q-N-T-VB
N-VB	$N-V-N_o$-Tag Q	T-VB-N
N-T-VB-N	Q-N-VB-N-S	VB-N-S
Q-N-VB-N	Q-N-VB-N-N	N-says S
$N-V-N_o$	Q-N-VB-VB	N-S-VB-N
VB-N	N-VB-N-Tag Q	N-VB-VB
N		S-because-S
$Q-N-V-N_o$	*Linguistic Level V*	N-VB-S
N-T-VB		N-VB-N-N-S
$N-V-N_{loc}$	N-VB-N	N-VB-VB-N
Q-N-T-VB	N-T-VB-N	VB-N-VB
N-S	N-VB	$Q-N-S-V-N_o$
Q-N-V-N	N-T-VB	Q-N-VB-N-N
Q-N-VB	$N-V-N_{loc}$	N-T-VB-N-Tag Q
$N-V-N_o-S$	VB-N	N-VB-N-VB-N
VB-N-N		

Construction types pooled in order of their frequency of occurrence across five linguistic levels of development for the deviant group.

Linguistic Level I	*Linguistic Level I*	*Linguistic Level II*
VB-N	T-VB-N	VB-N-S
N-S	$N-S-V-N_{loc}$	$N-V-N_o$
N-VB		N-VB-N-S
N	*Linguistic Level II*	N-S-VB-N
VB		N-N
$N-V-N_{loc}$	VB-N	VB-N-N
$Q-N-V-N_{loc}$	N	N-T-VB
N-VB-N	VB	N-S-VB
$N-V-N_o-S$	N-S	
VB-N-S	N-VB	*Linguistic Level III*
T-VB	N-VB-N	
	$N-V-N_{loc}$	N

Appendix F

Linguistic Level III	*Linguistic Level IV*	*Linguistic Level V*
VB-N	VB-N	N-VB-N
N-VB-N	N-VB-N-S	N-T-VB-N
N-VB	N-T-VB-N	N-VB
VB	N-S	N-VB-N-N
N-V-N_o	VB	N-VB-N-S
N-V-N_{loc}	N-VB-N-N	N-T-VB
N-S	N-T-VB-N-S	N
Q-N-V-N_o	Q-N-VB-N	N-T-VB-N-N
Q-N	N-T-VB	VB-N
N-VB-N_o-S	N-S-VB	N-V-N_o
N-VB-N-N	T-VB-N	N-S
N-T-VB-N	Q-N	N-V-N_o-N_{loc}
N-S-V-N_{loc}	N-V-N_o	N-VB-N-N-S
Q-N-V-N_o	N-VB-VB-N	N-T-VB-N-S
Q-N-T-VB-N	N-S-VB-N	N-VB-N-S-N
Q-N-VB-N	N-T-VB-N-N	N-V-N_{loc}
T-V-N-N	N-V-N_{loc}	VB
T-VB-N	VB-N-S	N-VB-N-VB
VB-N-N	N-say-S	N-VB-VB-N-S
N-T-VB-N-N	N-VB-S	Q-N-VB-N
VB-N-S	N-T	N-S-VB-N
N-T-VB-N-S	S-because-S	N-V-N_o-S
Q-N-T-VB-N-N	Q-N-VB	N-say-S
Q-N-V-N_{loc}	VB-VB-N	VB-N-S
N-T-VB	N-N	N-S-V-N_o
	N-VB-VB-N-S	N-T
Linguistic Level IV	Adverb-S-S	Q-N-V-N_{loc}
N-VB-N	N-VB-N-N-S	N-VB-N-S
N-VB	N-VB-S	N-T-VB-N-N-S
N		N-say-S
		Adverb-S-S

51

LANGUAGE ASSESSMENT:
Some Underlying Assumptions

JOHN R. MUMA

CLINICIANS should continually reexamine their underlying assumptions. Such examination could serve to direct clinicians toward more rationally based efforts. Locke's (1968) review of underlying assumptions in articulation research offered an opportunity for clinicians to reconsider the empirical-logical basis for articulation assessment and therapy. Similarly, a review of underlying assumptions in language assessment is needed because this clinical area is poorly understood.

Language assessment is typically predicated more by available tools than by a rationale which strives to match type of assessment and content area with apparent client needs. Typically the criteria for constructing and selecting language assessment devices are determined by what can be portrayed as in the PPVT (Dunn, 1965), varied as in the Auditory Discrimination Test (Wepman, 1958), situationally controlled as in the Picture Story Language Test (Myklebust, 1965), and quantified or scaled as in the ITPA (Kirk and McCarthy, 1961; Kirk, McCarthy, and Kirk, 1968) or the developmental sentence types or scores (Lee, 1966; Lee and Canter, 1971, respectively).

Many clinicians believe that language assessment should be conducted in a test format, presumably because language deviance (difference and pathology) can only be ascertained through normative comparison. Clinicians are typically not concerned about adequate sampling, either in the establishment of assessment procedures or in choosing assessment devices, even though inappropriate sampling could seriously jeopardize assessment. Clinicians seem to be preoccupied with language structure, often ignoring or underestimating language functions. Other issues such as the distinction between language knowledge and usage often become dismissed. These are important

ASHA, 1973, no. 15, pp. 331-338.

53

issues in language assessment; therefore, clinicians should examine the underlying assumptions of such practices in order to solve the maze of productive and nonproductive efforts.

Clinicians need to consider some implicit assumptions in at least seven major areas of language assessment. These are (1) quantitative and descriptive approaches, (2) language knowledge and usage, (3) language structure and function, (4) formal and informal approaches, (5) sampling, (6) data handling, and (7) validity.

Quantitative and Descriptive Approaches

Quantitative and descriptive approaches bring into question the basic reasons for assessment. Clinicians should ask why assessment is needed in a given circumstance. Is it needed to resolve an issue concerning deviance (difference and pathology)? Is assessment needed to determine the nature and course of intervention? Quantitative approaches are strong in resolving deviance, but weak in directing intervention. Descriptive approaches are strong in generating alternative courses of action in intervention, but weak in resolving deviance.

These distinctions can be readily appreciated by examples. Quantitative measures such as mean sentence length, ITPA, developmental sentence types and scores, transitional error probability scores (Johnson, 1966a,b), and complexity scores (Frank and Osser, 1970) can resolve issues of deviance through normative comparison—assuming, of course, that appropriate norms are used. However, what is the significance of an aberrant quantitative score in intervention? Clinicians typically circumvent the issue of significance. Once a category is found to be aberrant, intervention procedures become nothing more than a series of exercises in the category. The underlying assumption is that language assessment need only measure the products of a grammatical system and then predicate intervention on the issuance of these products.

Whereas quantitative approaches are addressed to products of language, descriptive approaches are addressed to functional relationships between grammatical systems and to referential functions of language. Functional relationships between grammatical systems pertain to inquiries concerning the status of certain

54

grammatical systems in the context of other systems. For example, studies on the development of the negation and interrogative systems not only reveal stages in the development of these systems, but also acquisition patterns partially defined by other co-occurring grammatical systems (Bellugi[1]; Klima and Bellugi-Klima, 1969; Brown, Cazden, and Bellugi-Klima, 1969). Similarly, in the auxiliary system, the "progressive" and "perfect" systems show an acquisition pattern in which restricted forms appear when the negation system or expanded verb complement systems co-occur (Muma, 1967). In addition, certain nonrestricted transformational operations occur more frequently in the context of certain sentence frames (Muma, 1971). Harris (1965) and Johnson (1966a, b) have shown that variations in phrase structure reflect significant differences in structional relationships between co-occurring grammatical systems. Other descriptive procedures of this type include transformational analysis, certain types of phrase structure analysis, co-occurring and restricted structures analysis, distinctive feature analysis, and coarticulation analysis.

Valuable descriptive evidence is not only available in terms of co-occurring and restricted grammatical systems, but also in terms of referential functions of language. Referential functions pertain to the communicative roles of speech. The delineation of referential functions should probably have priority over structure in ascertaining one's language capacity, according to Bloom (1970). She specifically called for a reinterpretation of the evidence on the development of questions and negations. She provided a compelling argument for an examination of referential functions as the determinants of structure. A series of papers reflect this shift (Glucksberg and Krauss, 1967; Krauss and Glucksberg, 1969; Glucksberg, Krauss, and Weisberg, 1966; Rosenberg[2]; and Gruber, 1967). This shift not only defined reference as a viable dimension of verbal behavior, but it also provided for an operational definition of the relationships between thought and language (Olson, 1970; Macnamara, 1972; Carroll and Freedle, 1972). Accordingly, referential functions

---

[1] U. Bellugi, unpublished study on the development of questions and negatives in the speech of three children, personal communication, 1965.

[2] S. Rosenberg, unpublished paper on the development of referential skills in children, personal communication, 1970.

constitute an important dimension in language assessment. An assessment of referential functions can be carried out in terms of topic-comment, antecedents, representation, and situational referents.

In short, quantitative assessment approaches are oriented toward products of linguistics systems and beget taxonomic intervention, whereas descriptive approaches are oriented toward a portrayal of underlying systems in grammatical and referential contexts. The underlying assumption of the former is that assessment can be satisfactorily carried out in terms of the products of a system. The descriptive assumption is that assessment must be done in terms of the functional status of grammatical systems under various structural and referential constraints. Descriptive evidence portrays relationships between and within grammatical systems and referential functions. Such information is directly relevant to intervention because it suggests alternatives. These alternatives are defined according to the contextual relationships that obtain in an individual's functional use of language. Notice that information of this sort contrasts sharply with nonfunctional-categorical evidence found in the quantitative approaches. To reiterate, quantitative approaches are strong in resolving deviance; descriptive approaches are strong in generating alternative courses of action for intervention.

Language Knowledge and Usage

Most clinicians do not draw a distinction between one's knowledge of language and his use of this knowledge. This distinction is important (Cazden, 1966a) because clinicians are prone to assume that any given language performance, or even lack of performance, can be taken as an index of one's knowledge.

There are several underlying assumptions about language knowledge and usage which clinicians should attend to in language assessment. First, knowledge and usage are always confounded. Second, evidence concerning one's language knowledge and applications of his knowledge (usage) are always derived from performance (comprehension and production). Actually, usage is also a form of knowledge—selectively using language for communicative purpose and even problem solving. Thus, the knowledge-usage distinction entails two types of knowledge—knowledge of grammatical and referential systems and knowledge of when, where, why, and how to use grammatical and referential systems (Cazden, 1972; Hymes, 1971; Ervin-Tripp, 1971).

Third, language assessment procedures reflect a continuum in the degree to which they seem to index one's language knowledge and usage. Fourth, situational constraints can obscure evidence on language knowledge of grammatical and referential systems. Stewart (1968) indicated that dialect speakers are more reticent in foreign situations such as school or tests. Typical test conditions greatly constrain performance of disadvantaged children (Sroufe, 1970). Palmer (in Kagan, 1969) showed that intelligence test performance of disadvantaged children probably does not assess intelligence, but the constraining biases of the test situation. Thus, conclusions that dialect speakers' language is both qualitatively and quantitatively inadequate on the basis of performance on the ITPA and PPVT (Gerber and Hertel, 1969) represents an unfortunate abridgement of important underlying assumptions (Holland, 1970). Fifth, procedural issues regarding segmentation, quantification, and a priori or normative comparisons may obscure evidence on language knowledge. In short, clinicians should not always conclude that when they have obtained verbal data, it is adequate evidence of one's language knowledge or usage.

Certain language assessment procedures reflect language usage more than knowledge of grammatical and referential systems. Even though the ITPA is offered as a test of psycholinguistic abilities, it is probably a measure of language usage (between modalities) rather than language knowledge of grammatical and referential systems (Severson and Guest, 1970; Weener, Barritt, and Semmell, 1967). Similarly, the mean length of utterance (MLU) reflects situational variation more than grammatical competence, especially when calculated in words as opposed to morphemes, and when calculated for children over four years of age (Shriner, 1969). Assessment procedures of this type are addressed to the products of a linguistic system rather than the structural and funtional relationships of the underlying grammatical and referential systems.

Certain other language assessment procedures reflect knowledge of grammatical and referential systems more than usage. Those procedures that attempt to describe what an individual knows about his gram-

57

matical systems provide relatively more information about one's language knowledge for grammatical systems than product-oriented procedures. It is necessary, however, that the language samples under consideration be obtained from natural and varied situations (Plumer, 1970). Bloom's work (1970) exemplifies a clinical assessment of referential and grammatical systems. The studies on the development of communicative competence exemplify more sophisticated assessment approaches in the area of language usage. These studies are addressed to issues such as the acquisition of topic-comment (Gruber, 1967), role-taking (Flavell et al., 1968), and code shifting (Bernstein, 1970).

Structure and Function

Most clinicians view language assessment in terms of language structure, particularly syntax. Bloom (1970), Lewis and Freedle (1972), and Lewis (1972) have shown quite convincingly that to consider language only in these terms is a major oversight. Contextual referents vindicate structural forms; in assessment, they delineate specific structures. There are several implications of assessment and intervention which bring an appreciation of language structure and function together. First, language assessment out of a natural context provides dubious information about one's language knowledge. Second, language intervention that is essentially context free or functionally sterile is questionable. To learn a core vocabulary or certain restricted and controlled word combinations is a marked departure from normal language functions (McNeill, 1965). Language drill and labelling objects and actions may be no more than an exercise for clinicians because they are addressed only to products of language (surface structure) rather than underlying linguistic systems for issuing products. Labelling is a relatively minor aspect of language acquisition (Menyuk, 1971a, p. 13).

It is necessary to question the common emphasis on structure because it often excludes an interest in function. This emphasis has been both too narrow and misplaced, too narrow because most assessment procedures focus on word order (syntax) and word tagging (morphology), and semantics is generally ignored. Phonology is typically viewed as distinctly sep-

58

arate from syntax, and the modalities of language are often viewed as independent. The emphasis is misplaced because most assessment procedures are oriented toward the products of one's grammatical system(s). An assessment of the status of one's system(s) should be in terms of the system(s) and its (their) functions. A fundamental assumption of language assessment of knowledge is that it should be carried out in optimal conditions—in a functional context—and structure and function should be ascertained together. This assumption is flagrantly dismissed in the structure-only approaches.

An underlying assumption of the structure-only approaches is that language can be compartmentalized. While there are certain major grammatical dimensions, a conversion of dimensions to compartments is a distortion with unfortunate ramifications in assessment and intervention. Bloom's (1970) admonishment that function predicates structure serves to underscore the impropriety of separating syntax from semantics. Menyuk (1964c, 1968, 1971b) showed that syntax (morphology) was intimately related to phonology (articulation). Lees' (1966) account of derivational mechanisms clearly showed that significant interrelations exist between grammatical forms and functions. In two recent works, Hamilton and Deese[3] (in press) showed that grammatical structure is more than the sum of its parts. Menyuk (1971a, p. 23) and others have argued very convincingly that language modalities are intimately related, indeed governed by the same grammatical system. In short, the essence of linguistic behavior resides in the integrity between structure and function. An assessment procedure predicated on an underlying assumption that separates or compartmentalizes structure and function distorts essential mechanisms under assessment.

Formal and Informal Approaches

Formal approaches are those in which an individual participates in specific kinds of verbal performance. There are several underlying assumptions of formal assessment. First, it is assumed that the particular

---

[3] H. Hamilton and J. Deese, unpublished paper on a study of associations to combinations of words, personal communication, 1971.

dimensions of verbal behavior under consideration are relevant to an individual's behavior. On an empirical level, relevance is usually handled by either scaling difficulty as in the ITPA or by establishing developmental norms as in developmental sentence scores (Koenigsknecht and Lee, 1971). Are scaled or developmental norms truly relevant to one's underlying grammatical system? It is likely that the substitution of norms for individual relevance is tenuous. This assumption is problematical because of the corresponding shift from individual to group criteria for the determination of relevance.

Group needs are by definition summaries or composites of individual needs. If group needs are useful referents for individual needs in language assessment, it must be assumed that everyone in a group learns language the same way. The evidence on language learning does not support this assumption. Bloom (1970) showed quite convincingly that individuals have prerogatives to employ individual strategies, probably superimposed on developmental universals (Ervin-Tripp, 1972). In addition, individuals adopt alternative strategies of language learning (Nelson[4], 1971).

Second, formal approaches are based upon the assumption that rate and sequence of language acquisition can be quantified and used as an assessment index. While verbal behavior can be quantified and scaled to reflect developmental trends, there is a major problem concerning the legitimacy of this procedure. The problem is that rate of acquisition is notoriously variable, whereas sequence is highly stable (Cazden, 1966b, 1972; Brown, Cazden, and Bellugi-Klima, 1969). This means that developmental norms for various dimensions of language obscure major issues in language acquisition. In assessment, normative information does not provide differential evidence concerning an individual's rate of learning and stage of acquisition for a given grammatical system. Both types of information are needed by a clinician who wishes to devise an intervention program. He needs differential information about rate and sequence rather than a composite index. Accordingly, a normative reference is limited to issues of deviance. Informal descriptive evidence derives its assessment power by account-

---

[4]K. Nelson, unpublished paper on word and phrase learning strategies in early language acquisition, personal communication, 1970.

ing for individual variations in rate of learning through a careful examination of grammatical and referential contexts. Sequence is accounted for through stages and sequences within systems as opposed to norms and profiles of products.

Third, formal approaches are contextually highly constrained. That is, verbal performance is limited to highly specific tasks. Performance is elicited in a contrived manner under specific conditions and limited to certain verbal dimensions. Thus, the resulting performance is highly biased, which frequently contrasts sharply with one's typical spontaneous behavior and can hardly be considered representative. Yet, representativeness is a major criterion for assessment. Under such limitations, formal or a priori approaches could be relegated to a supplementary role to informal approaches.

Informal approaches are those in which language samples are sought from a series of typical situations. Unlike formal approaches, an individual controls the dimensions of grammar that are available for assessment. Certainly, these dimensions are constrained by the nature of the situations, but they are not limited to specific forms and functions as are found in formal tasks or in a priori scales. The primary assumption of informal approaches is that assessment will correspond closely with one's typical performance. Accordingly, evidence and conclusions derived therefrom will be representative and relevant. Moreover, such evidence can be translated directly into an intervention program that is itself predicated on performance in functionally relevant ways.

A major limitation of informal approaches is the possibility of obtaining meager data in any dimension of interest. This may mean that additional informal evidence or formal evidence specific to the area of interest must be obtained. Another limitation is the determination of a target dimension. Informal approaches offer a clinician innumerable areas of assessment. One must decide, often intuitively or by scanning the data, which dimensions and specific aspects to examine in detail. Obviously, this is also a strength, for it allows the client to direct the selection of dimensions by virtue of his performance. Thus, informal procedures do not assess verbal behavior on an a priori basis.

The goal of language sampling is to obtain a sufficiently representative sample to display one's typical performance so that any conclusions drawn from this performance will be valid. The same goal holds whether one is primarily assessing knowledge of grammatical and referential systems or knowledge of appropriate application. Several variables should be considered in obtaining representativeness. These variables include stimulus types, sample size, situational variation, and familiarity.

Stimulus types frequently constrain verbal performance. For example, pictures typically result in naming, labelling, and short narrative word combinations. Picture sequences give naming and labelling, but also include brief serial utterances. Puppets often provide active participation and a wide range of utterances. Situational play such as a doll house encourages spontaneous activities and a relatively wide range of linguistic performance. The underlying assumption is that as variety of linguistic performance increases, the likelihood of exhausting one's linguistic repertoire also increases. A corrollary of this is that as sample size increases, one's linguistic capacity becomes increasingly available for observation. Both of these assumptions have certain limitations. The most obvious of course is that variability of performance may stabilize over repeated or extended samples. Thus, variability and sample size become merely relative operational criteria for representativeness.

Age, sex, familiarity of participants, ethnic affiliation, and socioeconomic background influence the amount and variety of verbal production. Given these possible influences, clinicians should obtain language samples across a variety of situations which are representative of one's normal environment. Bloom (1967) criticized Lee (1966) for inadequate sampling in an attempt to show the clinical value of developmental sentence types. Menyuk (1963b, 1964a) obtained language samples from three different situations—child/adult, child/child, and child samples in a variety of circumstances in the children's home. Sroufe (1970) pointed out that situational variations significantly alter verbal behavior. Lewis and Freedle (1972) and Lewis (1972) provided evidence of various influences in mother-child interactions which affect verbal behavior.

The commonly held assumption that language should be assessed in a standardized condition merely reflects a strong empirical tradition. This assumption, however, is contradictory to others concerning language learning and behavior. Specifically, a standardized condition places too great of a constraint on the opportunities for representativeness. From Sroufe's perspective, a standardized condition simply biases performance in favor of individuals who identify with the condition, and against individuals who do not identify with it.

On what bases can we say that a language sample is representative? On one hand, it is desirable to achieve shortcuts, such as short language samples, to obtain economy of effort. On the other hand, a language sample must be sufficiently long to reflect characteristic attributes. Appropriate sample size and variability are very tricky matters. Three common strategies for obtaining representative samples are standardization, stabilization, and repeated samples. Consider the underlying assumptions of each.

In the standardized condition, samples are taken at the same time in the same circumstance and an assessment is usually conducted on the same number of utterances (typically the initial 50 utterances). The assumption is that all speakers should respond to the same stimuli in the same way. This is a tenuous assumption in language assessment. Aside from individual variation (alternatives inherent in grammar) which is considerable by itself, there are major cultural variations that would make this assumption untenable. Bernstein (1970) has argued that stylistic variations in verbal performance differ as a function of cultural background. Similarly, Lesser, Fifer, and Clark (1965) showed that ethnic background accounts for different cognitive styles (not levels). The point is that the underlying assumption concerning standardization contrasts directly with the principle of representativeness.

Stabilization refers to a sampling procedure in which samples are obtained until the behavior of interest stabilizes. That is to say, the degree of variability remains relatively stable with subsequent samples. The assumption is that when performance stabilizes, a sufficient range of performance is obtained to practically exhaust the capacity of one's grammatical system. Variations within this range would reflect situational differences, whereas overall performance would reflect one's grammatical knowledge. Unfortunately, there are two major problems with this assumption. First, there is the problem of what stabilizes. A clinician can arbitrarily select something such as a dimension of grammar (auxiliary system, negation system, or nominal transformations) or a product of verbal performance (mean length of utterance). Under this strategy, a clinician must be sure that his criterion of stabilization is consistent with his assessment inquiry. If his inquiry concerns grammatical knowledge, the criterion should be in terms of the operations of a grammatical system (patterns of co-occurring and restricted structures) rather than a product of the system. If his inquiry concerns language usage, his criterion should be in terms of products or contingencies between products and communicative intent.

Ironically enough, stabilization is not particularly desirable for assessing either knowledge or usage, even though the empiricists might have us believe that it is (Darley and Moll, 1960). Moreover, stabilization is transient in verbal behavior. When one dimension of grammar is relatively stable, other dimensions vary (although not in free variation). Menyuk (1963a, 1964b) reported a dampened oscillatory function in the reduction of errors in children's utterances. This function apparently pertains to the concept of stability and variation in co-occurring structures. Presumably, fewer errors occur when children constrain their verbal behavior to those structures within their repertoire, but more errors occur when new structures are used. This raises the second problem of the stabilization strategy—namely, it is incompatible with language acquisition. Language learning occurs in spurts associated with frequent rapid developments. Stabilizations are typically brief with significant variations in co-occurring structures and alternative functions. The stabilization procedure may be nothing more than a convenient ploy superimposed on a dynamic system.

The assumption of repeated sampling is that variability across situations will be representative of one's normal situational variability. Further, this variability will be reflected in language performance; that is, the situational variables are primary determinants of verbal behavior. The issues then become how many samples and how many and varied situations are necessary to obtain representativeness. There is no simple answer because of the numerous variables that influence language performance. As a general rule, perhaps it is best to take a minimum of three language samples in three different but typical situations for an individual. These language samples should contain a sufficient number of structures for the target system to establish a pattern of restricted structures (Menyuk, 1963b, 1964b, c) and co-occurring structures (Brown, Cazden, and Bellugi-Klima, 1969; Bloom, 1970). This usually means that a minimum of 20 utterances containing the target system is needed. The number and extent of sampling is highly variable, contingent upon the particular target area of interest and its frequency of occurrence. Sometimes a sufficient number of target structures are available in relatively short samples from only three situations. Other times extensive samples or greater variation in situations yields a sufficient sample. Clearly, the commonly used assessment strategy of 50 utterances from one sample from one situation or the responses to categories on a specific test are highly suspect from the point of view of representativeness.

Data Handling

Clinicians should be cognizant of underlying assumptions and biases in data handling during assessment. Consider three primary areas—recording and transcription, segmentation, and quantification. The assumption in recording and transcription is that one's performance is faithfully transposed but not transformed. Most recording and transcription procedures violate this assumption. Written transcription is notoriously inadequate; omissions of verbal material and referents are common. Tape recording carries the limitations of clarity and the identification of speakers and situational referents. Video taping overcomes most of the former limitations, but it is too expensive, conspicuous, and very time consuming in translation (Bloom, 1972). Transcription can be a serious problem when the transcriber is not familiar with the communicative context and untrained to accept deviations.

Segmentation pertains to decisions that are made in data handling concerning the relevancy of material. All language samples must be segmented. Some aspects are superfluous for certain inquiries, but others are not. For example, an assessment of grammar would segment a language sample into fluent (grammatical, including restricted structures) and nonfluent (hesitation phenomena) (Maclay and Osgood, 1959; Muma, 1967) portions. Further segmentation issues deal with junctures of utterances (sentences, clauses, phrases, and even words and morphemes). Depending upon one's training, segmentation issues can materially alter a language sample.

Quantification pertains to the units of assessment. Clinicians should employ assessment units that are consistent with the ultimate conclusions that will be drawn. If conclusions are to be drawn about one's knowledge of grammar, the quantification units must be in terms of grammatical systems, that is, transformational operations (Chomsky, 1965; Menyuk, 1963a, b, c, 1964a; Muma, 1971), derivational mechanisms (Lees, 1966; Rosenbaum, 1967), phrase structure (Johnson, 1966a, b), recursiveness (Menyuk, 1969, p. 96), co-occurring and restricted structures (Muma, in press), and generative phonology (Compton, 1970; Crocker, 1969; Menyuk, 1968). On the other hand, conclusions on usage could also be made in terms of grammatical systems, and they could be drawn from units of linguistic products, that is, mean length of utterance, sentence types, or number of nouns. Evidence on syntax should not be generalized to phonology, semantics, and functions. Similarly, evidence on vocabulary alone should not be generalized to the whole semantic domain.

Validity

With so many variables influencing verbal behavior, how can one be sure he is truly assessing what he intends to assess? There is no absolute assurance, only relative assurance. When a dimension of grammar varies according to a pattern and the pattern (rule) is predictable and relates to or integrates with other patterns, the assumption is made that the observation is valid. Admittedly, this assumption is circular and relative. Indeed, any statement pressed to its limits about an autonomous mechanism is circular and relative. The circularity, however, is not a serious problem when it appears at the most specific levels of a conceptual hierarchy, because one must pass through higher levels of integrated generality which characterize the system.

Language assessment is a very complicated undertaking, one which clinicians should consider carefully, particularly at an operational level. Clinicians must understand the assumptions underlying various assessment approaches, particularly formal and informal. Clinicians should at least recognize the distinction between approaches that resolve issues of deviance (difference and pathology) and approaches that provide alternatives for directing the nature and course of intervention. Clinicians should also be cognizant of assessment approaches that are oriented toward products of grammar and those oriented toward grammatical and referential terms. Clearly, there is no such thing as a simple, clear-cut language assessment.

REFERENCES

BERNSTEIN, B., A sociolinguistic approach to socialization. With some reference to educability. In F. Williams (Ed.), *Language and Proverty: Perspectives on a Theme*. Chicago: Markham (1970).

BLOOM, L., A comment on Lee's developmental sentence types: A method for comparing normal and deviant syntactic development. *J. Speech Hearing Dis.*, 32, 294-296 (1967).

BLOOM, L., *Language Development: Form and Function in Emerging Grammars*. Cambridge, Mass.: MIT Press (1970).

BLOOM, L., Cognitive and linguistic aspects of early language development. Paper presented at the Annual Convention of the American Speech and Hearing Association, San Francisco (1972).

BROWN, R., CAZDEN, C., and BELLUGI-KLIMA, U., The child's grammar from I to III. In J. Hill (Ed.), *Minnesota Symposia on Child Psychology*. (Vol. 2) Minneapolis: Univ. of Minnesota Press (1969).

CARROLL, J., and FREEDLE, R. (Eds.), *Language Comprehension and the Acquisition of Knowledge*. New York: Wiley (1972).

CAZDEN, C., On individual differences in language competence and performance. *J. spec. Ed.*, 1, 135-150 (1966a).

CAZDEN, C., Some implications of research on language development for preschool education. Paper presented to the Social Science Research Council Conference in Preschool Education (1966b).

CAZDEN, C., *Child Language and Education*. New York: Holt, Rinehart, and Winston (1972).

CHOMSKY, N., *Aspects of the Theory of Syntax*. Cambridge, Mass.: MIT Press (1965).

COMPTON, A., Generative studies of children's phonological disorders. *J. Speech Hearing Dis.*, 35, 315-339 (1970).

CROCKER, J., A phonological model of children's articulation competence. *J. Speech Hearing Dis.*, 34, 203-213 (1969).

DARLEY, F., and MOLL, K., Reliability of language measures and size of language sample. *J. Speech Hearing Res.*, 3, 166-173 (1960).

DUNN, L., *Peabody Picture Vocabulary Test.* Los Angeles: Western Psychological Services (1965).

ERVIN-TRIPP, S., Social backgrounds and verbal skills. In R. Huxley and E. Ingram, (Eds.), *Language Acquisition: Models and Methods.* New York: Academic (1971).

ERVIN-TRIPP, S., Developmental universals. Paper presented at the Annual Convention of the American Speech and Hearing Association, San Francisco (1972).

FLAVELL, J., BOTKIN, P., FRY, C., WRIGHT, J., and JARVIS, P., *The Development of Role-Taking and Communication Skills in Children.* New York: Wiley (1968).

FRANK, S., and OSSER, H., A psycholinguistic model of syntactic complexity. *Lang. Speech,* 13, 38-53 (1970).

GERBER, S., and HERTEL, G., Language deficiency of disadvantaged children. *J. Speech Hearing Res.,* 12, 270-280 (1969).

GLUCKSBERG, S., and KRAUSS, R., What do people say after they have learned how to talk? Studies of the development of referential communication. *Merrill Palmer Quart.,* 13, 309-316 (1967).

GLUCKSBERG, S., KRAUSS, R., and WEISBERG, R., Referential communication in nursery school children: Method and some preliminary findings. *J. exp. child Psychol.,* 3, 333-342 (1966).

GRUBER, J., Topicalization in child language. *Found. Lang.,* 3, 37-65 (1967).

HAMILTON, H., and DEESE, J., Does linguistic marking have a psychological correlate? *J. verb. Learn. verb. Behav.* (in press).

HARRIS, Z., Co-occurrence and transformation in linguistic structure. Chapter 6 in J. Fodor, and J. Katz., *The Structure of Language: Readings in the Philosophy of Language.* Englewood Cliffs, N.J.: Prentice-Hall (1965).

HOLLAND, A., Comment on language deficiency of disadvantaged children. *J. Speech Hearing Res.,* 13, 440-441 (1970).

HYMES, D., Competence and performance in linguistic theory. In R. Huxley and E. Ingram (Eds.), *Language Acquisition: Models and Methods.* New York: Academic (1971).

JOHNSON, N., On the relationship between sentence structure and the latency in generating the sentence. *J. verb. Learn. Verb. Dis.,* 5, 375-380 (1966a).

JOHNSON, N., The influence of associations between elements of structured verbal responses. *J. verb. Learn. verb. Behav.,* 5, 369-374 (1966b).

KAGAN, J., Inadequate evidence and illogical conclusions. *Harv. ed. Rev.,* 39, 274-277 (1969).

KIRK, S., and MCCARTHY, J., The Illinois Test of Psycholinguistic Abilities: An approach to differential diagnosis. *Amer. J. ment. Defic.,* 66, 399-412 (1961).

KIRK, S., MCCARTHY, J., and KIRK, W., *The Illinois Test of Psycholinguistic Abilities.* (rev. ed.) Urbana, Ill.: Univ. of Illinois Press (1968).

KLIMA, E., and BELLUGI-KLIMA, U., Syntactic regularities in the speech of children. In D. Reibel and S. Schane (Eds.), *Modern Studies in English.* Englewood Cliffs, N.J.: Prentice-Hall (1969).

KOENIGSKNECHT, R., and LEE, L., Validity and reliability of developmental sentence scoring: A method for measuring syntactic development in children's spontaneous speech. Paper presented to the Annual Convention of the American Speech and Hearing Association, Chicago (1971).

KRAUSS, R., and GLUCKSBERG, S., The development of communication: Competence as a function of age. *Child Develpm.*, 40, 255-266 (1969).

LEE, L., Developmental sentence types: A method for comparing normal and deviant syntactic development: *J. Speech Hearing Dis.*, 31, 311-320 (1966).

LEE, L., and CANTER, S., Developmental sentence scoring: A clinical procedure for estimating syntactic development in children's spontaneous speech. *J. Speech Hearing Dis.*, 36, 315-340 (1971).

LEES, R., *The Grammar of English Nominalizations.* Bloomington: Indiana Univ. (1966).

LESSER, G., FIFER, G., and CLARK, D., Mental abilities of children in different social and cultural groups. *SRCD Monogr.*, 30 (1965).

LEWIS, M., State as an infant-environment interaction: An analysis of mother-infant behavior as a function of sex. *Merrill Palmer Quart. Behav. Develpm.*, 18, 95-121 (1972).

LEWIS, M., and FREEDLE, R., Mother-infant dyad: The cradle of meaning. Paper presented at a symposium on Language and Thought, Univ. of Toronto (1972).

LOCKE, J., Questionable assumptions underlying articulation research. *J. Speech Hearing Dis.*, 33, 112-116 (1968).

MACNAMARA, J., Cognitive basis of language learning in infants. *Psychol. Rev.*, 79, 1-13 (1972).

McCLAY, H., and OSGOOD, C., Hesitation phenomena in spontaneous English speech. *Word,* 15, 19-44 (1959).

McNEILL, D., Some thoughts on first and second language acquisition. Paper presented to the Modern Foreign Language Title III Conference, Washington, D.C. (1965).

MENYUK, P., A preliminary evaluation of grammatical capacity in children. *J. verb. Learn. verb. Behav.*, 2, 429-439 (1963a).

MENYUK, P., Syntactic structures in the language of children. *Child Develpm.*, 34, 407-422 (1963b).

MENYUK, P., Syntactic rules used by children from preschool through first grade. *Child Develpm.*, 35, 533-546 (1964a).

MENYUK, P., Alternation of rules in children's grammar. *J. verb. Learn. verb. Behav.*, 3, 480-488 (1964b).

MENYUK, P., Comparison of grammar of children with functionally deviant and normal speech. *J. Speech Hearing Res.*, 7, 109-121 (1964c).

MENYUK, P., The role of distinctive features in children's acquisition of phonology. *J. Speech Hearing Res.*, 11, 138-146 (1968).

MENYUK, P., *Sentences Children Use.* Cambridge, Mass.: MIT Press (1969).

MENYUK, P., *The Acquisition and Development of Language.* Englewood Cliffs, N. J.: Prentice-Hall (1971a).

MENYUK, P., Direction of language processing. *Quart. Rep. Electron.*, MIT, 101, 182-188 (1971b).

MUMA, J., A comparison of certain aspects of productivity and grammar in speech samples of fluent and nonfluent four year old children. Doctoral dissertation, Pennsylvania State Univ. (1967).

MUMA, J., Frequency of aspect in oral and written verbal samples by children. *Project Report B & A Section, R & D Center* (Technical Report), University of Georgia (1967).

MUMA, J., Syntax of preschool fluent and dysfluent speech: A transformational analysis. *J. Speech and Hearing Res.*, 14, 428-441 (1971).

MUMA, J., Language assessment: The co-occurring and restricted structures procedure. *Acta symbol.* (in press).

MYKLEBUST, H., *Development and Disorders of Written Language.* (Vol. 1) Picture Story Language Test. New York: Grune and Stratton (1965).

NELSON, K., Pre-syntactic strategies for learning to talk. Paper presented to the Biennial Meeting of SRCD, Minneapolis (1971).

OLSON, D., Language and thought: Aspects of a cognitive theory of semantics. *Psychol. Rev.*, 77, 257-273 (1970).

PLUMER, D., A summary of environmentalist views and some educational implications. In F. Williams, (Ed.), *Language and Poverty: Perspectives on a Theme.* Chicago: Markham (1970).

ROSENBAUM, P., *The Grammar of English Predicate Construction.* Cambridge, Mass.: MIT Press (1967).

SEVERSON, R., and GUEST, K., Toward the standardized assessment of the language of disadvantaged children. In F. Williams (Ed.), *Language and Poverty: Perspectives on a Theme.* Chicago: Markham (1970).

SHRINER, T., A review of mean length of response as a measure of expressive language development in children. *J. Speech Hearing Dis.*, 34, 61-67 (1969).

SROUFE, L., A methodological and philosophical critique of intervention-oriented research. *Developm. Psychol.*, 2, 140-145 (1970).

STEWART, W., A linguistic approach to nonstandard speech (with special emphasis on Negro dialects). Paper presented to the Annual Convention of the American Speech and Hearing Association, Denver (1968).

WEENER, P., BARRITT, L., and SEMMELL, M., A critical evaluation of the Illinois Test of Psycholinguistic Abilities. *Except. Child.*, 373-384 (1967).

WEPMAN, J., *Auditory Discrimination Test.* Chicago: Language Research (1958).

A STANDARDIZED METHOD
FOR OBTAINING A SPOKEN
LANGUAGE SAMPLE

MARGO E. WILSON

The stimulus picture from the Picture Story Language Test was used to elicit a spoken language sample from 40 subjects ranging in age from three to seventeen years. Our results showed the stimulus picture to be useful for the standardized elicitation of a spoken language sample which seems to be representative of the subject's language maturity. The method was found to have temporal reliability with the exception of the Words Per Sentence measure. The method required a minimum amount of time and equipment. The scoring procedures, with the exception ·f the Syntax Quotient, were found to be highly reliable with regard to interscorer and intrascorer agreement. All the language measures used in this study correlated satisfactorily with judged language maturity.

A sample of spoken language has been found useful for the clinical evaluation of the language development of an individual child and for various research studies dealing with language development and measures of language proficiency.

The technique most commonly used for spoken language sampling is that first described by McCarthy (1930) and later modified by Davis (McCarthy, 1954), Templin (1957), Winitz (1959), and others, which consists of obtaining 50 responses to pictures and toys. Other methods include recording the subject's responses during a classroom situation and as he identifys objects (Hahn, 1948), gives noun definitions (Schneiderman, 1955), or describes pictures from the Children's Apperception Test (Siegel, 1962; Brannon and Murray, 1966).

None of these methods is standardized with regard to either: (1) a definite set of instructions for the examiner and for the examiner to give to the subject, or (2) a standardized set of stimulus materials easily available and convenient to use. Many of the methods do not appear to be designed to elicit representative speech and may actually encourage naming responses and short sentences. Since the method of elicitation is not standard, the use of McCarthy's and Templin's norms is of questionable appropriateness, yet they are used routinely for clinical evaluations. Furthermore, there is evidence that the norms are outdated (Minifie, Darley, and Sherman, 1963).

JOURNAL OF SPEECH AND HEARING RESEARCH, March 1969, vol. 12, no. 1, pp. 95-102.

In addition to a need for a standardized method of obtaining the language sample, there is a need for accurate and adequate methods of evaluating the obtained sample. The reliability of various scoring techniques currently in use has been investigated and found wanting (Minifie et al., 1963; Darley and Moll, 1960.)

Since none of the methods currently in use is entirely satisfactory for eliciting a representative sample of spoken language and since the reliability and appropriateness of some of the scoring techniques have been questioned, another method was sought.

The Picture Story Language Test (Myklebust, 1965) was reviewed and found to be a standardized, reliable, and apparently valid method of obtaining and evaluating written language samples.

The primary purpose of this study was to determine whether the stimulus picture from the Picture Story Language Test could be used as a standardized method of eliciting a representative sample of spoken language and whether the five language measures described by Myklebust could be adapted for use with a spoken language sample. These are the measures: (1) Total Words, a count of all written units recognizable as elements that could stand alone and convey meaning; (2) Total Sentences, a division of the sample ". . . according to the most deducibly correct grammatical units on the basis of the established relationships among words, and also, according to the logical sequence of the ideas being expressed." (Myklebust, 1965, p. 101); (3) Words Per Sentence, computed by dividing the total number of words by the total number of sentences; (4) Syntax Scale, a penalty system employed to designate errors of word usage, word endings, and punctuation on the basis of additions, omissions, and substitutions with error totals being entered in a formula that yields a Syntax Quotient; and (5) Abstract-Concrete Scale, for which each sample is assigned to 1 of 25 levels depending upon degree of abstraction of ideas in the sample. Specifically, test-retest reliability, interscorer reliability, and intrascorer reliability were determined and the validity of the method of elicitation and scoring was investigated.

METHOD

Selection of Subjects

Forty subjects were selected from a normal (not speech defective) population on the basis of age, sex, and hearing acuity. There were four subjects, two male and two female, at each of the following age levels: 3, 4, 5, 6, 7, 9, 11, 13, 15, and 17. Any subjects not able to pass a hearing screening test at 500, 1000, and 2000 Hz at 25 dB HL (ISO) were eliminated from the study.

Adaptation of Scoring Procedures

The first step in the adaptation of the scoring instructions developed by Myklebust (1965, pp. 95-146) was the omission of all discussion of situations and examples that could only occur in written language samples: punctuation, meaningless language (scribbling), spelling errors, etc. Allowance was made for verbal dysfluencies through the use of instructions from Johnson, Darley, and Spriestersbach (1963) concerning word and phrase repetitions. The measure Total Words Corrected used in the present study reflects these changes from Myklebust's Total Words. McCarthy's criterion (1930) for designating responses was added to Myklebust's (1965). The common verbal overuse of the word *and* and the phrase *and so* made it necessary to exempt these words from addition penalties in Myklebust's Syntax Quotient.

Experimental Procedures

Each subject was tested individually in the same room; distractions and environmental noise were kept to a minimum. Each subject was given a hearing screening test. The subject was then shown the picture from the Picture Story Language Test. The picture, a black and white photograph 10½" by 13½", portrays a young boy seated at a table arranging doll figures and doll furniture. The following instructions were given:

I'd like you to tell a story about this picture. You can look at the picture while you tell the story. Begin whenever you are ready.

Each subject's story was tape-recorded as told spontaneously. No effort was made to force lengthiness through questioning, use of additional pictures, etc. Following the testing of all subjects, typescripts of each subject's story were prepared by the investigator. To determine test-retest reliability, a second language sample was obtained in exactly the same manner as the first from one-fourth (ten) of the subjects. The second sample was recorded no earlier than two days and not later than two weeks after the first sample was obtained to minimize possible maturational factors.

All the language samples were scored by the investigator using the adapted scoring instructions. Ten of these samples were also scored by a graduate student in speech pathology using the same scoring instructions. The interscorer reliability correlation coefficient was computed using the Pearson *r* formula (Adkins, 1964). Ten of the samples were scored by the investigator three weeks after initial scoring to obtain an intrascorer reliability correlation. The same Pearson *r* formula was used.

Validity of the Scoring Procedures

One accepted means of testing for validity is the comparison of scores obtained from the method under study to those obtained by another method of testing the same, or what is assumed to be the same, concept. A comparison of the results of the present study to the norms currently in use did not seem to be an acceptable means of determining the validity of the scoring procedures used in the present investigation since these norms have been questioned. Since overall language maturity is what is being evaluated when language samples are obtained and scored for clinical purposes, the finding of Marge (1964) that judges' ratings of samples obtained from his Picture Description Test had a high loading on the factor of Language Maturity made a rating technique the logical choice for a validity comparison.

Acquisition of language is a continuous process of growth. A ranking of the language samples from most proficient to least proficient in language ability seemed therefore more appropriate than interval scale ratings. Two speech pathologists from the Department of Speech at the University of Nebraska ranked unscored language samples from 1 to 40, with 1 representing the most proficient use of language and 40 the least proficient. The samples were presented to the judges in typescript form as suggested by Shriner and Sherman (1967) to eliminate the possible influence of such irrelevant factors as pitch, intonation, stress, articulation errors, and clues to the age of the subject being evaluated. The judges were asked to read all the typescripts first, to obtain an idea of the range and variability of the samples. The samples could be reread as often as required to estimate the degree of language maturity as defined by the following criteria: variety and complexity of sentence structure; correctness of usage of vocabulary and syntax; and organization (Marge, 1964). Each judge evaluated all the samples and ranked each in comparison to all the rest of the samples. The two judges' rankings for each sample were then averaged for computation of the rank difference correlation coefficient, using the Spearman Rho formula (Adkins, 1964) to compare the judges' rankings of the language samples to the rankings for each scored language measure and to chronological age. Interjudge reliability was determined, using the Pearson r formula (Adkins, 1964).

RESULTS

Every subject verbalized willingly about the picture, with Total Words Corrected ranging from 895 to 13, and Total Sentences ranging from 61 to 2. The longest time required for the instructions and the recording of the language sample, which corresponded to the longest language sample obtained, was eight minutes. All subjects were able to understand the instructions without any need for further elaboration. The instructions were in some cases repeated. Young subjects who tended to point to the picture were reminded to tell a story about it.

The reliability of the sampling technique was determined through the test-retest method. Correlation coefficients were computed using the Pearson r formula for the following language measures: Total Words Corrected, 0.98; Total Sentences, 0.80; Words Per Sentence, 0.42; Syntax Quotient, 0.04; and Abstract-Concrete Scale, 0.89. The reliability of Total Words Corrected, Total Sentences, and Abstract-Concrete Scale was found to be significant beyond the 0.01 level of confidence. (See Table 1.)

The reliability of the scoring procedures was determined for both inter-

TABLE 1. Coefficients of correlation obtained for the measures of spoken language.

	Test-Retest	Inter-scorer	Intra-scorer	Judges' Rankings	Chrono-logical Age
Total Words Corrected	0.98°	0.99°	0.99°	0.89°	0.83°
Total Sentences	0.80°	0.93°	0.96°	0.71†	0.58
Words Per Sentence	0.42	0.94°	0.99°	0.93°	0.95°
Syntax Quotient	0.04	−0.28	0.57	0.76†	0.68
Abstract-Concrete Scale	0.89°	–	–	0.93°	0.93°
Judges' Rankings	–	0.93°	–	–	0.95°

°Significant beyond the 0.01 level of confidence.
†Significant beyond the 0.05 level of confidence.

scorer and intrascorer agreement. With regard to interscorer reliability, three measures—Total Words Corrected, 0.99; Total Sentences, 0.93; and Words Per Sentence, 0.94—were found to be satisfactorily reliable and the coefficients of correlation for these measures were significant beyond the 0.01 level of confidence. The Syntax Quotient, −0.28, was not satisfactorily reliable.

The intrascorer coefficients were as follows: Total Words, 0.99; Total Sentences, 0.96; Words Per Sentence, 0.99; and Syntax Quotient, 0.57. All but Syntax Quotient were found to be satisfactorily reliable with the coefficients being significant beyond the 0.01 level of confidence.

It can be concluded from the evidence just cited that Total Words Corrected, Total Sentences, and the Abstract-Concrete Scale are highly reliable based on test-retest, interscorer, and intrascorer comparisons. The Words Per Sentence measure attains a high reliability for scoring agreement, but was not found to be satisfactorily stable over a period of time. The Syntax Quotient was found to be highly unreliable in all three aspects: test-retest, interscorer, and intrascorer reliability.

All the language measures showed a high positive correlation with the combined judges' rankings. The two judges, working independently, achieved satisfactory agreement with each other, obtaining a correlation coefficient of 0.93. The rank difference coefficients of correlation between the language measures and the combined judges' rankings of overall language maturity were as follows: Total Words Corrected, 0.89; Total Sentences, 0.71; Words Per Sentence, 0.93; Syntax Quotient, 0.76; and Abstract-Concrete Scale, 0.93. The coefficients for Total Words Corrected, Words Per Sentence, and Abstract-Concrete Scale were significant beyond the 0.01 level of confidence and the Total Sentences and Syntax Quotient coefficients were significant beyond the 0.05 level. The judges' rankings correlated 0.95 with chronological age of the subject. Table 1 summarizes the reliability coefficients for the language measures.

DISCUSSION

Of the five language measures used for analysis of the samples, Total Words Corrected was most reliable. The scoring instructions for this measure were apparently adequate and easily understood. Total Words Corrected is also reliable in that it is stable. That is, it does not vary extremely from time to time. Total Words Corrected appears to be a valid measure of language maturity based on the high correlation with the judges' rankings.

The Total Sentences measure also appears to be satisfactory for use in analyzing a spoken language sample when used as described in this study. The criteria for determining response sentences were evidently unambiguous since the interscorer and intrascorer reliabilities were high. The measure is not quite as stable as Total Words Corrected, but attained an acceptable correlation coefficient. The Total Sentences score correlated satisfactorily with judged overall language maturity.

The Words Per Sentence score was reliable with respect to interscorer agreement and intrascorer agreement. The measure was not shown to be satisfactorily stable, however, on the basis of the test-retest correlation. A larger number of subjects retested might have resulted in an acceptable test-retest coefficient, or the reliability if tested by age groups might be satisfactory for the older subjects, as found by Myklebust (1965). He states that the reliability coefficients were influenced by the age of the child, with the stories by the younger children being less reliably scored and less stable on test-retest measures. The Words Per Sentence score correlation with the judges' rankings indicates that this measure is strongly related to language maturity as judged by the listener.

The Syntax Quotient, as adapted for use in this study, was found to be highly unreliable for evaluation of the obtained language samples. The two scorers, both untrained, differed greatly in their interpretation of the rules for scoring the Syntax Quotient. The reliability of the scoring of this measure might be improved in several ways. With training and practice in the use of the measure, the scorers might agree better with each other and with themselves. More examples of the level of stringency to be applied to the area of word usage would aid the scorers. A revision of the scoring instructions to include more detail and examples might be helpful. It seems most likely, however, that an entirely different set of criteria for measuring this aspect of spoken language would be more appropriate. The Syntax Quotient as used by Myklebust for analysis of written language considered punctuation. When this aspect of the scoring criteria was deleted, the Syntax Quotient may have lost an important factor in its reliability and validity, although Myklebust did find that only trained scorers could reliably score this measure. It might become a more meaningful measure of spoken language if it were broadened to include structure, and grammatical usage. McCarthy (1930) found increases in the percentages of compound, complex, and elaborated sentences with increases in age, and thus with increased language maturity. Menyuk (1964) and Lee (1966) each found that children with normal speech and language development used more transformations and structures which required increasingly complex rules for their use. This evidence suggests that a different, broader, and more complete evaluation of language usage would be desirable.

The Abstract-Concrete Scale was found by Myklebust (1965) to be a highly reliable measure when used by either trained or untrained scorers. This scale also showed high agreement with the judges' rankings.

Examination of the data shows that each of the language measures with the exception of the Syntax Quotient and Total Sentences demonstrates an orderly progression of increasing language facility as age increases, as can be seen by the rank difference coefficients of correlation between the language measures and the judges' rankings and the chronological age of the subjects in Table 1. On the basis of these coefficients it can be concluded that the spoken language samples obtained from the individual subjects were representative of their language maturity with respect to amount of verbalization in the standardized situation (Total Words Corrected and Words Per Sentence) and their ability to abstract (Abstract-Concrete Scale) since these measures correlated strongly with chronological age. A much larger sampling would be required, however, to evaluate completely the effects of maturation on Total Words Corrected and Total Sentences.

The greatest value of the method used in this study, in our opinion, is the standardization of the stimulus and instructions. This method is easy to administer, requires a minimum of equipment, and the required equipment is easily available. Too, a great deal of time is not required, and the instructions are designed to elicit sequential speech rather than definitions or object descriptions, and therefore a more typical sample of the subject's language ability. When and if normative data are accumulated, the norms can be used with confidence since the method of obtaining the sample to be evaluated will be consistent and the scoring procedures have been found to be generally reliable and valid.

ACKNOWLEDGMENT

This report is based upon a master's thesis completed in the Department of Speech and Dramatic Art at the University of Nebraska under the direction of William F. Shrum.

REFERENCES

ADKINS, DOROTHY, Statistics. Columbus, Ohio: Charles E. Merrill (1964).

BRANNON, J. B., and MURRAY, T., The spoken syntax of normal, hard-of-hearing and deaf children. J. Speech Hearing Res., 9, 604-610 (1966).

DARLEY, F. L., and MOLL, K. L., Reliability of language measures and size of language sample. J. Speech Hearing Res., 3, 166-173 (1960).

HAHN, E., Analyses of the content and form of the speech of first grade children. Quart. J. Speech, 34, 361-366 (1948).

JOHNSON, W., DARLEY, F., and SPRIESTERSBACH, D. C., Diagnostic Methods in Speech Pathology. New York: Harper & Row (1963).

LEE, L., Developmental sentence types: A method for comparing normal and deviant syntactic development. J. Speech Hearing Dis., 31, 311-330 (1966).

McCARTHY, D., The Language Development of the Pre-School Child. Minneapolis: Univ. Minn. (1930).

McCARTHY, D., Language development in children. In L. Carmichael (Ed.) Manual of Child Psychology. New York: Wiley (1954).

MARGE, M., A factor analysis of oral communication skills in older children. *J. Speech Hearing Res.*, **7**, 31-46 (1964).

MENYUK, P., Comparison of grammar of children with functionally deviant and normal speech. *J. Speech Hearing Res.*, **7**, 109-120 (1964).

MINIFIE, F. D., DARLEY, F. L., and SHERMAN, D., Temporal reliability of seven language measures. *J. Speech Hearing Res.*, **6**, 139-149 (1963).

MYKLEBUST, H., *Development and Disorders of Written Language. Vol. I., Picture Story Language Test.* New York: Grune & Stratton (1965).

SCHNEIDERMAN, N., A study of the relationship between articulatory ability and language ability. *J. Speech Hearing Dis.*, **20**, 359-364 (1955).

SHRINER, R. H., and SHERMAN, D., An equation for assessing language development. *J. Speech Hearing Res.*, **10**, 41-48 (1967).

SIEGEL, O. M., Interexaminer reliability for mean length of response. *J. Speech Hearing Res.*, **5**, 91-95 (1962).

TEMPLIN, M., *Certain Language Skills in Children: Their Development and Inter-relationships.* Minneapolis: Univ. Minn. (1957).

WINITZ, H., Language skills of male and female kindergarten children. *J. Speech Hearing Res.*, **2**, 377-386 (1959).

COMMENT ON "A STANDARDIZED METHOD FOR OBTAINING A SPOKEN LANGUAGE SAMPLE"

Jerry Griffith

The purpose of this paper is to take issue with the basic conclusions drawn by Wilson (1969) that the Picture Story Language Test is a reliable method of evoking and scoring an oral language sample and that the sample obtained by the PSLT is representative of the language that would be obtained in any other sampling procedure. Evidence is cited that a child's verbal output is significantly affected by stimulus, examiner, and subject variables and that the language measures applied interact with the method used to evoke the sample.

The Wilson (1969) study makes an important contribution by highlighting major theoretical and clinical problems associated with sampling child language. She points out that traditional procedures fail to control the relevant variables, namely, stimulus and examiner effects. In addition, she comments on the need for a more sensitive measure of linguistic proficiency. The basic purpose of her study was to evaluate the Picture Story Language Test (Myklebust, 1965, p. 71) as a method of evoking and scoring oral language samples. In other words, her intent was to investigate the applicability of a graphemic system of language analysis to a phonological system.

Examination of Wilson's data revealed that several PSLT language measures correlated highly with judges' ratings of linguistic proficiency and chronological age. She concluded (p. 101):

> On the basis of these coefficients it can be concluded that the spoken language samples obtained from the individual subjects were representative of their language maturity with re-

spect to amount of verbalization in the standardized situation (total words corrected and words per sentence) and their ability to abstract (Abstract-Concrete Scale) since these measures correlated with chronological age.

By challenging traditional language sampling procedures, the purpose of this study raises a valid question of sufficiency. However, its conclusions seriously fail in their quest for sufficiency. How can one reliably state that a representative language sample was obtained without comparing a subject's linguist performance in various testing environments to PSLT performance? The results of a number of studies (Cowan, Weber, Hoddinott, and Klein, 1967; Mintun, 1968; Strandberg and Griffith, 1969; Strandberg, 1969; Quereshi, 1908; Brent and Katz, 1968) provide strong evidence that a child's verbal output is a function of the particular language measure, stimulus, examiner and subject variables and their resulting interactions. It may be that for a given subject different stimuli and different language measures are required to evaluate habitual linguistic performance when examiner bias is minimized. Until all of these factors are systematically varied and assessed, it seems premature to conclude that verbal output in one stimulus situation is representative of verbal output in nearly all situations. I would hesitate to make an unqualified endorsement of this sampling technique without additional data, although the Wilson (1969) study does make an attempt in the right direction.

One further point deserves comment. Since Wilson found the Syntax Quotient to

JOURNAL OF SPEECH AND HEARING RESEARCH, 1970, vol. 13, no. 2, pp. 438-439.

79

be highly unreliable, she suggests that a revision of this measure might increase its reliability. It may be for some research and clinical purposes that the length-complexity index (LCI) as recently reported in the literature (Shriner, 1967; Miner, 1969) is a useful tool in analyzing syntactic structures. Prior research (Barlow and Miner, 1968) demonstrated the reliability of the LCI.

Wilson is to be commended for tackling a problem with which many of her professional colleagues have been wrestling. However, her data do not justify her ambitious inductive leap to conclusions. It may be, indeed, that the PSLT does provide a representative sample of a child's linguistic performance. Nevertheless, this judgment should not be accepted without supportable convincing evidence.

REFERENCES

BARLOW, M. C. and MINER, L. E., Temporal reliability of the length-complexity index. *J. commun. Dis.*, 2, 241-251 (1969).

BRENT, S. B., and KATZ, E. W., A study of language deviations and cognitive process. Progress Report No. 3, O. E. O., Job Corps Research Contract 1209 (1967).

COWAN, P. A., WEBER, J., HODDINOTT, B. A. and KLEIN, J., Mean length of spoken response as a function of stimulus, experimenter, and subject. *Child Developm.*, 38, 191-203 (1967).

MINER, L. E., Scoring procedures for length-complexity index: A preliminary report. *J. commun. Dis.*, 2, 224-240 (1969).

MINTUN, SHIRLEY, A preliminary investigation of certain procedures for eliciting verbalizations in EMH children, unpublished master's thesis, Eastern Illinois University (1968).

MYKLEBUST, H. R., *Development and Disorders of Written Language*, New York: Grune & Stratton (1965).

QUERESHI, M. Y., Intelligence test scores as a function of sex of experimenter and sex of subject. *J. Psychol.*, 29, 277-284 (1968).

SHRINER, T. H., A comparison of selected measures with psychological scale values of language development. *J. Speech Hearing Res.*, 10, 828-835 (1967).

STRANDBERG, T. E. An evaluation of three stimulus media for evoking verbalizations from preschool children, unpublished master's thesis, Eastern Illinois University (1969).

STRANDBERG, T. E. and GRIFFITH, J., A study of the effects of training in visual literacy on verbal language behavior. *J. commun. Dis.*, 2, 252-263 (1969).

WILSON, M. E., A standardized method for obtaining a spoken language sample. *J. Speech Hearing Res.*, 12, 95-102 (1969).

THOMAS C. LOVITT
JAMES O. SMITH

Effects of Instructions on an Individual's Verbal Behavior

Abstract: The subject for this experiment was a 9 year old boy with specific learning disabilities. Using experimental analysis of behavior techniques, his verbal responses to pictures were directly affected and controlled by oral instructions. This study involved four experimental conditions and daily as well as pre- and posttest data were obtained. The potential effects of the teacher's instructions to children are discussed.

TEACHERS and clinicians use many and varied instructions in their efforts to teach children. These instructions are intended to serve many functions. They are used to inform pupils which response to make. Pupils are requested to walk, run, sing, or write. Instructions are employed to tell pupils how to respond. They are asked to walk more softly, run faster, sing louder, or write more neatly. Furthermore, instructions are used to inform students when to respond. They are told to perform now, in 5 minutes, when the bell rings, or tomorrow.

That teachers frequently use instructions is supported by some cursory data obtained from two classrooms in the Seattle area. In both instances, to obtain these data an observer tallied each instruction given by the teachers within specified time periods. Instructions were verbal prompts or requests the teachers directed toward a child or a group of children. In one class, where the teacher was working with five exceptional children, several 5 minute observations were scheduled throughout a day. These data revealed that the teacher's instructions ranged during the observation periods from 0 to 4.8 instructions per minute. The median rate for a 5 minute period was 1.3 instructions per minute. If these data were indicative of an overall rate throughout a 200 minute day, the teacher might be expected to deliver about 260 instructions.

In the second class, a regular fourth grade of 26 pupils, similar observations were conducted throughout a day. In this class the instruction rates ranged from 2 to 4.5 per minute. The median rate for an observation period was 3.1 instructions per minute. If that median rate was an indicator of the general rate of instructing, 620 instructions could be expected to occur in a school day.

Presumably, teachers and clinicians expect their instructions to influence certain pupil behaviors. Obviously, some teachers regard the giving of instructions as one strategy to alter behavior much as other teachers arrange contingencies of reinforcement to change behavior. The fact that instructions are frequently employed is not, however, reflected in the experimental literature concerning their effects.

Past Studies

Bijou and Baer (1967), in reviewing experimental studies with children, cited but one study that dealt with the effects of instructions on the behavior of children. They reported a 1960 study conducted by Walters and Ray that investigated the effects on the behavior of children of instructions preceding a marble game. Some

EXCEPTIONAL CHILDREN, May 1972, pp. 685-693.

81

subjects were told about the game they were to play, whereas others were not instructed. Their results showed that the pupils who were instructed were more sensitive to experimenter approval than their peers who were not informed.

Recently, a few experiments aimed at determining relationships between examiner instructions and the behavior of children have appeared. Rosenthal and Whitebook (1970) assessed the ability of third and fourth grade children to copy sentences under conditions where incentives were provided and where only instructions were given. Their results indicated that performance was as good when instructions were offered as when an incentive was granted.

Herman and Tramontana (1971) attempted to modify inappropriate behaviors of preschoolers by using reinforcement procedures, reinforcement plus instruction, and instructions alone. While the reinforcement procedures alone reduced inappropriate behaviors somewhat, the addition of instructions to the reinforcement reduced the behaviors to near zero.

Burgess, Clark, and Hendee (1971) conducted an ecological experiment investigating the differential effects of instructions and reinforcement contingencies on the amount of litter picked up by youngsters in a theatre. Although reinforcement contingencies caused more litter to be deposited, instructions alone were quite influential.

That so little research attention has been given to the effects of instructions on the behaviors of children, particularly when compared to the number of studies that have assessed the effects of reinforcement contingencies, is indeed remarkable. It is likely that while teachers give from 260 to 620 instructions each day, they may arrange only one or two systematic contingencies. Teachers, generally, are more apt to say "behave yourself" to the naughty boy than they are to withdraw some prized activity contingent on bad behavior. Correspondingly, they are more inclined to say "be careful and answer your problems correctly" than to arrange a situation whereby the pupil receives one point for each correct answer.

The need for systematic research dealing with instructions was pointed out by Lovitt and Curtiss (1968) when they stated that many "antecedent alterations, such as instructions . . . could possibly affect academic performance. However, evaluations of their functions are generally casual; rarely have . . . common classroom teaching aids been subjected to an experimental analysis [p. 329]."

Bijou and Baer (1967) also encouraged research dealing with instructions when they concluded that, if differences in instructions can produce significant statistical differences in the behaviors of children, then many of the instructions in child studies are probably at least as effective as are the reinforcement contingencies in contributing to differences in performances.

Rosenthal and Whitebook (1970) also stressed the importance of instructions and their influence on the behaviors of children. They conjectured that telling pupils what is wanted may be as effective in altering behavior as is the dispensing of goodies.

This study was designed to determine the effects of two different instructions on a boy's ability to describe pictures. Since three components of verbal behavior were measured, and the instructions were focused on one element, the experimenters were concerned with the direct and indirect effects of instructions. Two types of measurement were used to assess verbal behavior throughout this study: continuous (daily measurement) and intermittent (pre- and posttest).

Method

Subject

The subject was a 9 year old boy who was attending a class for children with learning problems at the Experimental Education Unit (EEU), Child Development and Mental Retardation Center, University of Washington.

His referral form pointed out that he "can't remember words previously learned; has a reading problem." The referring teacher described the subject as a boy who worked determinedly yet had difficulty in learning. He was further described as having problems forming words (orally) and being understood; he was "almost unintelligible at times." His teacher stressed, however, that his speech and reading problems did not seem to be a result of an inferior intellect. The subject was also described as being eager to learn, well adjusted, competitive, and not easily discouraged and as having a short attention span. It was further mentioned that during the summer preceding this study, the subject was enrolled in a remedial reading class and a clinical speech program.

When he was placed at the EEU, two achievement tests were given. These tests and other diagnostic surveys are routinely administered to new students. On the *Wide Range Achievement Test* (Jastak, Bijou, & Jastak, 1965) the following scores were obtained: 1-7 in reading and 2-4 in arithmetic. His grade equivalent scores on the *Metropolitan Achievement Test*, Primary II Battery (1960), were as follows: 1-8 in word knowledge, 1-9 in word discrimination, 1-6 in reading, 1-9 in spelling, and 2-3 in arithmetic. The *Goldman-Fristoe Test of Articulation* (1965) was also administered with the following results: no consistent sound substitutions, omissions, or distortions. Casual observations of his speech seemed to indicate that he inconsistently articulated the medial and final *th* (breathe). It was also noted that he rarely used the syllable *ing* as a suffix. Generally, the subject's voice quality was husky and he spoke rapidly. In summary, he was difficult to understand.

Procedures

Pre- and posttest. Before the daily sessions began, a sample of the subject's descriptive speech was obtained. To elicit the speech, three of the six Large Story Making Pictures from the *Peabody Language Development Kit* (PLDK), Level #3 (Dunn & Smith, 1967), were used. After the third phase of the experiment the same three pictures plus three new pictures were used to elicit speech. The comparison of verbal responses to the same pictures before and after the experiment provided an indication of change as a function of the daily language training. The three new pictures served as a control for familiarity. If improvement was noted from beginning to end of the study on the first set of pictures, it could be argued that the gain was as much a function of familiarity as of the daily language program; therefore, the second set of pictures was given.

Phase one. Throughout this investigation the daily sessions began at 11:30 a.m.

and were conducted by an experimenter who was a former classroom teacher and speech clinician. The sessions were held in a small room adjacent to a classroom which contained a table, two chairs, and a tape recorder. Each period lasted 10 minutes; timing was controlled by a 60-minute dial egg timer. This timer was checked several times for 10 minute settings with a stopwatch. It was found that the experimenter could consistently set the timer within 20 seconds of the 10 minute period.

All the picture cards used to elicit verbal responses during the four phases of the experiment were from the *Peabody Language Development Kit,* Levels #P, 1, 2, 3 (Dunn & Smith, 1965, 1966, 1967; Dunn, Horton, & Smith, 1968). These cards were randomly chosen and presented, with the exception of Numbers-in-Color and Shapes-in-Color Cards, which were not used.

During phase one (6 sessions), the instructions were: "I am going to show you some cards. Please make a sentence about the picture on each card." When the subject had finished describing a card, the next one was shown. He could respond to each card as long as he wished.

Throughout the study data were kept for the rate of correct and incorrect sentences that were said (number of correct or incorrect sentences divided by 10 minutes). A sentence was defined as a group of words which contained a subject and a verb. In addition, data were kept concerning the mean length of response (MLR) per picture (total number of words divided by total number of pictures) and the ratio of different sentence beginnings (different beginnings divided by total beginnings). Following each session the experimenter listened to a taped playback of the interview. While listening to the tape, the experimenter prepared a verbatim report of the session. This transcript was then used to determine the three language measures.

Throughout phase one, it was noticed that the subject consistently used "this is" to begin his sentences. On the basis of this repetition, the next phase of the study was conceived.

Phase two. During this phase, totaling 9 sessions, the daily instructions were the same as those used in phase one, plus the

83

following: "Most of your sentences have started with 'this is.' 'This is' is a way to start a sentence; however, there are many different ways to start sentences. Today, let's try to start our sentences in many different ways." On the first day of phase two the child asked, "You mean say them different?" To this the experimenter replied, "We want to see how many different ways you can start your sentences."

During this phase the manner in which he began his sentences was affected, but his MLR was not significantly influenced. It was, therefore, decided to see if this latter item could be influenced by instructions.

Phase three. During phase three (5 daily sessions), the instructions were: "You are making sentences. You have learned to start your sentences in many different ways. However, many of your sentences are very short. For example, look at this card [picture card A-12 of PLDK Level #2]. I could say: 'This is a woodpecker.' That is a sentence, but it only has four words and doesn't tell me very much. I could say: 'This is a red-headed woodpecker looking for bugs to eat.' Now, we have an 11 word sentence that tells me more. Let's see if you can start your sentences in many different ways *and* make your sentences longer so that they tell me more."

Phase four. No instructions were given throughout this phase. At the beginning of each of the 9 daily sessions the experimenter merely said, "Hello," then set the timer, turned on the recorder, and began to show the pictures.

Results

Sentence Construction

Throughout the experiment nearly all the sentences used by the pupil were correct. In the first phase, 456 correct sentences were noted while only 8 were incorrect. In phase two, when he was instructed to vary sentence beginnings, most of his sentences (570) continued to be correctly formed, with only 13 being incorrectly formed. In phase three, when the subject was requested to increase the length of his responses, he continued to use correct sentences. Throughout this phase 185 sentences were correctly stated; none were incorrect. During phase four, when no instructions were given, 2 sentences were incorrect, while 272 were correct.

Sentence Beginnings

Figure 1 shows the subject's ratio of different sentence beginnings throughout the four experimental phases. As stated earlier, during phase one the subject began nearly all his statements with "this is." On days three and five, for example, all responses began in this manner. His mean ratio of varied beginnings throughout this phase was .025; the range was .01 to .05.

When instructions to vary beginnings (phase two) were given, the effect was immediate. On the first day of phase two, the subject used 20 different beginnings for 67 sentences; his ratio, therefore, was .30. His ratios on subsequent days throughout this phase were: .37, .31, .34, .46, .27, .40, .21, and .45. The mean ratio in phase two was .35.

During phase three, when instructions continued to request varied beginning and additionally asked for longer sentences, the ratio of varied beginnings continued to increase. The phase three ratios ranged from .43 to .60, with a mean ratio of .51. During phase four, when no instructions were given, the subject continued to vary his sentence beginnings. In this phase his ratios of beginnings ranged from .36 to .57, with a mean of .51.

Mean Length of Responses

During phase one when the only instruction was to look at a picture and make a sentence, the subject's responses were generally limited to, "This is a _____." His MLR in this phase was, obviously, rather brief. Throughout phase one daily MLR's ranged from 4.2 to 6 words per card, with a phase mean of 4.9 words per card. During phase two his daily MLR's ranged from 5.7 to 8.9 with a phase mean of 7.1 words per card. The range of MLR's in phase three was 10.2 to 20.9 with a phase mean of 14.3 words per card. Throughout phase four his MLR's ranged from 12.9 to 40 words per card with a phase mean of 25.3. Daily MLR data are shown in Figure 2.

Pre- and Posttest

In the pretest situation the subject used 151 words to describe the three pictures. Under the same instructions and with identical pictures, the subject's verbal output at the conclusion of phase three (post-

84

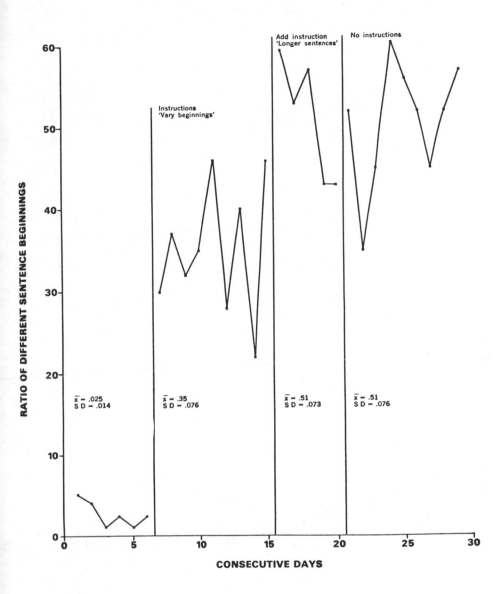

FIGURE 1.Ratio of different sentence beginnings throughout four experimental phases.

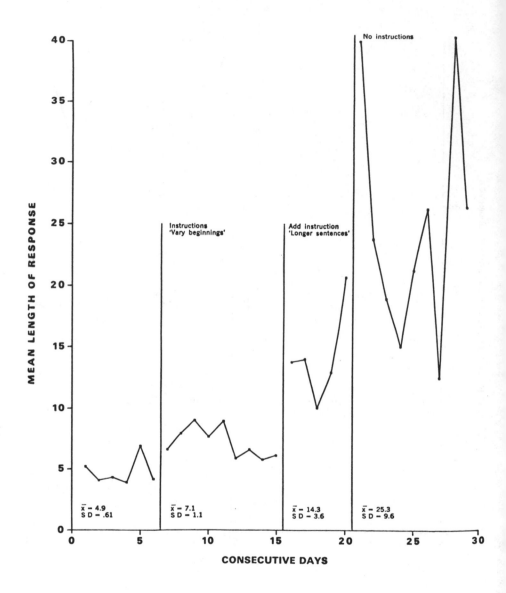

FIGURE 2. Mean response length throughout four experimental phases.

test) was 528 words. This was a gain of 377 words from the pretest score. The subject's verbal responsiveness to pictorial stimuli more than tripled from pre- to posttest assessment. His total responses for the three comparable but different pictures at the conclusion of phase three was 587 words.

Since time was not controlled in the pre- or posttest situation (the sessions lasted until the subject's responses expired), the duration of each session was noted. His pretest total response of 151 words to the three pictures required 1 minute and 52 seconds. However, his posttest responses of 528 words to the same three pictures took 6 minutes and 37 seconds. While the subject increased the number of words used to describe the pictures and used much more time to do it, the words per minute rate remained virtually the same. The pretest rate was 80.4 words per minute compared to a posttest rate of 79.8 words per minute.

Discussion

Throughout all phases of this study, the subject's responsiveness to oral instructions was excellent. When instructed, he, in turn, used sentences to describe pictures, then varied the beginnings of the sentences, and later used more words to describe pictures.

The extreme variability of sentence length during phase four could be a further indication of the subject's responsiveness to instructions. The subject behaved as though he wanted to comply with the experimenter's wishes, but he was not sure what they were. Did the experimenter want more sentences, longer sentences, varied beginnings? The subject's behavior could indicate that he was testing each of these hypotheses, attempting to satisfy the examiner.

Since no attempt was made to teach sentence construction or diverse beginnings and since only one example was given for a longer sentence, it is apparent that the words used and their arrangement were within the child's repertory. Performance then for this boy was apparently influenced by the oral instructions he received each day.

The teacher in this experiment merely told the child what was expected; no training period, instructional materials, or reinforcement contingencies were required. The implications of using consistent and clearly stated instructions for parents and teachers in their efforts to change the behaviors of children appear obvious. If parents or teachers want something, they should ask for it. This is not to say that all child behaviors can be influenced irrespective of training and contingency management, but the initial approach toward altering a behavior, certainly the least expensive, could be to describe clearly and consistently the behavior that is desired.

It could be that one of the reasons children in schools do not perform as their teachers would like is that they are not certain what their teachers expect of them. Possibly, the reason some children do not write neatly, read fluently, or compute accurately is that they have never been told to do so. Other children could be performing inadequately because the instructions they have received have not been precisely stated or consistently given. Some children have been instructed to "do better work," to "think before they act," to "improve their performance." Such directives could confuse children; their efforts, following such instructions, could be erratic and disorganized. At other times instructions are clearly stated but not consistently administered. In a writing session, for example, perhaps one day the teacher requests more words, the next day neater writing, then more imaginative content, then "watch the capitalization" or "be careful of the punctuation." Although some children can handle such a barrage of instructions, others flounder.

A second consideration to emerge from this study is in regard to those experimental studies that have manipulated some contingency of reinforcement and observed effects on a measured behavior. It could be in certain of those studies, particularly when a reinforcement contingency has been verbalized, that the modification effects resulted as much from instructions either stated or implied as from the contingencies of reinforcement. For example, in an experiment that followed contingency contracting techniques the following instructions could be given to the student: "If you read at a rate in excess of 75 words per minute for 5 minutes, you will be allowed 15 minutes of free time." The data from such an experiment could reveal that during the phase of contingency contracting the pupil's reading rates surpassed those during the no contingency phase. The investigator could conclude that the performance effects were due to the free time contingency when in fact the pupil's efforts may have been altered as much or more by the instruction to read faster as by the prospect of being able to earn leisure time.

A final comment should be made in regard to response generalization. The pre- and posttests that were administered in this study involved two sets of cards. One set of cards was presented before the daily measurement and following the third experimental phase, while one set was scheduled only after phase three. The subject's task was to describe the cards. Not only did the subject's performance improve (more words) from pre- to postmeasurement on the first set of cards, but his performance on the second set was superior to that on the second administration of the first set of cards (59 more words). As the pupil used more words to describe pictures during a situation in which he was instructed to do so (daily sessions), he also used more words to describe pictures when no instructions were used (pre- and posttest); response generalization had occurred.

In contrast, however, slight generalization from one response topography to another was observed. When the second phase data of the two charts are compared, it can be noted that as the instructions directed toward sentence beginnings influenced that behavior, the pupil's mean length of response was minimally altered.

The results of this study corroborate the findings of those studies noted earlier in the report. It appears that instructions can affect a wide range of motoric, social, and academic behaviors of young children. Recently, other projects have been conducted at the EEU which show that precise and consistent instructions can influence other academic behaviors. Lovitt and Smith (1971) found that instructions influenced certain writing patterns of an 11 year old girl. When she was instructed to write neater, write more, and use more correct punctuation, each element of writing was successively affected. In a reading project (Smith & Lovitt, 1971) when a boy was instructed to read faster, his rate of reading correctly was positively influenced.

Studies such as these showing that academic behavior such as speaking, writing, and reading can be influenced by carefully given instructions should be encouraging to teachers, parents, and others who are trying to influence the behavior of children. It would appear that if the student is capable of performing the requested skill, the first attempt to stimulate that behavior should be a clearly stated instruction. Further, if that behavior is desired over a period of time, the same instruction (s) should be given.

Obviously, other teaching techniques will have to be used with the nonmotivated student, the one who can but will not perform the requested task. One recommended technique would be to couple instructions with reinforcement contingencies; ask for the behavior and pay off when it occurs. In this regard, Herman and Tramontana (1971) speculated "that although instructions can be used to prompt very specific behavior. . ., consistent reinforcement is needed to maintain it [p. 118]."

Instructions would also need to be coupled with or supplanted by other teaching techniques if the desired behavior was not in the pupil's repertory of skills. If, for example, the pupil was requested to say the sound of /d/, or add 2 + 2 and had never done so, instructing him to perform these tasks could be futile. Some other form of prompting those behaviors, such as modeling, would be recommended.

Instructions, like other teaching methods and procedures, should be judiciously administered. When used prudently, they can, like modeling or contingency management, be effective in modifying behavior. An effective teacher's instructional portfolio should contain expertise in all three procedures.

References

Bijou, S. W., & Baer, D. M. *Child development: Readings in experimental analysis.* New York: Appleton-Century-Crofts, 1967.

Burgess, R. L., Clark, R. N., & Hendee, J. C. An experimental analysis of anti-litter procedures. *Journal of Applied Behavior Analysis*, 1971, **4**, 71-75.

Dunn, L. M., & Smith, J. O. *Peabody Language Development Kits.* Levels #1, 2, 3. Circle Pines, Minn.: American Guidance Service, 1965, 1966, 1967.

Dunn, L. M., Horton, K., & Smith, J. O. *Peabody Language Development Kit.* Level P. Circle Pines, Minn.: Amer. Guidance Service, 1968.

Goldman, R., & Fristoe, M. *Goldman-Fristoe Test of Articulation.* Circle Pines, Minn.: American Guidance Service, 1969.

Herman, S. H., & Tramontana, J. Instructions and group versus individual reinforcement in modifying disruptive group behavior. *Journal of Applied Behavior Analysis,* 1971, 4, 113-119.

Jastak, J. R., Bijou, S. W., & Jastak, S. R. *Wide Range Achievement Test.* (Rev. ed.) Wilmington, Del.: Guidance Associates, 1965.

Lovitt, T. C., & Curtiss, K. A. Effects of manipulating an antecedent event on mathematics response rate. *Journal of Applied Behavior Analysis,* 1968, 1, 329-333.

Metropolitan Achievement Test. Primary II Battery. New York: Harcourt, Brace and World, 1960.

Rosenthal, T. L., & Whitebook, J. S. Incentives versus instructions in transmitting grammatical parameters with experimenter as model. *Behavioral Research and Therapy,* 1970, 8, 189-196.

Smith, D., & Lovitt, T. Using instructions to increase oral reading rate. Unpublished manuscript, University of Washington, 1971.

Lovitt, T. C., & Smith, J. O. Using instructions to teach certain writing skills. Unpublished manuscript, University of Washington, 1971.

Walters, R. H., & Ray, E. Anxiety, social isolation and reinforcer effectiveness. *Journal of Personality,* 1960, 28, 358-367.

MEAN LENGTH OF SPOKEN RESPONSE AS A FUNCTION OF STIMULUS, EXPERIMENTER, AND SUBJECT

PHILIP A. COWAN

J. WEBER and B. A. HODDINOTT

J. KLEIN

Mean length of response (MLR) is the average number of words per remark emitted by Ss in responding to stimuli; in this case the stimuli were pictures. 96 Ss, equal numbers of male and female upper- and lower-socioeconomic status children at each of 4 ages (5, 7, 9, and 11), were individually tested by 1 of 2 Es. It was found that the stimulus influenced the length of response; that age, sex, and socioeconomic status effects interacted; and that the E effect interacted with the age and sex of Ss. While few studies now use the MLR measure, current textbooks are consistently drawing invalid conclusions based on previous MLR research. The present results also reemphasize the necessity for including an analysis of E effects in any developmental study.

Mean length of response (MLR) is a measure of the average number of words per remark spoken in fifty responses. These responses are elicited in free play or in a semistructured test situation where the child is en-

---

Appreciation is expressed to the Board of Education of Etobicoke Township and to Mr. Patten, the principal of the school in which this research was conducted, for their generous cooperation. Thanks are also due to Dr. D. Abbey for some of the analyses used in the report and also for his general comments on the results.

CHILD DEVELOPMENT, 1967, pp. 191-203.

couraged to talk about toys or pictures. Thirteen years ago, McCarthy summarized previous research in language development and declared that no measure seems to have superceded MLR "for a reliable, easily determined, objective, quantitative and easily understood measure of linguistic maturity" (McCarthy, 1954, p. 550). The statement was based upon the results of a large number of studies which used MLR as an important dependent measure for assessing the effects of subject variables (age, sex, IQ, class, family constellation) on the development of language.

Despite McCarthy's unqualified optimism, the use of MLR in language research has declined drastically since 1954. It appears that this decline has resulted from the impact of the new field of psycholinguistics with its emphasis on structural analysis of language development (Ervin & Miller, 1963). However, McCarthy's article and the studies to which she referred continue to be widely cited in current textbook accounts of language growth (see Johnson & Medinnus, 1965; Munn, 1965; Mussen, Conger, & Kagan, 1963; Watson, 1965). In light of the psycholinguists' present lack of concern with subject differences, authors have returned to the older literature to fill in the gaps.

The prevailing tendency in the textbooks is to combine a description of language development based on psycholinguistic studies with an account of individual differences in development based on studies using MLR as a primary measure. This procedure is obviously questionable on logical grounds. It is the purpose of the present paper to show that it may also be questionable because of gaps and inadequacies in MLR research.

While it is evident in at least nine studies that MLR increases with age, and that there are small but consistent class differences in length of response (McCarthy, 1954; Templin, 1957), other subject variables have not shown such consistent or clear-cut effects. Sex differences in favor of girls are prevalent in the early studies (Davis, 1937; Day, 1932; McCarthy, 1930), but are either minimal or nonexistent in the later studies (Templin, 1957; Winitz, 1959). Several investigators have concluded that individual differences in MLR may be attributable, in part, to IQ scores (Webster & Shelton, 1964; Winitz, 1959), but the correlations between MLR and IQ are very low. Possible interaction effects of sex, class, and IQ variables on MLR have never been adequately assessed.

At the same time that Es were investigating the social and intellectual sources of individual differences in MLR, they began to be disturbed by rather large between-study differences in MLR when samples of children of the same age were compared. In McCarthy's table summarizing a number of studies (1954, pp. 546–549), the reported average MLR for 5-year-olds varies as much as 2.9 words—from 3.2 to 6.1 words per response. A difference as large as 2.9 words per response *within* most of the studies which McCarthy cites is equivalent to approximately 3 years of developmental growth. The between-study range is far larger than the modest

MLR differences attributable to sex, class, and IQ which have been found within any one study. Differences in subject characteristics do not appear to be sufficient to account for the obtained discrepancies in results.

Usually, before studies are compared, attention is paid, or should be paid, to methodological equivalence. In the MLR field, however, the lack of concern with methodological variables reaches epic proportions. The present research focuses attention on two of these variables—the stimulus which has been inadequately studied and the E who has been completely ignored.

The stimulus—By comparing MLR scores obtained in free play and in test situations, a few investigators have explored the possibility that MLR is specific to particular experimental settings (Hahn, 1948; McCarthy, 1929; McConnon, 1935; Williams & Mattson, 1942; Young, 1941). The fact that contradictory results have been obtained may be due to the large number of variables in the two settings which may have been confounded. With the exception of Williams and Mattson (1942), who systematically varied the number of people in the test situation, Es have not been concerned with specific stimuli which might affect MLR.

Mean length of response has usually been obtained in a one-to-one test situation, where the E presents pictures or objects and elicits comments from the child. All previous Es have considered the particular stimuli so unimportant that they do not make certain that each child within the study is presented with the same material. Recording is stopped after fifty responses, regardless of what stimuli the children have seen or played with. No two studies have used the same sets of stimulus material. This procedure implies that MLR is solely a characteristic of the person and not of the person and stimulus, an interpretation with more than passing similarity to the outmoded interpretation of the results of IQ tests.

The experimenter (E).—No previous MLR study has considered the possibility that different Es would obtain different results. Several studies have "avoided" the problem by using only one E. Recent emphasis on the possibility of E bias suggests that we can no longer afford to ignore E's role, especially if E variables interact with subject and stimulus variables (e.g., McGuigan, 1963).

Even though MLR may not represent a currently popular research measure, it provides the basis for a number of current statements concerning language development. These statements are often based upon trends inferred from a comparison of several experiments. Noting that more contemporary studies yield larger MLR's than early studies, a number of authors (Johnson & Medinnus, 1965; McCarthy, 1954; Minifie, Darley, & Sherman, 1963; Mussen et al., 1963; Watson, 1965) believe that children have in fact changed over the years.

The present authors have chosen to explore the effects on MLR of the stimulus and the E, and to investigate the way in which these may interact with age, sex, and class characteristics of the subjects. The results suggest that methodological divergences may well account for findings previously accepted as substantive.

METHOD

One elementary school in a suburban district of metropolitan Toronto was chosen as most representative of the population of that district. Approximately 250 5-, 7-, 9-, and 11-year-olds from that school and all the 11-year-olds in the nearby junior high school constituted the subject pool for the present experiment. The occupation of the father (or the employed parent) of each child was classified on a seven-point socioeconomic scale developed on a Canadian population (Blishen, 1958). In the experimental sample, 48 per cent of the Ss were in the upper four of seven socioeconomic status groups (USES), 40 per cent were in the lower three socioeconomic status groups (LSES), and 12 per cent of the parents listed occupations which were unclassifiable, mostly because of inadequate information in the school records. As would be expected of a suburban population, socioeconomic status was above average for the country as a whole, but a full range was obtained.

At each age level, six children were randomly selected from male and female USES and LSES subgroups. Thus, there were 96 Ss, 24 at each of four age levels, with an equal number of male and female upper and lower socioeconomic status Ss. All Ss were given a WISC IQ test during the period of the study. The mean full-scale IQ was 110.

Two of the authors who are experienced speech therapists (Klein & Weber) administered the tests for MLR; both Es are male. In preparation for the study, they tested eight children with both Es in the room writing responses verbatim. There appeared to be little advantage in tape recording Ss' responses since the reliability of MLR scores transcribed by different typists is low (Siegel, 1962). After each pilot S had been tested, responses were scored separately, and the results were discussed in order to resolve scoring differences. After the testing of eight Ss, agreement in recording and scoring was extremely high. Mean length of response varied between Es no more than .05 words per response. In the experiment proper, each E tested Ss by himself and later scored the protocols which he had collected.

Since no set of stimuli has been used in more than one MLR study, a new set was collected. The test stimuli were ten pictures, approximately 5 × 7 inches, mounted on colored paper. All were taken from a popular magazine's cover paintings. The pictures were chosen as ones which would probably be of interest to children and showed varying numbers of adults and children engaged in different activities. Stimuli were limited to pictures, rather than a mixture of pictures and objects, in order to ascertain whether systematically different MLR scores would be elicited by stimulus items within a relatively homogeneous category.

Each child was brought by E to an empty classroom in the school. As a warmup, he was presented with three or four pictures not included in the test proper. The E then said: "I'm going to show you some pictures. In these pictures people are doing things. I want you to tell me what they are doing and what is happening in the pictures." The E attempted to elicit a total of ten responses. The S was encouraged ("uh huh" or "that's right"), especially for longer responses. He was prevented from just naming objects.

During the test phase, S was shown pictures one at a time and was asked to "Tell me what you see in the picture" or "Tell me what is happening" or "Tell me what the people are doing." Approval was given for most responses, but systematic dispensing of rewards was avoided. The E attempted to elicit at least three responses per picture; however, this was not always possible. It was necessary to present the same pictures to each S in order to test for stimulus effects. Therefore, S was allowed to continue, even after the traditional fifty responses had been made, until he had seen all ten pictures. If, at the end of ten pictures, it was apparent that S had given *fewer* than fifty responses, he was shown more pictures until he reached approximately fifty. This rarely required more than five additional stimuli. There were, then, two MLR scores for each S—a ten-picture score and a fifty-response score. Since the correlation between them was extremely high ($r = .94$), only the ten-picture score was used in the presentation of results. Scoring was performed according to the rules described by Winitz (1959).

The ten test pictures were presented in random order to each S. When additional stimuli were used, their order of presentation was also randomized.

In summary, at each of four ages (5, 7, 9, and 11) there were 24 Ss each shown at least ten pictures. The Ss were divided into four equal subgroups of male and female USES and LSES. In each subgroup, two Ss were randomly assigned to be tested by Klein and four by Weber. This arrangement of cells represents a $4 \times 2 \times 2 \times 2 \times 10$ mixed-models design.

The basic statistical analysis performed in the study was a five-factor analysis of variance (see Lindquist, 1953, chaps. xi, xiii). Age, sex, class, and E variables were analyzed as between-S effects, while the picture variable (the stimulus) represented a within-S repeated measure. The E effect was treated as a fixed rather than random variable since it was unreasonable to assume that the present two speech therapists represented a random sample from the hypothetical population of experimenters.

RESULTS

In Table 1 is presented an abbreviated summary of the analysis of variance. It includes all main effects and all statistically significant interactions. Since the main effect of the stimulus was so clear-cut, it will be described first.

TABLE 1

ABBREVIATED SUMMARY TABLE OF ANALYSIS OF VARIANCE

Effects	df	MS	F
Between Ss:			
Age (A)...................	3	772.5	12.08***
Sex (B)..................	1	38.2	<1
SES (C)..................	1	15.9	<1
Experimenter (D)	1	77.0	<1
A × D....................	3	215.8	3.37*
B × C....................	1	213.5	3.33*
B × D....................	1	244.0	3.81*
A × B × C...............	3	229.6	3.58*
A × B × D...............	3	243.2	3.80*
Error between.............	64	64.0	...
Within Ss:			
Stimulus.................	9	126.2	7.63**
Error within..............	576	16.5	...

* $p < .05$.
** $p < .01$.
*** $p < .001$.

The average MLR for each stimulus, arranged in ascending order, is shown in Table 2. The difference among pictures was significant at the .01 level ($F = 7.63$; 9/576 df). Critical difference tests indicated at the .05 level that picture A elicited significantly lower MLR than pictures B through J and that picture J elicited significantly higher MLR than pictures A through I. Adjacent differences from B through I were nonsignificant, although picture B differed significantly from picture I. This difference among eight stimuli was less than the separation between either A and B or I and J. Even in a relatively homogeneous set of stimuli, average MLR may vary as much as 4.49 words per response. The largest obtained mean difference between stimuli in the present study was far larger than any of the between-study discrepancies reported above.

No significant lower- or higher-order interactions involving stimuli were found. The main effect attributable to pictures remained constant across age, sex, class, and E subgroups. Stimulus effects also remained relatively constant across Ss. For each stimulus, Ss were ranked in order of MLR, and Kendall coefficients of concordance (W) were calculated separately for each age group (see Table 3). The W's, ranging between .43

TABLE 2

MEAN LENGTH OF RESPONSE FOR TEN STIMULI (ARRANGED IN ASCENDING ORDER)

	A	B	C	D	E	F	G	H	I	J
MLR................	8.85	10.25	10.41	10.66	10.71	10.72	10.80	11.18	11.46	13.44
Adjacent differences..........		1.40*	0.16	0.25	0.05	0.01	0.08	0.38	0.28	1.98*
Largest difference A–J = 4.49										

* Critical difference, significant at the .05 level, is 1.16.

96

TABLE 3

KENDALL COEFFICIENT OF CONCORDANCE (*W*) AT EACH OF FOUR AGE
LEVELS (THE EXTENT TO WHICH CHILDREN'S MLR SCORES REMAIN
IN THE SAME RANK ORDER ON EACH PICTURE)

	AGE			
	5	7	9	11
W....................	.43	.49	.57	.45
Associated χ^{2*}........	98.9	112.7	131.1	103.5

* All χ^2 significant; $p < .001$.

and .57, were all significant beyond the .001 level. All Ss tended to remain in the same rank order even when there were absolute differences
among stimuli. This consistency held even when the two extreme stimuli
were eliminated and the *W*'s were recalculated on the remaining eight
pictures. The stimulus effect, then, was solely a main effect.

When MLR performance was averaged for each age (*N* = 24), it
was apparent that MLR increased from the 5-year-olds (8.29 words per response) through 7-year-olds (11.14) to 9-year-olds (12.31), with a slight
decline in the 11-year-old group (11.69). However, this highly significant
age effect (*F* = 12.08; *df* = 3/64; *p* < .001) tended to be obscured by a
number of interactions with subject and examiner variables.

The effects of age, sex, and SES on MLR are presented in Figure 1.
Sex and class variables produced no overall differences, but they entered

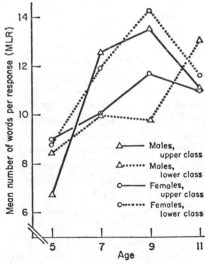

FIG. 1.—MLR as a function of age, sex, and socioeconomic status.

into a significant two-way interaction in which USES males and LSES females obtained higher scores than LSES males and USES females. Since the interaction of sex and class varied with age, the triple interaction of age, sex, and SES was also statistically significant. It is not possible, then, to discuss the effect of one subject variable on MLR without reference to specific values of the other two subject variables investigated in this study.

The complexity involved in interpreting MLR as an index of language development is compounded by the fact that subject variables interacted in various ways with E. The effects of age, sex, and E on MLR are shown in Figure 2. In the significant age $\times$ E interaction, Klein elicited longer

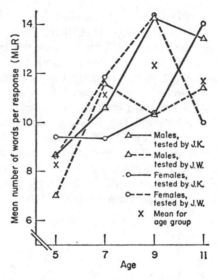

Fɪɢ. 2.—MLR as a function of age, sex, and E.

responses from 5- and 11-year-olds, while 7- and 9-year-olds performed performed better with Weber. Across all age groups, males showed higher MLR with Klein, while females emitted longer responses with Weber.

The age $\times$ sex $\times$ E triple interaction is also statistically significant. Nine-year-old males tested by Klein and females tested by Weber were above their age mean, while the 9-year-old females tested by Klein and the males tested by Weber were not only below their own age mean but also below three of four subgroup means of the 7-year-old Ss.

Both for males (*triangles* in Fig. 2) and for females (*circles*), the discrepancies in MLR attributable to E increased with Ss' age. Even in the 7-year-old female group, however, there was a mean difference between Ss tested by Klein and by Weber as large as 2.5 words per response. In 9- and 11-year-old females, the discrepancy reached 4.0 words per response.

It must be noted in addition that the discrepancy changed in direction between these latter two age groups; Weber elicited four more words per response than Klein in the 9-year-old group but four fewer words per response in the 11-year-old group. As in the case of stimulus effects, E created larger differences than those commonly found between studies. In contrast with stimulus effects, language expression was affected in different amounts for Ss in each age and sex subgroup.

DISCUSSION

The present study reconfirms the developmental properties of MLR, but introduces a number of important qualifications to the interpretation of previous results. Of the three subject variables, only age emerged as a major factor affecting MLR, with sex and class variables entering into interaction with age. However, the largest difference attributable to age—approximately four words per response—was no larger than effects produced by stimulus and by E variables when age was held constant.

It seems likely children would talk more about some pictures than others, but there is no immediately apparent reason why their sentences would be longer. Perhaps different stimulus content elicits sentences of different complexity, and the length may follow from the complexity. Unfortunately, in the present study, it was impossible to isolate specific stimulus variables associated with response length. The picture with the smallest MLR showed a great number of children and adults (possibly everyone in the neighborhood) gathered around the proud owner of a shiny new convertible. Perhaps the large number of details prevented any concerted effort to describe the picture, thus lowering MLR. However, the number of people in other pictures was uncorrelated with MLR. The picture with the largest MLR showed five children at a birthday party sitting in a row on chairs, with a sixth child standing on a chair trying to catch a balloon. This picture was different from many of the others in that it had no pattern in the background or foreground, only a neutral wall and floor. However, another picture with a similar background elicited one of the lower MLR values. All the present authors and two psychology interns tried to rank pictures in order of what they thought would be the elicited MLR. Although the speech therapists were able to pick the picture with lowest MLR, no rater showed a significant correlation of predicted and actual results. Future research is needed in which pictures are systematically varied in a number of content and form dimensions in order to track down the specific origins of the stimulus effect.

The E effects in the present study are difficult to interpret. Since each E recorded the responses of his own S and scored his own protocol, the effect of E as a social stimulus was confounded with effects attributable to his recording and scoring habits. In addition, the task presentation was not completely standardized. "Tell me what you see in the picture" and "Tell me what the people are doing" are not the same instructions.

In terms of interpretation of MLR literature, the present confounding is not terribly important, since E variables have always been confounded both between and within previous studies. The present study simply demonstrates that the cluster of variables associated with E interacts with subject variables of age and sex. The precise nature of the E effect can only be isolated if tape recordings are made and each E transcribes and scores some of the tapes in which the other functions as E.

In the present authors' opinion, such a study would find that the E effect *is* attributable to person variables rather than recording, scoring, and questioning habits. Even though MLR to the total ten pictures varied as a function of age, sex, and E, the ranking of stimuli within subgroups was remarkably consistent. Stimulus A elicited average MLR's within the lowest three of ten pictures in 14 of the 16 age, sex, and E cells. Stimulus J elicited responses within the highest three pictures in 11 of 16 cells. It is unlikely that idiosyncratic recording, scoring, and questioning methods would have allowed such persistent stimulus differences to emerge.

It may be argued that the present criticism attached to previous MLR studies should be tempered because these studies have used other measures of language development in addition to MLR. McCarthy especially cites evidence that the proportion of sentences with more than one clause (per cent complex) increases with increasing age of Ss and that the proportion of grammatically incomplete sentences (per cent incomplete responses) decreases with increasing age. It must be remembered that these percentages are calculated from the same data used to obtain MLR measures. In the present study, MLR was correlated .79 with per cent complex responses and $-.11$ with per cent incomplete responses. The multiple correlation of MLR with per cent complex and per cent incomplete was .91 (all $df = 94$). In view of the high correlations, it is evident that the above criticisms can be applied to at least some of the McCarthy grammatical measures as well.

The results of the present study indicate that stimulus and examiner variables could well account for the commonly obtained absolute differences in MLR between studies. Since the examiner variables interact with subject characteristics, caution must be used in assessing results of individual studies using MLR, and assessing inferences drawn from comparison of studies. No two studies are sufficiently methodologically comparable for firm inferences to be drawn.

The above discussion does not necessarily lead to the conclusion that MLR is a "bad" measure of language expression or development. It cannot be denied that older children speak longer sentences than very young children. However, the results of the present study indicate that the specific course of this development, the magnitude of the developmental changes, and the precise nature of individual differences cannot be described precisely, using McCarthy's approach to language measurement, without specifying the particular examiner, stimulus, and child. Like the now discredited assumption concerning the magnitude of IQ scores, the implicit assumption that magnitude of MLR is a property of the subject independent of his setting should be permanently discarded.

REFERENCES

Blishen, B. R. The construction and use of an occupational class scale. *Canadian Journal of Economics and poltical Science,* 1958, 24, 521–531.

Davis, E. A. *The development of linguistic skill in twins, singletons with siblings, and only children from age five to ten years.* Minneapolis: University of Minnesota Press, 1937.

Day, E. J. The development of language in twins, I: A comparison of twins and single children. *Child Development,* 1932, 3, 179–199.

Ervin, S. M., & Miller, W. R. Language development. In H. Stevenson, J. Kagan, & C. Spiker (Eds.), *Child psychology: the sixty-second yearbook of the National Society for the Study of Education.* Chicago: University of Chicago Press, 1963.

Hahn, E. Analyses of the content and form of the speech of first grade children. *Quarterly Journal of Speech,* 1948, 34, 361–366.

Johnson, R. C., & Medinnus, G. R. *Child psychology: behavior and development.* New York: Wiley, 1965.

Lindquist, E. F. *Design and analysis of experiments in psychology and education.* Boston: Houghton Mifflin, 1953.

McCarthy, Dorothea. A comparison of children's language in different situations and its relation to personality traits. *Journal of genetic Psychology,* 1929, 36, 583–591.

McCarthy, Dorothea. *The language development of the preschool child.* Minneapolis: University of Minnesota Press, 1930.

McCarthy, Dorothea. Language development in children. In L. Carmichael (Ed.), *Manual of child Psychology.* (2d ed.) New York: Wiley, 1954.

McConnon, K. The situation factor in the language responses of nursery school children. Unpublished doctoral dissertation, University of Minnesota, 1935. Cited in McCarthy (1954).

McGuigan, F. J. The experimenter: a neglected stimulus object. *Psychological Bulletin,* 1963, 60, 421–428.

Minifie, F. D. Darley, F. L., & Sherman, D. Temporal reliability of seven language measures. *Journal of speech and hearing Research,* 1963, 6, 139–148.

Munn, N. L. *The evolution and growth of human behavior.* (2d ed.) Boston: Houghton Mifflin, 1965.

Mussen, P. H., Conger, J. J., & Kagan, J. *Child development and personality.* (2d ed.) New York: Harper & Row, 1963.

Siegel, G. M. Interexaminer reliability for mean length of response. *Journal of speech and hearing Research,* 1962, 5, 91–95.

Templin, M. C. *Certain language skills in children: their development and inter-relationships.* Minneapolis: University of Minnesota Press, 1957.

Watson, R. I. *Psychology of the child.* (2d ed.) New York: Wiley, 1965.

Webster, M. J., & Shelton, R. L., Jr. Estimation of mean length of response in children of normal and below average intellectual capacity. *Journal of speech and hearing Research,* 1964, 7, 101–102.

Williams, H. M., & Mattson, M. L. The effect of social groupings upon the language of preschool children. *Child Development,* 1942, 13, 233–245.

Winitz, H. Language skills of male and female kindergarten children. *Journal of speech and hearing Research,* 1959, 2, 377–386.

Young, F. M. An analysis of certain variables in a developmental study of language. *Genetic Psychology Monographs,* 1941, 23, 3–141.

A STUDY OF THE EFFECTS OF TRAINING
IN VISUAL LITERACY ON VERBAL LANGUAGE BEHAVIOR

Twila E.STRANDBERG and Jerry GRIFFITH

The purpose of this study was to examine the language behavior of four and five-year old children when they are talking about pictures they have taken themselves with a still camera. Language samples were obtained from the children when they were describing their pictures made under three conditions: 1) pictures of ten individual toys; 2) pictures taken at home; 3) for an experimental group pictures taken at home following instruction in ways in which pictures go together to tell a story. Measures obtained in condition three were compared to a control group who received no training. Four language measures were applied to the samples obtained. Differences within measures for the three conditions were tested statistically for significance and the statistical relationships among the measures were determined. The incidence of picture sequencing before and after training was noted.

Introduction

In regard to the disadvantaged child and the learning process, Deutsch (1963) says:

"...emphasis on the importance of variety in the environment implies the detrimental effects of lack of variety. This in turn leads to a concept of 'stimulus deprivation'. But it is important that it be correctly understood. By this is not necessarily meant any restriction of the quantity of stimulation, but, rather, a restriction to a segment of the spectrum of stimulation potentially available... In addition to the restriction in variety, ...it might be postulated that the segments made available to these children tend to have poorer and less systematic ordering of stimulation sequences, and would thereby be less useful to the growth and activation of cognitive potential" (p.168–169).

Inherent in Deutsch's position is a concept currently identified as "visual literacy". Debes (1967) asserts that children can be trained to use their existing "passive visual vocabulary" more creatively and thereby enhance their verbal communication. He suggests that the still camera is a tool which can be used by the child to express himself visually. He goes on to say that in education, emphasis is placed on the acquisition of verbal skills rather than on visual skills, since verbal vocabulary and verbal skills develop later. Visual vocabulary and visual skills are assumed to be acquired early in an informal manner so that visual learning is passive. This visual learning or "visual memory", as it is sometimes called,

JOURNAL OF COMMUNICATION DISORDERS, 1969, vol. 2, 252-263.

is used by the child to interpret the meaning of his surroundings. Further, this type of learning may manifest itself in the form of picture sequences taken by the child which convey ideas or "tell stories" reflecting the child's reaction to his environment.

If, as Deutsch suggests, learning is facilitated when a child's attention is drawn to "stimulation sequences" and, if, as Debes suggests, a child's verbal communication skills are related to his visual vocabulary, a method of determining the parameters of visual literacy, or at least the relationship between visual and verbal expressive skills, is suggested. Available linguistic measures of length and structural complexity of spoken language could serve as the dependent variable in an investigation in which visual behavior is the independent variable.

To the authors' knowledge there have been no previous investigations of an experimental nature in which an attempt has been made to study "visual literacy". There is considerable literature, however, which deals with ways in which verbal behavior mediates such tasks as reproduction of visually perceived forms and other visual recall tasks (Carmichael, Hogan and Walter 1932; Hanawalt and Demarest 1939; Prentice 1954; Herman, Lawless and Marshall 1957). The present study attempts to determine if visual behavior can mediate verbal behavior. Undoubtedly the concept of visual literacy transcends basic visual perceptual skills just as spoken language transcends the mere utterance of phonemes and words. Taking the metaphorical approach (Turbayne 1962) that visual literacy involves visual language and thereby resembles verbal language, certain preliminary steps in the investigative process are allowed.

The present study was undertaken as a preliminary attempt to measure the relationship between visual experiences and the verbal behavior associated with the visual experiences. The purposes of the investigation were four: (1) to compare the length and structural complexity characteristics of verbal language samples of young children obtained from pictures the subjects had made themselves with a still camera under different conditions; (2) to study the effects of training in sequential activities and demonstrations as to ways in which pictures go together to tell stories on the length and structural complexity of verbal language samples obtained from pictures following training; (3) to determine instances of picture sequencing in the children's pictures before and after training and to describe the length and structural characteristics of the language behavior they use in describing these sequences; and (4) to determine the relationship between a child's pictures taken under different conditions and the spontaneity of his language behavior.

Procedure

Subjects in this study were selected from a university laboratory school population and were children of university faculty members. There were six children (three four-year-olds and three five-year-olds) in the experimental and control groups. The mean age of the experimental group was five years two months with

104

a range of four years five months to five years nine months. The mean age of the control group was five years three months with a range of four years four months to five years ten months. There were three males and three females in each group. Subjects were selected on the basis of normal intelligence as determined by the Ammons Ammons Quick Test of Intelligence (Ammons and Ammons 1965) and the Peabody Picture Vocabulary Test (Dunn 1965). Normal hearing was required as determined by an audiometric sweep hearing test at 500, 1000, 2000 and 4000 Hz at 30 dB (ISO 1964). These subjects were also recommended by the teacher as children who would be likely to cooperate and to understand the use of the camera. Subjects were assigned to the two groups in such a manner as to counterbalance the groups for age and sex.

The success of the study hinged in part on the subject's independent use of the camera and his selection of subject matter for his pictures. The parents of the subjects were brought together for an orientation session. They were informed as to the nature and purpose of the investigation. They were instructed in the operation of the camera and told that the extent of their involvement with their child during his picture-taking periods should be restricted to loading and unloading the film cartridge. All subjects were given training in the operation and use of the camera. The camera used in this study was the Kodak Instamatic 154, cartridge load, with flashcubes and color film.

The subjects took pictures on three occasions. On the first occasion all subjects were taken to a large room in which toys were arranged so that a picture could be taken of each individual toy. The toys had been chosen as being of universal appeal to both male and female subjects of this age and had been selected for use in two other studies of children's language (Mintun 1968; Strandberg 1969). The toys were: horse, dog, chick, piano, fire truck, airplane, tractor, car, cash register and telephone. Each child was asked to take two pictures of each toy thereby providing him with practice in the use of the camera and providing one source of stimuli for evoking language samples.

When the processed film and prints were returned, the subjects met with the examiner individually. A lapse of ten to twelve days occurred between the time a subject took his pictures and the time language samples were evoked. All of the language samples were obtained within a six week period. The subject was shown each picture taken and asked to tell about it. He was encouraged to respond as much as possible until, in the examiner's judgement, he was no longer stimulated to respond. The next picture was then introduced. All responses were tape recorded. Throughout the study the examiner variable was held constant.

On the second occasion all subjects were given a camera, two film cartridges of twenty exposures each and ten flashcubes. The parents were alerted that the children were bringing the cameras home. They were instructed to have the children shoot both film cartridges during the ensuing weekend and to return the cameras and exposed film with the child on Monday morning. Following the return of the processed film the individual prints were numbered in the order they were taken. This was for the purpose of identifying the individual pictures in each occurrence of picture sequencing and to code the language samples corresponding to a given picture sequence.

A subject was first given all the pictures in a set in a stack and asked "Tell me about your pictures". He was allowed to talk about them in any manner he wished, i.e. one at a time, two at a time. Following this, the same set was spread before him in a random fashion and he was asked, "Can you tell me more about any of these pictures?" This procedure allowed the subject to sequence pictures either in terms of the order in which he had taken them or by seeing relationship between pictures.

Between the second and third sessions the subjects were randomly assigned to experimental and control groups. The experimental group received specific training for forty-five minutes in visual sequencing activities. Following training, subjects in both groups took cameras, film and flashcubes home for the second time. The same instructions as to procedure were given parents. The parents were unaware as to whether their child was part of the experimental or control group. Following the receipt of this group of pictures, language samples were again evoked following the procedure used in the second session.

The tape recorded language samples were transcribed for the purpose of analysis. The same examiner conducted the training session, evoked and analyzed all language samples. She has had extensive experience in evoking language samples and in the use of the language measures applied. Four major language measures were used. They are the Length-Complexity Index (LCI), the Spontaneity Index, Total Number of Words (TNW) and Number of Different Words (NDW). The Length-Complexity-Index, as developed by Shriner and Sherman (1967) and modified by Miner (1968) is derived from the Mean Length Response measure (McCarthy 1954), and the Structural Complexity Score (Templin 1967). It measures both sentence length and complexity together according to a numeric weighting system. Numeric values are assigned to parts of speech and grammatical structures within an utterance and the index is computed by finding the ratio of the total number of points assigned to the number of sentences analyzed.

The Spontaneity Index, as used by Morris (1962), is defined in this study as follows. If a response came about as the result of direct questioning or prompting from the examiner it was scored as an evoked response. If a response came freely as the result of a child first being told to "tell me about these pictures" his first response was scored as evoked and the remainder as spontaneous. In some instances, the child began talking without prompting or direction when the examiner laid the pictures on the table. The number of evoked and spontaneous responses were tallied and calculated as their respective percent of the total number of responses so analyzed.

The Total Number of Words and the Number of Different Words are measures obtained by means of a specially written computer program. The transcribed langauge samples are transferred to computer cards. Each word is tallied for occurrence, counted for frequency of occurrence and the words alphabetized. TNW equals the sum of the frequency of occurrence tallies and the NDW equals the sum of all individual words tallied.

The data were analyzed statistically by means of IBM 1620 computer programming. The student t and Pearson Product-Moment Coefficient of Correlation were used.

Results

Table 1 shows a summary of the Length-Complexity Index measures obtained for the experimental and control groups across the three sessions. Session I designates measures on language samples obtained when the subjects were describing pictures of toys. Session II designates measures on samples obtained from the first round of pictures taken at home. Session III, the post-treatment session, designates measures on samples obtained from the second round of pictures taken at home following training in picture sequencing for the experimental group.

Table 1

Summary of mean comparisons of Length-Complexity-Index measures by sessions within groups and by sessions by age within groups.

Groups	Means			Sessions (t values)		
	I	II	III	I–II	I–III	II–III
Control	7.260	10.382	13.532	2.768**	4.332*	1.890
Experimental	6.900	8.432	11.822	1.658	4.412	2.635**
Control						
four years	7.437	9.617	14.140	1.110	2.534***	1.519
five years	7.083	11.147	12.923	2.960**	3.330**	.882
Experimental						
four years	7.660	9.333	12.850	2.486	4.791**	3.409****
five years	6.140	7.530	10.793	.893	2.518***	1.412

* $p < .01$; d.f. = 5.
** $.02\ p < .05$; d.f. = 5.
*** 2.571 is required for significance at .05 level.
**** $p < .02$; d.f. = 5.

The LCI measures for Session II are significantly higher than those for Session I for the control group but not the experimental group. The LCI's for Session III are significantly higher than for Session I for both groups. Significantly higher LCI's were obtained in Session III over Session II for the experimental group but not for the control group. This is interpreted as clear evidence of the effects of training in visual literacy on the LCI measure.

When the LCI's are compared on the basis of age within the experimental

107

and control groups, measures for Session III are significantly higher than for Session II for four-year-old subjects but not for the five-year-old subjects. This finding perhaps accounts for the major portion of the difference between the experimental and control groups. The four and five-year old subjects in the control group showed no significant changes between Sessions II and III in LCI measures. The five-year-old subjects in the control group evidently account for the difference between Sessions I and II.

Table 2

Summary of mean comparisons of spontaneity index measures by sessions within groups and by sessions by age within groups.†

Group	Means						Sessions (t values)		
	I		II		III		I	II	III
	E	S	E	S	E	S			
Control	.455	.545.	.123	.877	.075	.925	.773	18.341*	31.999*
Experimental	.455	.545	.103	.897	.123	.877	.632	24.616*	16.791*
Control									
four years	.587	.413	.143	.857	.097	.903	1.176	11.516*	20.667*
five years	.323	.677	.103	.897	.053	.947	3.404**	13.016*	27.091*
Experimental									
four years	.337	.663	.107	.893	.163	.837	5.521*	27.104*	9.108*
five years	.573	.427	.100	.900	.083	.917	.553	12.308*	22.541*

Intercomparison of Sessions (t values)

Experimental	I–II	I–III	II–III
elicited	3.412*	3.147*	.512
spontaneous	3.412*	3.146*	.512
Control			
elicited	3.804*	4.502*	1.387
spontaneous	3.804*	4.502*	1.387

† Spontaneity Index is the percent of evoked (E) and percent of spontaneous (S) responses.
* $p < .01$; d.f. = 5.
** $p < .05$; d.f. = 5.

Table 2 shows comparisons of the mean number of evoked and spontaneous responses obtained within the sessions. It can be seen that in Session I the number of evoked responses is significantly higher than spontaneous responses for both the experimental and control groups. Some exceptions are shown for the five-year-olds in the control group and the four-year-olds in the experimental group. In Sessions II and III the number of spontaneous responses significantly exceeds the evoked responses for both the experimental and control groups and for the four and five-year-olds in each group. When inter-comparisons are made between sessions for evoked responses and for spontaneous responses separately,

108

significant differences are found between Session I and II and I and III for both response categories for both groups. However, Sessions I and III are not significantly different for either group. The absence of a difference for the experimental group demonstrates the failure of training in visual literacy to effect this measure. However, it clearly points up the superiority of pictures taken at home over pictures of designated single objects in increasing the spontaneity of a child's language behavior. It should be pointed out, however, that the pictures taken at home often involved only one object and the subject's responses were quite spontaneous. The difference is that at home the subject chose the object, perhaps in some context.

Table 3 shows analysis of the Total Number of Words (TNW) and the Number of Different Words (NDW) between sessions for the experimental and control groups. None of the differences for either measure are significant.

Table 3

Summary of mean comparisons of total number of words and number of different words by sessions within groups.

	Total number of words		Number of different words	
	means	t values	means	t values
Control group				
I	290.00	1.811	107.00	1.956
II	718.00		187.17	
I	290.00	2.163	107.00	2.186
III	575.33		173.83	
II	718.00	.531	187.17	.268
III	575.33		173.83	
Experimental				
I	326.67	.767	123.67	.500
II	455.50		144.17	
I	326.67	1.145	123.67	.662
III	449.17		141.00	
II	455.50	.003	144.17	.070
III	449.17		141.00	

$p < .01 = 3.106$; d.f. = 11.
$p < .05 = 2.201$; d.f. = 11.

Table 4 is a summary of a correlation analysis for the measures TNW and NDW among sessions. The values underlined indicate the comparisons that are of the greatest relevance for the study. Specifically, the question to be answered by the analysis is whether the number of different words a child uses increases if his total output increases. This is clearly the case for Sessions II and III. Session

Table 4
Summary of correlation analysis (Pearson Product-Moment Coefficient of Correlation) for the measured total number of words and number of different words.

Group		I		II		III	
		TNW	NDW	TNW	NDW	TNW	NDW
Experimental							
I	TNW		.33	.37	.94	.40	.49
	NDW			.63	.37	.99	.68
II	TNW				.35	.57	.99
	NDW					.48	.45
III	TNW						.635
	NDW						
Control							
I	TNW		−.75	−.38	.69	−.74	−.37
	NDW			.82	−.18	.99	.81
II	TNW				.13	.84	.99
	NDW					−.16	.07
III	TNW						.83
	NDW						

$p < .01 = .92$; d.f. = 4.
$p < .05 = .81$; d.f. = 4.

I, however, is the exception for both the experimental and control groups. The low correlation for the experimental group and the moderately high negative correlation for the control group reflects the restrictive influence of pictures of designated single objects on a child's verbal behavior. The repetitive use of essentially the same sentence structures substituting only the name of the objects from picture to picture accumulates words but not different words. These results are consistent with the significant increases in LCI shown in table 1.

Table 5 is a description of the occasions in Sessions II and III in which the subjects sequenced some of their pictures and verbalized about these sequences. LCI's have been computed for the samples related to the sequences. In addition the number of sequences per subject, the number of pictures in the sequence and the number of varbalizations for each seqeunce are shown.

It is interesting to note that there are three five-year-olds and one four-year-old in both the experimental groups and control groups.

There are nearly twice as many instances of sequencing in Session III as compared to Session II for the experimental group. However, there are nearly twice as many instances in Session II as compared to Session III for the control group. There are nearly three times as many instances of sequencing in Session III for the experimental group compared to Session III for the control group. However,

Table 5
Description of subject performance in sessions II and III for picture sequencing and the associated language behavior.

Group	Session II				Session III			
	no. of seq.	no. of pic.	no. of sen.	LCI	no. of seq.	no. of pic.	no. of sen.	LCI
Control								
A. (5 yr)	1*	3	3	22.67	1	2	6	16.67
	1*	2	4	11.22	1	2	6	15.67
	1*	2	3	8.33				
N. (5 yr)					1	5	2	18.00
E. (4 yr)					1	4	5	21.20
D. (5 yr)	1	2	8	10.00	1	2	5	11.80
	1	2	11	10.54				M16.66
	1*	4	6	15.50				
	1*	3	13	11.07				
	1*	2	4	14.50				
	1*	2	4	13.00				
				M12.98				
Experimental								
K. (5 yr)	1*	2	2	7.50	1*	2	2	7.00
					1*	2	3	6.50
S. (5 yr)	1*	3	8	9.13				
C. (4 yr)	1	2	3	13.00	1	5	2	12.00
					1	2	1	22.00
R. (5 yr)	1*	4	2	12.00	1	2	3	10.67
	1*	4	12	12.42	1	10	10	14.10
	1	5	6	8.00	1*	9	8	12.88
	1	2	4	22.25	1	2	3	11.67
				M12.04				
					1*	2	4	11.22
					1*	2	1	13.00
					1*	2	2	18.00
					1	2	1	17.00
					1*	2	3	30.67
								M14.36

* spread.   stacked.

more than half the sequences can be accounted for in the experimental group in one subject's performance. Therefore, it is difficult to say to what extent specific training in picture sequencing effected the increased occurrence of sequences. Further study with more subjects will shed light on this.

An inspection of mean LCI's for both groups and both sessions show only small differences. However, considerable inter-subject variability is evident. Note, too, that the size of LCI is not necessarily related to the number of pictures in a sequence. This inconsistency is most dramatically shown in R's performance in which he has one sequence of ten pictures about which he verbalized 10 separate sentences with an LCI of 14.10. Compare this to his last sequence involving only two pictures and three sentences with an LCI of 30.67. These latter are clearly long and complex language structures.

Eighteen sequences occurred when the pictures were presented spread compared to sixteen sequences when the pictures were stacked. Evidently these two methods of presentation did not differentially effect sequencing for these subjects, but both should be used to give the subject every opportunity to sequence.

Discussion

It has been demonstrated that with a small population of four- and five-year-old subjects specific instruction and demonstration as to how pictures go together to tell "stories" significantly affect the length and complexity of the language a child uses to describe his pictures. The effects of this kind of training appear to be greater for four-year-olds than for five-year-olds.

A child's experiences with a camera even without training in picture sequencing affects his language behavior, depending upon the content of the pictures he takes. If he takes pictures at home of varied settings and situations of his own choosing as opposed to taking pictures of specified single objects, the length and complexity of his language is significantly increased, he uses more words and more different words and his language output becomes more spontaneous when he describes these pictures. In the present study the five-year-old subjects saw relationships between pictures (arranged picture sequences) more so than the four-year-olds. Whether sequencing ability is more characteristic of fives than fours needs to be studied. In terms of the present data it is not clear as to the effects of training on picture sequencing, i.e. whether or not it increases the frequency of sequencing. Perhaps a longer period of training with more examples of sequential activities and picture sequences would demonstrate an effect. In addition, the sequences that do occur vary greatly in terms of length, the amount of verbalization associated with them and the length and complexity of the verbalizations. There seems to be no systematic relationship among these three factors. Further investigation of these relationships is implied. Another important observation is that adult logic does not apply to children's picture sequences. In fact it is difficult at times to fully appreciate the relationship between or among pictures about which the child verbalizes. Perhaps this is true only for very young children.

The children seemed to enjoy manipulating their pictures and frequently commented about the quality of the pictures. One subject was quite amused with himself because he had taken a picture of the ground and his feet. The most frequently used "subjects" in the pictures were paintings and photographs in the home, the television set, books, light fixtures and members of the family. The children seemed to remember specific pictures they had taken and would frequently remain silent for rather long periods while they collected their thoughts about the pictures and formulated what they wanted to say about them. They were also aware when a picture was missing, i.e., not printed evidently due to faulty exposure.

Conclusions

The principal findings are as follows:

1. The subjects language responses were significantly longer and more grammatically complex when they were talking about pictures they made at home compared to pictures they made of specified individual objects.

2. Training in picture sequencing significantly increased the length and complexity of the subjects' language responses. This effect was greater for the four-year-old subjects than for the five-year-old subjects.

3. The subjects' language behavior was significantly more spontaneous when they described pictures taken at home compared to the pictures of toys. Training in picture sequencing did not significantly affect spontaneity. When the subjects talked about pictures of toys a significantly greater number of responses had to be prompted by the examiner.

4. The subjects did not differ significantly in the total number of words they uttered in the three conditions nor did they differ in the number of different words uttered. However, the relationship between TNW and NDW did change significantly when samples obtained for pictures of toys and pictures taken at home are compared. This relationship is such that when talking about pictures of toys a subject used the same number of words as when talking about pictures taken at home but the variety of words was not as high or may actually have been reduced. This finding, when considered in relation to the fact that significantly more responses had to be evoked when subjects were talking about the pictures of toys, points up the restrictive influence of this type of stimulus upon a child's language behavior. Training in visual literacy does not seem to affect either of these two measures.

5. Of the language measures used the LCI seems to be the most sensitive to changes in language behavior brought about by training in visual literacy or the content of the pictures a child has made.

6. There is evidence that children do sequence pictures without special training and the length and complexities of the language they use to describe these sequences is highly variable and not related to the number of pictures in the sequence.

This study was supported in part by the Eastman Kodak Company, Education and Youth Section, Consumer Markets Division, Rochester, New York.

References

Ammons, R.B. and C.H.Ammons, 1965, *Quick Test (QT)*. Psychological Test Specialists, Missoula, Montana.

Carmichael, L., H.P.Hogan and A.A.Walter, 1932, An experimental study of the effect of language on the reproduction of visually perceived forms. *J. Exper. Psych.* 15, 73–86.

Debes, J.L., 1967, *Visuals are a language,* volume 2. Eastman Kodak Company, Rochester, New York.

Deutsch, M., 1963, *The disadvantaged child and the learning process.* In: Education in depressed areas, edited by A.Harry Passow, Teachers College, Columbia University, New York, 163–179.

Dunn, L., 1965, *Manual for the Peabody Picture Vocabulary Test.* Minneapolis: American Guidance Service.

Hanawalt, N.G. and I.H.Demarest, 1939. The effect of verbal suggestion in the recall period upon the reproduction of visually perceived forms. *J. Exper. Psych.* 25, 159–174.

Herman, D.T., R.H.Lawless and R.W.Marshall, 1957, Variables in the effect of language on the reproduction of visually perceived forms. *Percep. and Motor Skills* 7, Monograph. Suppl. 2, 171–186.

McCarthy, D.A., 1930, The language development of the preschool child, Institute of Child Welfare Monograph, no. 4, Minneapolis: University of Minnesota Press.

Miner, L.E., 1968, *Scoring procedures for the Length-Complexity Index: A preliminary report.* Department of Speech Correction, Eastern Illinois University, Charleston.

Mintun, S., 1968, *A comparison of three stimulus media for eliciting verbal language samples from EMH children,* unpublished masters thesis, Department of Speech Correction, Eastern Illinois, Charleston.

Morris, H.L., 1962, Communication skills of children with cleft lips and palates, *J. Speech Hearing Res.* 5, 79–90.

Prentice, W.C.H., 1954, Visual recognition of verbally labeled figures. *Am. J. Psych.* 67, 315–320.

Shriner, T. and D.Sherman, 1967, An equation for assessing language development. *J. Speech Hearing Res.* 10, 41–48.

Strandberg, T.E., 1969, *A comparison of three stimulus media for evoking verbal language samples, masters thesis in progress,* Department of Speech Correction, Eastern Illinois University, Charleston.

Templing, M.C., 1966, Certain language skills in children, their development and interrelationships. *Inst. Child Welf. Mongr. Ser.,* no. 26. Minneapolis: University of Minnesota Press.

Turbayne, C.M., 1962, *The Myth of Metaphor.* Yale University Press: New Haven and London.

PROTOTYPES OF INSTRUCTIONS TO TYPISTS

Gerald M. Siegel

Tape recordings have been obtained for a series of experimental sessions, each session involving an adult and a child. Each session is on a separate tape. The tapes have been randomized and divided into two groups, and it is now necessary to have typed transcripts prepared from them. Each of you will be responsible for one set of tapes. The order in which you are to type the tapes has been indicated on the last page of these instructions. Be sure to follow this order faithfully.

In preparing these transcripts or protocols, you will be asked to perform a number of functions simultaneously:

1. You will have to do a careful and accurate job of representing all the verbal activity that occurred within each session. This is extremely important since all subsequent analyses will derive from the transcripts you type.
2. You will have to differentiate the verbal activity of the child from that of the adult.
3. You will have to learn several rules concerning the designation of 'vocal response units' so that you can mark off responses on transcripts as you prepare them. You will also have to indicate whether each vocal response unit is a statement or a question.

Before discussing specific rules for marking off responses on the transcripts, I would like to present some general instructions for your consideration:

A. General Instructions:
1. Type the transcripts in the predetermined random order.
2. Differentiate verbalizations of the adult from those of the child by placing the identifying symbol (a) in the margin for adult verbalizations and (c) for remarks made by the child.
3. *Do not use capitals* (except for proper names or for the pronoun 'I'), commas, question marks, or any other form of punctuation in preparing these transcripts. You will use apostrophes, however, to indicate a contraction (I'm, he's) or to indicate possession (the aide's house).
4. Some of the remarks made by either the child or the adult will be completely or partially incomprehensible. This may be because the speaker was particularly soft-spoken, mumbled, had unintelligible speech, or because some noise obscured what the speaker was saying. If a response (to be defined later) is either *partially or completely* incomprehensible, exclude it from the transcript. Even if the response has only one incomprehensible word, leave out the entire response.
5. Sometimes the adult or the child will make some non-communicative noises during the session. For example, the adult may say, 'The dog goes *bow-wow* and the lion goes *grr.*' If, as in the above remark, the noise is an integral part of the response, type it in. If, however, the noise is not essential, omit it. For example the child may say, '*Bow-wow*, here comes the dog.' In this instance omit the expression '*bow-wow.*'
6. Interjections such as 'uh,' 'er,' should be omitted except when they are used as words. Examples: Give me the *er* book. *Uh uh*, you can't have it. The 'er' should be omitted. 'Uh uh,' meaning 'no' should be typed.
7. If the speaker starts but does not finish a word and you are quite sure what he was going to say, in-

JOURNAL OF SPEECH AND HEARING DISORDERS, 1963, Monograph 10, pp. 100-102.

clude the word, but place it between parentheses. For example:
I th— I know he's coming.
I (think) I know he's coming.
If you can't tell what the started word was meant to be, simply exclude it.

B. *Designating 'vocal response units.'* In this study we are concerned with the *speech* behavior of the adults and children rather than with how their responses would look on paper. We are preparing these transcripts as a convenience, but more basically we are concerned with how the individuals used speech in the actual experimental sessions. We are not interested in whether or not a given response was grammatically complete and accurate. Rather we want to know whether it was functionally complete in terms of the ongoing exchange between the adults and the children. In normal conversation we don't always have a well defined predicate and nominative; and we indicate the beginning and end of our expressions by pauses, inflections, shifts in topics, etc., rather than by commas, periods, or exclamation points. That is why we have asked you not to put these punctuation marks in the transcripts you prepare. A little later I will describe the system you will use to indicate when a *vocal response unit* begins and ends. First, let us consider some of the rules that will help you decide when such a unit has occurred.

1. In general, a vocal response unit is a unit of spoken language marked off on either side by a pause or by some change in inflection.

2. A vocal response unit is considered finished when the speaker come to a complete stop and allows his voice to fall.

3. A vocal response unit is considered finished when the speaker comes to a complete stop with either a questioning or exclamatory inflection.

4. A vocal response unit is considered finished when the speaker in some manner clearly indicates he does not intend to complete the remarks.

5. A vocal response unit is considered completed when one speaker terminates and the other begins speaking.

6. A vocal response unit may include several simple utterances. If one simple utterance or remark is immediately followed by another with no pause for breath, they are considered only *one* response unit if the second remark is clearly subsidiary to the first.

7. A vocal response unit may be a single word such as 'yes' or 'uh huh' or it may comprise many words such as, 'I'm going to the movies with my brother and sister and mother and father tomorrow if it doesn't rain.'

8. A single expression of affirmation ('yeah,' 'yep,' 'uh huh,' 'yes'), or of negation ('no,' 'nope,' 'nah,' 'naw'), or of interrogation ('huh,' 'what,' 'eh') may be complete responses. You are to determine by listening to the tape whether an utterance is simply a non-communicative grunt (see No. 9 below) or serves communicatively to indicate affirmation, negation, or interrogation. Examples:
   (a) do you like me (one response)
   (c) huh (one response)
   (a) I said do you like me (one response)
   (c) oh yeah (one response)

9. Expressions such as 'aw,' 'aah, 'ow,' 'haha,' 'uh,' 'oop,' when they are not used as either affirmation, negation, or interrogation do not count as responses and should be omitted from the transcripts.

10. Utterances that are not recognizable as words or word approximations do not count as responses. Examples:

(a) what color is that (one response)

(c) pa (no response)

11. Occasionally the child and adult will be talking simultaneously. For example, the adult may start to speak and the child may interject a remark so that they are both talking at the same time. If this occurs, simply separate the response of the adult from that of the child on the transcript. That is, complete typing the adult responses and then indicate the child responses on the next line.

C. *Differentiating Statements from Questions.* All responses will be marked as either statements or questions. In normal conversation questions are typically indicated by the use of particular words, by the way the words are arranged in the response, or simply by inflection.

1. Occasionally a response may start out as a question but end as a statement. When this occurs, score the response a *question.* Examples:

   (c) can I I'm going to eat my candy now

   (a) would you like me to here let me help you with that

   Both of these examples would be scored as questions.

2. A response that starts out as a statement but ends as a question is also scored a question. Examples:

   (c) I think I'll do you think it is ok to tell the aide

   (a) if I let you will you no I don't think I had better

D. *Marking the Transcripts.* You are to mark the responses in the following manner:

1. Indicate the beginning of a response by (a) underlining the first word and by (b) placing the number of the response above the first word. Number adult and child responses separately.

2. You will indicate the end of a response by placing either a single stroke (/) or a double stroke (//) after the last word.

   (a) Use the single stroke (/) when the response is a statement.

   (b) Use the double stroke (//) when the response is a question.

3. Even if the response unit consists of only one word, it is important to underline that word and follow it by the appropriate number of strokes.

4. Responses that contain words that are incomprehensible or for some other reason are excluded from the transcript will not be counted.

5. Don't forget, number adult and child responses separately.

6. It is very important that you do not fail to indicate both the beginning and ending of each response and that you number the responses accurately.

PROTOTYPES OF CRITERIA FOR COUNTING WORDS

Gerald M. Siegel

1. All contractions, whether negative or affirmative, are to be considered two words (or more). Thus, contractions in expressions such as I'm, can't, won't, he's, John's talking now, etc., count as two words. Combinations such as gonna or hadda are counted as two words.

2. Expressions of affirmation (yes, yeah, uh huh), of negation (no, nope, nah, uh uh), of interrogation (what, huh), or of exclamation (oops, hey, wow) count as one word.

3. Hyphenated words and compound nouns which seem to function as single words are counted as one word each. For example:

Betty Lou	one word
Betty Lou Smith	two words
high school	one word
2-south-3	one word

4. Exclamations which tend to occur as a unit are counted as one word. For example: darn it; doggone it; oh boy; gee whiz   one word each

5. Where the child is counting or is spelling, each unit (number or letter) counts as a separate word.

6. Descriptive noises such as meow-meow, grr, or bow-wow are counted as single words.

JOURNAL OF SPEECH AND HEARING DISORDERS, 1963, Monograph 10, p 103.

JUNCTURE PHENOMENA AND THE SEGMENTATION OF A LINGUISTIC CORPUS*

ELAINE P. HANNAH and LEO ENGLER

The present study was an attempt to check the usefulness of the terminal juncture as a means of segmenting a linguistic corpus. Of importance are scorer agreement as to the occurrence of both juncture and hesitation phenomena, and consistency in perception of both types of phenomena. The perception of the pitch contour accompanying a terminal juncture is also examined.

The problem of segmenting a linguistic corpus for analysis is being handled through a variety of procedures. The traditional sentence has proven most useful for an analysis based on the transformational approach (Menyuk, 1961). Another quite frequently used segment has been the "response" (Minifie, et al., 1963) or "utterance" (McCarthy, 1930; Templin, 1957; Albright and Albright, 1956). These latter units have been described generally as occurring between two "pauses." It is fairly obvious that when one is involved with speech development at the $2\frac{1}{2}$ year level and below, as in the research of Albright and Albright (1956), there is little problem in determining the extent of the segment. Frequently such utterances are holophrastic and are clearly separated by "pauses." After the 3 year level, the child has perfected not only the intonational pattern of his native tongue but also an increasing vocabulary and greater preoccupation with the subtleties of style which are reflected in hesitation phenomena. Although Minifie, Darley and Sherman (1963) found 96 per cent. agreement among three sophisticated recorders as to an "utterance" and a consistency of 0.98 to 1.00 between first and second scorings, the determination of the limits of an "utterance" or a "response" becomes more difficult, particularly for the unsophisticated scorer, when one is scanning more mature linguistic development.

A number of recent linguistic studies (Strickland, 1962; Loban, 1963) have been making use of still another unit, the linguistic segment, which is said to exist between discourse initial and terminal contour or subsequently, two terminal contours (Hockett, 1958). For purposes of a current research project, this linguistic unit seemed to the present researchers to have some potential as a means of segmenting the linguistic corpus under consideration. However, after initial experimentation had indicated that scorers showed some confusion with respect to the difference between the true terminal juncture and hesitation phenomena, it was decided to check the discrimination patterns

* The authors acknowledge the assistance of R. B. Shackelford, Psychology Division, U.S. Veterans Administration Hospital, Topeka, Kansas.

LANGUAGE AND SPEECH, Oct-Dec., 1967, vol. 10, part 4, pp. 228-233.

of a group of relatively naive linguistics students who might possibly serve as research assistants. Dittman and Wynne (1961), in a previous study, indicate 93 per cent. agreement in coding junctures, with 87 per cent reliability between codings. Boomer and Dittman (1962) indicate significantly better discrimination for hesitation pauses than terminal juncture pauses in controlled sentence material. Since it was proposed that the juncture pauses be used to determine linguistic segmental limits, and since the corpus to which the scorers would listen was to be the spontaneous unedited speech of a group of school age subjects, it was decided to investigate possible differences in discrimination between the two types of pause within this context.

This investigation was also interested in the degree of consistency with which the individual scorer discriminated each of the two classes of pause phenomena. In addition, for purposes of future research, the subjects of the present study were asked to indicate a rising /↑/, falling /↓/, or sustained /→/ pitch contour (Hockett, 1958), for each pause perceived.

PROCEDURE

A tape of two first grade children talking with an adult was selected for examination. This section was two minutes in length and was played to a group of sixteen linguistics students who had previously had four one hour lectures on the American Structuralist view of the suprasegmental aspects of English. The students were asked to follow a transcript of the unedited tape as it was played and to indicate by means of a slash (/) the points at which they thought they heard pauses. They were also advised that the playback would be interrupted in order to allow them to register their judgments. The tape was then segmented by the experimenter operating the tape recorder, with care being taken to stop at approximately two second intervals throughout the tape, avoiding any obvious grammatical juncture points. Once an interval had been selected, it was replayed three times to allow time for the student to scan the tape and confirm his judgement. Twelve students followed the same process with identical segmenting of the tape a second time after a lapse of two days. Any juncture points indicated by the scorers were registered on a master copy of the transcript and categorised, by a trained and uninvolved linguist, from the nature of the context and the original tape recording, as either terminal in nature or as hesitation phenomena. The percentage of the total terminal juncture points and hesitation pauses identified by each scorer was determined and the two sets of percentages compared by means of a one-tailed Wilcoxon Matched Pairs Signed Ranks procedure. The number of changes in perception of the two types of pause made by each scorer from the first to the second trial was also compared by means of the same procedure. The relationship between ability to discriminate terminal juncture phenomena on the one hand and hesitation phenomena on the other was then examined by means of a Spearman Rank Correlation Coefficient procedure.

As previously indicated, the scorers were also asked to identify the pitch contour accompanying each pause phenomenon perceived. These were categorised according to the structuralist classification of rising /↑/, falling /↓/ and sustained /→/ (Hockett, 1958). Since it became apparent that, in this research situation, individual subject discrimination and re-test reliability for hesitation phenomena would be low, only the terminal juncture set was ultimately examined for discrimination of pitch contour. On this basis, it might be expected that a significant difference in discrimination between sustained, on the one hand, and rising or falling on the other hand would appear, since the latter, rather than the former are generally hypothesised to accompany the terminal juncture pattern. The terminal contour pitch patterns indicated by each of sixteen subjects for each terminal juncture perceived were compared by means of a Cochrane Q test procedure. A χ^2 procedure was then applied to the distribution of scores composed of those showing a significant difference beyond the 0.01 level and those showing no significant difference in choice among the three possible terminal pitch contours.

RESULTS

The analysis of the data indicated that individual subject discrimination of the terminal juncture phenomena ranged in this experiment from 80 to 100 per cent. On the other hand, individual discrimination of the hesitation phenomena ranged from 6 to 48 per cent., indicating a much wider range of perception and considerably less agreement upon the existence of the latter. The difference betwen the distributions was significant ($p < 0.01$) and the null hypothesis of no difference in perception for the two types of phenomena was rejected.

A similar analysis of the re-trial consistency with which each scorer perceived the two types of terminal indicated that, again, terminal juncture points were perceived with a re-trial consistency of from 80 to 100 per cent. The re-trial consistency for hesitation phenomena ranged from 0 to 80 per cent. The difference between the distributions was again significant ($p < 0.01$), allowing for a rejection of the null hypothesis with respect to re-trial consistency.

As was indicated previously, the correlation between the subject's pattern of perception for terminal junctures and that for hesitation phenomena was investigated through use of the Spearman Rank Correlation Coefficient. It was found that $r_s = -0.416$ and that this relationship closely approximated the 0.05 level of significance (0.425), suggesting that an individual's perception for terminal phenomena may be in an inverse relationship to his perception of hesitation phenomena. The subject who noted a greater number of the total juncture points tended to also perceive fewer of the points at which hesitation phenomena occurred. With respect to individual consistency of discrimination for the two classes of phenomena, a correlation of $r_s = 0.29$, which did not reach the 0.05 level in terms of significance, was obtained. A summary of this data appears in Table 1.

With respect to the discrimination of pitch contour, the examination of only the terminal juncture points would lead one to expect a significant degree of discrimination

TABLE 1

Summary of comparison scores: Wilcoxon Matched Pairs Signed Ranks and Spearman Rank Order Coefficient of Correlation procedures.

COMPARISON	RESULT
Perception (Terminal Juncture: Hesitation Pause)	0**
Coefficient of Correlation	−0.42
Consistency of Perception	1**
Coefficient of Correlation	0.29

between rising or falling as contrasted with the sustained pitch contour. In fourteen comparisons out of the twenty-five terminal juncture points indicated, there was a Cochrane Q score significant beyond the 0.01 level, leading to a rejection of the null hypothesis for the pitch contours relative to these terminals. In each of the fourteen instances, there was a very obvious agreement in choice as to the rising or falling pitch contour, with nine contours indicated as falling and five indicated as rising. However, there were also eleven terminal contours which were identified with agreement greater than the 0.05 level of significance. One would expect that, in order to reach the 0.05 level with respect to such discrimination, expected proportions of 1:24 would need to exist. Since the observed proportions (11:14) differ from the expected proportions beyond the 0.01 level of significance ($p < 0.01$ by χ^2), one would have to conclude that contours accompanying the terminal juncture cannot be identified by the human ear with significant agreement.

DISCUSSION

It is apparent from such results that, even in rapid speech, the human ear discriminates, with a high percentage of agreement among scorers, the terminal juncture points in speech. This was not true in this experiment for the hesitation phenomena, a finding which varies from the results of Boomer and Dittman (1962) mentioned earlier. Apparently the perception of the present subjects for hesitation and stylistic phenomena in spontaneous, unedited speech varied widely from subject to subject and might give rise to some concern with respect to examiner perception of the less obvious non-fluencies of the stuttering pattern. A negative and substantial correlation between identification scores on the two types of pause phenomena would possibly suggest that the scorers in this experiment who had better perception for terminal juncture points did not note as many hesitation phenomena, thereby adding less confusion and possibly giving greater validity to the process of segmentation. A positive, although non-significant, relationship between consistency in identification of terminal juncture points and hesitation phenomena might also support the use of this procedure for the selection of the more useful scorers.

122

It might be further added that, since the use of the terminal concept produced linguistic segments which in reality included a number of macrosegments (Hockett 1958), and since it proved difficult to computerize for tabulation such a large segment, another cut was arbitrarily made and a smaller unit, more closely resembling the idealised Hockett macrosegment, was ultimately utilised. This also tended to control any confusion created by variations in perception with respect to hesitation phenomena.

The examination of the terminal juncture points in terms of hypothesised pitch contours indicated other lines for further investigation. The relationship of the terminal pitch contour to the perceived impression of termination does not seem to be an integral one in this data. Despite the fact that all twenty-five terminal junctures were discriminated with from 80 to 100 per cent. agreement, in eleven instances the pitch contours accompanying them did not show an agreement in any direction which reached the 0.05 level of significance. In other words, in eleven instances, the scorers agreed upon the speaker's intent to terminate that particular linguistic segment but could not agree to any significant degree which of the pitch contours usually hypothesised to accompany the termination of a segment actually occurred. One would, therefore, have to suspect that, in rapid speech, the terminal pitch contour does not function as a primary indicator of thought termination and may actually depend for its recognition upon the presence of other factors.

It is interesting to note, from a graphic analysis[1] of the tape used for this experiment that, although twenty-five terminal junctures were discriminated with from 80 to 100 per cent. agreement and fourteen were accompanied by terminal contours on which there was agreement beyond the 0.01 level, there were only 11 returns to the base line of the graph in terms of amplitude. Apparently, as indicated by Fodor and Bever (1965), it is not necessary to have a complete return to the base line in order for the ear to perceive a terminal juncture. In other words, a change in amplitude pattern apparently contributes to the total signal pattern perceived by the ear but a complete cessation of the sound pattern is not necessary for the perception of termination.

SUMMARY

Sixteen scorers were asked to listen to a tape of two minutes duration and to indicate, on a transcript of the tape, the pause phenomena which they perceived. The results indicated a variation in degree of agreement on these, generally favouring the terminal junctures. There was also an individual scorer tendency for the percentage of agreement on the perception of hesitation phenomena to fall as the percentage of agreement on the perception of terminal junctures rose, thereby indicating a possible criterion for the selection of scorers who might be able to segment a linguistic corpus using the terminal juncture concept. Results also indicated that terminal pitch contours could not be discriminated in rapid speech with a significant level of agreement.

[1] *By means of an Offner Model R.P. Graphic Write-out unit.*

123

REFERENCES

ALBRIGHT, R. W. and ALBRIGHT, JOY B. (1956). The phonology of a two-year old child. *Word*, 12, 382.

BOOMER, S. and DITTMAN, A. T. (1962). Hesitation pauses and juncture pauses in speech. *Language and Speech*, 5, 215.

DITTMAN, A. T. and WYNNE, L. C. (1961). Linguistic techniques and the analysis of emotionality in interviews. *J. abn. soc. Psychol.*, 63, 201.

FODOR, J. A. and BEVER, T. G. (1965). The psychological reality of linguistic segments. *J. verb. Learning verb. Behav.*, 4, 414.

HOCKETT, C. F. (1958). *A Course in Modern Linguistics* (New York).

LOBAN, WALTER D. (1963). *The Language of Elementary School Children*. National Council of Teachers of English Research Report No. 1.

MCCARTHY, D. A. (1930). *The Language Development of the Preschool Child* (Minneapolis, Minnesota).

MENYUK, PAULA (1961). *A Description of the Syntactic Structures in the Language of Children : Nursery School and First Grade*. Ph.D. Dissertation, Boston University.

MINIFIE, F. D., DARLEY, F. L. and SHERMAN, DOROTHY (1963). Temporal reliability of seven language measures. *J. Sp. Hrg. Res.*, 6, 139.

SIEGEL, S. (1956). *Non-Parametric Statistics* (New York).

STRICKLAND, RUTH G. (1962). The language of elementary school children: its relationship to the language of reading textbooks and the quality of reading of selected children. *Bulletin of the School of Education, Indiana University*, 38, 4.

TEMPLIN, MILDRED (1957). *Certain Language Skills in Children* (Minneapolis, Minnesota).

A REVIEW OF MEAN LENGTH OF RESPONSE AS A MEASURE OF EXPRESSIVE LANGUAGE DEVELOPMENT IN CHILDREN

Thomas H. Shriner

An often used and frequently reported measure of language development is mean length of response (MLR). MLR is usually defined as the number of words per response averaged over a sample of 50 responses. Most investigators, using MLR either for clinical evaluation or in theoretical studies of language, have recorded one sample consisting of 50 responses from each child. Customarily, the responses are tape recorded and usually are elicited by pictures and/or toys presented by the examiner. The individual responses of each child are then transcribed by tape replay, constituting a sample of language for that particular child. An MLR score is derived from the sample and used for individual comparisons or pooled for group analysis.

EXPERIMENTAL AND STIMULUS BIAS

Quite obviously, response length changes with age. Investigators apparently have assumed that, by sampling expressive language behavior in various situations or in response to various stimuli, these changes could be quantified. The methods which have been used, however, have varied considerably and make it extremely difficult to make comparisons between studies.

McCarthy (Carmichael, 1954, pp. 546-549), apparently aware of various methods, tabulated MLR data from a number of studies. She claimed that the studies which employed similar methods yielded fairly comparable results. Inspection of her Table 5, however, reveals many discrepancies, not only between studies, but within the studies as well. Moreover, Minifie, Darley, and Sherman (1963) point out that response variability is sufficiently large to place a given child as much as two years ahead of or two years behind his age level; this is true even though he may be operating at about average for his

JOURNAL OF SPEECH AND HEARING DISORDERS, 1969, vol. 34, no. 1, pp. 61-68.

age level. McCarthy also states that most of the discrepancies between the studies which she reviewed could be accounted for by known selective factors or by differences in the methods of recording and analysis. According to McCarthy, the length of the child's response will vary: (1) with CA and IQ (Fisher, 1934); (2) if the child is a twin (Day, 1932); (3) in conversation with an adult (Smith, 1935); (4) in conversation with peers (Smith, 1935; Hahn, 1948); (5) in classroom situations (Hahn, 1948); (6) with socioeconomic status (Templin, 1957); and (7) with stimulus materials (McCarthy, Carmichael, 1954, p. 545, citing Shire, Davis, and Templin procedures). Various other factors such as the time of day, emotional state of the child, the examiner's so-called "practice" effect, and the physical condition of the child or examiner also may account for differences between responses.

Cowan, Weber, Hoddinott, and Klein (1967) designed a study to focus specifically on MLR as a function of stimulus materials, the experimenter, and the subject. They found that the stimulus materials influenced response length; that age, sex, and socioeconomic status effects interacted; and that the experimenter effect interacted with the age and sex of the subjects. MLR was not simply a product of the subject alone, but a joint product of subject, experimenter, and stimulus interaction. Their results indicated that stimulus and experimenter variables could well account for the commonly obtained absolute differences in MLR between studies. They stated that caution must be used in assessing results of individual studies using MLR, and that examiners should be cautious of inferences drawn when comparisons are made between studies. The Cowan et al. study (1967) emphasizes the need for a specific methodology and a reduction in experimenter bias if the results of one study are to be compared with those of another.

The McCarthy review and Cowan study demonstrate that MLR scores vary as a function of several manipulations and situational factors. This makes it extremely difficult to make comparisons between or among studies unless the examiner can minimize and specify the manipulations and situational factors which could enter into experimental bias. An example would be the remarks or questions used by the examiner in presenting the task: "Tell me what they are doing in the picture," "Tell me a story about the picture," and "Tell me what you see in the picture," are not the same instructions. If the experimental approach is one of behavior modification, the effectiveness of MLR may not be reduced; rather, MLR may be a more or less sensitive indicator of these various experimental arrangements. What may be important is not whether MLR remains the same in different situations, but, rather, whether the difference between situations is replicated on subsequent occasions. To the extent that a child's behavior reflects "systematic" changes in stimulus materials, this may not be a source of bias; bias would be measuring more of the experimenter and less of the verbal behavior of the child. Whether the examiner is evoking responses in the classical structured sense or establishing a baseline and concentrating on the control of variables in the instrumental sense, the exact procedures must be specified to permit comparisons and minimize biases. The examiner should be aware of the many variables which can influence a child's responses and also aware that different stimuli or consequent events may alter response length.

RELIABILITY AND VALIDITY

Investigators have assumed a "true" or relatively invariant MLR for children in specific age categories. This assumption appears to be based on the obvious observation that response length changes as the child matures from birth. The nature and the situational factors which bring about this change have only recently come under experimental observations. Whether or not this change is linear or continuous from birth to the age of three, four, five, is unknown.[1] As a first step, however, examiners apparently have taken for granted the invariant MLR concept, their task simply being to sample the child's changing responses at discrete points. Any sampling procedure raises the problem of reliability and validity.

Since the validity of any test is difficult or practically impossible to prove directly, earlier investigators have placed added importance on the reliability of MLR. Reliability is a necessary component of validity, but high reliability does not necessarily permit the conclusion that a sampling procedure is valid. From 50 response samples, correlation coefficients have been recorded for assessing reliability for various purposes: that is, to evaluate and to estimate the degree of agreement among: (1) examiners in preparing the transcripts (Siegel, 1962) ; (2) an examiner's repeated measures obtained from the transcripts (McCarthy, 1930; Day, 1932; Williams, 1937; Davis, 1937; Spriestersbach, Darley, and Morris, 1958; Winitz, 1959; Minifie, Darley, and Sherman, 1963) ; (3) examiners in obtaining measures from the same transcripts (Day, 1932; Davis, 1937; Spriestersbach et al., 1958; Winitz, 1959; Miller, 1961; Minifie et al., 1963; and others) ; and (4) the same measures obtained in the same manner over a period of time from the same children (Fisher, 1934; Minifie et al., 1963) .

To obtain an estimate of agreement between two persons in preparing transcripts, Siegel (1962) had two typists independently transcribe the same magnetic tapes for each of 30 children. The correlation coefficient (0.94) was high, indicating good agreement between the typists. They were typists, however, who had participated in an earlier study. The reliability coefficient for this earlier study was 0.64; this much lower coefficient indicates the importance of reliability checks of MLR, including transcript preparation when recordings

---

[1]The "within" discrepancies in McCarthy's Table 5 suggest that the growth is not linear. MLR obviously increases in length with increases in chronological age. There are, however, reversals in the data which are not easily explained, unless stimulus or experimental bias is operating. See Templin's Table 39 (1957, p. 79) for an example of the reversals in question. The five year old boys have a lower MLR score than the four and a half year old boys, with not much difference (probably not significant) appearing between the MLR scores of the four and five year olds. There is also a reversal in the MLR scores for the girls.

are used. Siegel cautioned that it is methodologically important to provide specific training for those who prepare the transcripts and to include a description of their behavior in the study. He concluded that, given adequate training, typists can reliably prepare transcripts of tape recorded responses.

Intra- and interexaminer reliability coefficients from the language transcripts are in general agreement and show relatively high correlations (0.90 and above). This indicates that children's utterances can be recorded and analyzed reliably for a single sample of 50 responses. It does not, however, indicate to what extent the 50 response samples represent the children's language development in general; that is, whether or not "the items constituting the test adequately represent the entire universe of items which the test undertakes to sample" (Anastasi, 1954, p. 97).

Darley and Moll (1960) were concerned specifically with the size of language sample needed to obtain an adequate reliability coefficient for MLR. They summarized previous research methodology by noting that some investigators do not discuss their choice of sample size while others have suggested or used 100 sentences (Nice, 1925), 50 sentences (McCarthy, 1930, p. 32), 40 sentences (Williams, 1937), and 15 sentences (Schneiderman, 1955). Darley and Moll concluded from their reliability analysis that a sample of 50 responses would have an estimated reliability coefficient of 0.85, adequate for most purposes; however, the adequacy would depend on the precision needed by an examiner in a particular situation. By increasing the sample beyond 50 responses, the estimated reliability

coefficients also increase. Because fairly large increases beyond a sample size of 50 are required to improve the reliability coefficient appreciably, increases in sample size beyond 50 produce only small increments in reliability. At least 100 responses are needed, for example, for a reliability coefficient of 0.92. Theoretically, the larger the sample and the greater the reduction in variability, the more closely the measure approaches the "true" mean. The time required, however, to record, transcribe, and analyze any more than 50 responses would make MLR impractical as a clinical tool.

Depending on the precision needed by an examiner, it appears as if 50 responses are sufficient for obtaining a reliable MLR measure for most purposes. If one accepts the invariant MLR concept, however, it is obviously necessary for a 50 response sample taken from a child at one point in time to agree highly with the second or possibly third 50 response sample taken at different but closely adjacent times. If more than one 50 response sample is gathered from the same child at different times, then close agreement between the 50 response samples should be obtained. This is referred to as temporal or test-retest reliability, and reveals the consistency of an individual's performance on the same test over a period of time. In only two studies (Fisher, 1934; Minifie, Darley, and Sherman, 1963) are coefficients for estimating temporal reliability for MLR reported. Fisher recorded 50 responses from 23 children on different days and reported a reliability coefficient of 0.58; she did not state the exact time between samples. She suggested (p. 79) that one sampling of 50 remarks does not assure a "true" MLR for any particular child. Minifie et al. recorded 50 responses from each of 96 children—24 males and 24 females who were five years, six months of age, and 24 males and 24 females who were eight years of age—on separate, adjacent days. They reported, in accordance with their results from intraclass correlation analyses, that

> none of the language measures (including MLR) based on single 50 response language samples appears to have a high temporal reliability for individual measures; that is, individual children were not consistent in their language usage from day to day. (p. 146)

They do report, however, that measures consisting of means of three 50 response language samples (150 responses) have adequate reliability for most research purposes. Their results in this respect are in agreement with those of Darley and Moll (1960), who state that a fairly large number of responses is needed to increase reliability appreciably. Generally, from the results of Darley and Moll, it appears that 50 responses are adequate for obtaining MLR scores for most purposes, depending on the precision needed by the examiner. According to Minifie et al. (1963), however, any single mean obtained from a 50 response language sample is only a gross estimate of the child's "true" MLR.

Since reliability is a necessary component of validity, and children's MLR scores do not appear reliable when taken on different days, the validity of MLR as a measure of language is questionable. The need for an outside criterion to evaluate MLR as a measure was considered important by Shriner and Sherman (1967) and Shriner (1967). An answer was needed to the question of whether MLR, singly or in combination with other language measures, would satisfactorily assess language development with reference to an outside criterion. Sherman, Shriner, and Silverman (1965), Shriner and Sherman (1967), and Shriner (1967) assumed that the impression language makes upon others might serve as the outside criterion. They assumed that, if a child's language development is correctly assessed as retarded, normal, or superior on the basis of MLR or other presently used language indices, the psychological impressions made upon observers by the child's language should agree with the assessment. They further assumed that, if observers' ratings of language development were not in agreement with assessment of children's language as determined by our present measures, then measures such as MLR are neither useful nor valid for making such an assessment. The impact of expressive language in communication with others must be considered an important criterion of validity.

Shriner and Sherman (1967) designed a study to evaluate relationships between presently used expressive language measures (including MLR) and scale values (outside criterion) of language development obtained by a psychological rating scale method. They obtained speech samples, consisting of 50 responses from each of 200 children ranging in age from 2 years and 6 months, to 12 years. In accordance with their results from a linear multiple-regression analysis, they reported deletion of MLR as a predictor variable. Their explanation for its nonsignificant contribution was that it correlated highly with other retained predictors. Although deleted from the final prediction equation, MLR had a higher correlation with scale values than any other predictor variable. They concluded that

> if a single measure is to be used for assessment of language development, this one (MLR) thus would appear to be the most useful among those studied. (p. 47)

In a related study, Shriner (1967) used four linear multiple-regression analyses to determine the best composite of several language measures (including MLR) for predicting psychological scale values of language development for children of four different age categories. For the youngest age group (mean age four years, seven months), a new measure, referred to as a modified length-complexity index, also was evaluated. The results revealed that, as the mean age of the groups for analysis increased, MLR lost significance as a predictor; that is, little systematic relationship was observed between the criterion, scale values of language development, and MLR for children above the age of approximately five years. For children younger than five years, the best single predictor was the length-complexity index. This index, however, did correlate highly with both MLR and with Templin's method (1957) for deriving a structural complexity score. This was expected because the new index is a measure of the length and complexity of utterance. The results of this study apparently indicate that response length does not appear to be a significant indicator of expressive language for children who are approximately five years of age and older, because of increased response variability. For older children, other factors such as those measured by the structural complexity score are coming to play a more important role for assessing expressive language. Whether or not one sampling of 50 responses is representative of a "true" MLR for children below the age of approximately five years has not been determined.

SUMMARY

Mean length of response probably has been one of the most frequently used measures in the study of children's language development since it was first reported by Nice in 1925. The purpose of this report was to review and discuss MLR as a measure with respect to experimenter and stimulus bias in obtaining the responses, and to review and discuss the reliability and validity of the obtained responses. Response length, as reviewed, has been shown to vary with several manipulations and situational factors.

This variability probably could be reduced if a specific methodology were employed and experimenter and stimulus bias could be kept at a minimum. If the approach is one of behavior modification, then the examiner may wish to isolate the factors which contribute to this variability. MLR, as far as I am aware, has not been used in this manner. If response length and variability are not studied with respect to both the experimental manipulations and the situational factors, then the usefulness of MLR is questionable. Even though examiners, given adequate training, can reliably prepare transcripts from tape replay and then analyze them reliably, 50 responses may or may not represent the child's "true" MLR.

Recent developments in descriptive linguistics which emphasize the structural aspects of language, and the influence of behaviorists who emphasize behavior modification have contributed to a decline in use of MLR, for MLR provides relatively scant information about morphological and syntactical developmental changes which occur with age. More systematic research should permit an examiner not only to describe the developmental changes which occur in the child's language as he matures, but to describe adequately the manipulations and situational factors which bring about these changes. Further research also should provide better ways to assess and quantify both the state and growth of syntax and lexicon in children, factors which MLR does not directly assess.

ACKNOWLEDGMENT

This paper was supported by Public Health Research Grant NB-07346 from the National Institute of Mental Health.

REFERENCES

ANASTASI, ANNE, Psychological Testing. New York: Macmillan (1954).

COWAN, P. A., WEBER, J., HODDINOTT, B. A., and KLEIN, J., Mean length of spoken response as a function of stimulus, experimenter, and subject. Child Developm., 38, 191-203 (1967).

DARLEY, F. L., and MOLL, K. L., Reliability of language measures and size of language sample. J. Speech Hearing Res., 3, 166-173 (1960).

DAVIS, EDITH A., Mean sentence length compared with long and short sentences as a reliable measure of language development. Child Developm., 8, 69-79 (1937).

DAY, ELLA J., The development of language in twins: I. A comparison of twins and single children. Child Developm., 3, 179-199 (1932).

FISHER, MARY S., Language patterns of preschool children. Child Developm. Monogr., New York: Teach. Coll., Columbia Univ. (1934).

HAHN, ELISE, Analyses of the content and form of the speech of first grade children. Quart. J. Speech, 34, 361-366 (1948).

McCARTHY, DOROTHEA A., Language development in children. Chap. 9 in L. Carmichael (Ed.), Manual of Child Psychology. New York: Wiley (1954).

McCARTHY, DOROTHEA A., The language development of the preschool child. Inst. Child Welf., Monogr. Ser., No. 4. Minneapolis: Univ. Minn. Press (1930).

MILLER, JUDITH C., Linguistic skills of physically handicapped children. M.A. thesis, Univ. Iowa (1961).

MINIFIE, F., DARLEY, F. L., and SHERMAN, DOROTHY, Temporal reliability of seven language measures. J. Speech Hearing Res., 6, 139-149 (1963).

NICE, MARGARET M., Length of sentences as a criterion of a child's progress in speech. J. educ. Psychol., 16, 370-379 (1925).

SCHNEIDERMAN, NORMA, A study of the relationship between articulatory disability and language ability. J. Speech Hearing Dis., 20, 359-364 (1955).

SHERMAN, DOROTHY, SHRINER, T. H., and SILVERMAN, F., Psychological scaling of language development of children. Proc. Iowa Acad. Sci., 72, 366-371 (1965).

SHRINER, T. H., A comparison of selected measures with psychological scale values of language development. J. Speech Hearing Res., 10, 828-835 (1967).

SHRINER, T. H., and SHERMAN, DOROTHY, An equation for assessing language development. *J. Speech Hearing Res.*, **10**, 41-48 (1967).

SIEGEL, G. M., Inter-examiner reliability for mean length of response. *J. Speech Hearing Res.*, **5**, 91-95 (1962).

SMITH, MADORAH E., A study of some factors influencing the development of the sentence in preschool children. *J. Genet. Psychol.* **46**, 182-212 (1935).

SPRIESTERSBACH, D. C., DARLEY, F. L., and MORRIS, H. L., Language skills in children with cleft palates. *J. Speech Hearing Res.*, **1**, 279-285 (1958).

TEMPLIN, MILDRED C., Certain language skills in children, their development and interrelationships. *Inst. Child Welf., Monogr. Ser.*, No. 26. Minneapolis: Univ. Minn. Press (1957).

WILLIAMS, H. M., An analytical study of language achievement in preschool children. *Univ. Iowa Stud. Child Welf.*, No. 2, Part 1, 13 (1937).

WINITZ, H., Language skills of male and female kindergarten children. *J. Speech Hearing Res.*, **2**, 377-386 (1959).

Interexaminer Reliability for Mean Length of Response

GERALD M. SIEGEL

One of the frequently reported measures of linguistic skill in children has been the mean length of response (MLR). The measure is usually obtained by placing the child in a situation in which he is encouraged to verbalize while a single examiner attempts to record the child's first 50 or 60 responses verbatim and in longhand. MLR is then computed simply as the arithmetic mean of the number of words divided by the number of responses. Estimates of interexaminer agreement for MLR require that two or more persons simultaneously transcribe the child's responses in either a live situation or from recordings. The present study reports interexaminer reliability in judgments of MLR independently obtained from two sets of typed transcripts, both sets deriving from the same tape recordings.

Related Literature

The use of longhand recording in deriving MLR increases the possibility of obtaining values that are inaccurate or even biased. McCarthy (6), for example, cites a study by Betts (1) in

Gerald M. Siegel (Ph.D., University of Iowa, 1957) is Assistant Professor of Speech, University of Minnesota. This study was completed while the author was a Research Associate, Bureau of Child Research, University of Kansas, and was supported by National Institutes of Mental Health Grant OM-111.

which longhand recording of oral compositions of children yielded only 32% of the flow of speech with approximately 84% accuracy. Systematic factors of familiarity, complexity, or length of the child's responses may determine which responses the scorer misses. McCarthy (5) obtained an average correlation of .99 among four examiners who independently scored previously prepared transcripts for a sample of 14 preschool children. The accuracy with which the transcripts were prepared and responses were designated, however, was not considered. Day (4) had three examiners prepare transcripts for a total of 250 responses elicited in a live testing situation. The reported interexaminer reliability was .99. The possibility of systematic differences among examiners, which would not be revealed by a correlation procedure, was not considered, however, since means and standard deviations for the various examiners were not presented. Spriestersbach, Darley, and Morris (9) reported indices of interexaminer reliability for two observers scoring MLR among 40 cleft palate children that 'were judged to indicate that the method of recording was sufficiently reliable.' The authors do not report the obtained coefficient, however.

Winitz (11) has been one of the few investigators to use tape recordings to

JOURNAL OF SPEECH AND HEARING RESEARCH, Mar. 1962, vol. 5, no. 1, pp. 91-95.

facilitate MLR analyses. Winitz tape recorded and subsequently typed children's responses to Children's Apperception Test cards. The average percentage of agreement in response identification between the examiner and one other person in the live testing situation was 94%. Winitz also rescored 10 of the transcripts, and obtained self-agreement of 99%. He did not, however, check the accuracy with which the transcripts were prepared originally. Darley and Moll (2) used the Winitz protocols to study the effects of sample size on MLR and found that 'MLR scores based on 50 responses are of adequate reliability for most research purposes.'

Siegel (7) used MLR as a measure of adult verbal behavior in two-person assemblies involving adults and mentally retarded children. The sessions were tape recorded and subsequently divided between two secretaries for typing and scoring. Word counts were then obtained independently by a third person. Typist reliability was determined for a random sample of 10 sessions and the obtained Pearson r was only .64. In many instances the typists appeared to have been more influenced by 'conversational probabilities' than by what occurred in the sessions. These data served to indicate the importance of reliability checks of MLR, including transcript preparation when recordings are used.

In order to determine whether reliable estimates of MLR for children could be obtained with these procedures, a study was designed in which tape recordings were obtained, two sets of transcripts independently prepared, and comparisons made of MLR values from the two sets of protocols.

Procedures

Children. The subjects in this study were 30 children (15 boys and 15 girls) from the Parsons (Kan.) State Hospital and Training Center, a residential institution for retarded children. They ranged in age from 11 to 17 years with a mean age of 14 years and six months. The children were further selected from among the upper 15% of the population on the Parsons Language Sample (*8*), a recently developed test that measures both vocal and nonvocal verbal behavior. Higher level children were selected in order to insure that some verbal activity would occur in response to the stimulus materials.

Test Sessions. A set of Children's Apperception Test cards was used as the stimulus materials. Assistant A, a research assistant, presented the cards sequentially to each child with the invitation to 'tell me what is in this picture.' Consistent with previous applications of this procedure, the assistant was instructed to remain as neutral as possible in the situation and to 'make only as many remarks as are necessary to encourage the child to talk.' The assistant was a male of 22 years who worked part time for the Research Department of the Hospital. He had no specific training in speech pathology. Assistant B, also employed by the Research Department, was responsible for bringing the children into the experimental room and for taping the sessions. This assistant was a female of 27 years who had been given some previous instruction in procedures for determining response units though she had no formal training in speech pathology.

The experimental room was a sound treated cubicle, wired for recording, and attached to an adjoining observation room. During the test sessions Assistant B monitored the recording equipment from the observation room. In order to establish time limits for each interview, Assistant B kept an informal check of the number of responses. When, in her judgment, 100 responses had occurred, she interrupted the procedures and the child was dismissed.

Preparation of Transcripts. The same two secretaries who had participated in the previously cited study by Siegel (7) served as the typists in the present study and each prepared a set of transcripts for the 30 interviews. Only the first 60 responses on each transcript were typed and, in accord with procedures suggested by McCarthy (5), the first 10 of these responses were discarded so that MLR was computed for 50 responses in every instance. The order of typing was randomly determined except that while Typist I worked on the first 15 sessions Typist II worked on the last 15. Thus each typist used the same tapes but worked independently. The typists were required to mark off vocal response units as they typed, indicating the beginning of each response by underlining the first word and the end of each response by a stroke (/). The response number (from 1 to 60) was also placed above the first word of the response. The procedures for designating responses were drawn from and essentially similar to those suggested by McCarthy (5), Davis (3), Templin (10), and Winitz (11). Instructions were read by the typists and discussed with the experimenter. These typists had also received previous training in this procedure in the Siegel (7) investigation.

Counting Words. Once the responses had been indicated on the transcripts, it was necessary to obtain a word count in order to get a measure of the MLR. Two 'word counters' were used, each randomly assigned a set of transcripts. Explicit instructions and practice in determining word counts were given. Criteria for determining number of words were again derived from the McCarthy (5), Davis, (3), Templin (10), and Winitz (11) procedures. The transcripts were presented to the counters in a random order. MLR was subsequently computed by dividing the number of words by 50 for each transcript. The two sets of data, one from each of the two secretaries, were then compared by a Pearson correlation coefficient and the mean difference between the two sets was evaluated.

Results

The mean and standard deviation for each set of transcripts were computed. For one set the obtained mean was 6.36 and the standard deviation 2.62. For the second set of transcripts the mean was 6.44 and the standard deviation was 3.05. The mean difference between the two sets of transcripts was only .08 and was not significant at the 5% level. The correlation between the two sets of data was .94, indicating considerable agreement. Thus, the scores obtained from the two sets of transcripts correlated highly and were similar with respect to means and variability.

Discussion

Templin's (10) data concerning MLR of normal eight-year-olds (based on a sample of 30 boys and 30 girls) indicated that the average response for these children was 7.6 words with a standard deviation of 1.6 words. Combining the two sets of data obtained in the present study (since they were very similar), the average MLR is 6.4 and the standard deviation 2.8 words. The present data refer to a sample of children ranging in age from 11 to 17 years, however, with a mean age of 14.5 years. Thus it is quite apparent that, despite the relatively advanced age of the institutionalized retarded children, their MLR values in the present study were considerably less than those obtained by Templin.

The data concerning reliability may be taken as evidence that tape recordings provide a practical method for obtaining and analyzing language samples into MLR and that MLR so obtained is a reliable measure. The data also indicate that, given adequate training, typists can reliably prepare transcripts from these recordings. The use of persons untrained in the areas of speech pathology or language development as 'word counters' further indicates that it is possible adequately to train inexperienced persons to carry out this procedure.

In view of the heavy responsibility typists carry in studies involving typed transcripts, it seems methodologically important to provide specific training for these persons and to include a description of their behavior in the study. Certainly a consideration of the reliability data in the study by Siegel (7) indicates that even experienced secretaries may differ markedly in their response to tape-recorded sessions. To the degree that later analyses derive from these transcripts, errors in transcription may become confounded with the criterion measures obtained.

Despite these cautions, tape recordings greatly facilitate interexaminer comparisons with respect to measures such as MLR. Where such comparisons are not made, it becomes difficult to interpret the obtained data. A comparison of Templin (10) and McCarthy (5) data relative to MLR, for example, indicates that Templin obtained estimates of MLR that are systematically longer than those obtained earlier by McCarthy. An interpretation often placed on this difference is that contemporary children do indeed use longer and more complex responses than did children of 30 years ago and that this may in part be attributable to the influences of radio and television and to the changing patterns of child-parent relationships. Another possible interpretation, however, is that there were systematic differences in the manner in which responses were elicited and/or scored by McCarthy and the examiners used by Templin. McCarthy did all the MLR testing herself and Templin, though she used several examiners, reports no interexaminer comparisons. A comparison of data obtained by McCarthy and Templin must presuppose that had they tested the same children the examiners involved would have obtained comparable results both with respect to reliability and to absolute score. In the absence of interexaminer comparisons these assumptions cannot be checked.

Summary

Tape recordings were made of the verbalizations of 15 boys and 15 girls in response to Children's Apperception Test cards. The children were all residents of the Parsons (Kan.) State Hospital and Training Center for retarded children and ranged in age from 11 to 17 years (mean = 14.5). The tape recordings were typed and responses marked by two secretaries specifically trained for this task. Two other persons were trained to count the number of words in the 50 responses analyzed for each child. Statistical comparisons between MLR values for the two sets of transcripts were made and an r of .94 was obtained. Means and standard deviations were also compared and found to be quite similar.

The average MLR used by the retarded children in the present study was considerably shorter than that used by the normal eight-year-old school children studied by another investigator.

Summario in Interlingua

Reproductions esseva facite de le verbalizations de dece-cinque pueros e dece-cinque pueras in responsa a Children's Apperception Test cardos. Le pupos esseva tote residentes de le Parsons (Kansas) Stato Hospital e Trainante Centro pro retardate pupos e rangiate in etate de dece-un a dece-septe ancians (medio = dece-quatro comma cinque). Le reproductions esseva dactylographate e responsas marcate per duo secretarios specificamente trainate pro iste carga. Duo altere personas esseva trainate contar le numero de vocabulos in le cinquanta responsas analysate pro cata pupo. Statistic comparations inter Medio-Longitude-Responsa valutas pro le duo series de transcriptions esseva facite e un r (correlation) de comma novanta-quatro esseva obtenite. Medios e standard deviations esseva comparate alsi e trovate esser bastante similar.

Le medie Medio-Longitude-Responsa usate per le retardate pupos in le presente studio esseva considerablemente plus breve que le qual usate per normal octo-anno-ancian schola pupos studiate per un altere investigator.

References

1. Betts, E. A., An evaluation of certain techniques for the study of oral composition. *Res. Stud. Elem. Sch. Lang. Univ. Ia Stud. Educ.*, 9, 1934, 7-35.
2. Darley, F. L., and Moll, K. L., Reliability of language measures and size of language sample. *J. Speech Hearing Res.*, 3, 1960, 166-173.
3. Davis, Edith A., The development of linguistic skill in twins, singletons with siblings, and only children from age five to ten years. *Inst. Child Welf., Monogr., Ser.*, No. 14. Minneapolis: Univ. Minn. Press, 1937.
4. Day, Ella J. The development of language in twins: I. A comparison of twins and single children. *Child Develpm.*, 3, 1932, 179-199.
5. McCarthy, Dorothea, A., The language development of the preschool child. *Inst. Child Welf., Monogr. Ser.*, No. 4, Minneapolis: Univ. Minn. Press, 1930.
6. McCarthy, Dorothea A., Language development in children. Chap. 9 in L. Carmichael (Ed.), *Manual of Child Psychology*. (2nd ed.) New York: Wiley, 1954.
7. Siegel, G. M., Verbal behavior of adults as a function of linguistic level of retarded children in 'play therapy' sessions. *Parsons Res. Proj. Work. Paper*, No. 36, Dec., 1960.
8. Spradlin, J. E., Assessment of the speech and language of retarded children: The Parsons Language Sample. *Parsons Res. Proj. Work. Paper*, No. 29, June, 1960.
9. Spriestersbach, D. C., Darley, F. L., and Morris, H. L., Language skills in children with cleft palates. *J. Speech Hearing Res.*, 1, 1958, 279-285.
10. Templin, Mildred C., Certain language skills in children, their development and interrelationships. *Inst. Child Welf., Monogr. Ser.*, No. 26. Minneapolis: Univ. Minn. Press, 1957.
11. Winitz, H., Language skills of male and female kindergarten children. *J. Speech Hearing Res.*, 2, 1959, 377-386.

Reliability of Language Measures and Size of Language Sample

FREDERIC L. DARLEY

KENNETH L. MOLL

The study here reported was designed to answer the question of how large a sample of children's connected speech must be elicited in order to obtain reasonably reliable scores representing the average length and the structural complexity of linguistic utterances.

Two Language Measures

Studies of the manner in which children's language develops have typically included some description of connected speech samples in terms of amount of verbal output and grammatical complexity of sentences used. Two measures of children's linguistic achievement which have been used in several studies are the mean length of response and the structural complexity of response.

Mean Length of Response. In the first of a series of related studies on children's linguistic skills done at the University of Minnesota Institute of Child Welfare, McCarthy (*5*) wrote down verbatim 50 consecutive verbal re-

sponses elicited from each of her 140 subjects. In the hope of obtaining spontaneous responses she used picture books and toys to overcome self-consciousness and establish rapport, and she addressed the child as little as possible during the observation. McCarthy developed a set of rules for identifying a response, counting the words in each response, and classifying each response with regard to grammatical completeness and complexity.

McCarthy used mean length of response (MLR) as her main measure of children's linguistic achievement, a measure earlier advocated by Nice (*6*) and used by Smith (*8*) in her analysis of hour-long samples of spontaneous speech recorded by hand in a group free-play situation. Nice (*6*) had suggested that 'this average sentence length may well prove to be the most important single criterion for judging a child's progress in the attainment of adult language.' McCarthy (*5*, p. 50) originally called MLR 'the simplest and most objective measure of the degree to which children combine words at the various ages'; more recently (*4*, pp. 550-551) she has stated that no measure 'seems to have superseded the mean length of sentence for a reliable, easily

Frederic L. Darley (Ph.D., University of Iowa, 1950) is Associate Professor, Department of Speech Pathology and Audiology, University of Iowa. Kenneth L. Moll (M.A., University of Iowa, 1959) is Research Associate, Department of Speech Pathology and Audiology, University of Iowa.

JOURNAL OF SPEECH AND HEARING RESEARCH, June 1960, vol. 3, no. 2, pp. 166-173.

determined, objective, quantitative, and easily understood measure of linguistic maturity.'

McCarthy (5, p. 46) calculated the reliability of the responses by correlating the odd- with the even-numbered responses in order 'to see how consistently the children used responses of a certain length.' She reported (5, p. 47) that 'the mean reliability coefficient for the analysis according to length of response was +.91, the range being from +.82 to +.97 for the various age levels' (seven levels at six-month intervals from 1.5 years to 4.5 years). She also broke her samples of 50 responses into five groups of 10 responses each (first 10, second 10, . . .). She found (5, pp. 66-67) that 'the children's responses tended to be somewhat shorter at first, but that there is little change in the mean length after the first ten or twenty responses.'

Structural Complexity of Response. McCarthy's (5, p. 42) analysis of responses classified into structural complexity categories (functionally complete but structurally incomplete responses, simple sentences without phrase, simple sentences with phrase, compound sentences, complex sentences, elaborated sentences, and incomplete responses) was adopted in an attempt 'to indicate the stage of grammatical complexity that the child has reached, or in other words, how closely his sentence structure approximates adult conversation, his sole criterion upon which to model his speech.' She reported high agreement among four judges in classifying responses with regard to structural complexity and considered the method reliable enough for use with groups.

Day (2) used McCarthy's procedures, definitions, classifications, and methods of analysis in her study of two-to-five-year-old twins, again recording manually 50 consecutive verbal responses. Davis (1) used McCarthy's procedures with minor modifications in her study of 436 children (twins, singletons with siblings, and only children) at three age levels, 5.5, 6.5, and 9.5 years. She too collected samples of 50 responses, usually consecutive, and for their analysis she amplified and clarified McCarthy's definitions and rules for sentence classification. Most recently Templin (10, p. 15) 'duplicating as nearly as possible the technique developed by McCarthy' elicited 50 verbal utterances, usually consecutive, from 480 children, 30 boys and 30 girls at each of eight age levels (3, 3.5, 4, 4.5, 5, 6, 7, and 8 years). Her analysis in terms of MLR and structural complexity was based upon Davis' modification of McCarthy's rules.[1]

In an earlier study Williams (12) used measures comparable to but not identical with those developed by McCarthy and used by Day, Davis, and Templin. He made a phonetic transcript of the spontaneous speech of children in a group play situation, the sampling unit (12, p. 10) being 'what seems preferable to be called an expression unit rather than a sentence. . . . Forty such units were sampled for each child.' Williams calculated the mean length of the expression units and devised two quantitative scores to indicate expression unit completeness and complexity. 'The classifications of un-

---

[1]The most convenient presentation of these rules is to be found in Templin (10, pp. 160-161).

intelligible, incomplete, and complete were weighted arbitrarily as 0, 1, and 2. . . . Arbitrary weights of 0, 1, 2, 3, and 4 were given to unintelligible, simple, [compound], complex, and compound-complex units.'

Templin also devised a quantitative method of representing sentence completeness-complexity. She assigned weights as follows to the categories of the McCarthy-Davis outline in order to obtain a structural complexity score (SCS):

Weight	Classification of Remark
0	Incomplete remarks (even if functionally complete)
1	Simple sentences (with or without phrases)
2	Simple sentences with two or more phrases or a compound subject or predicate with a phrase
3	Compound sentences
4	Complex and elaborated sentences

Templin found the SCS to be not quite as stable as other language measures used in her study, but she points out its advantage in being a quantitative measure, permitting comparison with other quantitative language measures such as MLR and vocabulary size.

Further use of MLR and SCS, generally following Templin's procedures, has been reported by Spriestersbach, Darley, and Morris (9) in a study of the language skills of 40 children with clefts of the palate and by Winitz (13) in a study of the language skills of 150 normal kindergarten boys and girls. In both of these studies 50 responses were elicited in the usual way, but the procedures followed by Templin and her predecessors were modified in the light of McCarthy's finding that children's first 10 or 20 responses tend to be shorter than subsequent responses: the first 10 responses were disregarded, the next 50 being recorded. Winitz (13) tape recorded his samples for analysis and also provided supplementary definitions and directions for counting and classifying words and remarks.

Size of Language Sample

The research and clinical usefulness of MLR and SCS as indices of children's linguistic developmental status is somewhat limited by the expenditure of time required to record and analyze the by now almost traditional 50 responses. The question arises as to whether equally reliable information can be obtained from an analysis of fewer than 50 responses.

Nice (6) offered the following comment concerning size of speech sample: 'Although as few as 30 such sentences ought to show clearly a child's stage of speech development, for any comparative or detailed study there should be at least 100 sentences and preferably more.' McCarthy (5, p. 32) explained her choice of speech sample size (50 responses) thus: 'This number was decided upon because it would give a fairly representative sample of the child's linguistic development in a relatively short period of time, without tiring the child with a prolonged observation.' She commented that the reliability of structural complexity measures would be increased if longer samples of each child's conversation were obtained. Day, Davis, Templin, Spriestersbach, Darley, and Morris, and Winitz do not discuss their choice of similar sample size.

It was noted above that Williams

TABLE 1. Means and standard deviations for two language measures, mean length of response (MLR) in words and structural complexity score (SCS) in scale points, computed from language samples of seven different sizes obtained from 150 normal five-year-old children.

Measure	Statistic	Number of Responses in Sample						
		5	10	15	20	25	35	50
MLR	Mean	5.87	5.63	5.84	5.76	5.56	5.54	5.62
	SD	3.2	2.3	2.3	2.1	1.9	1.9	1.8
SCS	Mean	39.93	39.76	41.18	40.33	39.45	39.06	40.40
	SD	30.45	22.89	20.78	18.76	17.15	15.52	14.39

(12, p. 10) used only 40 expression units in his study and considered these to constitute 'a fairly representative sample of the child's expressive control over language.' Schneiderman (7) in a study of the relationship between articulatory ability and language ability used for her measure of sentence length the mean length of 15 sentences (oral definitions of 15 common nouns after a practice session defining five other nouns). The question may be asked as to whether it is possible that a sample as small as 10 or 15 responses may yield MLR and SCS values dependable for group or individual prediction.

Procedure

A large group of connected speech protocols was available following the completion of the study reported by Winitz (13). The protocols represented 50 responses elicited from each of 150 randomly selected, physically normal, white, five-year-old kindergarten children (75 boys, 75 girls) from monolingual Iowa City homes. The two sex groups were essentially equivalent with regard to chronological age, IQ, socioeconomic status, and family constellation. The sexes-combined mean chronological age was 63.50 months,

mean Full Scale IQ on the Wechsler Intelligence Scale for Children was 100.51, and mean score on the Index of Status Characteristics (11) was 42.29 (lower middle class). Of the total group 11 were only children, 48 had older siblings, 38 had younger siblings, and 53 had both older and younger siblings; none were twins. All children were considered normal in intelligence (had Full-Scale WISC IQs of 70 or above), were currently considered by their parents not to stutter, and were found by a hearing-screening procedure with a pure-tone audiometer to have normal hearing. Children of university students and rural dwellers were not included in the sample.

The 50 consecutive responses were elicited and tape recorded in each child's home through the presentation of Children's Apperception Test cards one at a time, the examiner engaging the child in conversation with neutral comments such as 'Tell me about this picture.' Only the examiner was present with the child.

Used in the present study were the typewritten transcripts of the tape-recorded responses and from these MLR and SCS were calculated (a) on the basis of the first five, first 10, first

15, first 20, first 25, first 35, and the total of 50 responses and (b) for each of 10 groups of five responses, the first five, the second five, . . . , through the tenth five responses, each group of five responses being considered a response segment.

Results

Analysis of Samples of Increasing Size. Table 1 presents the means and standard deviations for MLR and SCS calculated for speech samples of seven different sizes (5, 10, 15, 20, 25, 35, and 50 responses). Inspection of the means indicates that the differences between them are small: the range of mean MLR scores is from 5.54 words to 5.87 words, while the range of mean SCS values is from 39.45 points to 41.18 points. On the basis of these data it appears that for a group of subjects the group mean would remain essentially the same regardless of the number of responses on which the scores are based.

Further inspection of Table 1 shows that the fewer the number of responses obtained, the greater the variability of the scores. This added variability can be accounted for primarily by the addition of greater 'measurement error' as the number of responses used becomes smaller. This finding demonstrates that the primary consideration in reaching a decision about the number of responses to use is the reliability of the individual scores obtained from varying numbers of responses.

Analysis of Response Segments. In order to study the reliability of these language measures, an analysis of variance was carried out on the MLR and SCS values based on 10 separate response segments in a Response-Segments-by-Subjects design (Table 2). From the analysis of variance data several reliability estimates were obtained by the following formula (3, p. 361):

$$r_{\bar{X}_k \bar{X}_k} = (ms_S - ms_{RS \times S}) / (ms_S + [n/k - 1] ms_{RS \times S})$$

where n = number of response segments used in sample (that is, n = 10)

k = any number of response segments from zero to infinity

$r_{\bar{X}_k \bar{X}_k}$ = estimated reliability coefficient of the mean of k response segments

The interaction mean square ($ms_{RS \times S}$) was considered to be the appropriate error term in this reliability analysis, rather than the total within-subjects variability, estimated by $ms_{RS \times S} + ms_{RS}$. When scores are based on the same response segments for all subjects and when stimulus materials (which could cause systematic variability between response segments) are standardized, between-response-segments variability is a constant and does not represent error.

By varying the value of k in the above formula it was possible to estimate the reliability of the mean of any

TABLE 2. Summary of analyses of variance performed on mean length of response and structural complexity scores for 10 five-response segments.

Source	df	ms
Mean Length of Response		
Response Segments (RS)	9	2397.12
Subjects (S)	149	3273.42
RS x S	1341	493.42
Total	1499	
Structural Complexity Score		
Response Segments (RS)	9	13.30
Subjects (S)	149	20.84
RS x S	1341	6.52
Total	1499	

TABLE 3. Estimated reliability coefficients of means of k response segments (five responses per segment) for mean length of response (MLR) and structural complexity score (SCS).

k	MLR	SCS
1	.36	.18
2	.53	.31
3	.63	.40
4	.69	.47
5	.74	.52
6	.77	.57
7	.80	.61
8	.82	.64
9	.84	.66
10	.85	.69
11	.86	.71
12	.87	.72
13	.88	.74
14	.89	.75
15	.89	.77
16	.90	.78
17	.91	.79
18	.91	.80
19	.91	.81
20	.92	.81
25	.93	.85
30	.94	.87
35	.95	.88
40	.96	.90
45	.96	.91
50	.97	.92

particular number of response segments. These estimated reliability coefficients appear in Table 3 for the two language measures studied and are plotted, together with their 98% confidence limits, as a function of the number of response segments in Figure 1.

Discussion

The results of the reliability analysis indicate that the decision as to how many responses to elicit in order to obtain MLR and SCS values depends on the precision needed in a particular situation. For 50 responses (10 response segments), the number most commonly used in previous research, the reliability of MLR scores (.85) seems adequate for most purposes; however, the reliability of SCS values derived from this number of responses (.69) may represent less precision than is desired in some situations.

Increasing the number of responses taken would improve the reliability of the scores. For MLR, however, the curve in Figure 1 begins to plateau

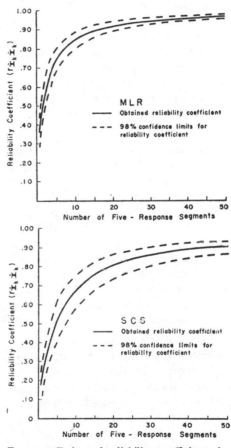

FIGURE 1. Estimated reliability coefficients for mean length of response (MLR) and structural complexity score (SCS), together with their 98% confidence limits, as a function of number of five-response segments.

soon after 50 responses. Thus, a fairly large increase in number of responses would be required to improve reliability appreciably. For SCS the use of a few more responses would bring about a sizable change in measurement precision.

For some research it may be necessary to elicit fewer than 50 responses. A necessary consequence of this restriction of sample size is loss of precision resulting in an increase in the error term of any statistical test used. The loss of precision can be overcome, to some extent, by the use of more subjects; however, obtaining and testing a larger number of subjects would seem to be a less efficient procedure, in terms of the time and effort required, than eliciting more responses from a smaller number of subjects.

The curves in Figure 1 indicate that SCS values are less reliable than MLR scores when both are based on the same number of responses, possibly because the structural complexity of a child's speech is a more variable phenomenon from response to response than is length of response. It is also possible that the arbitrary weights assigned in the Templin scheme to the different grammatical categories may not be entirely appropriate.

In general, it appears that eliciting 50 responses is adequate for obtaining MLR scores but that more than 50 responses should probably be obtained if SCS values are desired. Interpretation of the results of this study must be made with the realization that language samples of children of only one age were used. The fact that the standard deviations reported by Templin (10, pp. 79, 82) for MLR and SCS are fairly similar at all age levels from three to eight years suggests that the reliability of these language measures probably does not vary greatly with age within the age range studied by Templin.

Summary

Speech samples collected from 150 five-year-old kindergarten children were used to evaluate the reliabilities of two language measures, mean length of response (MLR) and structural complexity score (SCS) in relation to the size of the language sample. Each sample was divided into 10 five-response segments and MLR and SCS were calculated for each segment. Reliability estimates were obtained for the two language measures for varying numbers of response segments.

The reliability analysis suggests that MLR scores based on 50 responses are of adequate reliability for most research purposes; however, the reliability of SCS values based on 50 responses may represent less precision than is desired in some situations. From the data presented the number of response segments necessary to achieve given levels of reliability can be estimated.

Acknowledgments

The authors express their appreciation to Dr. Harris Winitz for the use of his language sample protocols, to Miss Sumiko Sasanuma for assistance in tabulation, and to Dr. Arnold M. Small for computer programming.

References

1. DAVIS, EDITH A., The development of linguistic skill in twins, singletons with siblings, and only children from age five

to ten years. *Inst. Child Welf., Monogr. Ser.*, No. 14. Minneapolis: Univ. Minn. Press, 1937.

2. DAY, ELLA J., The development of language in twins: I. A comparison of twins and single children. *Child Develpm.*, 3, 1932, 179-199.

3. LINDQUIST, E. F., *Design and Analysis of Experiments in Psychology and Education.* Boston: Houghton Mifflin, 1953.

4. McCARTHY, DOROTHEA A., Language development in children. Chap. 9 in L. Carmichael (Ed.), *Manual of Child Psychology.* (2nd ed.) New York: Wiley, 1954.

5. McCARTHY, DOROTHEA A., The language development of the preschool child. *Inst. Child Welf., Monogr. Ser.*, No. 4. Minneapolis: Univ. Minn. Press, 1930.

6. NICE, MARGARET M., Length of sentences as a criterion of a child's progress in speech. *J. educ. Psychol.*, 16, 1925, 370-379.

7. SCHNEIDERMAN, NORMA, A study of the relationship between articulatory ability and language ability. *J. Speech Hearing Dis.*, 20, 1955, 359-364.

8. SMITH, MADORAH E., An investigation of the development of the sentence and the extent of vocabulary in young children. *Univ. Ia. Stud. Child Welf.*, 3, No. 5, 1926.

9. SPRIESTERSBACH, D. C., DARLEY, F. L., and MORRIS, H. L., Language skills in children with cleft palates. *J. Speech Hearing Res.*, 1, 1958, 279-285.

10. TEMPLIN, MILDRED C., Certain language skills in children, their development and interrelationships. *Inst. Child Welf., Monogr. Ser.*, No. 26. Minneapolis: Univ. Minn. Press, 1957.

11. WARNER, W. L., MEEKER, MARCHIA, and EELLS, K., *Social Class in America* (a manual of procedure for the measurement of social status). Chicago: Science Research Assoc., 1949.

12. WILLIAMS, H. M., An analytical study of language achievement in preschool children. *Univ. Ia. Stud. Child Welf.*, 13, No. 2, Part 1, 1937.

13. WINITZ, H., Language skills of male and female kindergarten children. *J. Speech Hearing Res.*, 2, 1959, 377-386.

145

Temporal Reliability of Seven Language Measures

FRED D. MINIFIE

FREDERIC L. DARLEY

DOROTHY SHERMAN

The purpose of this study is to investigate the consistency, from day to day, of language performance of young children. Speech pathologists and students of child development have devised various research and clinical tools for the purpose of describing and evaluating children's language development. Knowledge of whether these language abilities are variable or consistent within short periods would appear to be useful since both the researcher and the clinical worker need to know whether measures of language development may be considered fairly valid and reliable.

In an important contribution to knowledge about the language development of preschool children, McCarthy (11) in 1930 focused attention on the development of language as it is manifested in the connected speech of 'normal speaking children.' Day (8) and Davis (6) extended the knowledge of language development through their investigations of twins and school-age

children. Other investigators have studied relationships between the verbal output of children and their mental age (20), environment (23), and sex (21, 22). Recent investigators have concerned themselves with the language development of cleft palate children (14) and severely handicapped children (13).

The most comprehensive study to date is that of Templin (18), who compiled normative data concerning the speech and language development of children between the ages of 3.0 and 8.0 years. Among the language variables she investigated are mean length of response, number of one-word responses, mean of the five longest responses, number of different words, structural complexity of responses, and size of recognition vocabulary.

During these 30 years of research, investigators appear to have assumed that the numbers they obtained with their scales and measures were isomorphically related to 'real' language development. Before such an assumption of isomorphism can be made, two important variables must be considered: validity and reliability.

The validity of a test, of course, cannot be proven directly. In the last analysis, reliance must rest upon its agreement with other tests. To date,

Fred D. Minifie (M.A., University of Iowa, 1962) is Research Associate, University of Iowa. Frederic L. Darley (Ph.D., University of Iowa, 1950) is Consultant in Speech Pathology, Mayo Clinic, Rochester, Minnesota. Dorothy Sherman (Ph.D., University of Iowa, 1951) is Professor of Speech Pathology and Audiology, University of Iowa.

JOURNAL OF SPEECH AND HEARING RESEARCH, June, 1963, vol. 6, no. 2, pp. 139-148.

no study has been done to evaluate the validity of these measures by establishing agreement with some outside criterion.

Since it is difficult to evaluate the validity of language measures, added importance is placed on their reliability. According to Anastasi (3, p. 94), 'The reliability of a test refers to the consistency of scores obtained by the same individuals on different occasions or with different sets of equivalent items.' In theory, therefore, the term *reliability* means the consistency, repeatability, or predictability of a test. In other words, measures of reliability are used in an attempt to define quantitatively the errors of measurement underlying the test scores.

Typically the reliability of language measures has been approached in terms of four aspects: internal consistency, adequacy of item sampling, examiner reliability, and temporal reliability.

The internal consistencies of the measures of mean length of response, structural complexity, mean of the five longest responses, and the number of one-word responses have been calculated using odd-even and split-half reliability measures (7, 12, 17, 20, 21, 22). The obtained correlations range from approximately .79 to .95, indicating a rather high internal consistency for all of these measures.

Anastasi (3, p. 97) states that adequacy of item sampling 'concerns the extent to which the items constituting the test adequately represent the entire universe of items which the test undertakes to sample.' Darley and Moll (5), in a study related to adequacy of item sampling, derived intraclass correlation coefficients from 50-response language samples of 5.0-year-old speakers. They concluded that mean length of response scores based on 50 responses were of adequate reliability for most research purposes ($r = .85$). Analysis of the structural complexity scores based on 50 responses, however, did not indicate sufficient reliability for most research purposes ($r = .69$).

Consideration of examiner reliability is generally divided into two parts: evaluation of the reliability of the observer who collects the data (recorder reliability) and evaluation of the accuracy with which the data are scored (scorer reliability). The only data reported in the literature concerning examiner reliability are restricted to mean length of response and structural complexity measures. Reliability among scorers is reported in several investigations and is above .90 in all but one case (8, 12, 17, 19, 21, 22). References to recorder reliability usually are concerned with the agreement between the records independently obtained by two or more observers (15). Recorder reliability on language development measures is not easily observed, and reports in the literature often have included subjective evaluations. Those who have attempted to make analyses, however, without exception have concluded that observers generally agree in the recording of spoken remarks.

Temporal reliability is often referred to as test-retest reliability. It reveals the consistency of individual performance, on the same test, over a period of time. Only one author, Fisher (10), has computed the temporal reliability of any of the language measures referred to above, and her study is limited to the temporal reliability of mean length of response. Fisher recorded 50 responses from 23 subjects, twice, over an interval of approximately one month (the age of the children is not reported). She obtained a Pearson r of .58 and suggested that 'one sampling of 50 remarks does not give the assurance that a true mean length of response for any particular child had been obtained.'

The dearth of literature on the temporal reliability of language measures indicates a need for the present study, the purpose of which is to test the temporal reliability of seven language measures: mean length of response, standard deviation of response length, number of one-word responses, mean of the five longest responses, number of different words, structural complexity score, and the type-token ratio (the number of different words divided by the total number of words).

Procedure

Selection of Subjects. Subjects were children living in Iowa City, Iowa, from January through June, 1960, selected on the basis of age, sex, intelligence, socioeconomic status, hearing, physical status, and language background.

Age and Sex. Two groups of children were selected on the basis of age. Group I consisted of 48 5.5-year-old children (24 boys and 24 girls). A comparable group of 8.0-year-old children made up Group II. The children in each group were tested within two months of the age level they represented.

Intelligence. Only those children receiving IQ equivalents of 80 or more on the Ammons Full-Range Picture Vocabulary Test (*1, 2*) were selected. This cutoff score was used because the IQ equivalents obtained on the Ammons tend to be systematically higher than the IQ scores on a test such as the Stanford-Binet. As it developed, no children were eliminated from the study because they failed to pass the screening test. Either the sample of children tested was an unusually bright group, or the Ammons Full-Range Picture Vocabulary Test yields IQ equivalents that are considerably elevated in comparison to the more widely used intelligence tests. The inability of three or four children to respond to certain commands throughout the study and to handle certain language forms suggests that the latter is a likely possibility.

Socioeconomic Status. Only those children were included whose families could be evaluated on the basis of the Index of Status Characteristics (*19*). Children were selected from all of the elementary schools in Iowa City in equal proportion to the percentage of children of each sex in each age group attending each school. The children were randomly selected from groups of a particular age, sex, and school from lists made available through the office of the Iowa City Superintendent of Schools. It was assumed that such a proportional sampling procedure would result in a cross-sectional sampling of the socioeconomic levels present in Iowa City. Included were only those children for whom parental permission had been given to participate in the study.

Hearing. Children were included in the study who could pass a pure-tone sweep-check test of three frequencies: 500, 1 000, and 2 000 cps. Since the children were tested in their homes, a less than optimal hearing testing situation, a special hearing-screening technique was utilized. The examiner, whose hearing was known to be normal at the test frequencies, determined his own absolute threshold in each testing situation. A sweep-check test was then administered to the child 15 db above the examiner's threshold.

Physical Status. Children who exhibited obvious neuromuscular involvement were excluded from the study.

Language Background. A child was eliminated if he came from a bilingual home or was a twin. Previous research has shown that twins differ systematically from the 'normal' language development pattern (6, 8). Children with a history of stuttering also were eliminated.

Testing Situation. All children were tested in their own homes. One-third of each group was tested in the morning, one-third in the afternoon, and one-third in the evening. From each child 50 verbal responses were elicited on three separate occasions. Speech samples were elicited no less than one day apart and all three samples were elicited within a period of less than three weeks; the speech samples thus occurred sufficiently close together that any influence of language maturation upon the results could be considered negligible.

Three separate sets of pictures were used to elicit the responses. Order of the three sets of pictures for the three trials was constant. One set of pictures used was the Children's Apperception Test Cards (4). The other two sets of pictures were constructed by the examiner and were judged to be of interest to children at both age levels.

The cards were presented one at a time, and the child who was being recorded was encouraged to 'tell a story about the picture.' In a few instances, when the child had difficulty responding to the cards, the examiner attempted to stimulate conversation by interjecting such statements as 'What is happening in this picture?' The order of presenting the pictures within a given set was randomized for each subject.

Each session was tape recorded. The examiner listened to the tapes and typed off transcriptions of the first 50 responses elicited from each child in each recording session. Measures from analyses of each speech sample included mean length of response, mean of the five longest responses, number of one-word responses, standard deviation of response length, number of different words, structural complexity of the responses, and the type-token ratio. The rules for making these analyses have been defined by Templin (18), who followed rather closely the McCarthy-Davis (11, 7) procedure. The speech samples used in this study were analyzed by a strict application of these rules as modified by Winitz (21, 22).

Recorder Reliability. Recorder reliability was estimated to evaluate the examiner's ability to identify spoken responses. What constitutes a verbal response is sometimes difficult to determine: (a) not all pauses represent breaks between responses; (b) some responses are made up of two short sentences; and (c) a single response may include a change in thought content.

The McCarthy-Davis (11, 7) procedure was used to determine how well the examiner agreed with other observers in identifying spoken responses. The examiner and two other observers, graduate students in speech pathology with experience in scoring language samples, independently recorded the first 25 remarks of three 5.5-year-old subjects. Each observer independently listened to the tape-recorded speech sample of each child and prepared a typed script of what he considered to represent the first 25 remarks uttered. The number of agreements and disagreements between the examiner and each of the other two observers was tabulated for each subject. Number of agreements ranged from 20 to 25. Agreements with one of the other two

TABLE 1. Means, standard deviations, and ranges at two age levels for seven language measures: mean length of response (MLR), mean of the five longest responses (M5LR), number of one-word responses (N1W), standard deviation of response length (SD-RL), number of different words (NDW), structural complexity score (SCS), and the type-token ratio (NDW/TNW). Included in the table below are the results of the present study (a); Templin's (18) study (b); and Winitz' (21, 22) study (c). The data from the present study are based on the verbal responses of 5.5-year-old children while those of the Templin and the Winitz studies are of 5.0-year-old children.

Measure	Study	Mean	SD	Range*
5.5-year-olds				
MLR	a	6.79	2.20	1.70 to 13.50
	b	5.70	1.50	
	c	5.39	1.66	1.74 to 13.76
M5LR	a	15.77	4.58	4.40 to 26.40
	b	11.73	3.43	
	c	14.92	7.01	4.40 to 52.80
N1W	a	5.78	4.55	0.00 to 30.00
	b	2.40	1.70	
	c	7.87	4.80	1.00 to 34.00
SD-RL	a	4.27	1.26	0.81 to 7.00
	c	3.85	1.46	1.20 to 16.19
NDW	a	134.02	27.14	47.00 to 203.00
	b	132.40	27.20	
	c	106.27	25.53	43.00 to 181.00
SCS	a	46.60	23.37	0.00 to 122.00
	b	56.90	21.50	
	c	40.40	14.39	1.00 to 73.00
NDW/TNW	a	0.41	0.08	0.26 to 0.63
8.0-year-olds				
MLR	a	10.31	2.18	3.10 to 14.22
	b	7.60	1.60	
M5LR	a	20.62	4.21	8.00 to 28.20
	b	14.15	2.85	
N1W	a	1.02	1.81	0.00 to 14.00
	b	0.60	0.30	
SD-RL	a	5.17	1.09	1.86 to 7.85
NDW	a	175.75	26.75	91.00 to 226.00
	b	166.50	29.50	
SCS	a	89.27	29.63	7.00 to 146.00
	b	77.70	33.80	
NDW/TNW	a	0.35	0.05	0.28 to 0.59

*Ranges for the Templin study are not available.

observers were 24, or 96%, for each of the three subjects. The high percentages of agreement indicate satisfactory reliability of the examiner's recording of responses.

Scorer Reliability. Intrascorer agreement for the examiner was found for two verbalization measures: mean length of response and structural complexity score. From the typed speech samples, a random selection of the records of four subjects, a total of 200 responses, was made and each response was rescored. The obtained Pearson correlations between the first and second scorings were 1.00 and .98 for the mean length of response and structural complexity scores, respectively, indicating that the experimenter was satisfactorily consistent in scoring responses.

Results and Discussion

Comparison with Previous Studies. Table 1 shows the means, standard deviations, and ranges obtained for each of the language measures at each age level in the present investigation and the values obtained by Templin (*18*) and Winitz (*21, 22*). It must be recognized that the younger children of the present investigation were 5.5 years old while those of the Templin and the Winitz investigations were only 5.0 years old. The results, therefore, are not directly comparable, but the ages are similar enough to merit discussion. Initial examination of the table indicates some rather large differences among the findings of the three studies. A consideration of the sizes of the standard deviations for each measure, however, shows that only two of the measures in the present investigation fail to fall within one standard devia-

tion of the mean values of at least one of the other two studies. These two measures are the mean length of response and the mean of the five longest responses for 8.0-year-old children. The close agreement among the other language measures suggests that the present investigation yields results that are typical for groups of subjects at each of the age levels.

Several general statements can be made concerning the slight differences that do exist among the results of the three studies. First, data from the present investigation and those from Winitz are in closer agreement than are Templin's data and those of either of the other two studies. This result is probably due to the fact that the present investigation was designed in essentially the same way as the Winitz study, that is, the techniques for eliciting and scoring the language samples more nearly approximate those used by Winitz than those used by Templin. Whereas in the Templin study the verbal responses were recorded in longhand, in both the Winitz study and the present study verbal responses were identified from tape-recorded speech samples. The latter technique allowed replaying of the tapes several times for identifying responses. Also, by tape recording the speech samples, the examiner can be sure of obtaining 50 consecutive responses while with handwritten responses there may often be difficulty in keeping up with the spontaneous speech of children, with a possible tendency to omit some longer responses. The examiner also tends to fill in missing words, for example, he may record 'He went to *the* store' instead of 'He went to store.' It is the subjective impression of the present investigators that differences between the results obtained by recording the responses by hand and by recording the responses on tape are real and important.

The apparent discrepancy between the mean number of one-word responses reported on the one hand by Templin (*18*) and on the other by Winitz (*21, 22*) and the present investigators may be partially accounted for by differences in technique. Winitz and the present investigators both asked questions to stimulate children who had difficulty responding to picture stimuli. It is probable that more one-word responses were uttered by the children as answers to questions than were uttered spontaneously.

Templin did not report that she interjected such questions and her results for 5.0-year-old children show lower mean values of one-word responses than either of the other studies. One would expect the increase in the number of one-word responses in the present investigation to be reflected in lower mean length of response values. Higher mean length of response values, however, are reported in the present study than were reported by Templin (see Table 1).

When Templin analyzed the mean length of response measure in her study, she was impressed with the fact that the verbalizations of children at each age level were longer than those of children in the studies done 15 to 25 years before. At the older age levels

TABLE 2. Summary table of the obtained mean squares and intraclass correlation coefficients for mean length of response (MLR), mean of the five longest responses (M5LR), number of one-word responses (N1W), standard deviation of response length (SD-RL), number of different words (NDW), structural complexity score (SCS), and the type-token ratio (NDW/TNW).

Measure	Between Subjects	Within Subjects	Interaction	r_i*	r_{ave}†
5.5 years					
MLR	13.03	0.90	0.90	0.82	0.93
M5LR	50.33	6.81	6.56	0.68	0.87
N1W	53.23	5.07	5.05	0.76	0.91
SD-RL	3.53	0.64	0.59	0.60	0.83
NDW	1 728.85	258.78	229.72	0.65	0.87
SCS	1 384.97	141.38	143.99	0.75	0.90
NDW/TNW	0.01	0.00	0.00	0.60	0.60
8.0 years					
MLR	12.35	1.10	1.00	0.77	0.92
M5LR	43.37	5.31	5.12	0.70	0.88
N1W	6.79	1.58	1.58	0.52	1.00
SD-RL	2.79	0.43	0.43	0.65	0.85
NDW	1 666.96	257.54	188.77	0.65	0.89
SCS	2 189.95	244.40	247.31	0.73	0.89
NDW/TNW	0.01	0.00	0.00	0.70	0.88

*$r_i = [ms_b - ms_w]/[ms_b + (k-1) ms_w]$; $df = 47$ and 96 for calculation of ms_b and ms_w, respectively.

†$r_{ave} = (ms_b - ms_{it})/ms_b$; $df = 47$ and 94 for calculation of ms_b and ms_{it}, respectively.

in her study these results were even more apparent than at the younger age levels. Templin (*18*) suggests that 'The increased talkativeness found in the present study would seem to reflect an increased amount of adult language in the child's environment whether as a result of increased viewing of TV, or inclusion in family activities, general permissiveness toward the child's behavior, or other factors.' It would appear that the trend suggested by Templin is still existent. Although the difference in mean length of response may be accounted for by differences in recording technique, it is also likely that environmental influences have been important. A consideration of this possibility is particularly important with reference to normative data since comparisons are of little value if the norms are obsolete, whatever the reason for the change.

The differences at each age level among mean lengths of response measures elicited in the morning, afternoon, and evening, evaluated by analysis of variance, were not significant (for 5.5 years, $F = 0.22$; $df = 2$ and 135; and for 8.0 years, $F = 0.76$; $df = 2$ and 135) at the 5% level.

Temporal Reliability. The main purpose was to determine the temporal reliability of seven language measures at each of two age levels. Two intraclass correlation coefficients (*9*) were computed for each measure at each age level (see Table 2). The first correlation coefficient (r_i) was computed to evaluate the reliability of individual measures on subsequent retests of single 50-response language samples. The second coefficient (r_{ave}) was computed to determine the reliability of averages over three trials for each language measure.

None of the language measures based on single 50-response language samples appears to have a high temporal reliability for individual measures (r_i), that is, individual children do not appear to be very consistent in their language usage from day to day. The language measures consisting of the means of three 50-response language samples appear to have adequate reliability for most research purposes (see Table 2).

The mean length of response measure appears to be the most reliable of any of the measures. The obtained reliability coefficients (r_i) of .82 and .77 for the 5.5-year-old and 8.0-year-old children, respectively, are significantly higher than the value of .57 reported in a previous study by Fisher (*10*). Any single mean obtained from a 50-response language sample, however, is only a gross estimate of the child's true mean length of response. The temporal reliability (measured by variability of speakers from day to day) of (a) the mean length of response and (b) the standard deviation of response length within a 50-response unit are sufficiently large to place a given child as much as two years ahead or two years behind his age level; this is true even though he may be operating at about the average for his age level (see Table 1).

For the structural complexity scores, the obtained temporal reliability coefficients (r_i) were .75 and .73 for 5.5-year-olds and 8.0-year-olds, respectively. In addition to the low temporal reliability of this measure there is some question of its validity. The omission of articles and prepositions can alter the assigned sentence weight as much as from a *four* to a *zero*. Consequently, a very complicated but technically incomplete sentence may be given a value of *zero* while a more simple but complete sentence is scored as a *one*.

Their low temporal reliabilities, r_i ranging from .52 to .76, make unnecessary any discussion of the remaining measures: number of one-word responses, mean of the five longest responses, standard deviation of response length, number of different words, and the type-token ratio.

Summary and Conclusions

The purpose of this study is to test the temporal reliability of seven language measures: mean length of response, mean of the five longest responses, number of one-word responses, standard deviation of the mean length of response, number of different words, structural complexity score, and the type-token ratio.

Subjects were children selected on the basis of age, sex, intelligence, socioeconomic status, hearing, physical status, and language background. Two groups of children were selected on the basis of age: Group I with 48 5.5-year-old children and Group II with 48 8.0-year-old children. Each group consisted of equal numbers of boys and girls.

With picture cards as stimuli, a 50-response language sample was elicited from each child on three separate occasions. The language samples were tape recorded, and typed scripts were prepared from the tapes.

Intraclass correlation coefficients were computed to determine the temporal reliability of each measure. In general, the results indicate relatively low temporal reliability for all of the language measures investigated at both age levels. The obtained correlations ranged from .52 to .82. It thus appears that language measures obtained from 50-response language samples are not very consistent from day to day. The means, however, for three separate 50-response language samples from children appear to be of adequate reliability for most research purposes.

References

1. AMMONS, R. B., and AMMONS, HELEN S., *Full-Range Picture Vocabulary Test*. Missoula, Mont.: Psychol. Test Specialists, 1948.
2. AMMONS, R. B., and HOLMES, J. C., The Full-Range Picture Vocabulary Test: III. Results for a preschool-age population. *Child Develpm.*, 20, 1949, 5-14.
3. ANASTASI, ANNE, *Psychological Testing*. New York: Macmillan, 1954.
4. BELLAK, L., and BELLAK, SONYA S., An introductory note on the Children's Apperception Test (CAT). *J. proj. Techniques*, 14, 1950, 173-180.
5. DARLEY, F. L., and MOLL, K. L., Reliability of language measures and size of language sample. *J. Speech Hearing Res.*, 3, 1960, 166-173.
6. DAVIS, EDITH A., The development of linguistic skills in twins, singletons with siblings, and only children from age five to ten years. *Inst. Child Welf., Monogr. Ser.*, No. 14. Minneapolis: Univ. Minnesota Press, 1937.
7. DAVIS, EDITH A., Mean sentence length compared with long and short sentences as a reliable measure of language development. *Child Develpm.*, 8, 1937, 69-79.
8. DAY, ELLA J., The development of language in twins: I. A comparison of twins and single children. *Child Develpm.*, 3, 1932, 179-199.
9. EBEL, R. L., Estimation of the reliability of ratings. *Psychometrika*, 16, 1951, 407-424.
10. FISHER, MARY S., Language patterns of preschool children. *Child Development Monographs*. New York: Bur. Pub. Teach. Coll., Columbia Univ., 1934.

11. McCarthy, Dorothea A., The language development of the preschool child. *Inst. Child. Welf., Monogr. Ser.,* No. 4. Minneapolis: Univ. Minnesota Press, 1930.
12. McCarthy, Dorothea, Language development in children. Chap. 9 in L. Carmichael (Ed.), *Manual of Child Psychology.* (2nd ed.) New York: Wiley, 1954.
13. Miller, Judith C., Linguistic skills of physically handicapped children. M.A. thesis, Univ. Iowa, 1961.
14. Morris, H. L., Communication skills of children with cleft lips and palates. *J. Speech Hearing Res.,* 5, 1962, 79-90.
15. Siegel, G. M., Interexaminer reliability for mean length of response. *J. Speech Hearing Res.,* 5, 1962, 91-95.
16. Smith, Madorah E., An investigation of the development of the sentence and the extent of vocabulary in young children. *Univ. Ia. Stud. Child Welf.,* 3, No. 5, 1926.
17. Spriestersbach, D. C., Darley, F. L., and Morris, H. L., Language skills in children with cleft palates. *J. Speech Hearing Res.,* 1, 1958, 279-285.
18. Templin, Mildred C., Certain language skills in children, their development and interrelationships. *Inst. Child Welf., Monogr. Ser.,* No. 26. Minneapolis: Univ. **Minnesota Press, 1957.**
19. Warner, W. L., Meeker, Marchia, and Eells, K., *Social Class in America, a Manual of Procedure for the Measurement of Social Status.* Chicago: Science Res. Assoc., 1949.
20. Williams, H. M., An analytical study of language achievement in preschool children. *Univ. Idaho Stud. Child Welf.,* **13, No. 2, 1937, 9-18.**
21. Winitz, H., Language skills of male and female kindergarten children. *J. Speech Hearing Res.,* 2, 1959, 377-386.
22. Winitz, H., Relationships between language and nonlanguage measures of kindergarten children. *J. Speech Hearing Res.,* 2, 1959, 387-391.
23. Young, Florene M., An analysis of certain variables in a developmental study of language. *Genet. Psychol. Monogr.,* 23, 1941, 3-141.

Psychological Scaling of Language Development of Children

DOROTHY SHERMAN, THOMAS SHRINER and FRANKLIN SILVERMAN

Abstract: Certain aspects of the use of psychological rating scale methods for measuring degrees of language development in the speech of children are evaluated. That typed samples from children's speech can be scaled reliably is demonstrated. Comparisons are made among correlation coefficients which were obtained for the purpose of estimating relationships among three measures of language development for the same set of 50 samples of children's language: structural complexity scores obtained by analysis of the samples; scale values of intricacy of language usage obtained by the psychological scaling method of Equal-Appearing Intervals; and mean estimates of age derived from sophisticated observers' judgments. The conclusion was drawn that psychological scaling of various aspects of children's language could provide new and useful tools for the study of and the assessment of children's language development.

The basic problem is to evaluate certain aspects of the use of psychological rating-scale methods for the purpose of measuring the degrees of language development exhibited in samples of children's speech. Both for experimental and clinical purposes a method for assessing children's language development is often needed by those who are concerned with speech pathologies. Presently, however, no single measure has been used which appears to be completely satisfactory for this purpose.

IOWA ACADEMY OF SCIENCE, 1965, vol. 72, pp. 366-371.

Indices which have been used have been based upon various single aspects of language which reasonably might be expected to change with increasing age. The ones primarily used have been these: mean length of response, mean of the five longest responses, number of one-word responses, standard deviation of response length, number of different words, structural complexity score, and the ratio of the different words over the total number of words (Johnson, Darley, and Spriestersbach, 1963). Each of these measures is based upon an analysis of 50 oral responses which have been obtained from a child in a standard manner (Winitz, 1959).

The above-named indices have often been used under the assumption that they provide a satisfactory basis for evaluating language development. These indices, although they apparently have been useful, have not been established as valid for their intended purpose; they have not been studied in relation to any outside criterion. The one obviously useful outside criterion is the impression language makes upon others. Psychological rating-scale methods thus might provide measures useful for evaluation of the validity of the indices currently used; they also might provide, in the form of speech samples scaled for degree of language development, a tool useful for evolving new indices which not only would be more valid than are those previously named but also would be more reliable. Satisfactory temporal reliability, that is, adequacy of sampling in obtaining the 50 responses from which the currently used indices are derived, has been questioned (Minifie, Darley, and Sherman, 1963).

The present experiment was designed for two purposes: first, to determine whether given samples of children's language will be consistently judged to display greater or lesser degrees of language development than will certain other samples; and, second, to evaluate the validity of a frequently used measure, the structural complexity score, by estimating the relationships, for the same samples, among three sets of measures: structural complexity scores, scale values of intricacy of language usage derived from observers' judgments, and mean estimates of age derived from sophisticated observers' judgments.

PROCEDURE

Language Samples

The language samples to be scaled were prepared for presentation to the observers in typed, mimeographed form. This method of presentation was chosen mainly to eliminate the influence of certain irrelevant cues which might operate if

157

observers were to make their ratings on samples presented by tape recordings. It seems likely that variables such as pitch usage, rhythm, and articulation skill might seriously contaminate the desired responses.

Transcripts of tape-recorded language samples from the speech of 96 children, 24 boys and 24 girls within two months of the age of five and one-half years, and 24 boys and 24 girls within two months of the age of eight years, were available from a previous experiment (Minifie, Darley, and Sherman, 1963). These samples, each consisting of 50 verbal responses, had been elicited from the children in response to Children's Apperception Test Cards.

From this larger pool of 50-response samples, 25 were chosen at random for experimentation aimed at determining the feasibility of employing the psychological scaling method of Equal-Appearing Intervals to obtain data for assessing language development by means of median scale values derived in the way described by Thurstone and Chave (1929). Each of these 25 samples was taken from a longer 50-response sample and consisted of the first 150 words to the nearest complete response.

Another set of 50 speech samples to be scaled with reference to some aspect of language consisted of portions of 50 of the longer 50-response samples. For the purpose of minimizing irrelevant influences upon observers' rating it seemed desirable to keep the topic constant for all samples; and, for this reason, the 50 portions consisted of the verbal output of each of 50 children in response to the same stimulus card. One result of this limitation was variation in lengths of samples to be rated, a result considered desirable because of the possibility that amount of verbal output may be an important and relevant factor with reference to certain aspects of language usage if measures are intended to reflect impressions characteristic of a true situation of communication. These 50 language samples were the experimental stimuli used for obtaining scale values of intricacy of language usage and also for obtaining estimates of chronological age.

The longer 50-response samples, portions of which were used for scaling intricacy of language usage, were analyzed to obtain corresponding structural complexity scores for each of the "intricacy" scale values. The structural complexity measures were derived by the usual method of assigning a weight of 0, 1, 2, 3, or 4 to each response according to differing classifications, such as "functionally complete but structurally incomplete", "simple sentence without phrase(s)", "simple sentence with phrase(s)" with several subcategories, "compound sentence" with subcategories, and "complex sentence" with subcategories. Exact instructions for the usual method of deriving these scores have been reported by Johnson, Darley, and Spriestersbach (1963).

Rating of Language Samples

To obtain data for evaluation of the reliability of scale values of language development obtained from observers' responses to typed language samples, 39 students of speech pathology were instructed to respond to 25 language samples by rating them on a 7-point equal-appearing-intervals scale extending from 1 for least language development to 7 for most language development. After an interval of eight to ten days the same 25 samples arranged in a new random order were again presented to each of the 39 students and the rating procedure was repeated.

An additional 29 students rated 50 samples on intricacy of language usage. None of these students had had any extensive course work in the language development of children; the purpose was to avoid the possibility that rating would be influenced by prior training in the use of the structural complexity score and its derivation. Observers were instructed to respond by the procedure already described. Since it was necessary for the purposes of the experiment to avoid artificial weighting of various factors which might influence the observers' responses, the following definition and instructions were included in "Instructions to Observers":

"Intricacy of language usage, for the purposes of this experiment, is defined as the intricacy of the arrangement of words for the purpose of conveying information. For example, consider the following four sets of words, which, without reference to the specific meanings, might be judged to vary with respect to intricacy of language usage as here defined:
  a) two good little boys
  b) boys in our school
  c) boys who are orphans
  d) really good little boys
Although each of the above sets contains four words, it is obvious that they vary with respect to type of arrangement of words for the purpose of conveying information.

"Make your judgment on the basis of the whole sample. Avoid being influenced by grammatical correctness; for example, 'we was' and 'we were' do not differ with respect to the intricacy of word arrangement. Also, do *not* give a rating based upon a judgment of the extent of vocabulary; for example, 'big size' and 'extensive area' are equivalent as far as the intricacy of arrangement is concerned, but they probably would not be considered

159

equivalent if judged for the purpose of rating extent of vocabulary."

Five sophisticated judges estimated the age of the 50 children from whom the 50 samples were elicited. All had had extensive associations with children of elementary school age. One was a supervisor of practice teaching, another was a country supervisor in education work, and the other three were elementary school principals. They were instructed to assume that each language sample was selected from the speech of a child with average intelligence and with average home environment. The experimental task consisted of recording for each of the samples an estimate of the age of the child who had spoken.

RESULTS AND DISCUSSION

The two sets of median scale values of degree of language development for 25 samples rated by 39 observers on two trials separated by eight to ten days are closely related. The Pearson r for estimating the relationship is .96. For the first trial a Q-value, the semi-interquartile range, which is a measure of the dispersion or scatter of judgments, was calculated for each of the 25 samples. These values were satisfactorily small, with a range from .47 to 1.02 and a mean of .78. Two additional sets of scale values were derived for the first trial by randomly assigning the 39 observers, and the corresponding raw data, to two groups. The Pearson r obtained for estimating relationship between these two additional sets of scale values is .90. Thus, with respect to placing samples in relative positions on the 7-point scale of language development, the measures obtained by the method of this experiment appear to be satisfactorily reliable.

Mean differences between the two sets of scale values for (a) the two trials and (b) the two smaller groups of the first trial were in both cases small, .36 and .49, respectively. These differences, however, according to results of a t test for related measures, were both significant beyond the .01 level. Scale values were quite consistently slightly lower for the second trial than for the first. Scale values of one of the two additional sets derived for the first trial were quite consistently lower than scale values of the other set. Certain precautions, then, in the interpretation of exact values of obtained scale positions are necessary. Pooling of scale values derived from responses of more than one judging session for the same group of observers, or for two groups of observers, make it necessary to follow a procedure which will ensure that the observers use the same standards for judging. If maintenance of the same standards is not possible, scale values of two sets of scale values might be pooled in those instances when one of the sets can be "adjusted" by the addition of an appropriately determined constant.

A set of 50 scale values of intricacy of language usage was derived from responses of 29 naive observers to 50 language samples, all on the same topic and varying in length. For the same samples, mean estimates of the ages of the children were obtained by averaging the estimates of five sophisticated observers. Structural complexity scores were computed from analyses of the 50 corresponding, longer 50-response samples.

Interrelationships among the three sets of measures were estimated by the Pearson r procedure. The Pearson r's for estimating these relationships for the indicated pairs of variables are as follows: structural complexity scores and scale values of intricacy of language usage, .63; structural complexity scores and mean estimates of age, .70; scale values of intricacy of language usage and mean estimates of age, .90. The high r of .90 is evidence not only of strong relationship between the last-mentioned sets of measures but also of their reliability. Comparisons among these three coefficients lead to the inference that the structural complexity score, as derived, may not be a good measure of the aspect of language for which it has been used. As previously mentioned, the validity of the weighting procedure has been questioned. The question arises also as to whether "complexity" may be at least partially dependent upon factors other than those used in derivation of structural complexity scores. The present results provide definite evidence leading to both questions. Possibly neither the categories of responses used in deriving these scores nor the weighting of them are satisfactory for the intended purpose.

That an extension of this experiment could result in useful new tools for the study of and the assessment of language development of children appears to be a reasonable assumption.

Literature Cited

Johnson, W., F. L. Darley, and D. Spriestersbach. 1963. *Diagnostic Methods in Speech Pathology.* New York: Harper and Row, 160-185.
Minifie, F. D., F. L. Darley, and D. Sherman. 1963. J. Speech Hearing Res., 6, 139-149.
Thurston, L. L. and E. J. Chave. 1929. *The Measurement of Attitude.* Chicago: University of Chicago Press.
Winitz, H. 1959. J. Speech Hearing Res., 5, 337-386.

AN EQUATION FOR ASSESSING
LANGUAGE DEVELOPMENT

THOMAS H. SHRINER

DOROTHY SHERMAN

Samples of language from the speech of 200 children, ranging in age from two
years and six months to twelve years, were used to obtain an equation for predicting
the degree of language development as measured by psychological scale values.
Predictors retained in the final equation are the mean of the five longest responses,
the number of one-word responses, the number of different words, and the structural
complexity score. A multiple-regression procedure yielded a final R of 0.85. Although
deleted from the final equation, the best single predictor is the mean length of response. The standard deviation of response length was found to have no systematic
relationship to psychological scale values of language development.

The need to assess children's language development has long been recognized. Customarily such development has been measured by analyzing the
child's use of language in response to stimuli (usually pictures) presented by
the examiner. Measures which have been used extensively include mean length
of response, mean of the five longest responses, number of one-word responses,
standard deviation of response length, number of different words, and structural complexity score (Johnson, Darley, and Spriestersbach, 1963, Ch. 7).
Their usefulness for such evaluation depends upon the accuracy of the assumption that they relate to changes in language which occur with increasing age,
as well as to changes in degree of language development. But are some of
the measures more closely related to judged degree of language development
than others? Can all noticeable changes in degree of development be accounted
for by using some or all of these measures, or do new measures of other aspects
of language need to be developed? Could modification of some of these measures result in a more accurate judgment of the degree of language development? Until recently no attempt has been made to examine these measures
in the light of the impact of language upon the listener (Sherman, Shriner, and
Silverman, in press).

The basic purpose was to examine, using a multiple-correlation procedure,

JOURNAL OF SPEECH AND HEARING RESEARCH, Mar. 1967, vol. 10, no. 1, pp. 41-48.

the relationships of the above-mentioned measures, both singly and in varying combinations, to psychological scale values of language development derived from observers' responses to samples of children's language.

METHOD

Experimental Design

Psychological scale values of degree of language development for samples of children's language provided the dependent variable of a multiple-regression analysis. Six measures currently used to assess children's language development were the independent variables. A prediction equation was determined and used for making a cross-validation analysis. This prediction equation was also used for making a validity generalization to the language of children with cleft palate and poor articulation skill.

An intraclass correlation technique was used to evaluate adequacy of sampling with reference to the dependent variable (the psychological scale value). For this purpose there were several samples and scale values for each of a selected group of children.

Language Samples

The experimental materials were 300 language samples obtained from 200 children who ranged in age from 2.5 to 12 years, with a mean age of six years, seven months. Although no attempt was made to select a sample representative of the population in general, all socioeconomic levels were included. None of the children had an educationally significant hearing loss.

Since language samples were obtained from several sources (see the acknowledgment), the criteria for hearing loss varied. With the exception of eight among those used for the validity generalization, all had IQ's above 80. All had articulation skills considered to be within the range of normal except for those chosen for the validity generalization, which was to children with cleft palate and with severe articulation problems.

The language samples were elicited from the children by a standard procedure (Templin, 1957) with slight modifications (Minifie, Darley, and Sherman, 1963). Each sample consisted of 50 responses to picture stimuli or, occasionally (especially for the younger children), to interjected remarks or questions from the examiner.

For each 50-response sample the following measures were obtained: mean length of response, mean of the five longest responses, number of one-word responses, standard deviation of response length by number of words, number of different words, and structural complexity score. The methods of obtaining these measures (except for the structural complexity score) are indicated by their names.

Structural complexity scores were obtained by the method outlined by Templin (1957, p. 81), that is, by assigning arbitrary weights of 0, 1, 2, 3, and 4 to five categories of responses ranging from a structurally incomplete response to a complex sentence or an elaborated sentence, such as a compound sentence with a subordinate clause.

The stimuli for which the psychological scale values of language development were obtained consisted of the first 150 words, to the nearest response, of the longer 50-response samples. The decision to use 150 words was based upon the results of a pilot study (Sherman, Shriner, and Silverman, in press) which demonstrated that 150 words constitute an adequate sample for satisfactory reliability of scale values.

Groups for Analyses

Multiple Correlation and Cross Validation. For multiple-correlation and cross-validation procedures, 160 of the samples were used: 110 for multiple correlation and 50 for cross validation. Those for cross validation were randomly selected.

Validity Generalization. A validity-generalization procedure (Mosier, 1951) was used to examine the results of applying the prediction equation to measures of speech samples from a population differing from the one for which the equation was derived. For this purpose, 40 speech samples were used from children with cleft palate whose articulation scores were lower than one standard deviation below the norms (Templin and Darley, 1960, p. 18). It seemed possible that children with severely deviant articulation, particularly those with additional problems likely to accompany cleft palate, might differ from the usual pattern of language development when evaluated by the independent variables under study. Generally, they might tend, for example, to use shorter responses but at the same time fewer one-word responses than would children without the same problems.

Adequacy of Sampling. To evaluate adequacy of sampling, with reference to psychological scale values, that is, to estimate reliability for different language samples from the same children, the experimental material consisted of three language samples for each of 50 children. These 50 were a random selection from the 96 children used in the study by Minifie et al. (1963), in which three 50-response samples had been elicited from each child within a 48-hour period. Thus, differences from one set of samples to another could not be attributed to language development; such differences, if important, would be the result of inadequacy of sampling, or possibly of the scaling technique. It is also possible that various irrelevant factors (time of day, emotional state of the child or the examiners, so-called "practice" effect, physical condition of the child or examiner, or, quite importantly, the stimuli employed to elicit the samples) might differentially influence the nature of samples from the same children from one time to another.

Scaling Procedure

The 104 judges who rated the experimental samples were students in the Department of Speech Pathology and Audiology at the University of Iowa. The single restriction placed upon their selection was the elimination of any student who had previously been enrolled in a course in language development. This restriction seemed necessary in order that ratings would not be unduly influenced by specific and extensive knowledge of the particular, often-used, language measures under study.

The language samples were presented to the judges in typed, mimeographed form. This method of presentation, rather than auditory, was necessary for the purpose of eliminating the irrelevant influence of such factors as pitch, intonation, stress, and articulation errors.

All samples were rated by the method of equal-appearing intervals (Thurstone and Chave, 1929) on a seven-point equal-appearing-intervals scale of language development. The scale extended from 1 to 7, with 1 representing least development of language and 7 representing most development. The judges were instructed to read the first 20 samples quickly to acquaint themselves with the experimental task and with the range of the samples with respect to language development.

From the judges' ratings, 350 median scale values (Thurstone and Chave, 1929) for quantifying degree of language development were derived, including two scale values derived for each of 50 samples from the responses of two groups of judges to provide for a reliability estimate.

One group of 37 judges rated the 150 samples with three samples from each of 50 children. The 150 samples were arranged in random order. Another group of 67 judges rated each of 200 samples. These 200 samples included (a) the 50 samples rated by both groups of judges, (b) the 110 samples selected for the multiple-correlation procedure, (c) the 50 samples selected for the cross-validation procedure, and (d) the 40 samples selected for the validity-generalization procedure.

RESULTS

Scale Values

A total of 350 psychological scale values were derived from observers' responses to samples of children's language. Judging was done by the method of equal-appearing intervals on a seven-point scale as previously described.

For the multiple-regression analysis and cross validation there are 160 scale values: 110 for the main analysis and 50 for cross validation. The 110 measures range from 0.77 to 6.03, with a mean of 3.47 and a standard deviation of 1.05. The 50 measures range from 0.65 to 6.38, with a mean of 3.45 and a standard deviation of 1.26. For the validity generalization to samples from children with cleft palate and severely deviant articulation there are 40 scale values.

These range from 0.94 to 5.32, with a mean of 3.26 and a standard deviation of 1.11. A Q value, that is, the semi-interquartile range, which measures the dispersion of judgments was calculated for each of the 200 scale values. These range from 0.31 to 1.34, with a mean of 0.81.

An additional 150 scale values were obtained for purposes of evaluating reliability and adequacy of sampling. A Pearson r of 0.91 was obtained as an estimate of the relationship between two sets of scale values for 50 samples derived from ratings made by two separate sets of judges. An intraclass correlation coefficient, r_i[1] (Ebel, 1951), was computed to evaluate adequacy of sampling. This coefficient, which is 0.89, provides a reliability estimate for the individual scale values of the three sets of values for samples elicited from the same 50 children.

Multiple-Regression Analysis

For the multiple-regression analysis in which all six predictor variables were used, a multiple R of 0.85+ was obtained. Two beta weights, those for mean length of response and standard deviation of response length, are nonsignificant (see Table 1) and were eliminated as predictors. With the elimination of these two, essentially no change is observed in the final R, which remains 0.85+.

TABLE 1. Beta weights and Rs for the three successive cycles of the multiple-regression analysis. The columns show the order of deletion of predictors; entries omitted in the second and third columns indicate that the corresponding variable is deleted. Predictors are mean length of response (MLR), mean of the five longest responses (M5LR), number of one-word responses (N1W), standard deviation of response length (SD-RL), number of different words (NDW), and structural complexity score (SCS).

		Beta Weights		
Predictors		Cycle 1	Cycle 2	Cycle 3
1.	MLR	0.026°	0.025°	—
2.	M5LR	0.317	0.319	0.334
3.	N1W	−0.176	−0.176	−0.179
4.	SD-RL	0.015°	—	—
5.	NDW	0.238	0.238	0.242
6.	SCS	0.231	0.229	0.234
	R	0.8544	0.8543	0.8542

°Beta weight is statistically nonsignificant at the 0.05 level.

By inspection of the intercorrelation matrix (see Table 2) it may be seen that standard deviation of response length does not correlate with either the dependent variable (the scale values) or any other predictor variable. How-

---

[1] $r_i = \dfrac{(ms_b - ms_w)}{[ms_b + (k-1)ms_w]}$, where ms_b = mean square between subjects, ms_w = mean square within subjects, and k = number of trials.

ever, mean length of response, which was the second predictor variable eliminated, does correlate more highly with the dependent variable than does any
other predictor variable. A reasonable explanation of its nonsignificant contribution may be based upon the fact that it also correlates highly with each of
the retained predictor variables.

TABLE 2. Intercorrelations for all possible pairings of variables, including both the predictors and the criterion score. The predictors are mean length of response (MLR), mean
of five longest responses (M5LR), number of one-word responses (N1W), standard deviation of response length (SD-RL), number of different words (NDW), and structural complexity score (SCS). The criterion score is the psychological scale value of degree of
language development (SV).

	2	3	4	5	6	7
1. MLR	0.91	−0.58	−0.02	0.82	0.81	0.80
2. M5LR	—	−0.49	0.01	0.75	0.71	0.77
3. N1W	—	—	−0.02	−0.51	−0.54	−0.59
4. SD-RL	—	—	—	−0.02	−0.05	0.00
5. NDW	—	—	—	—	0.82	0.78
6. SCS	—	—	—	—	—	0.76
7. SV	—	—	—	—	—	—

Cross Validation

In order to evaluate the accuracy with which ratings of language development might be predicted, a raw score prediction equation was determined.
This equation is:

$$Y = 0.0576X_2 - 0.0458X_3 + 0.00659X_5 + 0.00737X_6 + 1.359,$$

where Y = the predicted score for degree of language development, X_2 = mean
of the five longest responses, X_3 = number of one-word responses, X_5 = number
of different words, and X_6 = structural complexity score. The standard error of
estimate associated with this equation is 0.56.

This equation was used to predict scale values of language development for
50 language samples which constituted an independent group from the same
population from which the 110 samples were selected for the multiple-regression analysis. A Pearson r of 0.83 was obtained as an estimate of the relationship between the 50 observed scale values and the 50 predictions. The difference between the mean of predictions and the mean of obtained scale
values was evaluated by an F test. The obtained F ratio (0.43, $df = 1/49$) is
nonsignificant, less than 1.00. The mean difference between the observed and
predicted criterion scores is 0.54.

DISCUSSION

Future usefulness in applying these results depends largely upon the feasibility of making generalizations about language development in children from

whom language samples are elicited. For several sets of samples obtained from the same children under the conditions of this study, psychological scale values are closely alike. This is not to say, however, that these language samples are truly representative of the children's language development in general; nor can it be assumed that the degree of language development exhibited in such samples correlates with the degree exhibited in other situations. Important questions thus remain to be answered.

As evaluated in this study, standard deviation of response length cannot be said to increase systematically with psychological scale values of language development. The observed correlation between these two variables was 0.00. The fact remains that, as children mature, more variability would be expected because of increasing sentence length. Perhaps, in fact, there is a general correlation between variability of response length and chronological age. According to present results, however, the only reasonable assumption is that the measure of standard deviation of response length is of no practical use in the evaluation of language development for the population studied here. Mean length of response, on the other hand, although deleted from the prediction equation, had a higher correlation with scale values than did any other predictor variable. If a single measure is to be used for assessment of language development, this one thus would appear to be the most useful among those studied.

The obtained multiple R is quite high; and the predictor-composite performed more effectively than might have been expected, especially in view of the fact that scale values by their nature are somewhat unreliable. The coefficient of determination, R^2, is 0.72. This result can be interpreted as indicating that 72% of the variance of the criterion measures (the scale values) is associated with the variance of the predictors.

Possibly, with further experimentation, the efficiency of certain predictors could be improved. This seems particularly likely with the structural complexity score. The weighting procedure employed in deriving this score has been questioned (Darley and Moll, 1960; Minifie et al., 1963). Minifie et al. have reported that the omission of articles and prepositions can alter assigned weights as much as from 4 to 0. Ideas developed as a result of linguistic analysis might be of use for improving this measure. Menyuk (1964), for example, has referred to omissions of the type mentioned as "approximations," and, through use of the generative model of grammar formulated by Chomsky (1957), she found differences in the particular forms of approximations used from one age level to another. Grammar obviously becomes increasingly complex as the child matures. This complexity, however, is not related simply to increasing sentence length, or to more use of compound or complex sentences. According to Menyuk, increasing complexity is dependent on the child's improving ability to proceed from the application of the most general rule in the formulation of a syntactic structure, to increasingly differentiating rules, and then to a complete set needed for a particular structure. Evaluation, not only of the measures customarily used for assessing language development, but also of additional measures, particularly some which have been used in linguistic analyses, seems indicated.

Additional validity generalizations might provide useful information about other populations, for example, children who are hard of hearing, children from varying socioeconomic levels, or children who are mentally retarded. For some populations, new multiple regression analyses might be indicated.

Various methods of quantifying the listener's evaluations of language development should be compared and evaluated. A ratio-scaling method, for example, might be demonstrated to be superior to the method of equal-appearing intervals used in this study.

This article is based partially upon a doctoral dissertation completed under the direction of Dorothy Sherman.

We are indebted for some of the language samples to Hughlett L. Morris, University of Iowa (Research Project M-1158), Judith N. Moody, State College of Iowa, and Fred D. Minifie, University of Wisconsin.

REFERENCES

CHOMSKY, N., *Syntactic Structures*. Gravenhage, The Netherlands: Mouton (1957).

DARLEY, F. L., and MOLL, K. L., Reliability of language measures and size of language samples. *J. Speech Hearing Res.*, 3, 166-173 (1960).

EDEL, R. L., Estimation of the reliability of ratings. *Psychometrika*, 16, 407-424 (1951).

JOHNSON, W., DARLEY, F. L., and SPRIESTERSBACH, D. C., *Diagnostic Methods in Speech Pathology*. New York: Harper (1963).

MENYUK, P., Alternation of rules in children's grammar. *J. verb. Learn. verb. Behav.*, 3, 480-488 (1964).

MINIFIE, F. D., DARLEY, F. L., and SHERMAN, D., Temporal reliability of seven language measures, *J. Speech Hearing Res.*, 6, 139-149 (1963).

MOSIER, C. I., Symposium: the need and means of cross-validation. I. Problems and design of cross-validation. *Educ. Psychol. Measmt.*, 11, 5-11 (1951).

SHERMAN, D., SHRINER, T. H., and SILVERMAN, F., Psychological scaling of language development of children. *Proc. Iowa Acad. Sci.*, in press.

TEMPLIN, M. C., *Certain Language Skills in Children* (*Institute of Child Welfare Monograph Series*, No. 26), Minneapolis: Univ. Minn. (1957).

TEMPLIN, M. C., and DARLEY, F. L., *The Templin-Darley Tests of Articulation*. Iowa City: Univ. Iowa (1960).

THURSTONE, L. L., and CHAVE, E. J., *The Measurement of Attitude*. Chicago: Univ. Chicago (1929).

A COMPARISON OF SELECTED MEASURES WITH PSYCHOLOGICAL SCALE VALUES OF LANGUAGE DEVELOPMENT

THOMAS H. SHRINER

Four linear multiple–regression analyses were used to determine the best composite for predicting scale values of language development derived from children of four different age categories. For the youngest age group (mean age of four years, seven months), a new measure of language development was evaluated. The results showed that the relationship among the predictor variables change as a function of age. Little systematic relationship was observed between the criterion, scale values of language development, and the predictor variables for children above the age of approximately five years. For children who were younger than five years, the best single predictor was the new measure, a modified length-complexity measure. Until there is further improvement of the length-complexity measure, however, mean length of response is a satisfactory predictor of language for children who are approximately five years of age and younger.

Previous research conducted by Sherman, Shriner, and Silverman (1965) and by Shriner and Sherman (1967) demonstrated that psychological scaling of various aspects of children's language could provide new and useful tools for assessing children's language development. Shriner and Sherman (1967) reported that samples of language from the speech of 200 children were used to obtain an equation for predicting degree of language development as measured by psychological scale values of language development. Measures retained in the final prediction equation were the mean of the five longest responses, number of one-word responses, the number of different words, and the structural complexity score.

Their study demonstrated that selected measures can be evaluated, either singly or in combination, in relation to psychological scale values of language development for samples of language obtained from children who ranged in age from two years and six months to 12 years. The question arises as to whether the relationships among the predictor variables would remain the same or whether a new predictor-composite would be related more closely to judged degree of language development for children of specific age categories.

Shriner and Sherman (1967) used the linear multiple–regression procedure to obtain the desired estimate of relationships. This technique also may be used to evaluate new measures of language development which may be derived

JOURNAL OF SPEECH AND HEARING RESEARCH, 1967, vol. 10, no. 4, pp. 828-835.

170

through further experimentation. In this respect they proposed that results of current developments in structural linguistics might be used either to form new measures or to modify present measures of children's language development. A modified combination of two measures, mean length of response (Mc-Carthy, 1954, ch. 9) and structural complexity of response (Templin, 1957, p. 81), seems particularly likely.

Numerous investigators have analyzed length of response independently of complexity of response. Although mean length of response seems adequate for most purposes, the arbitrary weighting system proposed by Templin (1957) to evaluate the grammatical categories of children's language development was questioned (Darley and Moll, 1960; Minifie, Darley, and Sherman, 1963). Because language production increases in length as well as in complexity with increasing chronological age, and because the weighting system used to assess complexity of response was questioned, a procedure which combines both length and complexity of response into a single measure may prove to be more useful for research or clinical purposes than either of these measures used independently.

The purpose is to examine relationships between selected language measures and psychological scale values derived from language samples obtained from children of specific age categories. In addition, a new measure, a modified combination of length and complexity of utterance, also will be evaluated.

METHOD

Language Samples

The samples of children's language used were selected from a larger pool of samples which had been used in previous research (Shriner and Sherman, 1967). Each sample consisted of 50 responses and was elicited from the child by a standard procedure (Templin, 1957) with slight modifications (Minifie, Darley, and Sherman, 1963). In general, the standard procedure consisted of eliciting 50 responses by showing each child a picture stimulus and asking him about what he saw in the picture.

The larger pool of samples was obtained from 200 children who ranged in age from two years, six months, to 12 years with a mean age of six years, seven months. The primary criterion for the selection of the samples used in the present research was the child's chronological age. Each child from whom samples were obtained, however, had no hearing loss considered to be educationally significant. All levels of socioeconomic status were represented without any significant bias. With the exception of eight children, each child had an I.Q. above 80.

The first linear multiple–regression analysis consisted of language samples obtained from 45 children who ranged in age from three years to five years, six months, with a mean age of four years, seven months. The second and third analyses each consisted of samples obtained from 46 children who were five

171

years, six months, and eight years of age, respectively. The final group for analysis consisted of samples included in the third analysis plus 31 additional samples. These were obtained from children ranging in age from eight years, two months, to 12 years with a mean age of eight years, nine months.

Language Measures

The independent variables in each of the analyses consisted of: mean number of words per response (MLR); mean number of words of the five longest responses (M5LR); structural complexity score (SCS); and number of different words (NDW). (An excellent discussion of these measures and how they are derived can be found in Johnson, Darley, and Spriestersbach, 1963, ch. 7.) An additional predictor, the modified version of length and complexity of utterance (LC), was evaluated only in the first multiple–regression analysis.

The LC measure was formed by relying on the research of Menyuk (1964) and Cazden (1965). Menyuk (1964) reported that complexity was not related simply to increasing sentence length or proportion of usage of what have been termed compound or complex sentences. Increasing complexity, according to Menyuk, is proceeding from the most general rule to the application of increasing differentiating rules. She reported, for example, that to conjoin two sentences, or to delete and substitute as in relative clauses requires the application of certain rules. If a child uses a rule to generate a sentence and then proceeds to conjoin two or possibly three similar sentences, the utterance would be obviously increasing in length; however, the utterance would not be increasing in complexity. The observations of Menyuk were employed, as illustrated below, in making decisions regarding specific parts of utterances to be scored.

If, for example, a child has an internalized rule for generating a sentence which consists of a NP (noun phrase) + VP (verb phrase), then proceeds to use the same rule again simply by adding a conjunction, only the first part of the sentence was considered for scoring (see examples one, two, and three below). Again, by the same token, if a child generated a sentence consisting of a NP + NP + NP + VP, only one of the NPs was scored (see example four below). The italicized words were scored in the following:

1. *The momma wants it* and the poppa wants it and the baby wants it.
2. *The big bears might be in the big bed* and the little bears might be in the little bed.
3. *If this one got it I suppose he would tie those two up* and if those two got it I suppose they would tie him up.
4. A baby bear and a mother bear and *a daddy bear are holding onto the rope.*
5. *He would go get his* great, great, great, *great, big father.*

Utterances were scored by slightly modifying and combining the noun phrase and verb complexity indexes developed by Cazden (1965). She devised the two indexes largely on the unpublished data available from the work of

172

Roger Brown and Ursula Bellugi of Harvard University. In her noun phrase index, for example, a child was given points for the use of modifiers, articles, plurals, and possessive inflections with the child's final score being the total of his noun phrase points divided by the number of phrases. In the present research each child's final score was the sum of his noun phrase points plus his verb phrase points divided by the total number of sentences in the corpus.

The following are examples of the scoring method used in this study. Symbols used are N (noun), M (any modifier), A (article), MA (modifier other than an article), P (plural inflection), Poss (possessive inflection), Aux (auxiliary), PrP (present participle), V (verb), and PreV (preverb).

Symbols	Example	Score
N	Doggie	1
N + P	Cars	2
A + MA + N	A good idea	3
M + N + P	My lips	3
MA + MA + N	Some more red	4
N + Poss + N + P	Baby's balls	5
N + Aux + PrP[1]	I'm getting	4
N + PreV + V	Mommy gonna go	3

---

[1] N would receive a weight of one, Aux + PrP would receive 3.

A copula index also was developed by Cazden (1965) to measure the verb form *is*. In this study the verb *is* was not considered separately; rather, it was included and scored as part of the verb complexity index. Negatives were omitted from analysis in her study. With the exception of the elliptical responses, *no* and *I don't know*, negatives were included in the present research and given a weight of *one*. Obvious elliptical responses, such as *no, yes, I don't know, uh huh*, were eliminated from the corpus. Starters, such as *oh, hey, and, cause, then*, and *well* also were eliminated.

Scaling Method. The dependent variable in all of the analyses was median psychological scale values of language development. All samples were rated by the method of equal-appearing intervals (Thurstone and Chave, 1929) on a seven-point equal-appearing-intervals scale of language development. The scale extended from *one* to *seven* with *one* representing *least* development of language and *seven* representing *most* development. The judges were instructed to read quickly the first 20 samples to acquaint themselves with the experimental task and with the range of the samples with respect to language development.

The language samples were presented to the judges in typed, mimeographed form. This method of presentation, rather than auditory, was necessary for the purpose of eliminating the irrelevant influence of such factors as pitch, intonation, stress, and articulation errors.

All judges who rated the samples, a total of 104, were students in the Department of Speech Pathology and Audiology, University of Iowa. The single

TABLE 1. Summary of all four linear multiple-regression analyses. Symbols used are length complexity measure (LC), mean length of response (MLR), structural complexity score (SCS), and the mean of the five longest responses (M5LR).

Age Groups for Analysis	Mean Age (Yrs.-Mos.)	N	Predictor with Remaining Sig. Beta*	Initial R	Final R
1	4.7	45	LC	0.89	0.88
2	5.6	46	MLR	0.82	0.80
3	8.0	46	SCS	0.69	0.68
4	8.9	77	M5LR SCS	0.65	0.65

*Significant at the 0.05 level of confidence.

restriction placed upon their selection was the requirement that any student who had been enrolled previously in a course in language development should be eliminated. This restriction seemed necessary in order that ratings would not be unduly influenced by specific and extensive knowledge of the language measures under study.

RESULTS

The results of all four analyses are summarized in Table 1. In the first linear multiple–regression analysis in which all the predictors were used, a multiple R of 0.89 was obtained. The LC predictor had the only remaining significant beta weight. The other four predictors, MLR, M5LR, NDN, and SCS, were eliminated because their beta weights were not significant. When they were eliminated, relatively little change was observed in the final R, which is 0.88.

By inspection of the intercorrelation matrix (Table 2) it may be observed that LC correlates highly with both MLR and SCS. This was expected since the LC predictor is a measure of the length and complexity of the utterance. Table 2 also reveals that MLR, even though eliminated, correlates highly with the dependent variable, median scale values (SV) of language development. A reasonable explanation of its nonsignificant contribution may be that it also

TABLE 2. Intercorrelations for all possible pairings of variables for the first analysis which consisted of the youngest age group. Symbols used are mean length of response (MLR), mean five longest responses (M5LR), length complexity measure (LC), number of different words (NDW), and structural complexity score (SCS). The criterion score is the psychological scale value of degree of language development (SV).

	M5LR	LC	NDW	SCS	SV
MLR	0.91	0.97	0.68	0.91	0.86
M5LR		0.89	0.68	0.81	0.83
LC			0.67	0.91	0.87
NDW				0.56	0.56
SCS					0.77
SV					—

correlates highly with the only remaining significant predictor, the LC measure; therefore, only one is maintained for prediction.

The second group for analysis shows that as the mean age of the subjects increased from four years, seven months, to five years, six months, the final R decreased from 0.88 to 0.80 (Table 1). The predictor with the only remaining significant beta weight was MLR. When the other predictor variables were eliminated, the initial R decreased from 0.82 to 0.80.

In the third analysis where the mean age of the subjects was eight years, the relationships among the predictor variables changed. The best single predictor is no longer MLR; rather, SCS has the only remaining significant beta weight. As the mean age of the subjects increased to eight years, the final R continued to decrease from 0.80 to 0.68.

In the last group for analysis which includes 77 subjects with a mean age of eight years, seven months, the beta weights for two predictors, M5LR and SCS, were significant. Although M5LR did not remain as a significant predictor in the third group, it remained as a significant predictor in the fourth group. It probably remains as a predictor because of the increase in degrees of freedom for this population. The intercorrelation matrix for this particular analysis, however, revealed that SCS is contributing to most of the overall multiple R. Its correlation with the dependent variable (SV) is 0.63. The trend of a decrease in the final R continues as the mean age of the subjects increase.

DISCUSSION

The results indicate that the relationships among the predictor variables change as a function of age. In the first multiple–regression analysis the LC measure remained as the single, best predictor of psychological scale values of language development. Table 2 revealed, however, that both MLR and LC correlate highly with SV. The LC measure was not applied to the older age groups because of the impreciseness of the measure when applied to longer and more complex sentence structures. This measure should be considered as a preliminary and quite promising measure for future research. More systematic research should permit further modification and improvement of the weighting method developed by Cazden (1965). Although Cazden's noun phrase index was based primarily on emergence of development, her verb index was based primarily on complexity of development. Further research should lead to the quantification of the various verb forms with respect to the time they emerge in the verbal output of young children. Bellugi's research (1966), as yet unpublished, on the transformational analysis of children's negations and questions also may prove helpful in further improvement of the LC measure. As Cazden (1965) has stated: "Current research will eventually lead to the discovery of a developmental sequence of language acquisition common to all children learning a particular language."

In devising scales of developmental sequence, complexity, or correctness and assigning numbers to points on the scale, the experimenter should be aware of the differences between ordinal and interval-scale measurements. Further experimentation with transformations or psychological scaling procedures may help to develop a weighting method with equal units that will eventually prove worthwhile in clinical evaluation. As Carroll (1961, p. 334) has stated: "If such developmental scales could be established, they would probably be more meaningful than such indices of language development as mean sentence length."

Until such development scales are established for research or clinical purposes and further improvement of the LC measure is accomplished, MLR should still be considered the "simplest and most objective measure of the degree to which children combine words at the various ages" (McCarthy, 1930, p. 50). Although the LC measure may ultimately be shown to be more valuable than MLR, the results of the present research indicate that MLR is a satisfactory predictor of psychological scale values of language development for children who are approximately five years of age and younger.

As the mean age of the groups for analysis increases, MLR loses significance as a predictor. The coefficient of determination, R^2, for MLR in the first analysis is 0.74. This result is interpreted as indicating that 74% of the variance of scale values is associated with the variance of MLR. While MLR accounts for less variance with an increase in mean age, SCS gains significance as a predictor for the older children. These results are in agreement with an earlier study of MLR by Smith (1926). She reported a steady increase in MLR up to the age of four years, six months, and very great variability in the older children. Response length apparently reaches an asymptote for the older children, and other factors such as those measured by SCS are beginning to play a more important role. This may be expected because SCS as a measure is based primarily on the adult model for correctness, with older children conforming more to this model. The coefficient of determination, however, for SCS is 0.40, which means that only 40% of the variance of SV is associated with the variance of SCS. As previously mentioned, the weighting system used to derive the SCS measure to assess the different grammatical categories of children's language production was questioned and a new weighting system at this time appears warranted.

This study also supports the research of Darley and Moll (1960) and Minifie, Darley, and Sherman (1963) who reported for children five years and five years, six months, respectively, that MLR appears to be a satisfactory language measure. That an extension of the LC could result in a new and useful tool for the assessment of children's language development appears to be reasonable and warranted.

Suggestions of Dorothy Sherman are gratefully acknowledged. This investigation was supported in part by Public Health Service Research Grant NB-07346 from the National Institute of Mental Health.

REFERENCES

BELLUGI, URSULA, The development of questions and negatives in the speech of three children. Cambridge: Harvard Univ. (1966).

CARROLL, J. B., Language development in children. In S. Saporta (Ed.), *Psycholinguistics: A Book of Readings*. New York: Holt, Rinehart and Winston (1961).

CAZDEN, COURTNEY B., Environmental assistance to the child's acquisition of grammar. Unpublished doctoral dissertation, Harvard Univ. (1965).

DARLEY, F. L., and MOLL, K. L., Reliability of language measures and size of language samples. *J. Speech Hearing Res.*, 3, 166-173 (1960).

JOHNSON, W., DARLEY, F. L., and SPRIESTERSBACH, D. C., *Diagnostic Methods in Speech Pathology*. New York: Harper and Row (1963).

McCARTHY, DOROTHEA, A., *The Language Development of the Preschool Child*. Institute of Child Welfare Monograph Series, No. 4. Minneapolis: Univ. Minn. Press (1930).

McCARTHY, DOROTHEA, A., Language development in children. In L. Carmichael (Ed.), *Manual of Child Psychology* (2nd ed.) New York: Wiley and Sons (1954).

MENYUK, PAULA, Alternation of rules in children's grammar. *J. verb. Learn verb. Behav.*, 3, 480-488 (1964).

MINIFIE, F. D., DARLEY, F. L., and SHERMAN, DOROTHY, Temporal reliability of seven language measures. *J. Speech Hearing Res.*, 6, 139-149 (1963).

SHERMAN, DOROTHY, SHRINER, T. H., and SILVERMAN, F., Psychological scaling of language development of children. *Proc. Iowa Acad. Sci.* (in press).

SHRINER, T. H., and SHERMAN, DOROTHY, An equation for assessing language development. *J. Speech Hearing Res.*, 10, 41-48 (1967).

SMITH, MADORAH, E., An investigation of the development of the sentence and the extent of vocabulary in young children. *University of Iowa Studies in Child Welfare*, 3, No. 5. Univ. of Iowa (1926).

TEMPLIN, MILDRED C., *Certain Language Skills in Children*. Institute of Child Welfare Monograph Series, No. 26. Minneapolis: Univ. Minn. Press (1957).

THURSTONE, L. L., and CHAVE, E. J., *The Measurement of Attitude*. Chicago: Univ. of Chicago Press (1929).

SCORING PROCEDURES FOR THE LENGTH-COMPLEXITY INDEX: A PRELIMINARY REPORT

L.E.MINER

Shriner (1968) has reviewed the procedural and inherent weaknesses of the MLR. The sufficiency of the SCS has also been challenged. A new language measure, the length-complexity index (LCI), is currently regarded as the best single indicator of developmental changes in child language. The LCI makes a composite analysis of sentence length and sentence complexity concurrently according to a numeric weighting system. The methodology and implications for language therapy are discussed.

Future research should permit refinement of the LCI. Currently unanswered questions include (A) the emergence of transformations, (B) standardized sampling procedure, (C) size of language sample, and (D) generalizability for different dialect groups. Nevertheless, the LCI does provide more information regarding the morphological and syntactical features in the language of children than does either MLR or SCS.

Introduction

Recent developments in descriptive linguistics provide the clinician with new methodologies for the diagnosis and appraisal of verbal maturity in children. One approach has discussed the emergence of two and three word sentences in terms of certain "open" and "pivot" class constructions (Brown and Bellugi 1964; Brown and Fraser 1963; Brown, Fraser and Bellugi 1963; Ervin 1964; Miller and Ervin 1964; Braine 1963; McNeill 1966a,b). It examines the way in which children initially combine words into sentences. A second method proposes a tentative hierarchy of developmental sentence types. It proceeds from various kinds of two word combinations through noun phrase constructions and kernel sentences up to emerging transformations (Lee 1966). A third classification system purports to measure both the length and complexity of utterances (Shriner 1967). It consists essentially of a numeric weighting scale for assessing developmental changes in child language. Each of these three techniques attempts to describe the grammatical rules that children employ in generating sentences.

The first two methods, open-pivot constructions and developmental sentence types, have been discussed both from a theoretical and clinical viewpoint. While the theoretical rationale of the third approach, length-complexity index, has been reported in the literature, its application to the clinical setting remains

JOURNAL OF COMMUNICATION DISORDERS, 1969, vol. 2, pp. 224-240.

178

unspecified. The ultimate sufficiency of this or any language measurement tool can only be determined after it has been utilized at the clinical level. The purpose of this article is to describe the preliminary procedures for the analysis of verbalizations according to the length-complexity index (LCI). It attempts to bridge the gap from a theoretical perspective to the specific application of the LCI in a clinical setting.

Definition and description

The length-complexity index (LCI) is a linguistic measure designed to make a composite analysis of sentence length and sentence complexity. Both length and complexity are considered together (not independently) according to a numeric weighting system. It is a modified combination of two previous measures, the mean length of response (McCarthy 1954, chapt. 9) and the structural complexity score (Templin 1957, p. 81).

The LCI measure is based on the research of Menyuk (1964a), Cazden (1965) and Bellugi (1964) and was first synthesized by Shriner (1967). Menyuk (1964a) noted that sentence complexity relates to more than sentence length; it is also a function of the ability to apply increasingly differentiated rules for generating sentences. This notion suggests, for example, that conjoining several sentences with the conjunction *and* would result in longer but not necessarily more complex sentences. As an illustration, only the words in italics represent original grammatical rules within the following utterances.

1. *That's a bear there and* that's a bear there and that's a bear there.
2. *I rode on the train for a long,* long, long, long, long, long *time.*
3. *My mother and* my father and my brother and my sister *went to the store.*
4. *I like candy and* I like gum.
5. *I wish I could go to the show and* I wish I could see a cowboy show.

Consequently, the LCI was developed out of a discerned need for a more sensitive measure of verbal maturity in children, a measure which concurrently assesses sentence length and complexity.

The child's final LCI score is the sum of his noun phrase (NP) points plus verb phrase (VP) points plus additional points (AP) for each sentence divided by the number of sentences (NS). Put differently, LCI = NP + VP + AP/NS. Indicated below are examples of the scoring method. Symbols used are N (noun), M (modifier), A (article), P (plural inflection), Poss (possessive inflection), Aux (auxiliary), PrPt (present participle), V (verb), and PreV (preverb). The LCI scores are also contrasted with traditional MLR scores.

Symbols	Examples	LCI score	MLR score
N	dog	1	1
N + P	dogs	2	1
A + M + N	a big dog	3	3
M + M + N	big white dog	4*	3
N + Poss + N + P	dog's dishes	4	2
N + Aux + PrPt	dog's eating	4**	3
N + PreV + V	dog gonna bark	3	3

* Extra point derived from two consecutive modifiers for noun.
** N received 1 point, Aux + PrPt = 3.

179

Historical perspectives

The LCI had its origins in the recent developments from structural linguistics (Shriner and Sherman, 1967). Shriner (1968), in an extensive review of the literature, questioned the adequacy of the mean length of response (MLR) as a means of measuring developmental changes in language facility. Minifie, Darley and Sherman (1963) contend that the structural complexity score (SCS) fails to be an accurate predictor of language development, primarily because the omission of articles and prepositions can considerably alter the assigned sentence weight.

It is not the purpose of this report to review the literature relative to the adequacy of the MLR and SCS as linguistic measures; however, the objections to these measurements can be briefly summarized as follows: the MLR has been criticized for a lack of sufficiency (Carrol, 1961, p. 334), validity (Cowan, Weber, Hoddinott and Klein 1967; Minifie, Darley and Sherman 1963; Shriner, 1968) and reliability (Minifie et al. 1963; Siegel 1960; Fisher 1934; Shriner 1967, 1968). By the same token, the SCS has been questioned on grounds of sufficiency (Sherman, Shriner and Silverman 1965; Shriner and Sherman 1967; and Shriner 1967), reliability (Minifie et al. 1963; Darley and Moll 1960) and validity (Minifie et al. 1963). In brief, both MLR and SCS provide relatively scant information about morphological and syntactical developmental changes which occur with increased chronological age.

Utilization of the LCI presupposes familiarity with base structure rules for generating sentences. A partial list of the rewrite rules is indicated below.

S	$\rightarrow NP_1 + VP_2$
NP_1	$\rightarrow (A) + (PrPh) + (M) + N$
VP_2	$\rightarrow VP_1 + (NP_2)$
A	$\rightarrow$ a, an, the
PrPh	$\rightarrow Prp + NP$
M	$\rightarrow (adj) + (adv)$
N	$\rightarrow$ boy, dog, truth, etc.
VP_1	$\rightarrow (Aux_1) + (Aux_2) + V$
NP_2	$\rightarrow NP_1$
Prp	$\rightarrow$ in, to, for, etc.
Adj	$\rightarrow$ good, sad, happy, etc.
Adv	$\rightarrow$ quickly, there, soon, etc.
Aux_1	$\rightarrow$ tense + modal
tense	$\rightarrow$ present + past
modal	$\rightarrow$ will, can, may, do
Aux_2	$\rightarrow$ (be + present participle) + (have + past participle)
V	$\rightarrow$ think, jump, run, etc.

Further note that NP's can be embedded within VP's. Consider: "The man hit the ball". "The ball" is a noun phrase nested in the verb phrase "hit the ball". Consequently, it becomes necessary to distinguish between NP_1, VP_1, NP_2 and VP_2. Examine the tree branching diagram below

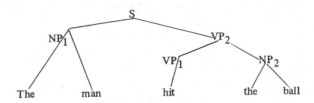

NP_1 consists of optional articles, prepositional phrases, modifiers and an obligatory noun. VP_1 is composed of optional auxiliaries and an obligatory main verb. NP_2 has the same structure as NP_1 but is embedded in VP_2. In other words, $VP_2 = VP_1 + NP_2$.

The following grammatical reminders may be helpful in scoring the LCI. Modifiers specify, restrict or explain another word or phrase. Modifiers are either adverbial or adjectival. Adverbs modify verbs, adjectives or other adverbs. Adverbs are usually formed by adding *ly*. Adverbs indicate time, place, manner or purpose. Adjectives indicate degrees of intensity: fast, faster, fastest. Adjectives modify nouns, pronouns, or phrases with nominal function. Conjunctions join words or phrases with similar grammatical functions. Common conjunctions are: and, but, for, although, since, because, unless, so and also. Caution: sometimes conjunctions can serve as adverbs or prepositions. Auxiliary verbs complete the forms of other verbs. Examples include: be and its various forms (are, is, am, was, were), can, do, have, may and must. Note that some auxiliaries can stand alone and function as main verbs. Infinitives are one type of verb forms consisting of to + the base: to bark. There are two types of participles: present (be + *ing*) and past (have + *ed, en*). Both occur in the NP and VP. If they occur in the NP, they commonly function as modifiers: the jumping rope, the tired man, her maiden name. In the VP, the present participle is preceded by an auxiliary form of *be*: He is running. Analysis of the past participle is more difficult because +ed may indicate either the past tense or the past participle for many regular verbs. For example, the word "jumped" by itself could be either a past tense verb or a past participle. The resolution of this ambiguity lies in examination of the auxiliary. The VP functioning as a predicate contains an auxiliary. It must indicate tense: present or past. The form following *have* in the VP, when have is part of the auxiliary, is the past participle. Other examples of past participles, regular and irregular: driven, walked, hurried, eaten, spoken, left. Both the past participle and past tense verbs are scored as two points according to the LCI procedures. This applies to regular and irregular verbs. For expansion of this grammatical review, see Chomsky (1965), Roberts (1964) and Thomas (1965).

Methodology

Eliciting language samples

Since no standardized procedure yet exists for eliciting verbalizations in children, the clinician must use his best judgment in selecting items of high stimulus value to children. The stimulus items employed in previous language studies may serve as guides. McCarthy (1930) utilized books illustrating animal pictures and Mother Goose rhymes as well as toys consisting of a little red auto, a cat that squeaked, a telephone with a bell, a little tin mouse, a music box and a small ball. Davis (1937) employed the same stimulus materials as McCarthy but added some cowboys and indians for more male interest. Templin (1957) relied solely on the McCarthy approach. Siegel (1962) selected the Children's Apperception Test (CAT) cards as appropriate stimuli for eliciting verbal output. Minifie, Darley and Sherman (1963) tested the temporal reliability of seven language measures using pictures to elicit the language samples. Menyuk (1963a) analyzed language samples obtained from three different situations: The Blacky Pictures, questions from the experimenter and role playing in a family setting. Cowan and his associates (1967) resorted to 10 pictures taken from a popular magazine's cover paintings. Povich and Baratz (1967) decided to present photographs of the child in his natural environment. Regardless of which specific stimulus items future clinicians decide to utilize in sampling a child's verbal output, it is recommended that the stimulus materials be selected from concept areas of interest to young children: work and occupations, home and family life, sex roles, animals, machinery, travel and transportation, and television.

When collecting the language samples, it is important for the examiner bias to be minimized by presenting the same verbal directives with all stimuli to each child being tested. This is done, of course, after the initial rapport building period. Until further research specifies the size of the sample necessary for a reliable analysis, collect 60 consecutively intelligible sentences unless greater precision is needed in research work. From the corpus of 60 sentences, discard the first 10 since they tend to be shorter and less complex than later responses. (McCarthy, 1930.)

Transcribing the responses

Record precisely, paying particular attention to inflected endings, pauses and repetitions. Mark off each grammatical or ungrammatical sentence with hash marks (/). Notice that the language segment under analysis is the sentence, not the traditional "per breath utterance" as in MLR. The sentence may be complete or incomplete and occasionally will extend across a pause. Example: "My mother irons clothes — (slight pause) — every day". While MLR would score this illustration as 2 separate responses, it would be counted as 1 sentence according to LCI. The intent of the LCI is to analyze a child's grammatical rules for his deep structure, not his surface structure. Many times the sentence and the per breath utterance will be the same language segment, but not always. Analysis of the child's grammatical rules should reveal whether a response is an immediate constituent of the preceding sentence. Number each sentence consecutively beginning with number 1. In each sentence underline NP_1 with a single line and VP_2 with a double line.

Word count

Subject and predicate contractions count as two words (same as MLR procedure). Note, some contractions occur in spoken English that are not considered grammatical in written English: it's, it'll, we're, we'll, that's, that'll, what's, waht'll, you've, you'll, I'm, I'll, they're, they'll, she's, she'll, he's, he'll, who's, who'll, mine'll, mine's, where's, where'll, I'd, you'd, he'd, she'd, it'd, they'd, we'd.

Contractions of the verb and negative are counted as one word: didn't, aren't, won't, don't, can't, ain't, wouldn't, couldn't, shouldn't, isn't. The verbs are counted in VP_1 with additional points given elsewhere for the negative element.

Hyphenated words and compound nouns, particularly proper nouns designating a single object, are counted as single words: merry-go-round, cowboy, bubblegum, Miss X, doughnut, ABC's, jack-o-lantern, kool-aid, Santa Claus, Mother Goose.

Starters are eliminated and not scored: oh, and, then, now, um, hey, cause, well, Miss X. However, if any of these words serve a sequencing function rather than as starters, they should be included and counted.

All prepositions are counted except in the following situations: (A) When it is considered part of the inifnitive construction: I'm ready *to eat*; I like *to read*. (B) When it is the last word in a sentence and is elliptical: Me want *to*; I like *to*.

Omit word and/or phrase repetitions when (A) The same word is repeated several consecutive times; count the word only once. (B) When a phrase is repeated or revised, count it only once unless one or more words is different; in that case, count only the phrase with the highest LCI point value. (C) If a word repetition occurs within a phrase repetition, count the word only once. (D) If a contraction is separated in a phrase repetition, count only the phrase repetition with the highest LCI score. (E) Repetitions for emphasis or constituting a fluency failure should be excluded.

Proper names in apposition are eliminated: *Joseph*, what are you doing? *Mister*, you got a flat tire. Also, delete elliptical responses.

Noun phrase

Adjectives which are functioning as nouns are counted as residing in the noun phrase: some more red; big fat two. Adjectives and adverbs are symbolized as M (modifier).

Pronouns serving in the nominative function are counted as noun phrases: I don't know *what* to do; I see *it*. Nouns and pronouns with a nominative function are symbolized as N (noun or pronoun). On the other hand, pronouns serving a possessive function are counted as N + Poss. Count possessive pronouns only if the correct form is used. The intent here, according to Cazden (1965), is not to penalize for incorrectness, but to give credit only where the structure is clear: *Your shirt* = 2 point; *you shirt* = 1 point.

Noun phrases are not considered to extend across pauses. Pauses frequently make structures ambiguous. Furthermore, Brown and Bellugi (1964) present a strong case for the psychological unity of the NP as a sentence constituent. In the following sentence, count only the underlined word: This is — *a dog.*

N + N combinations are counted as single nouns on the NP index. Score as one point: picture stove, telephone bell, tree bird, wrist watch, candy cane, department store.

A is not counted as an article when it is obviously a reduction of another word. It was considered a reduction of *of* in *some a this* and a reduction of *it* in *take a back* (Cazden, 1965).

Plural inflections are not counted separately for a few words which are frequently utilized only as pluralized nouns: scissors, pants.

Most nouns form their plurals by adding [s], [z], or [iz]. A few nouns change form: man, men; child, children. These should be considered appropriately as plural forms and scored as 2 points.

Noun phrase examples and assigned weights. Symbols: N (noun or pronoun), A (article), P (plural inflection), Poss (possessive inflection), Prp (preposition).

Symbols	Examples	Score
A	a, an, the	1
M	big, white, such	1
N	dog, dish	1
A + N	the dog	2
M + N	big dog	2
N + P	dogs	2
N + Poss	dog's, her	2
A + M + N	the big dog	3
A + N + P	the dogs	3
N + Poss + N	her dog	3
A + N + Poss	the dog's	3
M + N + P	big dogs	3
M + N + Poss	big dog's	3
Prp + A + N	by the dog	3
M + M + N	big white dog	4
A + M + N + P	the big dogs	4
A + N + Poss + N	the dog's dish	4
A + M + N + Poss	the white dog's	4
A + M + M + N	the big white dog	5
A + M + N + Poss + N	the big dog's dish	5
M + M + N + P	big white dogs	5
A + M + M + M + N	the great big old dog	6
A + M + M + N + Poss + N	a big old dog's dish	7
A + M + N + Poss + N + P	a big dog's dishes	6

Verb phrase

English verbs indicate 2 main tenses, present or past. For regular verbs, common suffices are *s*, *ed*, or *ing*: jumps, jumped, jumping. Regular verbs form their past tense by adding +d or +ed to its infinitive form. Irregular verbs form their tenses differently: go, went, gone; run, ran, run. Irregular verbs form their past tense usually, but not always, by a vowel change within a verb. Score present tense verbs, regular and irregular form, as 1 point. Assign 2 points to past tense verbs for both regular and irregular forms. Study these examples where the LCI point values are indicated for the VP only: He *gets* it = 1 (gets is 3rd person, irregular, singular); I *jump* = 1; We *ran* = 2; It *fell* = 2.

In infinitive constructions, the word *to* is considered to be part of the verb of the verb and not a preposition. Thus, the word *to* in this case is not scored. Furthermore, the word *to*, when it is an elliptical expression standing for an infinitive, is not scored.

Only lexical verbs and connectives are counted. This procedure eliminates the problem of deciding when particular prepositions are considered part of the verb and when they are not, especially for cases other than the infinitive. For example, in the sentence, "Think up an idea", the question of whether the verb is *think* or *think up* would depend on such factors as intonation, normal usage of the expression by the child and other considerations not determinable through a tapescript. One notable exception exists relative to the rule for counting only lexical verbs. Preverbs are frequently observed in the verbal output of children. Since they indicate the transitional development of a grammatical rule for verb forms, credit for this performance should be given. Score all preverbs as 1 point: gonna, oughta, shoulda, coulda, woulda, and halfta.

Since pauses always contribute some ambiguity to syntactic structures, a verb is counted only if it is on the same side of the pause as its subject. In *Mommy want me – put this on,* want receives a score of 1; similarly *wanna,* in *Her wanna – hold this.*

The verbs in each phrase are counted separately. In *You saw we had turkey, saw* and *had* each receive 1 point.

In the case of a compound predicate, both verbs are counted if they receive the same score; if not, only the verb closest to the subject is counted. In *Somebody jumps and bites,* each verb receives 1 point. In *He's coming and get out,* only the first verb is counted, for a score of 3. This rule prevents any penalty for a correct usage of ellipsis.

No penalty is computed for errors. Only correct responses or obvious approximations are tabulated. The verb phrase weights for some unique constructions are indicated as follows: I dood; it broked. Each verb is scored as two points (V + PsT). He's upped = 3 (Aux + V + PsT).

Scoring of verbs presents many complex and subtle problems. Regular verbs usually form the past tense by adding +ed: jump – jumped, look – looked. Each past tense suffix received one point. Irregular verbs indicate tense differently:

run — ran, come — came, think — thought. Score all irregular past tense verbs as 2 points. Frequent past tense irregular verbs include: went, fell, ran, swam, saw and got.

Verb phrase examples and assigned weights. Symbols: V (verb), PrPt (present participle), Aux (auxiliary), P (plural), PsT (past tense), PreV (preverb), PP (past participle).

Symbols	Examples	Score
PreV	gonna	1
V	go, is, jump	1
V + P	jumps	2
PrPt	going, jumping	2
Aux + PrPt	is going	3
Aux + PP	had jumped	3
Aux + V	can jump	2
Aux + PreV + V	is gonna go	3
Aux + Aux + PP	could have gone	4
V + V	try to go	2
Aux + PrPt + V	am going to get	4
Aux + PP	had arrived	3
Aux + Aux + PP + PrPt	could have been going	6
Aux + PrPt + V + V	am going to try to fix	5

Negatives

The following point system for negatives and questions was based on the research of Bellugi (1966). Four different point levels are operationally defined as regards the usage of negatives.

The negation appears either at the beginning or at the end of the utterance, not within, and consists of *no* or *not* and the rest of the sentence. Score as 1 point: no wash; no singing song; wear mitten no.

Two auxiliary verbs appear in the negative form, *can't* and *don't*. The negative element now appears within the sentence, but may or may not be connected to an auxiliary verb. Score as 2 points: nominal + no, can't, don't + main verb. Examples: I no bit you; I can't catch you; I don't know. Furthermore, at this point level, the negative also appears in the demonstrative form at the beginning of a sentence in the imperative form. Demonstrative + no or not + nominal: That no mommy; that no fish school. Also observed is don't + main verb: Don't leave me.

When the negative form appears between the noun phrase and the present participle, assign a weighting value of 3 points. NP + Ng + PrPt: Me not crying; I no peeking.

The last level exemplifies the adult version of the negative. The sentence includes appropriate intonation. Score as 4 points: *No, it isn't* or *No, I don't have the book*. Auxiliaries are contracted with the negative *n't*: *You didn't eat supper with us; I can't see it.* These sentences are of the form: Nominal + Aux + Ng + V. In child language the verb be is often missing but is now optional. Nominal + (be) + not + nominal objective: *That not a clown* or *I am not a doctor.*

Questions

Questions are formed primarily by a rising intonation, with and without a *wh* word. Bellugi (1966) distinguishes two levels of questions. For the first level, there are no auxiliaries and no subject-verb inversion. There are a few negative questions. Score as 1 point: Mommy eggnog? I ride train? What cowboy see? Who dat? No ear?

At the second level, yes—no questions contain an auxiliary or some form of do. Score as 2 points: Aux + nominal + V + ?; Is mommy talking? Did I hit? The auxiliary component can have an optional negative attachment. Aux + Ng + nominal + V + ?; *Can't you work*? Sometimes the auxiliaries are not inverted: *What he can ride* in? *Why the kitty can't stand* up? The auxiliary is option in *wh* questions: *What is he writing*? *What he is writing*?

Analysis of language samples

The language samples can be analyzed by two different procedures depending upon the diagnostic needs of the clinician. The first approach consists of a numeric analysis of the NP and VP constructions. This yields quantitative information regarding sentence length and complexity which can be used for intra- or inter-group comparisons. The second method specifies the kind and frequency of generative rules observed in the child's utterances. This linguistic analysis will be particularly helpful to the clinician in planning language therapy. Both the numeric and linguistic techniques of analyzing the language samples should prove beneficial to the clinician and researcher.

Numeric analysis

Determine the assigned weights for each sentence according to the scoring rules listed above. Since examples may be more helpful than precepts, scrutinize the following sentences. In doing so, recall that NP_1 is the grammatical subject of the utterance. VP_1 consists of the main verb and auxiliaries, if any. NP_2 is the NP nested in the VP which predicates NP_1. VP_2 is the predicate of NP_1 and consists of $VP_1 + NP_2$. According to the LCI procedure, additional points (AP) are given for the use of conjunctions (C), negatives (Ng) and questions (?). (See the table on next page.)

With this numeric analysis, three measures can be computed: noun phrase index (NPI), verb phrase index (VPI), and length-complexity index (LCI). The formula is NPI = No. of NP_1 points/no. of NP_1's. In the above example, NPI = 27/16, or NPI = 1.69. The formula for the VPI = no. of VP_1 points/no. of VP_1's. In the above example, VPI = 23/14 or VPI = 1.64. Finally, LCI = NP_1 points + VP_2 points + AP/no. of sentences. Usually 50 sentences are analyzed. However, for the above example, LCI = (27 + 57 + 17)/15, or LCI = 6.73.

187

Table 1
Scoring Procedures

	NP		VP		AP		
	NP_1	NP_2	VP_1	VP_2	C	Ng	?
1. A girl							
A + N	2	0	0	0	0	0	0
2. Playing with the ball							
PrPt + Prp + A + N	0	3	2	5	0	0	0
3. A bunny rabbit							
A + N + N	2	0	0	0	0	0	0
4. In our friends							
Prp + M + N + P	0	4	0	4	0	0	0
5. We play with trucks in it							
N + V + Prp + N + P + Prp + N	1	5	1	6	0	0	0
6. He's drawin							
N + Aux + PrPt	1	0	3	3	0	0	0
7. Sometimes we have dollies 'n							
sometimes we don't *							
M + P + N + V + N + P + C	3	2	1	3	1	0	0
M + P + N + V + Ng	3	0	1	1	0	4	0
8. Well, we win'in get to go							
to the root stand							
N + V + C +	1	0	1	1	1	0	0
N + V + V + Prp + A + N + N	1	3	2	5	0	0	0
9. We don't get to go to the ro-root stand							
N + Aux + Ng + V + V + Prp + A + N + N	1	3	3	6	0	2	0
10. But we wanna win							
C + N + PreV + V	1	0	2	2	1	0	0
11. A jack-in-the-box							
A + N	2	0	0	0	0	0	0
12. You wind it – you wind the thing around							
N + V + A + N + M	1	3	1	4	0	0	0
13. Well, if the girls give the man a ticket so							
the girl can get on the train							
Prp + A + N + P + V + A + M + A + N +	4	4	1	5	1	0	0
C + A + N + Aux + V + Prp + A + N	2	3	2	5	0	0	0
14. You know why?							
N + V + N + ?	1	1	1	2	0	0	2
15. Cause, so we won't fall out out the door							
C + N + Aux + Ng + V + Prp + A + N	1	3	2	5	1	4	0

* Treat compound, complex and compound-complex sentences as separate base structure sentences.

Linguistic analysis

Clinically, it is important to determine what rules a child employs for generating sentences before effective remedial instruction is initiated. In fact, knowledge of a child's rules for sentence production may be more therapeutically meaningful than any numeric score. The following illustrations show how the linguistic analysis can be applied to the 15 sentences cited above. However, not all generative rules for NP's and VP's are listed. Other grammatical rules for adult English exist. Furthermore, a child may exhibit knowledge of some rules which are restricted to child's grammar, such as *The momma'll* or *Put the hat.* Clinicians should not view the following list of rules as all inclusive but rather as guidelines for the more frequently occurring rules. When analyzing samples from children with the deviant language patterns, the therapist will probably have to expand the present list to include any ungrammatical rules observed. The language samples should be segmented into largest units possible for NP_1, NP_2 and VP_1.

Table 2
Linguistic analysis of noun phrase.

| NP Rule * | Frequency of occurrence | |
	NP_1	NP_2
N	8	1
A + N + (N)	4	2
M + N	2	0
N + P	0	1
Prp + N + P	0	1
Prp + M + N + P	0	1
Prp + A + N + P	1	0
Prp + A + N	0	4
Prp + N	0	1
A + N + M	0	1

* For list of other possible NP rules, see discussion of NP.

Table 3
Linguistic analysis of verb phrase

| VP Rule * | Frequency of occurrence |
	VP_1
V	7
PrPt	1
Aux + PrPt	1
Aux + V	2
V + V	1
PreV + V	1

* For list of other possible VP rules, see discussion of VP.

189

Clinicians can employ this same format in the analysis of grammatical rules observed in the verbal output of their specific children. Obviously, some different grammatical rules will be observed. These should be listed in their appropriate category. Future research employing this methodology should indicate the frequency of occurrence of grammatical rules to which a specific child's verbalizations can be compared.

Table 4
Linguistic analysis of AP's

Conjunctions		Negatives	Questions
and	= 2	level 1 = 0	level 1 = 0
but	= 1	level 2 = 0	level 2 = 1
so	= 2	level 3 = 0	
since	= 0	level 4 = 2	
because	= 0		
cause	= 0		
for	= 0		

Note that tables 2, 3 and 4 apply only to the 15 sentences exemplified under the linguistic analysis section.

Discussion

Interpretation of LCI

Both numeric and linguistic analyses of the LCI can be computed. The numeric procedure may be employed as a pre- and posttest of developmental changes occurring as a result of maturation and therapy. This technique enables the clinician to quantify the qualitative aspects of verbal maturity. Unfortunately, no normative data has yet been published which enables the therapist to compare a specific child with a large number of peers such as Templin (1957) did with the MLR. This is a problem awaiting further research efforts. Nevertheless, numeric scores may be helpful to the clinician in planning for therapy. Inspection of the NPI and VPI should identify the response variability in a child's verbal output. If a child produced more NP's than VP's, the clinician might want to augment his client's verbal maturity by teaching the child to embed NP's in VP$_2$. Thus, *the big dog* could become *I see the big dog, We ran after the big dog,* or *I saw the big dog and he chased me.* On the other hand, if more VP's than NP's were generated, it might be prudent to begin language therapy by teaching the development of NP's.

Inspection of the linguistic analysis should reveal many implications for therapy. For example, it would be important to identify those generative rules which are restricted to a child's grammar, those utterances which are considered ungrammatical by adult English standards. Possibly such utterances might be modified into adult grammatical rules by operant procedures. Furthermore, the list of NP and VP constructions can be viewed as a very tentative hierarchy of developmental levels for that child. If a child has a rule for NP which is A + N and another NP rule M + N, the clinician might want to begin teaching this NP rule: NP → A + M + N, and then proceed to NP → A + M + M + N. Knowledge of the child's environment and the relative frequency of occurrence of English words (see Thorndike, 1944) should indicate which specific words to teach. Other therapy approaches should also be considered. If a child has a rule for generating a noun, does he use the plural or possessive form of the noun? If he produces a verb, does he use both the present and past tense? Does he use auxiliaries? Auxiliaries must be mastered before grammatically acceptable questions and some other types of transformations can be produced.

The LCI procedure could also be applied to other categories of language impairment. To illsutrate, in aphasia it would be important to know what linguistic rules exist for generating sentences after the neuroloigcal insult. In cases of mental retardation, the clinician should know which grammatical rules a child possesses before attempting to expand his verbal maturity. Finally, with skillful interpretation the LCI approach should help distinguish between the child who is delayed in his language development and the child who uses atypical rules for generating sentences.

Sufficiency of LCI

At present, the LCI is the best single indicator of language development in children five years of age and younger (Shriner, 1968). It can be extended to children older than five when more definitive data on the emergence of transformations is available. This information will eventually yield a weighting system for the more complex utterances in children. The work of Menyuk (1964a) represents a large step towards the analysis of transformational abilities in children and is currently being extended by James (1968). It is also possible that different types of transformed sentences should be analyzed by a psychological scale value procedure to determine various levels of sentence complexity. This technique would represent an extension of Shriner (1967a) work but employing more complex utterances.

In order for the LCI to be considered a reliable measure, it is necessary that one language sample taken at a particular point in time agree closely with samples taken from different but closely adjacent times. Put differently, several language samples taken in close temporal proximity should yield similar results. This is known as temporal or test-retest reliability. Barlow (1968) investigated the temporal reliability of the LCI. Replicating the Minifie, Darley and Sherman (1963) procedure, Barlow attempted to determine the day to day consistency of verbal output in children as measured by the LCI. The resulting intraclass correlation coefficient (r_i) for the LCI was .80 in contrast to an MLR of .65. This was interpreted to mean that a language measure of length and complexity will yield a more reliable estimate of a child's verbal output than will a measure of length alone.

A recent study by Cowan (1967) has stressed the need for a standardized procedure for controlling experimenter bias when sampling a child's verbal output. The Cowan (1967) study underscores the notion that input and output are not separate events but rather are aspects of a unitary coding process. In other words, a child's verbal output is, in part, a function of the stimulus input. The most desirable procedure is to control the relevant variables of stimulus input and experimenter bias so differences in verbal output can be solely attributable to individual differences in children, not the result of contaminatory uncontrolled variables. The best method for eliciting verbalizations in children is, of yet, an unanswered question.

The size of the language sample necessary to compute a valid and reliable LCI is another unanswered but researchable question. Until this issue is empirically researched, the best *a priori* assumption is to follow the lead of Darley and Moll (1960). They conclude that the average of 3 samples of 50 responses each would determine a child's "true" MLR, depending on the degree of precision needed by the researcher. Admittedly, it is a large inductive leap to infer the MLR size of language samples should also prove meaningful for the LCI. It does seem theoretically plausible, however, to assume that the larger the sample, the more closely the LCI measure approaches the "true" mean for a particular child.

One final caution regarding the generalizability of the LCI must be noted. Consideration must be given to differences between the dialect on which the scale was developed and the dialect to which it is being applied (Cazden, 1966, p. 55). The present LCI was developed for analysis with a random selection of midwestern, white children. It presupposes that the generative rules for this particular dialect group and its sequential development are known. If the LCI measure is applied to different social dialects, one must first identify what different rules for generating sentences exist. As one brief example, some Negro dialects consider it acceptable to generate an auxiliary with an unmodified verb: *He's go* or *I'm put*. Such utterances cannot be considered grammatical errors but instead should be viewed as distinctive features of this particular social dialect. The norms of a child's speech community should be the yardstick against which his verbal maturity is evaluated.

References

Barlow, M.C., 1968, *Temporal reliability of the length-complexity index.* Eastern Illinois University, unpublished master's thesis, 1968.

Bellugi, U., 1964, *The emergence of inflections and negation systems in the speech of two children,* paper presented at New England Psychol. Assn. 1964.

Braine, M., 1963, The ontogeny of English phrase structure: the first phase. *Language* 39, 1–13.

Brown, R., and U. Bellugi, 1964, Three processes in the child's acquisition of syntax. *Harvard Educ. Rev.* 34, 133–151.

Brown, R. and C.Fraser, 1963, *The acquisition of syntax.* In: *Verbal Behavior and Learning,* edited by C.N.Cover and B.S.Musgrave. New York: McGraw-Hill.

Carroll, J.B., 1961, Language development in children. In: *Psycholinguistics: A book of Readings,* edited by S.Saporta. New York: Holt, Rinehard and Winston. p. 334.

Cazden, C.B., 1965, *Environmental assistance to the child's acquisition of grammar,* Harvard University, unpublished doctoral dissertation.

Chomsky, N., 1965, *Aspects of the Theory of Syntax.* Cambridge, Mass.: MIT Press.

Cowan, P.A., J.Weber, B.A.Hoddinott and J.Klein, 1967, Mean length of spoken response as a function of stimulus, experimenter and subject. *Child Development* 38, 191–203.

Darley, F.L. and K.L.Moll, 1960, Reliability of language measures and size of language sample, *J. Speech Hearing Res.*.3, 166–173.

Davis, E.A., 1937. Mean sentence length compared with long and short sentences as a reliable measure of language development. *Child Development.* 8, 69–79.

Ervin, S., 1964, Imitation and structural change in children's language. In: *New Directions in the Study of Language,* edited by E.Lenneberg, Cambridge: MIT Press.

Fisher, M.S., 1934, *Language patterns of preschool children.* Child Development Monogr. New York: Teach. Coll., Columbia Univ.

Fraser, C., U.Bellugi and R.Brown, 1963, Control of grammar in imitation, comprehension and production, *J. Verb. Learn. Verb. Behav.* 2, 121–135.

Freedman, M., 1965, *The Compact English Handbook.* New York: David McKay Co., Inc.

Hurley, O., 1967, *Linguistic Analysis of Verbal Interaction in Special Classes for the Mentally Retarded,* Report Project no. 7-0130, Bureau of Research, Office of Education, Dept. of Health, Education and Welfare.

James, S.E., 1968, *Transformational abilities of culturally advantaged and disadvantaged children.* Eastern Illinois University, Unpublished master's thesis.

Lee, L.L., 1966, Developmental sentence types: A method for comparing normal and deviant syntactic development. *J. Speech Hearing Dis.* 31, 311–330.

McCarthy, D.A., 1936, *The language development of the preschool child.* Inst. Child Welf., Monogr. Ser. no. 4, Minneapolis: University of Minn. Press.

McCarthy, D.A., 1954, *Language development in children.* In: *Manual of Child Psychology,* edited by J.Carmichael. New York: Wiley and Sons, chapter 9.

McNeill, D., 1966a, The capacity for language acquisition. *Volta Rev.* 68, 17–33.

McNeill, D., 1966b, Developmental psycholinguistics. In: *The Genesis of Language,* edited by F.Smith and G.A.Miller. Cambridge: MIT Press, pp. 15–34.

Menyuk, P., 1963a, Syntactic structures in the language of children. *Child Development.* 34, 407–422.

Menyuk, P., 1963b, A preliminary evaluation of grammatical capacity in children. *J. Verb. Learn. Verb. Behav.* 2, 429–439.

Menyuk, P., 1964a, Syntactic rules used by children from preschool through first grade, *Child Development* 35, 533–546.

Menyuk, P., 1964b, Alteration of rules in children's grammar. *J. Verb. Learn. Verb. Behav.* 3, 480–488.

Menyuk, P., 1964c. Comparison of grammar of children with functionally deviant and normal speech. *J. Speech Hearing Res.* 7, 109–121.

Miller, W. and S.Ervin, 1964, The development of grammar in child language. In: *The Acquisition of Language,* edited by U.Bellugi and R.Brown. Monogr. Soc. Res. Child Development 23, 9–34.

Minnifie, F., F.L.Darley and D.Sherman, 1963, Temporal reliability of seven language measures. *J. Speech.Hearing Res.* 6, 139–149.

Povich, E., and J.Baratz, 1967, *Grammatical constructions and the language of the Negro-preschool child.* Paper presented at Am. Speech. Hear. Assoc., Chicago.

Roberts, P., 1964, *English Syntax*. New York: Harcourt, Brace and World, Inc.

Sherman, D., T.H.Shriner and F.Silverman, 1967, Psychological scaling of language development of children. *Proc. Iowa Acad. Sci.* 72, 366–371.

Shriner, T.H., 1967, A comparison of selected measures with psychological scale values of language development. *J. Speech.Hearing Res.* 10, 828–835.

Shriner, T.H. and D.Sherman, 1967, An equation for assessing language development. *J. Speech Hear. Res.* 10, 41–43.

Shriner, T.H., 1969, A review of mean length of response as a measure of expressive language development in children. *J. Speech Hear. Dis.* 34, 61–68.

Siegel, G.M., 1960, Verbal behavior of adults as a function of linguistic level of retarded children in "play therapy" sessions. *Parsons Res. Proj. Work. Paper,* no. 36.

Templin, M.C., 1957, Certain language skills in children, their development and inter-relationships. *Inst. Child. Welf., Monogr. Ser.* no. 26. Minneapolis: Univ. Minn. Press.

Thomas, O., 1965, *Transformational Grammar and the Teacher of English*. New York: Holt, Rinehart and Winston.

Thorndike, E.L. and I.Lorge, 1944, *The Teachers Word Book of 30,000 Words,* New York: Teach. Coll., Columbia Univ.

TEMPORAL RELIABILITY OF LENGTH-COMPLEXITY INDEX

Margaret C.BARLOW

and

L.E.MINER

The purpose of this study was to determine the test-retest reliability of a new measure of children's language, the Length-Complexity Index (LCI). There were seventeen subjects who participated in this study, seven males and ten females. The subjects were five-year-old children attending Kindergarten in the Sullivan, Illinois Public Schools. Each of the subjects had normal hearing, average or above average intelligence as measured on the Peabody Picture Vocabulary Test (Dunn, 1965), no obvious neuromuscular disorders, and American English family language background. None were twins, or had a history of stuttering. All subjects came from middle or lower class socioeconomic level families. Language samples were elicited from these children on three separate occasions within a ten-day period by two examiners. The stimulus material constructed to elicit the verbalizations consisted of three sets of pictures judged to be of interest to five-year-old children. The intraclass correlation coefficient for MLR was $r_i = .65$ for the individual child's responses on subsequent retests of single 50-response language samples. This indicates the considerable variability of MLR as a measure of a child's daily verbal output. The intraclass correlation coefficient for the LCI was $r_i = .80$ for the individual child's responses on subsequent retests of single 50-response language samples. The results indicate that within the limits of this study as a language measure the LCI is not as variable as the MLR; that it tends to measure children's language output more reliably over time. This is interpreted to mean that a composite linguistic analysis of length and complexity will yield a more consistent picture of an individual child's verbal output than will a measure of length alone.

Introduction

A recent investigation (Sherman and Shriner 1967) has offered to researchers and language clinicians alike a new tool for measuring expressive language skills in young children. This new classification system, the length-complexity index (LCI), attempts to measure both sentence length and sentence complexity together according to a numeric weighting system. It purports to quantify the developmental changes that occur in child language. The LCI differs from the more traditional mean length of response (MLR) in that it makes a composite analysis of sentence length and syntactic structures, not just length alone.

JOURNAL OF COMMUNICATION DISORDERS, August 1969, vol. 2, no. 3, pp. 241-251.

Shriner (1967) has reported that the LCI is the best single predictor for psychological scale value judgments of verbal maturity in young children. His data, however, were concerned only with language samples elicited in a single testing situation.

In order for the LCI to be considered a reliable measure, it is necessary that several language samples taken over a short period of time yield similar results. This is known as test-retest or temporal reliability. Replicating the Minifie, Darley and Sherman (1963) procedure, the purpose of this investigation is to determine the day-to-day consistency of the verbal output of children as measured by the LCI.

The Length-Complexity Index (LCI) was synthesized by Shriner (1967), based on the research of Menyuk (1964), Bellugi (1964), and Cazden (1965). Menyuk noted that sentence complexity relates to more than sentence length; it is also a function of the ability to apply increasingly differentiated rules for generating sentences. If a child uses a rule to generate a sentence and then proceeds to conjoin two or possibly three similar sentences, the utterance would be obviously increasing in length; however, the utterance would not necessarily be increasing in complexity.

The scoring method for the LCI is derived from Shriner (1967), Bellugi (1964), Cazden (1965), Hurley (1967), and Miner (1968). The following are examples of the scoring method used in this study, scored both as to MLR and LCI. Symbols used are N (noun), M (any modifier), A (article), P (plural inflection), Poss (possessive inflection), Aux (auxiliary), PrPt (present participle), V (verb), PreV (preverb), Ng (negative), PP (past participle), and ? (question).

Example	Symbols	MLR	LCI
Kitties	N + P	1	2
My legs	M + N + P	2	3
The mother cat's tail	A + M + N + Poss + N	4	5
Big old dog's bones	M + M + N + Poss + N + P	4	7
He's going	N + Aux + PrPt	3	4
He'd walked home	N + Aux + PP + N	4	5
I don't want it	N + Aux + Ng + V + N	4	6
Is he going?	Aux + N + PrPt + ?	3	6

The complete rules for scoring the LCI are reported in detail by Miner (1968).

Procedure

Selection of subjects

The seventeen subjects who participated in this study were children living in Sullivan, Illinois from September through December, 1967. They were selected on the basis of age, sex, intelligence, socioeconomic status, auditory acuity, physical status, and family language background. These criteria for the selection of subjects are discussed below.

A. *Age and sex.* There were seven males and ten females selected on the basis of age and attendance at Kindergarten in the Sullivan Public Schools. The mean CA for the males was five years, one month, with a range from four years, eleven months to five years, three months, and a standard deviation of one and one-half months. The mean CA for the females was five years, two months, with a range from four years, ten months to five years, four months, with a standard deviation of two months. There was no statistically significant difference between the CAs of the males and females. The resulting student t ratio was .44 (df = 15).

B. *Intelligence.* Initially, only those children whose scores ranged from 80–130 on the Peabody Picture Vocabulary Test (Dunn, 1965) (a test of recognition vocabulary) were considered for inclusion in this study. This cutoff score was used because the IQ equivalents obtained on the Peabody tend to be systematically higher than the IQ scores on a test such as the Stanford-Binet (1951). The mean MA for the females was five years, three months, with a standard deviation of eight months. The mean IQ for the females was 101.4, with a standard deviation of 7.92.

The mean MA for the males was six years, two months, with a standard deviation of eight months. The mean IQ for the males was 111.71, with a standard deviation of 5.40. There was a statistically significant difference in the MAs between males and females. The resulting t ratio of 2.81 (df = 15) was significant beyond the .01 level. There was a statistically significant difference between the CAs and the MAs of the males. The resulting t ratio of 3.90 (df = 12) was significant beyond the .01 level.

C. *Hearing.* A pure-tone audiometric sweep-check at 500, 1000, and 2000 Hz in both ears was administered to all children. A Beltone audiometer, Model C calibrated to 1964 ISO standards, was used to present the pure tone at a level of 25 dB re: .0002 dynes per cm^2. No children were eliminated for participation in this study on the basis of insufficient auditory sensitivity. All children included in this study were considered to have essentially normal hearing for the speech frequencies.

D. *Physical status.* The subjects exhibited no obvious neuromuscular involvements as determined by observation of the experimenter.

E. *Family language background.* No subjects came from homes with bilingual background. This particular community has a minority Amish population, and these children were excluded from this study. No subject was a twin, since previous research has shown that twins differ systematically from the "normal" language development pattern (Day 1932; Davis 1934). Children who had a history of stuttering were also excluded from the study.

F. *Socioeconomic status.* The families of the subjects were evaluated on the basis of the Index of Status Characteristics (Warner 1949). Children were randomly selected from a list of all five-year-old children attending in Sullivan,

Illinois. It was assumed that such a procedure would result in cross-sectional sampling of the socioeconomic levels present in that community; however, ten of the seventeen subjects were level five, lower class. One subject was upper middle class, and the remaining six were lower middle and upper lower class.

Language samples were elicited from each child on three separate occasions. Nine of the subjects were tested in the morning, and eight were tested in the afternoon. Two examiners were utilized to elicit the verbalizations; each examiner saw the same child on each of the three testing situations. Both examiners were experienced in eliciting child language samples by virtue of their clinical and academic background.

The three speech samples were elicited within a ten-day period. The duration was short enough so that maturational influences on verbal output were assumed to be negligible. Sixty verbal responses were elicited from each child.

The experimenter constructed three sets of stimulus pictures judged by university speech pathologists to be of interest to five-year-olds. There was a random order of presentation between sets of pictures, but the order of presentation of pictures within a set was constant. These pictures were taken from pre-primers of several basic reading series. The pictures were presented to the child one at a time, and he was asked "to tell a story about the picture". In instances where the child had difficulty responding to the pictures, the examiners attempted to stimulate conversation by interjecting such questions as "What else is happening in this picture?"

Each session was tape recorded on a Wollensak tape recorder, model T-1500. The experimenter listened to the tapes and transcribed the first 60 responses elicited from each child for each of the three recording sessions. The first ten verbalizations were discarded because they tend to be shorter and less complex than later responses (McCarthy 1930). Measures from analysis for each speech sample elicited included mean length of response (MLR) and length-complexity index (LCI). The rules for computing the MLR have been defined by Templin (1957), following the McCarthy (1930) procedure. The rules for scoring the LCI were developed independently by Cazden (1965), Bellugi (1964), Hurley (1967) and Shriner (1967) and then synthesized by Miner (1969).

Recorder reliability

Recorder reliability was estimated in order to determine the examiner's ability to identify spoken responses. What constitutes a verbal response is sometimes difficult to determine: (a) not all pauses represent breaks between responses; (b) some responses are made up of two short sentences; and (c) a single response may include a change in thought content. The McCarthy (1930) procedure was used to determine how well the examiner agreed with other observers in identifying spoken responses. The examiner and two other observers, professors in speech pathology with experience in scoring child language samples, independently recorded the first 35 remarks of three five-year-old subjects. Each observer independently listened to the tape-recorded speech sample for three children and pre-pared a written script of what he considered to represent these 35 remarks uttered. The number of agreements and disagreements between the examiner and each of the other two observers were tabulated for each subject.

There was a 76% agreement among the experimenter and two independent observers relative to the trnscription of the utterances of each of three subjects. Further analysis of this data revealed differences between the experimenter and the independent observers were due to different views on segmentation of utter-ances rather than differences in lexical items. These differences in segmentation were factored out, and the percentage of agreement was recomputed. The result-ing agreement score was 99%. This was interpreted to mean that there was a high percentage of agreement between the experimenter and the independent re-corders, except on the matter of segmentation. Therefore, it was necessary to re-examine the operational definition of what constitutes an utterance, both for MLR and LCI. For the MLR, the experimenters used the Templin (1957) defini-tion of "per-breath utterance". For the LCI, the intent of the measure is to ana-lyze a child's grammatical rules for his deep structure, not his surface structure. Sometimes an utterance will extend across a pause in order to complete the grammatical unit. Many times the sentence and the per-breath utterance will be the same language segment, but not always. The experimenter discussed the operational definitions of the MLR and LCI with the two independent observers and all agreed that these were valid procedures to follow. Consequently, it was concluded that when the independent observers follow the same operational defi-nitions for transcribing utterances, the utterances can be reliably transcribed from tape recordings as evidenced by the 99% agreement obtained.

Scorer reliability

Intra-scorer agreement for the experimenter was found for two verbalization measures: MLR and LCI. From the typed speech samples the experimenter re-scored 300 responses from six different subjects, for both MLR and LCI. The obtained Pearson Product-Moment Correlation Coefficient between the first and second scorings were 1.00, for both measures, showing the experimenter was satisfactorily consistent in scoring responses.

Inter-scorer agreement for the experimenter and one independent observer were obtained for both the MLR and LCI. This independent observer rescored 200 responses from four different children. The resulting Pearson Product Mo-ment Correlation Coefficient between the first and second scorings was 1.00, indicating consistent scoring agreement between two examiners.

Results and discussion

Results

The temporal reliability for the MLR and the LCI were computed by means of the Intraclass Correlation Coefficient (Ebel 1951). The resulting correlations are indicated in table 1.

Table 1
Intraclass correlation coefficients for MLR and LCI

Language measure	r_i	r_{ave}
MLR	.65	.85
LCI	.80	.92

The first correlation coefficient (r_i) was computed to evaluate the reliability of an individual's responses on subsequent retests of single 50-response language samples. Inspection of (r_i) in table 1 reveals a higher temporal reliability for the LCI than the MLR. This is interpreted to mean that a composite linguistic analysis of length and complexity will yield a more consistent picture of an individual child's verbal output than will a measure of length alone.

The second coefficient (r_{ave}) was computed to determine the group reliability of averages over three trials for both language measures. The (r_{ave}) differs from (r_i) in that it is a measure of group consistency over three trials, whereas (r_i) is a measure of individual consistency over three trials. Inspection of (r_{ave}) in table 1 reveals a slightly higher correlation for LCI than MLR. This is interpreted to mean that the temporal reliability correlation coefficients are higher for both measures of a group, as opposed to an individual basis. Clinically, the experimenter's greatest concern is with the consistency of an individual's linguistic performance, (r_i), since language evaluations are concerned with individuals, not groups. In other words, it is important to know how representative a child's language sample is of his daily verbal performance over time. Consequently, Table 1 reveals that within the parameters of this study the LCI is a more consistent measure of verbal maturity than MLR.

Derived mean scores and standard deviations for MLR and LCI are reported in table 2.

Table 2
MLR and LCI scores for each sample time

Language measure	Time 1		Time 2		Time 3	
	M	SD	M	SD	M	SD
MLR	5.34	1.43	5.14	1.02	5.65	1.08
LCI	5.99	1.49	5.74	1.12	6.39	1.20

Inspection of table 2 reveals that the derived MLR scores approximate very closely the data reported by Templin (1957, p. 79), for this age group and socioeconomic status. Furthermore the LCI mean scores are consistently higher than

MLR mean scores, because complexity as well as length is included in the scoring system. Rank ordering the mean scores for the three sample times, it should be noted that the highest mean score was obtained in sample 3, followed by sample 1, and then sample 2. In an effort to assess the significance of the difference between the mean scores for the three sample times, student t tests were computed for both MLR and the LCI. The resulting t ratios within both the MLR and LCI were nonsignificant, less than 1.00. This is interpreted to mean that within each language measure the derived mean scores were not significantly different and that this population was homogeneous in their responses from sample to sample.

A further analysis was made in order to determine the correlations within and between the two language measures. The resulting Pearson Product Moment Correlation Coefficients are reported in table 3.

Table 3
Within and between correlation coefficients for MLR and LCI

Measure	MLR−2	MLR−3	LCI−1	LCI−2	LCI−3
MLR−1	.78	.64	.99	.79	.65
MLR−2	−	.46	.78	.96	.48
MLR−3	−	−	.65	.49	.97
LCI−1	−	−	−	.79	.69
LCI−2	−	−	−	−	.53

* r = .48 at 5% level, and .61 at 1% level (df = 15).

Inspection of table 3 reveals a wide range of correlations within and between the two language measures. For example, the Pearson r between MLR Sample 1 and LCI Sample 1 is .99. If one language sample only is taken, this might lead one to conclude that the correlation would always be high. Inspection of other *single* sample correlations is deceptive because of the range from .99 to .46. These ranges influence the interpretation of the reliability of the measures. The greatest variation in correlations obtained seems to be related to Sample 3 for both MLR and LCI. Note that within MLR neither Sample 1 nor Sample 2 correlate highly with Sample 3. However, Samples 1 and 2 correlate highly with each other. The same pattern is revealed within the LCI samples. However, MLR−3 and LCI−3 are highly correlated suggesting that whatever variable (s) affected Sample 3, the effects are revealed in both measures. The variation in correlations for single sample responses reinforces the importance of determining the temporal reliability of any language measure. By this type of analysis, clinicians and researchers can assess whether measures of language development may be considered reliable.

Discussion

There are several factors to consider in interpreting the data. One is the problem of examiner bias. There is the possibility that different examiners obtain different results, especially if examiner variables interact with subject and stimulus variables (Cowan et al. 1967).

Some intervening variable appears to have influenced the correlation with sample three since the obtained correlations for this sample time are the lowest observed. It is hypothesized that these low correlations are a result of a time differential between the sample times. Examiner no. 1 elicited samples two and three on consecutive days, while Examiner no. 2 had a five day period between Samples two and three. Examiner no. 1 was ill during the taking of Sample three also, and the questions interjected by her were not of the same quality as during the other two sessions.

Another problem of interpretation is that of stimulus material bias. Very few studies have used the same stimulus material to elicit verbalizations. The sets of pictures used may not have been the most interesting to children of this age-group, despite the fact that they were so judged by the experimenter. This factor underscores the need to develop a standardized procedure for eliciting verbalizations in children. Media studies are now underway which should indicate which stimulus material among toys, still pictures, and movies produce the most verbalizations in children (Strandberg 1968; Mintun 1968).

A fourth variable to be considered in the interpretation of the data is that of sample size. There were only seventeen subjects available for analysis, all of whom met the criteria for participation in this study. The factor of sample size, for example, could account, in part, for differences between this study and the one reported by Minifie, Darley and Sherman (1963). They obtained intraclass correlation coefficient for the MLR (r_i) = .82, in contrast to the (r_i) = .65 in this study. Besides differences in sample size, it must also be remembered that their subjects were slightly older and represented different socioeconomic levels. While there were only seventeen subjects in the study, 2550 sentences were analyzed. Consequently, the sample size is not as small as it might appear on first impression.

A fifth variable, which became evident after the samples were elicited, was the MA difference between the males and the females in the sample. The males had significantly higher MA's than the females, although there were only seven males and ten females.

The use of MLR in language analysis continues because McCarthy declared that no measure seems to have superseded it "for a reliable, easily determined, objective, quantitative, and easily understood measure of linguistic maturity" (McCarthy 1954, p. 550). The fact remains, however, that after MLR is computed, all the clinician has is a numerical score for linguistic performance. It tells nothing about the grammatical structures a child has, or his ability to generate grammatical rules.

When the LCI is computed, its greater temporal reliability, as indicated in table 1, shows it to be a more stable indicator of a child's verbal maturity than the MLR. The examiner has more information from its linguistic analysis. Computation of the LCI takes more skill and orientation of the part of the examiner, but the results justify the time spent. In addition, it has profound implications for planning therapy. For example, inspection of the noun phrase index (NPI) and the verb phrase index (VPI) should indicate the child's response strengths and weaknesses. If he has more VP's than NP's it might be wise to begin therapy with teaching the development of NP's. If a child has a rule for NP's which is A + N, and another rule which is M + N, the clinician may wish to begin teaching with the NP rule: A + M + N = NP. Other therapy approaches can be considered. If a child has a rule for generating a noun, does he also use the rule for forming plurals or the possessive form of that noun? If he produces a verb, does he use both the present and past tenses? Does he use auxiliaries? Auxiliaries must be mastered before grammatically acceptable questions can be produced.

The LCI could be applied to other categories of language impairment. In aphasia, it would be important to know what linguistic rules exist following neurological damage. With skillful interpretation, the LCI approach should help to distinguish between those children who are delayed in language development, and those who are disordered in their language development.

Conclusions

From the results of the present study on its temporal reliability, the LCI would seem to be a more reliable measure of verbal output in children than the MLR. Furthermore, on the basis of previous research by Shriner (1967) it would seem to be the best single measure of a child's language abilities.

References

Bellugi, Ursula, 1964, *The emergence of inflections and negation systems in the speech of two children,* paper presented at New England Psych. Assn.

Braine,, M., 1963, The ontogeny of English phrase structure: the first phase. *Language* 39, 1–13.

Brown, R. and U.Bellugi, 1964, Three processes in the child's acquisition of syntax, *Harvard Educ. Rev.* 34, 133–151.

Brown, R. and O.Fraser, 1963, *The acquisition of syntax.* In: Verbal behavior and learning, edited by O.M.Cofer and S.S.Musgrove. New York: McGraw-Hill.

Carrol, J.B., 1961, *Language development in children.* In: Psycholinguistics: a book of readings, edited by S.Saporta. New York: Holt, Rinehart and Winston, p. 334.

Cazden, C.B., 1965, Environmental assistance to the child's acquisition of grammar. Unpublished doctoral dissertation, Harvard University.

Chomsky, M., 1965, *Aspects of the theory of syntax.* Cambridge, Mass.: MIT Press.

Cowan, P.A., J.Wober, B.A.Hoddinott and J.Klein, 1967, Mean length of spoken response as a function of stimulus, experimenter and subject. *Child Development* 38, 191–203.

Darley, F.L. and K.L.Moll, 1960, Reliability of language measures and size of language sample, *J. Speech Hear. Res.* 3, 166–173.

Davis, E., 1937, Mean sentence length compared with long and short sentences as a reliable measure of language development. *Child Development* 8, 69—79.

Day, E.J., 1932, The development of language in twins: I. A comparison of twins and single children. *Child Development* 3, 179—199.

Dunn, L.M., 1965, *Manual for the Peabody Picture vocabulary test*. Minneapolis: American Guidance Service.

Ervin, S., 1964, Imitation and structural change in children's language. In: *New directions in the study of language*, edited by E.Lenneberg. Cambridge: MIT Press.

Fraser, C., U.Bellugi and R.Brown, 1963, Control of grammar in imitation, comprehension and production. *J. Verb. Learning, Verb Behavior* 2, 121—135.

Lee, L.L., 1966, Developmental sentence types: A method for comparing normal and deviant syntactic development. *J. Speech Hear. Dis.* 31, 311—330.

McCarthy, D.A., 1954, Language development in children. In: *Manual of child psychology*, chapter 9, edited by L.Carmichael. New York: Wiley and sons.

McCarthy, D.A., 1930. *The language development of the preschool child*. Inst. Child. Welf., Monogr. Ser., no. 4, Mineapolis: University of Minn. Press.

McNeill, D., 1966, The capacity for language acquisition. *Volta Rev.* 68, 17—33.

McNeill, D., 1968. Developmental Psycholinguistics. In: *The genesis of language*, edited by F.Smith and G.A.Miller. Cambridge: MIT Press 15—84.

Menyuk, P., 1963a, Syntactic structures in the language of children. *Child Development* 34, 407—422.

Menyuk, P., 1964a, Syntactic rules used by children from preschool through first grade. *Child Development* 35, 533—546.

Menyuk, P., 1964b, Alteration of rules in children's grammar. *J. Verb. Learning, Verb. Behav.* 3, 480—488.

Menyuk, P., 1964c, Comparison of grammar of children with functionally deviant and normal speech. *J. Speech Hear. Res.* 7, 109—121.

Miller, W. and S.Ervin, 1964, The development of grammar in child language. In: *The acquisition of language*, edited by U.Bellugi and R.Brown. *Monogr. Soc. Res. Child. Development* 28, 9—34.

Miner, L.E., 1969, Scoring procedures for the length-complexity index: a preliminary report. *J. Comm. Dis.* 2 (1969) 224—240.

Minifie, R., F.L.Darley and D.Sherman, 1963, Temporal reliability of seven language measures. *J. Speech Hearing Res.* 6, 139—149.

Mintun, S., 1968. *A preliminary investigation of certain procedures for eliciting verbalizations in EMH children*. Unpublished Master's Thesis, Eastern Illinois University.

Povich, E. and J.Baratz, 1967, Grammatical constructions and the language of the Negro Preschool Child, paper presented at the *Am. Speech Hear. Ass.*, Chicago.

Revised Stanford-Binet Intelligence Scale, Third Revision. Boston: Houghton-Mifflin, 1951.

Sherman, D., T.H.Shriner and F.Silverman, 1967, Psychological scaling of language development of children. *Proc. Iowa Acad. Sci.* 72.

Shriner, T.H., 1967, A comparison of selected measures with psychological scale values of language development. *J. Speech Hear. Res.* 10, 828—835.

Shriner, T.H. and D.Sherman, 1967b, An equation for assessing language development. *J. Speech Hearing Res.* 10, 41—48.

Shriner, T.H., 1969, A review of mean length of response as a measure of expressive language development in children. *J. Speech Hearing Dis.*

Siegel, O.M., 1962, Inter-examiner reliability for mean length of response. *J. Speech Hearing Res.* 5, 91—95.

Strandberg, T., 1968, *A preliminary investigation of certain procedures of eliciting verbalizations in normal children*. Unpublished Master's Thesis, Eastern Illinois University.

Templin, M.C., 1957, Certain language skills in children, their development and inter-relationships. *Inst. Child. Welf. Monogr. Ser.* no. 26, Minneapolis: Univ. of Minn. Press.

Thomas, O., 1966, *Transformational grammar and the teacher of English.* New York: Holt, Rinehart, Winston.

Thorndike, L.E., 1944, Teacher's Wordbook of 30,000 Words, Bureau of Pub. Teachers Coll. Columbia University.

Warner, W.L., M.Meaker and K.Eells, 1949, Social Class in America (a manual of procedure for the measurement of social status). Chicago: Science Research Assoc.

LCI RELIABILITY AND SIZE OF LANGUAGE SAMPLE

Jerry GRIFFITH and L.E.MINER

Language samples were evoked under four stimulus conditions from 36 children between the ages of four and five. The purpose was to evaluate the reliability of the LCI in relation to the size of the language sample. Each sample was divided into five response segments (5, 10, 15, 20 and 25) and was correlated with its total 50 response LCI score. The reliability analysis suggests that LCI scores based on 15 responses are quite satisfactory for most research purposes.

Introduction

The purpose of this study was to answer the question of how large a sample of children's verbal output must be evoked in order to obtain reasonably reliable length-complexity index (LCI) scores. The LCI is a linguistic measure designed to make a composite analysis of sentence length and sentence complexity according to a numeric weighting system. It is a modified offspring of two prior measures, the mean length of response (McCarthy 1954, ch. 9) and the structural complexity score (Templin 1957, p. 81). Recent articles have discussed the theoretical rationale (Shriner 1967) and clinical application (Miner 1969) of the LCI. Essentially, the LCI provides more linguistic information relative to morphological and syntactical developmental changes which occur with increased chronological age than do the older independent measures, mean length of response (MLR) and the structural complexity score (SCS). Shriner (1967) has reported that the LCI is the best single predictor of expressive language abilities in children five years of age and younger. His conclusion was based on the results of psychological scaling procedures which were subjected to multiple regression analyses. The LCI predictor was the only significant remaining weight.

The Shriner data discussed above deals only with verbal responses in single testing situations. In order for the LCI to be considered a reliable measure, several language samples taken over short time periods should yield similar results when relevant variables are controlled. This is referred to as test-retest or temporal reliability. Recently, Barlow and Miner (1969) investigated the day to day consistency of verbal output in children as measured by the LCI. The resulting intraclass correlation coefficient revealed a higher temporal reliability for the LCI ($r_i = .80$, $n = 17$) than for the MLR ($r_i = .65$; $n = 17$). This was interpreted to

JOURNAL OF COMMUNICATION DISORDERS, 1969, vol. 2, pp. 264-267.

mean that a composite linguistic analysis of length and complexity will yield a more consistent picture of an individual child's verbal output than will a measure of length alone.

In summarizing the current literature relative to the LCI, the following statements can be made within the context of the studies in which they were reported.

1. Increased verbal maturity is not only a function of increased sentence length but also of the ability to apply increasingly differentiating rules for generating sentences (Menyuk 1964).

2. The clinical sufficiency of the MLR is questionable (Shriner 1968).

3. The best single predictor of psychological scale values of language development in children five years and younger is the LCI (Shriner 1967).

4. The LCI has higher temporal reliability than the MLR and, consequently, yields a more stable picture of a child's expressive language abilities (Barlow and Miner 1969).

5. The LCI provides more linguistic information applicable to planning language therapy than indicated by the MLR (Miner 1969).

The data reported by Shriner (1967) and Barlow and Miner (1969) suggest that the LCI is an appropriate linguistic measure fully applicable to the verbal output of preschool children. Since the LCI appears to be sensitive to developmental changes in language facility, the question arises as to how large a language sample is needed in order to obtain reasonably reliable LCI scores. Traditionally, the MLR has required 50 responses in order to obtain reliable information. In the case of the LCI, it seemed plausible to ascertain whether a smaller sample might still yield reliable LCI values. If so, it would render a time-consuming procedure greater efficiency.

Procedure

The language protocols of 36 children constituted the data for analysis in this study. The protocols represented 50 responses evoked from 7 males and 10 females. The language samples were evoked under four different stimulus conditions: (1) in response to pictures commonly regarded as "reading readiness" material for 17 subjects, (2) in response to photographs of individual toys taken by 6 subjects, (3) in response to photographs taken in their home environment by 7 subjects, and (4) in response to photographs taken in their home environment by 6 subjects following receipt of visual literacy training. Stimulus condition one represents the subjects reported in the Barlow and Miner (1969) study, whereas stimulus conditions two through four constitute a portion of the subjects reported by Strandberg and Griffith (1969). The two sex groups were essentially equivalent with regard to chronological age, intelligence, and auditory acuity. The sexes combined mean chronological age was 5 years, 1 month with a range from 4 years, 5 months to 5 years, 9 months. Intelligence was determined in terms of performance on the Peabody Picture Vocabulary Test (1965) and the

Ammons Ammons Quick Test (1965). The mean mental age was 5 years, 10 months with a range from 4 years, 9 months to 8 years, 6 months. Normal hearing was required as determined by an audiometric sweep hearing test at 500, 1000 and 2000 Hz at 30 dB (ISO 1964).

The verbalizations of each child were tape recorded and a typewritten transcript of the responses was prepared for analysis. The first 10 verbalizations were discarded since they tend to be systematically shorter than subsequent responses (McCarthy 1930). From the remaining corpus, LCI scores were computed on the basis of the first five, first ten, first fifteen, first twenty, first twenty-five and first fifty responses. These scores were determined according to the procedure described by Miner (1969). Each of the five response segments was correlated (Pearson Product-Moment Coefficient of Correlation) with the total 50 response language sample.

Results and discussion

Table 1 describes the LCI scores obtained with different sample sizes and compares them with the LCI score obtained from a sample size conventionally accepted as adequate. A high correlation is obtained between scores based on a sample of fifteen utterances and scores based on fifty utterances with a $S.E._{measure}$ of less than one point. This means that an LCI based on fifteen utterances will be within 1.96 $S.E._{measure}$ 95% of the time or 2.58 $S.E._{measure}$ 99% of the time. That is, if a child's LCI is 12 based on his first fifteen utterances, we have 95% confidence that his true LCI is between 10.08 and 13.92 and 99% confidence that his true LCI is between 9.47 and 14.53.

The $S.E._{mean}$ was computed for each sample size as a means of predicting representativeness of a given sample compared to a large sample. With a sample size of fifteen utterances and a mean LCI for the sample of 8.267 we have 95% confidence that the true mean is that value ± 1.636.

The reliability of a measure increases with an increase in sample size. Further, the precision of measurement required in a given situation is determined by

Table 1

Descriptive comparisons of LCI scores based on the first five, first ten, first fifteen, first twenty and first twenty-five utterances with an LCI based on fifty utterances ($N = 36$).

Sample size	Mean LCI	S.D.	$S.E._{mean}$	$S.E._{measure}$	$r*$
5	8.322	4.313	.729	1.92	.80
10	8.456	4.269	.722	1.48	.88
15	8.267	3.754	.634	.98	.93
20	8.138	3.572	.603	.79	.95
25	8.154	3.694	.624	.69	.97
50	8.251	3.173	.536	–	–

* All r's are significant beyond the .001 level of confidence.

many factors and the purposes for making the measures, e.g. clinical prediction or research hypothesis testing. On the basis of the data in table 1 the reliability of the LCI measures is not significantly increased beyond those determined from a language sample of fifteen utterances. In addition, a child's true LCI score will be only slightly more than two and a half points (2.53) greater or lesser than his score based on this sample size. While this would appear to be an acceptable margin, those desiring a higher degree of precision can achieve it by increasing the sample size. A sample size of twenty-five utterances reduces the disparity between the obtained LCI and the predicted true LCI from two and a half points to slightly more than one and a half points (1.78).

Previously, Miner (1969) had recommended that 50 LCI samples be evoked for analysis. This recommendation was based on *a priori* assumptions following MLR procedures. It now appears that fifteen utterances will yield a reliable sample for analysis in most situations and, as a consequence, save the examiner time and effort in data analysis.

References

Ammons, R.B. and C.H.Ammons, 1965, *Quick Test (QT)*, Missoula, Montana: Psychological Test Specialists.

Barlow, M.C. and L.E.Miner, 1969, Temporal reliability of the length-complexity index. *J. Comm. Dis.* (in press).

Dunn, L.M., 1965, *Manual for the Peabody Picture Vocabulary Test.* Minneapolis: American Guidance Service.

McCarthy, D.A., 1954, Language development in children. In: *Manual of Child Psychology*, edited by L.Carmichael. New York: Wiley and Sons.

Menyuk, P., 1964, Syntactic rules used by children from preschool through first grade. *Child Developm.* 35, 533–546.

Miner, L.E., 1969, Scoring procedures for length-complexity index: a preliminary report. *J. Comm. Dis.* (in press).

Shriner, T.H., 1967, A comparison of selected measures with psychological sclae values of language development. *J. Speech Hearing Res.* 10, 828–835.

Shriner, T.H., 1968, A review of mean length of response of a measure of expressive language development in children. *J. Speech Hear. Dis.* (in press).

Strandberg, T. and J.Griffith, 1969, A study of the effects of training in visual literacy on verbal language behavior. *J. Comm. Dis.* (in press).

Templin, M.C., 1957, *Certain language skills in children: their development and inter-relationships.* Inst. Child. Welf., Monogr. Ser. no. 26, Minneapolis: Univ. Minn. Press.

SOME RELATIONSHIPS BETWEEN MEASURES OF EARLY LANGUAGE DEVELOPMENT

Donald J. Sharf

Some relationships between language measures based on verbal output (Mean Length of Response and Number of Different Words) and those based on structural analysis (Length-Complexity Index and Developmental Sentence Types) were investigated by longitudinally analyzing the early language development of 13 children. Seven recordings were made of eight boys and five girls at two- to four-month intervals beginning at an average age of 21 months. A method for quantifying the DST was devised, and all the recordings were analyzed to compare scores for the measures. It was found that (1) variability in the rate of increase in language development scores made age a poor basis for comparing children, using any language measure; (2) there was considerable agreement among measures in reflecting the rate of language development; (3) all the language measure scores seemed to be equally related to language growth, so each provided a reasonable index of the complexity of the underlying language structure; and (4) the reliability of trained scorers was as good for measures based on structural analysis as it was for those based on verbal output.

The development of objective standards with which to describe and quantify speech and language in children has long been a major goal of research. The most extensively studied measures have been those assessing verbal output, such as mean length of response (MLR) and number of different words (NDW).

Recently, through work in linguistics, measures have been developed involving structural analysis of the child's language. One such measure, based on a theoretical hierarchy of developmental sentence types (DST) (Lee, 1966), views a child's language development as cumulative, with success at lower levels necessary to the attainment of higher language development. Lee designates four levels of structural complexity. Level 1 is made up of the child's first two-word combinations. Level 2 is the noun phrase of more than two words. Level 3 is composed of four different types of phrase constructions: designative, predicative, verb phrase, and stereotyped. With the exception of stereotyped phrases, Level 3 phrases are noun phrases to which has been added a pivot word serving a more structurally complex function either as a predicate of the noun, a designator of the noun, or a verb. Level 4 is the complete sentence including subject, verb, and object of the verb, if necessary.

JOURNAL OF SPEECH AND HEARING DISORDERS, Feb. 1972, vol. 37, no. 1, pp. 64-74.

Shriner (1967) developed a language measure, length-complexity index (LCI), which is a modified combination of mean length of response (McCarthy, 1954) and the structural complexity score (Templin, 1957). The LCI is a numerical score obtained from a child's language sample by combining noun and verb phrase points and additional points for negatives and questions. A major problem with measures of verbal output, such as MLR, is that they do not provide information about grammatical and syntactical development. However, it seems logical to infer that, as MLR increases, there are systematic changes in the structural aspects of language. If so, it should be possible to relate such changes in measures like LCI to increases in verbal output in measures like MLR. The purpose of this study was to investigate some of the relationships between language measures based on verbal output (MLR and NDW) and those based on structural analysis (LCI and DST), by analyzing the early language development of a group of children.

OBTAINING THE LANGUAGE SAMPLES

The 13 children used as subjects were obtained by various means. Some were solicited through appeals to university students, church groups, and mothers of children treated in a well-baby clinic. An attempt was made to randomize the sampling procedure by using birth notices from approximately 18-month-old local newspapers as a source for soliciting volunteers. Even so, parents who volunteered their children for study and persevered long enough to be included in the data analysis probably represented a somewhat biased sample. For example, six parent pairs had college degrees and all parents had at least a high-school education.

Since it was not this study's purpose to obtain normative data, no attempt was made to record each child at a specific age. Instead, the child's age at his first recording was used as a base, and all the children were recorded at approximately the same intervals following that initial sample.

An attempt was made to start subjects on the sampling sequence as soon as they constituted a sample large enough for analysis. In a questionnaire, parents were asked to indicate whether the child had a vocabulary of 50 words. Children were brought in for their first recording when they reached this criterion.

Recordings of approximately 45 to 60 minutes were made of children at two- to four-month intervals beginning between 17 and 24 months of age. At each recording session, there were present the examiner, the child, and the child's mother or father, who was asked to repeat the utterances so as to identify them. The examiner sought to stimulate responses from the child by presenting a collection of toys and objects for the child to identify and discuss. In the course of the investigation, it was necessary to use two different examiners; they worked with the same test battery and followed the same test procedures.

Recordings were transcribed without the transcribers' knowing the actual chronological order of the tapes. From each of these tapes, 50 responses were transcribed after eliminating the first 10 responses. The criteria used in defining a response have been specified by Winitz (1959) and Miner (1969). Pauses and inflectional patterns were used in determining questions, declarative statements, and termination of utterances.

One-word utterances were accepted only if the child named an object independently of the examiner's question; automatic, echolalic, and unintelligible responses and "fill-in" answers were deleted. Fill-in answers were interpreted as specific replies to questions such as "What is this?" These answers were excluded on the basis that they were not expressive of spontaneous grammatical construction.

After the tapes were transcribed, the LCI, DST, NDW, and MLR measures were calculated. The MLR was computed by totaling the number of words in each response and dividing by the number of responses, usually 50. The criteria for word count were generally those outlined by Johnson, Darley, and Spriestersbach (1963). Criteria for the NDW measure were the same as those for the MLR. NDW was determined by counting the number of different words.

Utterances were classified into the four levels of the DST according to the criteria outlined by Lee (1966), except that one-word responses were classified at Level 0. The DST was not developed as a quantitative measure, but for comparative purposes a weighted score was computed for each child as follows: the number of utterances at each level was converted into a percentage of the total number of responses; Level 0 percentage was multiplied by 1, Level 1 by 2, Level 2 by 3, and so on, and the products were summed.

The LCI was calculated by scoring responses in terms of the whole subject noun phrase, the whole verb phrase, and additional points for conjunctions, negatives, and questions. Each word in the response was given numerical credit depending on its function in the utterance. Here there was strict adherence to the criteria described by Miner (1969). After each response had been broken down into the appropriate point values, the figures were totaled and then divided by the number of responses, to give the value for LCI.

EVALUATING THE LANGUAGE MEASURES

Scorer Reliability

Six graduate-level speech pathology students trained for the task analyzed the speech samples. No more than one scorer determined all of the scores for any individual child. As a check on the reliability of the scorers' analyses, each analyzed the same recording of a 27-month-old child. Kendall's coefficient of concordance was applied to the rank orders of the scores for all measures. Although the coefficient of 0.68 was found to be significant at the 0.01 level of confidence, it is only moderately high. However, the actual differences in the scores assigned by the six scorers for each measure were relatively small. For example, the differences between the high and low scores were approximately 15%, 13%, 14%, and 11% of the mean scores for LCI, MLR, NDW, and DST.

As an additional indication of reliability, three scorers analyzed the same seven tapes for one child. The values assigned by each scorer were rank-ordered for each of the measures. The extent of agreement among the three scorers for each measure was tested by means of Kendall's coefficient of con cordance. The coefficients obtained for DST, LCI, MLR, and NDW were 0.99, 0.98, 0.98, and 0.99, respectively. All of the coefficients were significant at the 0.01 level of confidence.

Subject Variability

To indicate the variability of the data, the MLR and LCI scores obtained for the 13 children are presented in Tables 1 and 2, respectively. In a number of recordings, fewer than 50 utterances were available for analysis. Small samples in the early recordings generally reflect limited vocabularies. In later

TABLE 1. Means for length of response (MLR) of 13 children analyzed longitudinally. (Child's age in months appears in parentheses.)

Child				Sequence of Recordings			
	1st	2nd	3rd	4th	5th	6th	7th
	(17)	(19)	(21)	(23)	(25)	(27)	(30)
1 (M)	1.60	1.98	2.32	3.00	3.44	3.04	3.24
	(18)	(20)	(22)	(24)	(26)	(28)	(30)
2 (F)	1.32†	1.68	2.00	2.24	2.14	3.58	3.10
	(19)	(21)	(23)	(25)	(27)	(29)	(32)
3 (M)	1.74†	2.30†	2.64	4.12	3.08	2.94	4.00
	(20)	(22)	(24)	(26)	(28)	(30)	(34)
4 (M)	1.02	1.20	1.82	3.64	3.88	3.42	2.76
	(20)	(22)	(24)	(26)	(28)	(30)	(33)
5 (M)	1.04	1.06	1.22	1.50	1.40	1.44	2.86
	(21)	(23)	(25)	(27)	(29)	(31)	(34)
6 (M)	1.11*	1.07†	1.80	2.20*	4.26	3.20	4.27*
	(21)	(23)	(25)	(27)	(29)	(31)	(34)
7 (F)	1.00§	1.03†	1.06†	1.30	1.10	1.50	1.78
	(21)	(23)	(25)	(27)	(29)	(31)	(34)
8 (F)	1.18‡	1.11†	1.63*	2.16	2.10	2.60	3.50
	(21)	(23)	(25)	(27)	(29)	(31)	(34)
9 (F)	1.05*	1.08‡	1.60	2.42	2.78	3.68	3.46
	(21)	(23)	(25)	(27)	(29)	(31)	(34)
10 (F)	1.10	1.28	2.16	2.98	3.94	4.32	4.98
	(22)	(24)	(26)	(28)	(30)	(32)	(35)
11 (M)	1.00§	1.02	1.20	1.36	1.48	2.38	4.00
	(22)	(24)	(26)	(28)	(30)	(32)	(35)
12 (M)	1.59‡	1.77†	2.28	2.86	3.22	2.84	3.58
	(24)	(26)	(28)	(30)	(32)	(34)	(37)
13 (M)	1.36	1.48	3.96	3.26	3.28	3.12	3.60

*Sample of 40-49 utterances
†Sample of 30-39 utterances
‡Sample of 20-29 utterances
§Sample of 10-19 utterances

TABLE 2. Length-complexity index (LCI) scores for 13 children analyzed longitudinally. (Child's age in months appears in parentheses.)

Child				Sequence of Recordings			
	1st	2nd	3rd	4th	5th	6th	7th
1 (M)	(17) 1.76	(19) 2.20	(21) 2.36	(23) 3.86	(25) 4.06	(27) 3.36	(29) 3.60
2 (F)	(18) 1.54†	(20) 2.00	(22) 2.26	(24) 2.48	(26) 2.80	(28) 3.90	(31) 3.44
3 (M)	(19) 1.68†	(21) 2.40†	(23) 2.86	(25) 4.28	(27) 3.44	(29) 3.40	(32) 3.60
4 (M)	(20) 1.02	(22) 1.22	(24) 2.02	(26) 4.14	(28) 4.34	(30) 4.10	(34) 2.96
5 (M)	(20) 1.14	(22) 1.10	(24) 1.32	(26) 1.70	(28) 1.74	(30) 2.00	(33) 3.24
6 (M)	(21) 1.11*	(23) 1.13†	(25) 2.42	(27) 2.50*	(29) 4.66	(31) 3.60	(34) 5.22*
7 (F)	(21) 1.00§	(23) 1.03†	(25) 1.13†	(27) 1.36	(29) 1.22	(31) 1.64	(34) 1.94
8 (F)	(21) 1.14‡	(23) 1.11†	(25) 1.65*	(27) 2.26	(29) 2.22	(31) 2.88	(34) 4.04
9 (F)	(21) 1.23*	(23) 1.28‡	(25) 1.80	(27) 2.56	(29) 2.96	(31) 4.04	(34) 3.68
10 (F)	(21) 1.30	(23) 1.36	(25) 2.14	(27) 3.22	(29) 4.74	(31) 4.98	(34) 5.50
11 (M)	(22) 1.00§	(24) 1.02	(26) 1.60	(28) 1.42	(30) 1.56	(32) 2.52	(35) 4.04
12 (M)	(22) 1.63‡	(24) 1.90†	(26) 2.30	(28) 3.12	(30) 4.34	(32) 3.64	(35) 4.62
13 (M)	(24) 1.40	(26) 1.52	(28) 4.38	(30) 4.02	(32) 3.90	(34) 3.60	(37) 4.40

*Sample of 40-49 utterances
†Sample of 30-39 utterances
‡Sample of 20-29 utterances
§Sample of 10-19 utterances

recordings, they may reflect lack of responsiveness due to such factors as mood and illness. The initial scores for all the children within each measure are similar and seem to represent a reasonable baseline, although the actual ages vary. With the exception of samples containing fewer than 20 utterances, initial MLR and LCI scores range between 1.02 and 1.74 and between 1.02 and 1.76, respectively. It is interesting that these variations in initial scores are not closely related to the actual age of the children.

If one attempts to follow the course of language development by examining the language scores for each child through the recording sequence, it becomes evident that the patterns differ. For example, the progressive increase in MLR scores for Child 7 was slow but regular, whereas that for Child 3 was rapid but irregular. These same patterns for Children 7 and 3 can be observed in the LCI scores. Although the regularity of the developmental process is evident in Tables 1 and 2, there were numerous sudden increases, reversals, and perseverations in continguous samples. For example, note the abrupt increases for Child 10 between the second and third samples, the abrupt decline between the fifth and sixth samples for Child 6, and the lack of change in the first three samples for Child 7. It seems likely that at least some of these irregularities were due to sampling error.

There was considerable variation in the rate of language development for the 13 children. For example, Children 7 and 11 both had initial MLR scores of 1.00, but 13 months later Child 7 had increased his score by only 0.78 while Child 11 had increased his score by 3.00. The same differences in rate of development can be observed in the LCI scores. Rate of growth did not appear to be necessarily indicated by high or low initial scores. For example, Child 1, who obtained very high initial scores on all measures, did not attain final scores as high as Child 6, who started with very low scores.

In an attempt to quantify the variations in rate of development, regression coefficients were calculated for each child for the four measures. The slope functions obtained from these coefficients (shown in Table 3 in rank order)

TABLE 3. Rank order of regression-coefficient slope functions calculated for 13 children for measures of mean length of response (MLR), length-complexity index (LCI), developmental sentence types (DST), and number of different words (NDW). (The numbers in parentheses identify the individual children.)

MLR	DST	NDW	LCI
(10) 0.326	(10) 29.73	(11) 6.37	(10) 0.364
(6) 0.273	(6) 27.30	(6) 5.25	(6) 0.331
(11) 0.229	(9) 25.65	(9) 5.01	(12) 0.244
(9) 0.227	(4) 21.96	(4) 4.83	(9) 0.234
(8) 0.178	(8) 21.11	(10) 4.78	(8) 0.220
(4) 0.172	(11) 21.09	(3) 4.50	(11) 0.220
(2) 0.155	(2) 18.27	(13) 4.48	(13) 0.212
(13) 0.155	(13) 16.45	(8) 4.14	(4) 0.201
(12) 0.153	(12) 16.22	(12) 3.89	(2) 0.167
(3) 0.144	(1) 15.99	(2) 3.84	(1) 0.157
(1) 0.135	(5) 13.22	(7) 3.49	(5) 0.148
(5) 0.113	(3) 12.72	(1) 3.25	(3) 0.102
(7) 0.057	(7) 6.84	(5) 2.85	(7) 0.071

indicate the rate of increase in scores per month during the interval analyzed for each child. There is a considerable range in the score increments for the group of children: 0.057–0.326 for MLR, 2.85–6.37 for NDW, 0.071–0.364 for LCI, and 6.84–29.73 for DST. However, there is a great similarity in the rank order of the children on each of the four measures. Using Kendall's rank order procedure, a coefficient of concordance of 0.84 was obtained. This value is significant at the 0.01 level.

Relationships Between Measures

To show the relationships between measures of language development more

215

clearly, 10-word samples were selected from various children at levels of increasing MLR covering the range of MLR scores from 1.50 to 3.50 in four equal intervals. Along with MLR intervals, the NDW, DST, and LCI score ranges which correspond to these samples were determined. As the range of the MLR score increases, so do the ranges for LCI and DST, with little overlap except for the NDW scores, where there is considerable overlap in ranges from sample to sample.

There appears to be some regularity between increases in score intervals and increases in complexity of the language samples. In samples for MLR scores between 1.50 and 1.99 (Table 4), two- and sometimes three-word

TABLE 4. Samples of the utterances of three children taken when MLR was between 1.50–1.99, NDW 25–65, LCI 1.60–2.45, and DST 150–235.

Child 17 Months Old	Child 25 Months Old	Child 34 Months Old
baby	it broke	I want toy
a car	airplane	blue
spoon	put away	boots mine
rabbit	socks on	mine
the ball	put up	what's this?
block	car	take home
where the toys?	hat off	put back
a ball	hat on	shoes off
off	up	nighty night
the baby	I don't want it	bites me

utterances predominate. Many of these are still noun phrases, but verbs are employed in simple phrases. In the samples with MLR scores between 2.00 and 2.49 (NDW: 40–60; LCI: 2.35–2.50; DST: 240–255), the children began to put nouns and verbs together to produce some basic sentences. In addition, they demonstrated some ability to use interrogatives and inflections to form questions. By the time MLR scores reached 2.50–2.99 (NDW: 55–70; LCI: 2.85–3.00; DST: 285–310), the samples included some verb phrases containing more complex noun phrases than previously employed. There is a fairly common use of personal pronouns. With samples ranging between MLR scores of 3.00 and 3.49 (Table 5), there appear the beginnings of sentences in which noun phrases are incorporated into verb phrases. Although some isolated noun phrases persist, even these have become somewhat more complex.

To indicate the nature of the changes occurring, the incidence of phrase types was plotted in relation to MLR levels between 1.00 and 4.49. Table 6 shows the noun phrases which were used as complete utterances. Each mark

216

TABLE 5. Samples of the utterances of three children taken when MLR was between 3.00–3.49. NDW 60–95, LCI 3.60–3.95, and DST 330–360.

Child 30 Months Old	Child 31 Months Old	Child 32 Months Old
oh, that's a bear there	a cracker	dog
that one, yeah, that one	a paper	he's going away
what's that?	it broke	he gots hair on his tail
I want backside	like my dolly	there's soup
see that man	up there	it's in there
that my finger	a coat	dish and cup
to see with	a choo choo train	baby doll
what's her sweater in the bathtub for?	daddy go in that one	don't know how
that kind way up there	that won't fit	she took a shower
hi	let's put the boat over here too	she's on the street

in the table represents one or more occurrences of the phrase type. A large number of different noun phrases are used at the lower MLR levels. At the 3.5–3.99 level, there is a sharp decline in the occurrence of isolated noun phrases. Noun and verb phrases occurring in sentences were also plotted in relation to MLR levels. These noun phrases do not begin to appear until the 2.0–2.49 level. Thereafter, they are used frequently until they appear to reach a maximum at the 3.49–4.00 and 4.00–4.49 levels. At very low levels, few verb phrases are employed. Their use increases gradually through the middle levels of MLR. There is a marked increase in the verb phrase types at the 3.5–3.99 level which coincides with the increase in noun phrase types noted in Table 6.

DISCUSSION

The results indicate that there is considerable individual variability in the pattern of early language development. The scores obtained for all the language measures administered exemplify this. Scores of successive samples obtained from individual children often represent reversals, sudden increases, or no change. Such sample-to-sample variations may be more indicative of the child's mood on the sampling day than of his language development. Only when several sampling intervals are considered do the scores for each child appear to reflect adequately the growth in language which is occurring.

The samples obtained in this study demonstrate the variability of early language development which follows the use of single-word, naming responses. Within a one-year period, some children develop to the point of using a variety

TABLE 6. Occurrence (indicated by x) of noun-phrase types used as complete utterances by children at increasing MLR levels.

Phrase Type	1.00– 1.49	1.50– 1.99	2.00– 2.49	2.50– 2.99	3.00– 3.49	3.50– 3.99	4.00– 4.49
Adj. + N (Prn.)	–	x	x	x	x	–	–
Adv. + Adj.	x	–	x	–	–	–	–
Art. (+ Adj.) + N	x	x	x	x	x	–	x
Int. + Art. + N + ?	–	x	–	–	–	–	–
Int. + Prn. + ?	–	–	–	–	–	–	x
N + Adj. (Adv.)	x	x	x	x	–	–	–
N (+ Conj.) + N	x	–	x	–	x	–	–
N + Prep. Ph.	–	–	x	–	–	–	–
Poss. + Adj. + N	–	–	–	–	–	x	–
Prep. + Prn.	x	–	–	–	–	–	–
Prn. (+ Poss.) + N	–	–	–	–	x	–	–
Prn. + Prep. Ph.	–	–	–	x	x	–	–

of sentence types including many different nouns and verb phrases. In these children the changes occur quickly, so that within the two-month sampling interval examined, there were considerable differences between contiguous samples. Some children progressed much more slowly but according to the same pattern. Their first two or three samples were dominated by one-word utterances and the next few by two-word noun or verb phrases. During the course of the study, they did not progress much beyond this level.

This study indicates the difficulty in comparing the language development of children on the basis of age. There was considerable disparity in the scores for given age levels and in the age-related samples from different children. It is quite possible that a child may be developing language normally but still may not fit age norms. Determination of normal development should probably require at least two language samples taken at intervals which adequately reflect rate of growth. Since some children show little change for several months, it may be necessary to obtain evaluations at least six months apart. The slope function values in this study should be of some aid in determining variation in rate of change which may be expected to occur over the sampling interval.

There are reliability problems involved in assessing language development which affected the results of this study. The nature of these problems has been well-documented for MLR assessment. Shriner (1969) has reviewed some, including response variability, transcriber agreement, and size of sample. Cowan, Weber, Hoddinott, and Klein (1967) have found that MLR varies depending upon the examiner; the age, sex, and socioeconomic status of the subject; and the type of stimulus materials used. It seems likely that the same problems found for measures based on verbal output also function in obtaining measures based on structural analysis. Since quantification of structural complexity requires more sensitive judgments than quantification of verbal output, one might expect that LCI and DST scoring would be affected more by problems of reliability than would NDW and MLR scoring. The results of this study indicate that the degree of disagreement among scorers is of the same magnitude in assessing MLR, LCI, NDW, and DST.

The results also indicate a close relationship between measures based on verbal output, such as MLR and NDW, and those based on structural analysis of language, such as LCI and DST. This relationship appears to be closer between MLR and the structural measures than between these measures and NDW. For the purpose of relating language growth to chronological age, it appears that quantification of structural analysis of language provides no more sensitive measure than quantification of verbal output. It seems likely that, at least for normal language development, even simple measures like MLR will adequately reflect the growth process. Shriner and Sherman (1967) found that MLR had a higher correlation with scale values of language development than any other variables studied. The close relationship between MLR, LCI, and DST may be due to a high correlation between length of response and complexity of language structure. It may be that the factor common to measures of verbal output and structural complexity is the limitation that memory span places on the length and complexity of responses during early language development.

In addition, the results of this study indicate that general inferences about the development of language structure can be drawn from verbal output measures such as NDW and MLR. The possibility for making such inferences would appear greater for MLR than for NDW. Even for MLR, however, the nature of these inferences must be limited. Nevertheless, it does seem clear that, within certain ranges of MLR scores, the frequency and variety of usage of noun phrase and verb phrase types will be somewhat restricted. Although such information does not permit detailed reconstruction of the language usage of a child, it may be useful in making inferences about the level of structural complexity at which he is functioning.

Verbal output measures do not substitute for the kind of language descriptions which are the basis for DST and LCI measures. This is certainly true when it becomes necessary to provide remedial aid for a given child. However, screening tests for language development are desirable and tests such as MLR will no doubt be utilized for this purpose. There are problems involved in making absolute comparisons between language measure scores and attributing significance to small differences. It is necessary to use caution in interpreting small differences between sample scores for all language measures. However, it does seem possible and worthwhile to employ language measures to make relative judgments about development. Results of this study indicate that all measures analyzed can be used in this way with good reliability. This may be because any reasonable measure of language will produce increases in score as language develops with age.

219

ACKNOWLEDGMENT

This study was supported in part by Grant No. 5 PO1 HD 01368-03 from the National Institute for Child Health and Human Development to the Center for Human Growth and Development, University of Michigan. Some of the results were reported at the Annual Convention of the American Speech and Hearing Association in Denver in 1968. A number of research assistants and students have contributed to the study in the process of data collection and analysis. The author is currently in the Departments of Speech and Physical Medicine and Rehabilitation. Requests for reprints should be directed to him in care of the Speech Clinic, University of Michigan, Ann Arbor, Michigan 48103.

REFERENCES

COWAN, P. A., WEBER, J., HODDINOTT, B. A., and KLEIN, J., Mean length of spoken response as a function of stimulus, experimenter, and subject. *Child Developm.*, 38, 191-203 (1967).

JOHNSON, W., DARLEY, F. L., and SPRIESTERSBACH, D. C., *Diagnostic Methods in Speech Pathology.* New York: Harper (1963).

LEE, LAURA, Developmental sentence types: A method for comparing normal and deviant syntactic development. *J. Speech Hearing Dis.*, 31, 311-330 (1966).

McCARTHY, DOROTHEA A., Language development in children. In L. Carmichael (Ed.), *Manual of Child Psychology.* New York: Wiley (1954).

MINER, L. E., Scoring procedures for the length-complexity index: A preliminary report. *J. Commun. Dis.*, 2, 224-240 (1969).

SHRINER, T. H., A comparison of selected measures with psychological scale values of language development. *J. Speech Hearing Res.*, 10, 828-835 (1967).

SHRINER, T. H., A review of mean length of response as a measure of expressive language development in children. *J. Speech Hearing Dis.*, 34, 61-68 (1969).

SHRINER, T. H., and SHERMAN, DOROTHY, An equation for assessing language development. *J. Speech Hearing Res.*, 10, 44-48 (1967).

TEMPLIN, MILDRED C., Certain language skills in children: Their development and interrelationships. *Child Welfare Monographs*, No. 26. Minneapolis: Univ. Minn. (1957).

WINITZ, H., Language skills of male and female kindergarten children. *J. Speech Hearing Res.*, 2, 377-386 (1959).

SECTION IV. Linguistic Analysis: LASS, ISCD and CORS

A Preliminary Evaluation of Grammatical Capacity in Children[1]

PAULA MENYUK

In previous studies (Menyuk, 1963a, 1963b), an explanatory model of grammar as presented in Chomsky's *Syntactic Structures* (1957) was used to describe a children's grammar. This transformational model of a grammar provides us with a technique for describing the rules from which the child may generate the sentences in his language.

The results of these studies showed that almost all the basic syntactic structures used by adults that we have thus far been able to describe are found in the grammar of children as young as 2 years 10 months. From 2 years 10 months to 7 years 1 month there was an almost steady increase in the number of children using these structures as an increasingly mature population was observed. However, most of the structures were used at an early age and used consistently. Many of the structures which were still in the process of being acquired by the nursery-school children were also in the process of being acquired by first-grade children. Structures restricted to a children's grammar (presumably nonconsistent with adult usage) occurred infrequently. Significantly more of the children from 3 to 4 years of age sometimes omitted rules which are obligatory once a structure has been

[1] This investigation was supported in part by the U.S. Army Signal Corps, the Air Force Office of Scientific Research, and the Office of Naval Research; in part by the National Science Foundation (Grant G-16526) and the National Institute of Health (Grant MH-04737-03); and in part by a fellowship (MPD-8768-C3) from the National Institute of Mental Health, Public Health Service.

optionally chosen than did older children. At other times they used the complete set of rules to produce a particular structure.

One might hypothesize from these results that at even a very early age language is not an imitative function and that the child has, indeed, the grammatical capacity for generating an infinite number of sentences of the language and for recognizing sentences versus nonsentences. He may produce sentences which do not follow the rules of a structure to completion, such as "You can't put no more water in it," but he does not easily produce or understand the nonsentence, "It in water more no put can't you."

Various authors have discussed this capacity in terms of a model of a perceiver or speaker (Matthews, 1961; Halle and Stevens, 1962; Miller and Chomsky, 1963). The perceptual model incorporates both the generative rules of the grammar and a heuristic component that samples an input (sentence) to extract from it certain cues as to which rules were used to generate it, selecting among alternative possibilities by a process of successive approximation. The device stores the rules of the grammar but only has enough computing space to understand or produce in the manner of the grammar a certain proper subset of the set of sentences of the language capable of being generated by the grammar. For example, a sentence theoretically can be indefinitely long, but no actual perceived or produced sentence ever exceeds some given length. However, behavior can be extended

JOURNAL OF VERBAL LEARNING AND VERBAL BEHAVIOR, Dec. 1963, vol. 2, no. 5-6, pp. 429-439.

systematically without additional instruction if additional memory aids are given. For example, a child may understand the rules for multiplication but may be able only to perform a proper subset of the set of possible operations, and there are instances in which he produces approximations to the "correct" answer. As he matures, the number of approximations decreases and this subset is expanded. When given pencil and paper the child expands this subset even further. However, at any level of performance he is applying the rules for multiplication. Miller and Chomsky (1963) conclude that a device that incorporates competence, whether or not it is realized in performance, provides the only model of psychological relevance, since only this kind of device can explain the transfer of learning that is known to occur when memory aids are in fact made available.

This study was undertaken as a *preliminary* examination of this hypothesis of grammatical capacity in children. An attempt was made to circumvent reliance on grammatical production for an evaluation of grammatical capacity since some of the primary claims of this hypothesis are that language production is not an imitative function; that although the speaker may not produce sentences which contain some possible syntactic structures within the proper subset of the set of sentences of his language, he has the capacity to do so; and that although the speaker may not always produce sentences which conform completely to the rules of the grammar, he has the capacity to do so. It was felt that by asking the children to repeat sentences containing syntactic structures found in the language they produced, the following questions might be explored: (1) would the children imitate the sentences heard up to the limits of their memory capacity or would they produce sentences in terms of the rules of the grammar as postulated; (2) could the children understand and produce sentences containing syntactic structures which are used infrequently and by few of them when given the memory aid of im-

mediate recall; and (3) were instances of non-grammaticalness found in children's language usage an indication that children have a different set of rules in their grammar or are they indications that children sometimes use a set of rules which deviates from complete grammaticalness to generate their sentences.

METHOD

Subjects and Procedure. The population was composed of 14 nursery-school children aged 2 years 10 months to 3 years 8 months and 50 kindergarten children aged 4 years 9 months to 6 years 1 month.[2] There were 9 boys and 5 girls in the nursery-school group and 27 boys and 23 girls in the kindergarten group. The mean age of the nursery-school group was 3 years 3 months and the mean age of the kindergarten group was 5 years 6 months. The mean I.Q. of the nursery-school children, as measured by the Full Range Picture Vocabulary Test (Ammons and Ammons, 1958), was 133.80 ($SD = 19.66$) and the mean I.Q. of the kindergarten children was 126.16 ($SD = 16.57$). All the children's parents had middle-class occupations (Institute of Child Welfare, 1950).

A language sample was obtained from each child and recorded in various stimulus situations: (1) responses to a projective test (Blum, 1950), (2) conversation with an adult, and (3) conversation with peers. The latter two situations took place both in controlled and free (classroom) environments. The language sample of each child was analyzed using a transformational model of a grammar. From this analysis the rules for syntactic structures used by children to generate all the sentences they produced were postulated. The transformational rules (rules which transform simple-active-declarative sentences into other types) and rules restricted to a children's grammar (rules which produce sentences which deviate from complete grammaticalness) were chosen for further study.

The nursery-school children were presented with a list of sentences which were representative of the various transformation types found in a children's grammar. The actual sentences were chosen from the language sample of children used in a previous study (Menyuk, 1962). After an intervening task (taking the Full Range Picture Vocabulary Test), the nursery-school children were then presented with a list of sentences containing the various restricted forms found in a children's grammar. These sentences were also selected from the language sample previously

2 Grateful acknowledgment is given to the children and teachers of the Beacon Nursery School and the Edith C. Baker School in Brookline, Massachusetts.

obtained. Twenty-five of the kindergarten children were given the same list of sentences representing the transformation types and another twenty-five were given the same list of sentences with the restricted forms.

The task was presented in the following manner:

The E said, "I'm going to say some sentences for you. I want you to say just what I say. If I say 'The sun is shining' I want you to say _____." If the correct response was obtained the E proceeded. If not, the E stated, "No, you say just what I say. If I say 'The sun is shining' you say _____." No more than these two examples of what was required was needed by any of the Ss. The E then read the list of sentences with head bent over the list so that no visual cues could be obtained, and waited for the response of the child to each sentence. If a child did not respond at all to a sentence, one repetition of that sentence was given. If the child did not respond again, the next sentence was presented. No second repetition was made and the one repetition was given only in the case of no response at all. Both the E's reading of the sentences and the children's responses were tape-recorded for later analysis.

In addition to the above, three older Ss were used for an elaboration of the procedure for exploratory purposes. Subject A was a girl aged 6 years 11 months, S B was a boy aged 8 years 6 months, and S C was an adult male. These Ss were asked to repeat the two lists in the same way previously stated. They were then asked to repeat the list containing the restricted forms in a manner which they thought correct. The E said, "I want you to say these sentences the way you think they should be." Finally they were given the list of sentences representing the various transformation types with each sentence in exact reverse word order and asked to repeat these sentences.

The list of the sentences presented for repetition is shown in Table 1.

Analysis of Data. A repetition was counted as correct when the Ss were able to repeat either the transformation type or the restricted form in a sentence. Errors of omission in repetition of the structure such as the preposition *over* in item 16 (Peter is here and you are there) and the article *a* in item 17 (I see a red book and blue book) were counted as correct and the omissions noted for separate analysis. Substitution in repetition such as expansion of a contracted verb form in item 20 (He will eat the ice cream because he wants to) or the substitution of *there* in item 16 (Peter is over here and you are over there) were also counted as correct repetitions and again noted for separate analysis.

Omissions, such as omission of the noun phrase or verb phrase and, of course, complete omission, were counted as nonrepetitions. Modification of the trans-formations such as simplification of nominalization to present participle in item 26 (She's shopping and cooking and baking) or the declarative of the question in item 3 (You are nice) were also counted as nonrepetitions.

All corrections of sentences in the repetition of restricted forms were counted as nonrepetitions and listed in a separate category called corrections. For example, if *childs* was replaced by *children* in item 1, *people* for *peoples* in item 2, and *teeth* for *tooth* in item 3, these were listed as corrections. In addition to the above modifications some redundant changes took place. They were very infrequent. A redundant pronoun form and redundant verb phrases occurred. These were also listed as corrections and noted for analysis.

Chi-square analyses were used to compare the number of nursery-school children and kindergarten children who repeated, did not repeat, and corrected the various transformations and restricted forms. Also, chi-square analyses were used to see which structures were repeated, not repeated, and corrected by a significant number of children in the total population.

Since data were available on the use of the various structures in the language produced by these children, regression analyses were used to determine the correlation between the number of transformations and restricted forms in each child's grammar and the number of transformations and restricted forms he repeated. This analysis was also used to determine the correlation between the number of children who used each syntactic structure in their language and the number of them who repeated each structure. Finally, regression analysis was used to determine the correlation between sentence length and non-repetition.

RESULTS

In the repetition of transformations all items were repeated by a significant number of the nursery-school children ($p < 0.05$) except the Question (3), Got (10), Auxiliary Have (12), Conjunction with So (19), Conjunction with Because (20), and Nominalization (26) transformations. A significant number of the kindergarten children repeated all transformations except Got (10) and Auxiliary Have (12) transformations. However, in comparing the numbers of nursery-school and kindergarten children who repeated these items, significantly more of the kindergarten children repeated the Question and Conjunction with So transformations but not the Conjunction with Because and Nominalization transforma-

TABLE 1
LIST OF SENTENCES PRESENTED FOR REPETITION

EXEMPLAR	List of sentences
EXEMPLAR	**Transformation types**
1. Passive	He got tied up.
2. Negative	He isn't a good boy.
3. Question	Are you nice?
4. Contraction	He'll be good.
5. Inversion	Now I have kittens.
6. Relative Question	Where are you going?
7. Imperative	Don't use my dough.
8. Pronominalization	There isn't any more.
9. Separation	He took it off.
10. Got	I've got a lollipop.
11. Auxiliary Be placement	He is not going to the party.
12. Auxiliary Have placement	I've already been there.
13. Do	I did read the book.
14. Possessive	I'm writing daddy's name.
15. Reflexive	I cut myself.
16. Conjunction	Peter is over here and you are over there.
17. Conjunction Deletion	I see a red book and a blue book.
18. Conjunction If	I'll give it to you if you want it.
19. Conjunction So	He saw him so he hit him.
20. Conjunction Because	He'll eat the ice cream because he wants to.
21. Pronoun in Conjunction	David saw the bicycle and he was happy.
22. Adjective	I have a pink dog.
23. Relative Clause	I don't know what he's doing.
24. Complement	I want to play.
25. Iteration	You have to drink milk to grow strong.
26. Nominalization	She does the shopping and cooking and baking.
27. Nominal Compound	The baby carriage is here.

NOUN FORM EXEMPLAR	Restricted forms
1. Substitution	We have childs in this school.
2. Redundancy	Where are the peoples?
3. Omission	I have two tooth.
VERB FORM	
4. Substitution	He growed bigger and bigger.
5. Redundancy	He liketed that game.
6. Omission	He wash his face.
7. Pronoun Restriction	Mommy was happy so he kissed Betty.
8. Relative Pronoun	I see a dog what's white.
9. Adjective Restriction	I write that numbers.
10. Tense in Conjunction	They get mad and then they pushed him.
11. Reflexive 3rd Person	He's washing hisself.
12. No Separation	You pick up it.
13. There Substitution	It isn't any more rain.
14. No Question	What that is.
15. Contraction Deletion	They sleeping.
16. Double Negation	You can't put no more water in it.
INVERSION RESTRICTIONS	
17. Verb Number	There's three babies.
18. Subject-Object	Brothers and sisters I have.

TABLE 1 (*Continued*)

EXEMPLAR	List of sentences
	Restricted forms
PARTICLE	
19. Redundancy	Take it in in there.
20. Omission	Put the hat.
ARTICLE	
21. Substitution	I see a teeth.
22. Redundancy	His name is a teddy bear.
23. Omission	Giant wakes up.
PREPOSITION	
24. Substitution	Daddy took me at the train.
25. Redundancy	You shop in over there.
26. Omission	I want to go New York.
NOUN PHRASE	
27. Redundancy	She took it away the hat.
28. Omission	Want it.
VERB PHRASE	
29. Substitution	Say the story.
30. Redundancy	He'll might get in jail.
31. Omission	The baby'll.

tions. On the whole, there was a great deal of similarity in the performance of the children in both groups in the repetition of transformations. It should be noted that no item was *not* repeated by a significant number of the children ($p < 0.05$). Table 2 lists the transformations repeated by an insignificant number of the nursery-school children and compares their performance with that of kindergarten children. The number of children in the total population who repeated these transformations is also listed and the level of significance of these totals noted.

In the repetition of restricted forms a different pattern emerged. Only 13 of the 31 items were repeated by a significant number of the nursery-school children. Twenty-three of the items were repeated by a significant number of the kindergarten children. Most of the nonrepetitions were due to corrections of the restricted forms. Five items were corrected by a significant number of the nursery-school children. They were Verb Form Omission (6), Tense Agreement in Conjunction (10), Contraction Deletion (15), Preposition Omission

(26), and Noun Phrase Omission (28). Three items were corrected by a significant number of the kindergarten children; they were Con-

TABLE 2

COMPARISON OF REPETITION OF TRANSFORMATIONS REPEATED BY AN INSIGNIFICANT NUMBER OF NURSERY-SCHOOL CHILDREN

(Entries are numbers of cases)

Transformations	Nursery school (N = 14)[d]	Kindergarten (N = 25)	Total (N = 39)
3. Question	10[a]	25[b]	35[b]
10. Got	9	15	24
12. Auxiliary Have	6	13	19
19. Conjunction So	7[a]	21[b]	28[b]
20. Conjunction Because	9	18[c]	27[c]
26. Nominalization	9	23[b]	32[b]

[a] Significantly different from kindergarten group at the 0.05 level.

[b] Number of repetitions significant at the 0.01 level.

[c] Number of repetitions significant at the 0.05 level.

[d] Number of cases.

TABLE 3

Comparison of Omissions and Corrections of Restricted Forms

Restricted forms	Omissions		Corrections		
	Nursery school (N = 14)	Kindergarten (N = 25)	Nursery school (N = 14)	Kindergarten (N = 25)	Total (N = 39)
2. Noun form Red.	1[e]	0	4	2	6
6. Verb form Omiss.			13[c]	14	27[d]
7. Pro. Restr.			5	3	8
8. Rel. Pro. Restr.			6	10	16
9. Adj. Restr.			5	2	7
10. Tense in Conj.	2	0	10[d]	14	24
13. There Sub.	6[b]	0	0	3	3
15. Contr. Del.			11[d]	21[c]	33[c]
16. Double Neg.	1	0	9[a]	3	12
19. Part. Red.			10	17[d]	27[d]
20. Part. Omiss.	1	0	3	1	4
22. Art. Red.			4	0	4
25. Prep. Red.			6	6	12
26. Prep. Omiss.			14[c]	25[c]	39[c]
27. Noun Ph. Red.			10	10	20
28. Noun Ph. Omiss.			14[a,c]	2	16
29. Verb. Ph. Sub.	5[b]	0	0	1	1
30. Verb. Ph. Red.			8	15	23

[a] Significantly different from kindergarten group at 0.01 level.
[b] Significantly different from kindergarten group at the 0.05 level.
[c] Number of corrections significant at 0.01 level.
[d] Number of corrections significant at 0.05 level.
[e] Items 2 and 29 were omitted completely.

traction Deletion (15), Particle Redundancy (19), and Preposition Omission (26). Significantly more nursery school children than kindergarten children corrected Double Negation (16) and Noun Phrase Omission (28). A significant number of the children in the total population corrected Verb Form Omission (6), Contraction Deletion (15), Particle Redundancy (19), and Preposition Omission (26). Some of the nonrepetition of restricted forms was due to complete and partial omission of items by nursery school children. The There Substitution Sentence (13) was partially omitted by significantly more of the nursery-school than kindergarten children ($p < 0.05$), and the Verb Phrase Substitution Sentence (29) was completely omitted by significantly more of the nursery school children ($p < 0.05$). Table 3 lists the restricted forms repeated by an insignificant number of the nursery-school children and compares the number of nursery-school and kindergarten children who omitted or corrected these forms. The number of children in the total sample population who corrected these forms is also listed and the levels of significance of these numbers noted.

A comparison was made of the mean number of items that were repeated, not repeated, and corrected in each group. Significantly more of the items were repeated in the kindergarten group than in the nursery school group ($t = 4.49$, $p < 0.001$). Significantly more of the items were changed by (1) correction ($t = 4.15$, $p < 0.001$) and (2) modification of the transformation ($t = 2.32$, $p < 0.05$) in the nursery-school group than in the kindergarten group. There were no significant differences in the mean number of items omitted completely or partially, substituted, or corrected with redundant forms by both groups.

Data were available on the number of syn-

TABLE 4

COMPARISON OF USE AND REPETITION OF TRANSFORMATIONS AND USE AND CORRECTION OF RESTRICTED FORMS

	Nursery school		Kindergarten	
	N = 16	N = 14	N = 50	N = 25
Transformations	No. using	No. repeating	No. using	No. repeating
EXEMPLAR				
1. Passive	5	14^a		
8. Pronominalization			16	24^a
12. Auxiliary Have	0	6	9	13
15. Reflexive 3rd Pers.	0	14^a		
18. Conjunction—If	6	12^a	10	23^a
19. Conjunction—So	4	7	18	21^a
25. Iteration	0	11^b	8	25^a
26. Nominalization	2	9	14	23^a
Restricted forms		No. correcting		No. correcting
EXEMPLAR				
6. Verb form Omiss.	6	13^a	15	14
10. Tense in Conj.	5	12^a	19	14
15. Contr. Del.	7	11^a	23	21^a
19. Part. Red.	0	10^c	0	17^c
26. Prep. Omiss.	0	14^a	7	25^a
30. Verb Ph. Red.	0	8	7	15

^{a} Number of repetitions or corrections significant at the 0.01 level.
^{b} Number of repetitions or corrections significant at the 0.05 level.
^{c} Number of repetitions or corrections significant at the .10 level.

tactic structures (both transformations and restricted forms) each child had in his grammar. Regression analysis showed that there was a significant correlation between the number of syntactic structures each child used in his grammar and the number of structures he repeated, both within the nursery-school group and the kindergarten group. For the nursery-school group $r = 0.65$ ($p < 0.001$) and for the kindergarten group $r = 0.41$ ($p < 0.01$). There was also a significant correlation between the number of children who used each syntactic structure in their grammar and the number who repeated each structure both for the nursery-school and kindergarten group. For the nursery-school group $r = 0.41$ ($p < 0.01$), and for the kindergarten group $r = 0.36$ ($p < 0.01$).

Despite these significant correlations a closer analysis of the use of the various structures in language production and the repeti-tion of these structures yields some interesting results. When one lists the transformations used by less than 50% of either the nursery-school or kindergarten population, the two lists match well, as seen in Table 4. On the whole, more children in both groups are able to repeat these transformations than were able to use them in their language. The kindergarten children are better able to repeat these structures than are the nursery-school children. All these transformations were repeated by a significant number of kindergarten children except the Auxiliary Have transformation, and all were repeated by a significant number of the nursery-school children except the Auxiliary Have, Conjunction with So, and Nominalization transformations.

Since restricted forms are used by comparatively many fewer of the children than the transformations, the criterion of 30% or more usage in the population was used to isolate the forms used by a sizeable number of the children. There is some overlap in the restricted forms used by 30% or more of the nursery-school and kindergarten children, but, on the whole, the groups are distinctive in the usage of these forms. However, when one looks at the restricted forms which are corrected by 50% or more of the populations, there is striking similarity, as seen in Table 4. It should be noted that the structures corrected by the greatest number of the children are about equally divided between the restricted forms most used and the restricted forms least used by the children in their grammar. Table 4 lists the transformations used by 50% or less of the population and the restricted forms corrected by 50% or more of the population and notes the significance of the number of children repeating and correcting these items.

Regression analysis was used to determine the correlation between nonrepetition of sentences and their length. One might hypothesize that the longer the sentence is the greater the number of children who would be unable to repeat it, especially at the younger age level. Sentence-word length ranged from 2 to 9 words with a mean of 5 words. The correlation between nonrepetition and sentence length for nursery school children was $r = 0.04$, and for kindergarten children was $r = 0.03$, both insignificant correlations.

Subjects A, B, and C

The results obtained from the performance of these three Ss illuminates the results previously described. All these Ss repeated exactly the list of transformations and the list of restricted forms. When asked to repeat the list of restricted forms in the way ". . . you think they're right," S A corrected all structures except Double Negation (16), Noun Phrase Omission (28), and Verb Phrase Substitution (29). Subject B corrected all forms except Double Negation (16), Inversion of Subject and Object (17), and Preposition Redundancy (25). Subject C corrected all items.

When given each exemplar of a transformation in exact reverse word order, the three Ss responded very differently than they had previously. Whereas no repetition of any sentence had been requested previously, all the Ss requested one or more repetitions of most items. Any inversion of word order or omission of two or more consecutive words or a hit-or-miss response were counted as nonrepetitions of the sentence. An example of the last type of response is the repetition of item 20 ("to wants he because ice cream the eat he'll"). Subject A responded with "to the ice cream because he wants eat he'll," S B responded with "he he wants see ice cream because he'll eat he'll," and S C responded with "because ice cream the wants he'll." The correlation between nonrepetition of a sentence and the number of words in each sentence was calculated for each S. The correlation was significant for all three Ss, with the correlation highest for the youngest S, and lowest for the oldest S. For S A, $r = 0.88$ ($p < 0.001$), for S B, $r = 0.68$ ($p < 0.001$), and for S C, $r = 0.65$ ($p < 0.001$).

DISCUSSION

One may state that within the bounds of a two- to nine-word sentence, the length of the sentence is not critical in determining the success of repetition even for children as young as 3 years. The differences in the ability of children to repeat the various sentences seems to be dependent on the particular rules used to generate these sentences rather than sentence length. This is shown by the insignificant correlation between length and nonrepetition when normal word order is maintained and the highly significant correlation between length and nonrepetition when the structure is broken down (sentences in reverse word order given to Ss A, B, and C).

This hypothesis of repetition being dependent on structure rather than mere imitation is further strengthened by the kinds of responses one obtains in the repetition of certain struc-

228

tures. The most frequent types of deviation from complete repetition found were modification of transformations and correction of restricted forms. The modifications always took the form of using a set of rules which come earlier in the grammar than those used in the sentence. They come earlier both in terms of an abstract formulation of a children's grammar (Menyuk, 1961) and in terms of the developmental trends observed. The structures substituted do not show significant changes in usage over the age range of 3 to 7 years, whereas the ones for which they were substituted do. For example, the question sentence was repeated as a declarative sentence, the conjunction sentence was repeated as two sentences, and the more complicated conjunctions with *if* and *so* were repeated as *and* conjunctions. Although the restricted forms used by a sizeable number (30% or more) of the nursery-school and kindergarten children were, on the whole, not very similar, the restricted forms corrected by a sizeable number of the children were very similar. Primarily, these corrections were of either omissions or redundancies at the phrase structure (parts of speech rules) and morphology (inflectional rules) levels of the grammar. Omissions and redundancies seem to occur in children's use of grammar before the completed rule in the production of certain structures. For example, in formulating the past tense of the verb "push," the child may produce first "push" (omission), then "pushted" (redundancy), and finally "pushed" (complete). Brown, Fraser, and Bellugi (in preparation) found that a 2-year-old child could not or would not make any judgments about the grammaticality of a sentence. These children, especially the nursery-school children, seemed to be exercising their judgment of grammaticality overtly and using the rules in their grammar to repeat and modify transformations and correct restricted forms. They were applying their grammatical capacity in the repetition of sentences.

Most of the sentences representing the various transformation types were repeated by a significant number of the children. When given the memory aid of immediate recall of these sentences, a significant number of the children reproduced transformations which they do not use in their own sentences. On the other hand, when given sentences where the rules for sentence generation were not maintained (reverse word order), Ss A, B, and C were unable to repeat with accuracy despite the aid of immediate recall.

In addition, when given sentences which contain some deviation from complete grammaticalness, the children, especially the younger ones, reproduced these sentences in their correct grammatical form despite the fact that these deviations are found in their language sample and that indeed significantly more of the younger children use these deviations. These results seem to indicate that children, even at the age of 3, have incorporated the rules of the grammar and are able to understand and produce sentences using these rules.

The differences obtained between the nursery-school and kindergarten children, primarily in the correction of restricted forms, may be due to factors which are interrelated. The more obvious factor is that of task orientation. The kindergarten children, when given the task of repeating, were much more apt to do so than were the nursery-school children, despite the distraction of a transformation which was used rarely and by few of them or a structure which deviated from complete grammaticalness. The fact that significantly more of the nursery-school children correct obviously does not imply that their grammatical capacity is superior. When older Ss (A, B, and C) were given the task of repeating the restricted forms, they did so without any alternations, but they did correct almost all these forms when asked to do so. Perhaps the kindergarten children and even younger children could approximate this performance if they were given the task. The question that remains is why are the younger children more distracted from the task of repetition of *some* transformations and restricted forms. Vigotsky (1962) and other theorists have discussed the development of language as a process which goes from the external to the internal. The younger children may be at the level at which they both evaluate the stimuli in terms of the rules of their grammar and reproduce what they hear primarily in accordance with these rules because their evaluation and production are still operating more externally than at a later age.

As was stated, the oldest Ss (A, B, and C) were able to understand and reproduce sentences containing the various restricted forms. However, these Ss, especially the adult, did show some initial hesitancy in repeating these forms. The time between presentation of these types of sentences and response may be an indication of the level of internalization of grammatical evaluation and, therefore, of grammatical sophistication, and will be a subject for further research. Also, many examples of each of the infrequently used transformation types and the task of repetition of the restricted forms in a "manner they think correct" should be presented to children further to explore this hypothesis of incorporation of the generative rules of the grammar.

SUMMARY

The purpose of this study was to examine the hypothesis that children have incorporated the generative rules of their grammar and are able to understand and produce sentences in accordance with these rules and to extend systematically their behavior without additional instruction if additional memory aids are given.

Fourteen nursery-school children (age 2 years 10 months to 3 years 8 months) and 50 kindergarten children (age 4 years 9 months to 6 years 1 month) were the subjects in this study. A language sample was obtained from each child in various stimulus situations. The children were then asked to repeat a set of sentences representative of the various transformation types (sentences which go beyond the simple-active-declarative type) and a set representative of the various restricted forms (deviations from complete grammaticalness) that were found in their usage of grammar. In addition, three older Ss were asked to repeat the two sets of sentences, to repeat the set containing the restricted forms in a manner they thought correct, and to repeat the set representing the transformations given to them in reverse word order.

It was found that when given the memory aid of immediate recall, these children were better able to produce than use in their own language both transformations and completely grammatical rules at all three levels of the grammar (phrase structure, transformations, and morphology). The 3 older Ss, although they had repeated all sentences containing transformation types with complete accuracy, were unable to do so when the structure of these sentences was removed (reverse word order) even though they were again given the aid of immediate recall. The children's deviations from complete repetition were due to the particular structure contained in the sentence and not sentence length. It was hypothesized that significantly more nursery-school than kindergarten children modified some transformations and corrected some restricted forms because the younger children were evaluating and producing sentences in accordance with the rules of their grammar at a more external level than the older children. Therefore, the older children were better able to perform the task of repeating regardless of the structure of the sentence.

The data obtained seem to indicate that the children in this population, at age 3, have incorporated most of the basic generative rules of the grammar that we have thus far been able to describe and are using these rules to understand and produce sentences. Some of the results obtained suggest areas for further examination of this hypothesis.

REFERENCES

AMMONS, R. B., AND AMMONS, H. S. *Full range picture vocabulary*. Missoula: Psychological Test Specialists, 1958.

BLUM, G. S. *The Blacky Pictures*. New York: Psychological Corp., 1950.

BROWN, R., FRASER, C., AND BELLUGI, U. Evaluation procedures for grammar. In preparation.

CHOMSKY, N. *Syntactic structures*. Gravenhage, the Netherlands. Mouton, 1957.

HALLE, M., AND STEVENS, K. Speech recognition: A model and a program for research. *I.R.E. Transactions on Information Theory*, IT-8, 1962.

INSTITUTE OF CHILD WELFARE. *The Minnesota scale for paternal occupation*. Minneapolis: University of Minnesota, 1950.

MATTHEWS, G. H. Analysis by synthesis of natural languages. London: National Physical Lab., 1961, No. 13, 531-542.

MENYUK, P. Syntactic structures in the language of children: Nursery school and first grade. Unpublished doctoral thesis, Boston University, 1961.

MENYUK, P. Syntactic structures in the language of children, *J. Child Developm.*, 1963, **34**, 407-422.

MENYUK, P. Syntactic rules used by children from pre-school through first grade, accepted for publication *J. Child Developm.*, 1963. (a)

MILLER, G. A., AND CHOMSKY, N. Finitary models of language users. In Handbook of Mathematical Psychology, Vol. II. New York: Wiley, 1963, 419-492.

VIGOTSKY, L. S. *Thought and language*. New York: M.I.T. Press and Wiley, 1962.

(Received April 15, 1963)

COMPARISON OF GRAMMAR OF CHILDREN WITH FUNCTIONALLY DEVIANT AND NORMAL SPEECH

PAULA MENYUK

A generative model of grammar was used to compare the grammar of 10 children diagnosed as using infantile speech with that of 10 matched children using normal speech to attempt to formalize the description of language simply characterized as infantile. The language of one child was periodically sampled from age two to three. A language sample from each child was analyzed and the syntactic structures used were postulated. A number of children in each group were asked to repeat a list of sentences containing syntactic structures found in children's grammar.

The term infantile seemed to be a misnomer since at no age level did the grammatical production of a child with deviant speech match or closely match that of a child with normal speech. It was hypothesized that the differences found in the use and repetition of syntactic structures between the two groups might be due to differences in the use of the coding processes for the perception and production of language. The children with deviant speech, in the terms of the model of grammar used for analysis, formulated their sentences with the most general rules whereas children with normal speech used increasingly differentiating rules for different structures as they matured.

In any description of children's speech disorders such as disorders of articulation or infantile perseveration we usually find some comments on the general language ability of the children with the disorder. For example, Powers (1957) in her discussion of functional disorders of articulation tells us to evaluate speech behavior as a whole and includes under this heading level of language organization, grammar, and pronunciation. In general, these speech disorders are no longer considered discrete phonemic anomalies but part of the total language production of the individual.

If we deem it necessary to observe and describe language production rather than just the production of a speech disorder for complete diagnosis, the problem then arises as to how to evaluate this language. One way of doing this is to describe the grammar of the child. Studies of the grammatical form in children's language have used traditional grammatical labels to classify aspects of language production. There are descriptions of sentence length, complexity of sentence structure, and proportion of usage of differently structured sentences at various age levels (McCarthy, 1954). Essentially equivalent conclusions are reached in these studies. As the child matures the proportion of complex sentences increases. The definition of complex, thus far intuitively defined, is more difficult. A technique for describing children's grammar should be able to provide a formalization of the notion of increasing complexity.

JOURNAL OF SPEECH AND HEARING RESEARCH, June 1964, vol. 7, no. 2, pp. 109-121.

The descriptive technique used in this study is a generative or transformational model of grammar. The model is analagous to a categorization theory of learning. This, in turn, is based on an hypothesis about the nature of the nervous system and its possibilities for storing information for later use. Because the nervous system is limited in its capacity to discriminate between all available stimuli it is postulated that the organism learns to categorize or assign class membership to given stimuli. In a generative model of grammar it is hypothesized that the perceiver or child has incorporated both the generative rules of the grammar and a heuristic component that samples an input sentence and by a series of successive approximations determines which rules were used to generate this sentence (Halle and Stevens, 1962; Matthews, 1961; Miller and Chomsky, 1963). In this way the child has the capacity to formulate categories of sentence types: the affirmative sentence, the negative sentence, the imperative sentence, and so on. Instead of memorizing every sentence he has been exposed to and imitating these sentences, he uses a set of rules to understand and generate not only sentences he has heard, but also other possible examples.

A generative grammar, as formulated in Chomsky's *Syntactic Structures* (1957), is viewed as having a tri-partite structure. The first level is phrase structure where kernel or simple-active-declarative sentences are formulated from rules for stringing together parts of speech. The second level is transformations where more complex sentence types are generated by rules for addition and/or deletion, permutation and substitution within or among kernel sentences. The rules which operate on one kernel sentence are termed simple transformations. Rules which operate on two or more kernels are termed general transformations. The third level is morphology where inflectional rules, dependent on the previous sequences are applied. For example, at the phrase structure level we may choose the sentence Noun Phrase + Verb Phrase expanded into "He play + past tense." At the transformational level we may add by an optional rule the *do* morpheme and derive "He do play + past tense." Then from another optional rule for a question we permute and derive "Do he play + past tense." From a final obligatory transformation we permute tense to attach to *do* and derive "Do + past tense he play." At the morphology level *do* + past tense becomes did and the sentence "Did he play?" is derived. In this way the model organizes previously compartmentalized measures of language production into an interdependent sequence of rules.

The purpose of this study was to use the model to compare the grammar of children diagnosed as using infantile speech with the grammar of children using normal speech in an attempt to formalize the description of language simply characterized as infantile. The following questions were explored: (1) what, if any, were the differences in the use of syntactic structures between the two groups? and (2) were these differences representative of a more immature language production?

METHOD

Language was elicited and tape-recorded with 10 children who were diagnosed, first by their teachers and then by a speech clinician, as using infantile speech. There was no evidence of any physiological impairment as the cause for the speech disorder. Language was elicited and recorded in three stimulus situations: first, responses to a projective test, *The Blacky Pictures* (Blum, 1950), second, conversation with an adult (the experimenter) generated by a proscribed set of questions, and third, conversation with peers generated by role playing in a family setting. Using the criteria of age, sex, I.Q., and socio-economic status, these children were matched with a group of 10 children using normal speech. Language samples had previously been obtained from these children in exactly the same stimulus situations. The age range of the groups was 3.0 (3 years, 0 months) to 5.10. The mean I.Q. of the infantile speech (I.S.) group was 125.70 and the mean I.Q. of the normal speech (N.S.) group was 126.40 as measured by the *Full Range Picture Vocabulary Test* (Ammons and Ammons, 1958). Parental occupation for all the children fell within the upper 24% range of a middle class population (Institute of Child Welfare, 1950). There was no significant difference in the mean number of sentences produced by the N.S. group (80.30) and the mean number produced by the I.S. group (73.60). Language was also elicited and tape-recorded in various stimulus situations with one child over a 12-month period beginning at age 2.0 to 3.0. This was done to examine the possibility that children with infantile speech were using syntactic structures which were similar, in fact, to those used by a much younger child.

The language sample produced by each child was analyzed using the model previously described and the syntactic structures used by the children in each group at all three levels of the grammar were postulated. (For more complete details on obtaining and analyzing language samples see Menyuk, 1963a.) The structures used by the children to generate their sentences produced both completely grammatical sentences and sentences which deviated from complete grammaticalness. The structures which deviated are designated as restricted forms. Using Fisher's exact probability formula (Fisher, 1925) comparisons were made of the number of children in each group who used both types of structures. The frequencies of usage of the restricted forms in both groups were computed. Regression analyses were used to determine the correlation between age and increase in use of transformations and decrease in use of restricted forms for each group.

In addition to the above, three children in the I.S. group and the three matching children in the N.S. group were asked to repeat a list of sentences containing exemplars of various transformation types. Also, four of the children in the I.S. group and four in the N.S. group were asked to repeat a list containing exemplars of the various restricted forms. The number of sentences that were repeated, not repeated, and corrected in each group was computed. Finally, regression analyses were used to determine the correlation between non-repetition and sentence length for each group.

234

The following is a list of the syntactic structures, with sentence examples, that were compared. All examples were taken from children's language samples.

Transformation Types	Examples
Passive	He got tied up.
	He was washed.
Negation	He isn't a good boy.
Question	Are you nice?
Contraction	He'll be good.
Inversion	Here is the toothpaste.
Relative Question	Where are you going?
Imperative	Don't use my dough.
Pronominalization	There isn't any more.
Separation	He took it off.
Got	I've got a lollipop.
Auxiliary Be Placement	He is not going.
Auxiliary Have Placement	I've already been there.
Do	I did read the book.
Possessive	I'm writing daddy's name.
Reflexive	I cut myself.
Conjunction	Peter is here and you are there.
Conjunction Deletion	I see a red book and a blue book.
If Conjunction	I'll give it to you if you want it.
So Conjunction	He saw him so he hit him.
Cause Conjunction	He'll eat it because it's good.
Pronoun in Conjunction	David saw the bicycle and he was happy.
Adjective	I have a pink dog.
Relative Clause	I don't know what he's doing.
Infinitival Complement	I want to play.
Participial Complement	I like painting.
Iteration	You have to drink milk to grow strong.
Nominalization	She does the shopping and cooking and baking.
Nominal Compound	The baby carriage is here.

Restricted Forms	Examples
Verb Phrase Omission	This green
Verb Phrase Substitution	He tries to take the knife from falling
Verb Phrase Redundancy	He'll might get in jail
Noun Phrase Omission	Look at
Noun Phrase Redundancy	I want it the paint
Preposition Omission	He'll have to go the doctor's
Preposition Substitution	He took me at the circus
Preposition Redundancy	Take it off from there
Article Omission	Daddy has new office

Article Substitution	I want a milk please
Article Redundancy	I like the Donny
Particle Omission	Put the hat
Particle Redundancy	The barber cut off his hair off
Contraction Deletion Be	I going
Contraction Deletion Have	I been thinking about that
Double Negation	You can't put no more water in it
Inversion Subject-Object	Crayons I want
Inversion Verb Number	Here's two clouds
No Question	Who he is kissing
Pronominalization Substitution	It was snow yesterday
No Separation	Take off it
Reflexive Third	They're hurting theirselves
Tense Restriction	They mixed paints and pour buckets
Pronoun Restriction	My mother washes and he cleans
Adjective Restriction	Do you like this papers
Relative Clause Restriction	I know what is he doing
Noun Form Omission	She has lots of necklace
Noun Form Substitution	Those are wolfs
Noun Form Redundancy	Where are the peoples
Verb Form Omission	She like that
Verb Form Substitution	He growed up fast
Verb Form Redundancy	She splashted herself
Adverb Form Omission	You play nice
Adverb Form Redundancy	You have to draw straightly
Pronoun Subject Substitution	Me like that
	Him is a bad boy
Possessive Form Omission	That's mes
Possessive Form Substitution	That's mys
Possessive Form Redundancy	That's mines

RESULTS

Use of Syntactic Structures

In comparing the number of children in both groups who used the various transformation types there were many structures which were used by more of the children in the N.S. group above the level of chance (.50). In all instances except in the use of So Conjunction, these are not structures which show significant changes in usage when three to four and six to seven-year-old children with normal speech are compared (Menyuk, 1963a). In fact, it was found that the transformations Negation, Auxiliary Be Placement, Do and Pronoun in Conjunction or Conjoining Sentences were used by all the children, and the transformations Question, Inversion, Separation, Possessive, Conjunction, and Conjunction Deletion were used by 85% or more of the children from three years on.

TABLE 1. Comparison of usage of transformations which show differences above the level of chance.

| Transformations | Number of Cases | | P value* |
	I.S. Group	N.S. Group	
Negation	6	10	.22
Question	6	10	.22
Inversion	6	10	.22
Imperative	6	10	.22
Pronominalization	0	8	.05
Separation	5	9	.23
Auxiliary Be Placement	6	10	.22
Do	3	10	.11
Possessive	6	9	.26
Reflexive	3	8	.20
Conjunction	4	10	.16
Conjunction Deletion	3	10	.11
So Conjunction	1	4	.42
Cause Conjunction	4	8	.23
Pronoun in Conjunction	6	10	.22
Relative Clause	5	10	.21

*P values were obtained by Fisher's exact probability formula

In addition, when one divides the population into the five youngest children in the N.S. group and the five oldest children in the I.S. group and compares the usage of these structures essentially the same results are obtained. The only structure which is not used by more of the N.S. group above the level of chance is the Reflexive transformation. The mean age of the five youngest N.S. children was 3.3 and of the five oldest I.S. children was 5.0. Table 1 lists the transformations which show differences in usage between the two groups above the level of chance and notes the probability of occurrence of such usage.

The results of the comparison of usage of restricted forms show that the forms used differently by the two groups above the level of chance can be divided into two categories. Almost all forms which are used by more of the children in the I.S. group are omissions at all three levels of the grammar. The only exception is Preposition Substitution at the phrase structure level. All restricted forms which are used by more of the children in the N.S. group are redundancies or substitution on the phrase structure level and non-observation of rules which are necessary for the formulation of transformations. Three of the four restricted forms used by more of the N.S. children in the generation of transformations concern general transformations or those which require operations on two sentences (Tense Restriction, Pronoun Restriction and Adjective Restriction). This seems a logical result since more of the N.S. children than I.S. children were using general transformations. All forms which are used with *greater frequency* by the children in the I.S. group are omissions. To some extent the same kinds of differences occurred when the use of restricted forms by three to four and six to seven-year-old children was compared. More of the older children used Noun Phrase Redundancy and more of the younger children omitted prepositions and particles. However, the clear-cut differences found between the

TABLE 2. Comparison of usage of restricted forms which show differences above the level of chance and frequency of usage.

Restricted Forms	No. of Cases I.S. Group	No. of Cases N.S. Group	P Value	Frequency I.S. Group	Frequency N.S. Group
Verb Phrase Omission	10	3	.11	54	3
Verb Phrase Substitution	3	5	.34	3	5
Noun Phrase Omission	9	5	.23	27	8
Noun Phrase Redundancy	2	4	.38	2	4
Preposition Omission	8	1	.13	14	2
Preposition Substitution	5	3	.34	7	3
Article Omission	8	2	.15	24	2
Article Redundancy	1	5	.24	1	7
Contraction Deletion	10	10	—	58	15
Inversion-Verb Number	2	5	.37	2	9
Tense Restriction	1	5	.24	1	7
Pronoun Restriction	2	4	.38	6	4
Adjective Restriction	3	5	.34	3	7
Verb Form Omission	9	7	.26	69	22
Noun Form Omission	4	2	.38	8	2
Pronoun Substitution	6	0	.14	24	0
Possessive Form Omission	5	3	.34	6	6

N.S. and I.S. groups were not found in the previous study since fluctuations in the number of children using all types of restricted forms occurred throughout the age range. In addition, when one compares the usage of these forms by the five youngest children in the N.S. group and the five oldest children in the I.S. group, the results obtained in the comparison of the two entire groups were again found. The only structures which did not show differences in usage above the level of chance were Verb Form Omission, Noun Form Omission and formulation of possessives at the morphology level of the grammar. Again, more of the children in the N.S. group used substitutions and redundancies and did not observe rules attendant on the use of transformations, and, again, more of the children in the I.S. group omitted structures. Also, all the same forms were used with greater frequency by the children in the I.S. group. Table 2 lists the restricted forms which show differences in usage between the two groups above the level of chance and notes the probability of occurrence of such usage. The frequency of occurrence of these forms is also listed.

The correlation between increased age and increased usage of transformations was insignificant for both groups with the correlation higher for the N.S. group. For the N.S. group $r = .25$ and for the I.S. group $r = .10$. This result might be predicted from the fact that with normal speaking children it was found that many of the transformations are used at an early age and used consistently. However, the correlation between increased age and decreased usage of restricted forms was significant for the N.S. group ($r = .91$, $t = 6.14$, $p < .001$) but was not significant for the I.S. group ($r = .20$).

Repetition of Syntactic Structures

The comparison of the two groups in their ability to repeat sentences containing the various syntactic structures seems to point up the differences found

TABLE 3. Comparison of repetition of sentences.

Types of Repetition	No. of Sentences	
	I.S. Group	N.S. Group
Complete Repetition	73	164
Complete Omission	2	2
Last Word/s Repeated	28	0
Phrase or Word Repeated	12	0
Sentence Two of Conjunction Omitted	2	1
Sentence One of Conjunction Omitted	11	0
Noun Phrase Omission	17	1
Verb Phrase Omission	16	2
Verb Form Omission	6	0
Article or Adverb Omission	3	2
Modification of Transformation	7	4
Correction of Restricted Form	20	27
Substitution	8	2

in the usage of these structures. More of the items were completely repeated by children in the N.S. group. More of the items were repeated with omissions by children in the I.S. group. Table 3 lists the categories which were used to compare the repetitions of the two groups and the number of items repeated in each manner by the children in the two groups. Modification of a transformation was the repetition of a sentence using a different transformation. An example is changing the question to a declarative: "You are nice." for "Are you nice?" Correction of a restricted form was changing the sentence to a completely grammatical one. An example is correction of Preposition Omission: "I'm going to go to New York!" for "I'm going to go New York." Substitution was any change of words that did not alter the grammaticalness of the sentence. Some examples are: "the" for "a," "here" for "there," and "he" for "she."

The correlation between sentence length and non-repetition of sentences was significant for the I.S. group ($r = .53$, $t = 4.58$, $p < .001$) but non-significant for the N.S. group ($r = .04$). In a previous study (Menyuk, 1963b) with normal speaking children the repetition capacity of nursery school and kindergarten children was compared. It was found that most of the non-repetitions, primarily those of the younger children, were due to modifications of transformations and corrections of restricted forms and not omissions. Also, it was found that non-repetitions and sentence length were not significantly correlated even for the younger children.

Grammar of Two Year Old

When we compare the grammar of the two year old and the youngest member of the I.S. group, and then note the trends occurring throughout the age range of the I.S. group, more dissimilarities than similarities exist. At the phrase structure level the two year old does not use some structures which he does use at age three. (The age at which he begins to use these structures is noted and those which are not used by the 3.0 I.S. child are marked by an asterisk.) He does not use: First and Second Person Subject (2.7), Be + Predicate (2.6), Adverb of Manner (2.7*), Time (2.9*), Location—here and there (2.9*), Modals Can, May, Will (3.0* May, Will), Article The (2.9), Prepositional Phrases of Location (2.6), Time (2.9*). In addition, the two year old often formulates sentences without the Verb Phrase (Judy's chair.) He sometimes formulates sentences with Noun Phrase Redundancy (Fix it mommy's shoes). The three-year-old I.S. child often formulates sentences without Noun Phrase (Want dat.) and without be in Be + Predicate sentences. All the phrase structure rules are being used throughout the rest of the age range of the I.S. group but the omissions noted for the 3.0 I.S. child are still occurring frequently.

At the transformation level all the structures used by the two year old are being used by the three-year-old I.S. child. However, by age three the N.S. child is using many more transformations than the three-year-old I.S. child. By age 2.0 the N.S. child is using the transformations: Negation, Contraction, Relative Question and Imperative. The following are the transformations not used by the two year old. (The age at which the N.S. child begins to use these structures is noted and those which are not used by the 3.0 I.S. child are marked by an asterisk.) He does not use Adjective (2.4), Nominal Compound (2.4), Possessive (2.6), Separation (2.6), Relative Clause (2.6), Conjunction (2.6), Infinitival Complement (2.7), Question (2.7*), Passive (2.9*), Nominalization (2.9*), Cause Conjunction (2.9*), Conjunction Deletion (2.9*), Inversion (2.9*), Do (2.9*). Less than 50% of the children in the I.S. group use the following transformations used by the child with normal speech as he reaches age three: Passive, Conjunction Deletion, Cause Conjunction, and Nominalization. In addition, throughout the age range in the I.S. group the do in the do + Verb constructions and the to in the Infinitival Complement transformation are very frequently omitted so that sentences of the following type are often found: "How that wheel come off?" and "I know how ride."

At the morphology level the two year old does not use or often omits the following structures. (The age at which he no longer does this is noted.) He does not use Third Person Singular Present (2.6) and Past (2.9) markers of verbs. He often omits Plural of Nouns (2.6) and Possessive 's (2.6). In addition, he often uses substitutions for other possessive forms until age 3.0 and sometimes substitutes a for prepositions to and for until age 2.7. The three year old often omits and substitutes all the above mentioned structures plus substituting object pronoun for subject pronoun (me/I, him/he, her/she) and omitting ing in the Present Participle construction ("He's play."). All the omissions and substitutions noted for the 3.0 I.S. child are still occurring with great frequency at the end of the age range of the I.S. group.

DISCUSSION

The results of the statistical analysis of grammatical production allow us only to observe trends since the population in this study was small. Using a generative model of grammar for description, three factors seem to emerge from this com-

240

parison of the grammar of children with normal speech and children diagnosed as using infantile speech. The first is that, in fact, the term infantile seems to be a misnomer. The grammatical production of the oldest members of the I.S. group did not match or closely match the grammatical production of the youngest members of the N.S. group. The three-year-old I.S. child used both more transformations and more restricted forms than did the two-year-old N.S. child, and some of these were restricted forms never used by the N.S. child at any point from age two to three or by any other normal speaking children from age three to seven. The two- to three-year period seems to be one of extremely rapid maturation in the use of syntactic structures for normal speaking children. Although at age two many structures were missing from the N.S. child's grammar, by age three he exceeded even the oldest I.S. child in grammatical production. To say, for example, that a five-year-old child with infantile speech uses the grammar of a normal speaking child at age four or three or two is incorrect. His grammatical usage is not simply more infantile than normal for his age or delayed in time.

The second factor is the two ways in which the I.S. group's use of grammar differed from that of the N.S. group. They were different both in their use of transformations and restricted forms. Earlier it was hypothesized that the child samples an input sentence and by a series of successive approximations determines which rules were used to generate this sentence. From the viewpoint of this hypothesis, the I.S. children seemed to be using the most generalized rules or first approximations to rules to formulate their sentences. They generated their sentences with transformations that involve the fewest numbers of operations and with restricted forms which seem to be early approximations to completed rules. Restricted forms are still being used by age seven in a normal speaking population. However, at that age, redundancies in structures generally occur more frequently than omissions and substitutions. In a previous study (Menyuk, 1963c) it was found that the usage of omissions peaked earliest and highest in an age range from three to seven. The peak for usage of substitutions and redundancies occurred later. It was hypothesized that this might indicate children's increasing ability to use more and more differentiated rules in the formulation of sentences as they mature. In addition to using more generalized rules, the children in the I.S. group used them much more frequently than did the N.S. children.

The third factor is the striking dissimilarity in the repetition ability of the N.S. group and the I.S. group. Powers has stated that despite many studies our information about the relationship of hearing processes to articulation remains equivocal and that ". . . the more carefully controlled studies in which functional articulatory defectives and good speakers were matched for age and intelligence show no differences in auditory memory span between speech ability groups." (Powers, 1957, p. 744). Hoberman and Goldfarb (1963) in a comparative study of the hearing acuity of normal and schizophrenic children found that there was no significant difference in pure-tone thresholds but that speech perception thresholds were significantly higher in the schizophrenic group. The results of these studies indicate that in functional speech disorders sound stimuli perception does not seem to be affected. On the other hand, the coding processes required in language perception may be.

In this study the I.S. children seemed to be either repeating the last things heard or applying the most general or elementary rules in perceiving and reproducing a sentence. Sentence length affected their ability to repeat. This was also the case with normal speaking subjects when the stucture of the sentence was broken down (sentences in reverse word order). The N.S. children seemed to be using the syntactic structure of the sentence to repeat. Most of their non-repetitions were due to some modifications of transformations and corrections of restricted forms and not sentence length.

In conclusion, the N.S. children rapidly acquired increasingly differentiated rules to formulate structures as an increasingly mature population was observed and therefore produced increasingly complex structures. The I.S. children seemed unable to move much beyond the use of sets of elementary and generalized rules. This seemed to be also the case with the articulation difficulties found in this group. The most frequent sound errors were omission and substitution. The initial s and final t were omitted by more than 50% of the I.S. children, and the following substitutions were also used by more than 50% of the children: the sound w was used for w and r and l, the sound t was used for t and k and the unvoiced th, the sound d was used for d and g and the voiced th. The results of this study indicate that the most significant factor may be the difference in the N.S. child and the I.S. child's ability to determine the complete sets of rules that are used to generate and differentiate structures at any level of the grammar.

SUMMARY

The purpose of this study was to use a generative model of grammar to describe and compare the language of children with deviant and normal speech in an attempt to obtain an adequate description of the deviant speech.

Language was elicited in various stimulus situations from 10 children diagnosed as using functionally infantile speech. Using the criteria of age, sex, socioeconomic status, and I.Q. they were matched with 10 normal speaking children from whom a language sample had previously been obtained in the same stimulus situations. Language was also obtained from one child over a 12-month period from 2.0 to 3.0 years. The language sample produced by each child was analyzed using a generative or transformational model of grammar and the syntactic structures used were postulated. Some of the children in each group were asked to repeat a list of sentences containing transformational types (sentences which go beyond the simple-active-declarative type) and sentences containing restricted forms (sentences which deviate from complete grammaticalness).

From the results obtained the term infantile seems to be a misnomer since at no age level did the grammatical production of a child with deviant speech match or closely match the grammatical production of a child with normal speech from two years on. The child with normal speech rapidly acquired structures which required increasingly complex rules for their generation over the two- to three-year period and exceeded even the oldest I.S. child at age three. Formally, the grammatical usage of the two groups differed in that the children with normal speech used more transformations and the children with deviant speech used more restricted forms and used them much more frequently.

The repetition ability of the two groups differed strikingly. The children with deviant speech, for the most part, repeated with omissions or just repeated the last words of sentences. Non-repetition was significantly correlated with sentence length. The repetition of sentences by children with normal speech seemed dependent on the structure of the sentence, and for them non-repetition was not significantly correlated with sentence length.

It was hypothesized that differences found in the use of syntactic structures and in the repetition of these structures between the two groups might be due to differences in how the coding processes for perception and production of language are used. Both in use and repetition of syntactic structures the children with deviant speech, in the terms of the model of grammar used for analysis, formulated their sentences with the most general rules whereas children with normal speech used increasingly differentiated rules to generate syntactic structures as an increasingly mature population was observed.

This investigation was supported in part by the U.S. Army Signal Corps, the Air Force Office of Scientific Research, and the Office of Naval Research; in part by the National Science Foundation (Grant G-16526), the National Institutes of Health (Grant MH-04737-03), and the National Aeronautics and Space Administration (Grant NsG-496). Additional support was received through Fellowship 5F2 MH-8768-03 from the National Institute of Mental Health, Public Health Service. Grateful acknowledgement is given to the children and teachers of the Young Israel and Beacon Nursery Schools and Edith C. Baker school in Brookline, Massachusetts.

REFERENCES

AMMONS, R. B., and AMMONS, H. S., *Full Range Picture Vocabulary*. Missoula, Montana: Psychological Test Specialists (1958).

BLUM, G. S., *The Blacky Pictures*. New York: Psychological Corp. (1950).

CHOMSKY, N., *Syntactic Structures*. The Netherlands: Mouton (1957).

FISHER, R. A., *Statistical Methods for Research Workers*. Edinburgh: Oliver and Boyd, Ltd. (1925).

HALLE, M. and STEVENS, K., Speech recognition: a model and a program for research. *I.R.E. Transactions on Information Theory*, IT-8 (1962).

HOBERMAN, S. E., and GOLDFARB, W., Speech reception thresholds in schizophrenic children. *J. Speech Hearing Res.*, 6, 101-106 (1963).

Institute of Child Welfare, *The Minnesota Scale for Paternal Occupation*. Minn: U. of Minn. (1950).

MATTHEWS, G. H., Analysis by synthesis of sentences of natural languages. *International Conference on Machine Translation of Languages and Applied Language Analysis*. London: National Physical Laboratory (1961).

McCARTHY, D., Language development in children. In Carmichael, L., (Ed.) *Manual of Child Psychology*. New York: Wiley (1954).

MENYUK, P., Syntactic structures in the language of children. *J. Child Development*, 34, 407-22 (1963a).

MENYUK, P., A preliminary evaluation of grammatical capacity in children. *J. Verbal Learning and Verbal Behavior*, 2, 429-439 (1963b).

MENYUK, P., Alternation of rules in children's grammar. In preparation (1963c).

MILLER, G. A., and CHOMSKY, N., Finitary models of language users. In Luce, D. et al. (Eds.) *Vol. II Handbook of Mathematical Psychology*. New York: Wiley (1964).

POWERS, M. H., Functional disorders of articulation—symptomatology and etiology. In Travis, L. E., (Ed.) *Handbook of Speech Pathology*. New York: Appleton-Century-Crofts, Inc. (1957).

Language Behavior of the Mentally Retarded: Syntactic Characteristics [1]

JAMES T. GRAHAM AND LOUELLA W. GRAHAM

Language samples from 9 mentally retarded subjects with CAs ranging from 10 to 18 years and MAs ranging from 3 years, 6 months, to 10 years were analyzed syntactically. The results indicated that certain indices of linguistic sophistication and subjects' MAs were correlated. It was tentatively hypothesized that nonmongoloid retardates develop rules of their language at a different rate but in much the same way as intellectually-average children.

Most modern philosophies concerning management of the mentally retarded embody some form of the concept that, consistent with his abilities, the mentally retarded individual should have every opportunity to approach a normal life style. It is the contention of the authors that each individual, whether retarded or nonretarded, is judged by those he meets primarily on the basis of his oral communication ability. The fact that the mentally retarded as a group have language difficulties has been well-documented (Jordan, 1967). Although several studies of language behavior of the mentally retarded have been reported (e.g., Goda & Griffith, 1962; Lenneberg, Nichols, & Rosenberger, 1964), many questions remain concerning the specifics of their difficulties.

In the study of language, one may choose one or more of four levels to examine. These are the semantic (meaning) level, the syntactic (organizational) level, the morphologic (word structure) level, and the phonologic (speech sound) level. While no single level alone will provide a total understanding of an individual's linguistic performance, it is the authors' belief that the syntactic level provides the best point at which to begin to unravel the language system used by the mentally retarded of various intellectual levels.

Analysis of syntactic structure provides one with several insights into a language system. It shows: (a) the ways in which propositions are argued, (b) the rules by which components of the language can be strung together, and (c) the way in which complex strings are generated from a number of simple propositions. It is well-accepted that language systems are based on a finite and relatively small number of rules, while the possible sentences that speakers of the language will agree are grammatical are infinite (Chomsky, 1965). The rules that a given speaker of a language has internalized about his language determine his competence in the use of that language.

Estimates of linguistic competence are not easily acquired, as has been pointed out (Chomsky, 1964). However, it is possible to gain information about an individual's language system through observing the language that he uses. An individual's performance can be analyzed and the rules by which that performance was probably governed can be formulated. Obviously, linguistic performance can be used as an estimate of an individual's underlying linguistic competence (Chomsky, 1964; McNeill, 1966). Furthermore, the confidence one can place in the estimate is, in part, a function of the type and extent of the sample that is available for analysis.

Two basic approaches can be used in the

[1] The project report herein was supported by Grant No. 7–1242 from the U.S. Department of Health, Education, and Welfare, Office of Education, Bureau of Education for the Handicapped. The authors wish to thank the staff of the Fort Wayne (Indiana) State Hospital and Training Center, especially Dr. Jeffrey H. Smith, for their cooperation.

AMERICAN JOURNAL OF MENTAL DEFICIENCY, 1971, vol. 75, no. 5, pp. 623-629.

study of an individual's understanding and use of the various rules that govern the structure of his language. One may collect a sample of relatively spontaneous language and establish rules that explain the subject's linguistic system. A second approach is the use of tests designed to probe specific facets of syntax and the speaker's ability to deal with these structures. In the present report, the first method has been used.

Method

Subjects

Three research assistants, all experienced speech therapists, gathered data from 15 male residents ranging in chronological age (CA) from 10 to 18 years, and in mental age (MA) from 3 years, 6 months, to 10 years, selected from the academic program of a state residential facility. The major concern of the investigators was that a sample of representative language be obtained under comparable conditions from each subject. Although the task of data collection required flexibility from session to session, two general techniques were used to elicit language: (a) Each subject was engaged in conversation about himself, his home, his work in school, or any other topic that seemed fruitful, and (b) he was asked to tell stories about or describe sets of pictures which showed scenes such as a farmyard, a boy washing a wagon, or a birthday party. In some cases, sufficient language was elicited in one 20-minute session while, in other cases, multiple sessions were required before a sufficient sample was obtained.

The authors previewed the recordings of each interview and decided, on the basis of the amount of language elicited and the quality of the recording itself, when the material from a given subject was acceptable for analysis. On the basis of preliminary work, it was decided that an "acceptable" amount of language would be operationally defined as 75 sentences that were other than simple naming responses. The recordings of six potential subjects were excluded at this time on the basis of excessive background noise or lack of sufficient responses.

The recordings from interviews with the nine remaining retarded subjects provided the data upon which subsequent analyses were based. Salient factors concerning each subject are presented in Table 1. The characteristics of this group of subjects were similar to the larger population of male residents in the institution's academic program.

Data Analysis

The recordings from the nine subjects were transcribed into rough drafts which the authors reviewed by listening to the original tape as many times as necessary to resolve all lexical items. The experience of the researchers with the task indicated that even when editors are practiced listeners, the use of two people to review such tapes is mandatory if an accurate final transcript is to be obtained.

TABLE 1

DESCRIPTION OF SUBJECTS

Subject	Chronological age [a]	Mental age [b]	IQ [b]	Etiology [c]
BD	10	3–6	36	Congenital cerebral deficit
MM	14	3–8	26	Encephalopathy
CW	18	4–10	26	Cultural-familial
RC	15	5–5	37	Cultural-familial
MB	15	5–6	39	Congenital cerebral deficit
DN	15	5–10	39	Encephalopathy
CN	14	6–10	56	Encephalopathy
BK	14	8–10	64	Encephalopathy
RK	15	10–0	62	Uncertain

[a] To nearest birthday at time of initial data collection.
[b] IQ and MA information (in years and months) are based on either Wechsler Intelligence Scale for Children (WISC) or Stanford-Binet data.
[c] This institution bases etiologic classifications on Heber (1961).

After all lexical items were resolved, the corpus was divided into sentences, using each subject's particular intonation and pause patterns as indicators of sentence boundaries. Therefore, sentences were not always complete in the traditional sense, but often were sentence fragments. Some examples of these are given below. Simple one-word responses of affirmation or negation were not counted as sentences, and were not included in the analysis.

A total of 1,436 sentences from the nine subjects provided the data from which formulations of syntactic rules were developed. (For descriptions of these procedures, see Chomsky, 1957). All utterances were rewritten in terms of underlying strings of the form

$$NP + tense\ (+ aspect) + \begin{Bmatrix} cop + pred \\ V_I \\ V_T + NP \end{Bmatrix},$$

which, in this case, involved a very small number of phrase-structure rules. A set of transformational rules then were developed to allow recovery of the original surface structure. These transformations were of two types: (a) elementary transformations which resulted in changes in the underlying base strings through such operations as addition, deletion, or substitution; (b) generalized transformations which acted on two (or more) underlying strings to produce a single derived structure through such operations as conjoining and embedding.

In almost any sample of casual speech, regardless of the intelligence of the speaker, many utterances are ellipses (fragments) of complete sentences. Although a grammar of English ellipses has yet to be fully developed, it is possible to use one's basic intuitions about his native language to decide whether an elliptical response seems acceptable or lacks some necessary elements. For example, although a complete response to the question "Where is he going?" would be "He is going home," one accepts that the exchange "Where is he going?" "Home" is acceptable even though omissions have occurred. On the other hand, the responses in exchanges such as "What's she doing?" "She eating" and "Tell me about this picture" "All playing in the box. Dog's got Easter Bunny" seem to be incomplete in some sense. Intuitively, the deletions here do not seem acceptable.

In analyzing transcripts, items that had been omitted incorrectly were added in order to make the utterance acceptable. All items then were assigned to grammatical categories (parts of speech), and a deletion error-rate was computed for each subject by starting with his expanded sentences and computing the percentage of required lexical items that had been omitted (see Table 2).

Results

It has been hypothesized (and some support now exists for the proposition) that, in the process of developing his language system, a child first uses primarily base structure rules (along with a few elementary transformational rules) and then proceeds to add more—and more complicated—transformational rules. It has been suggested that the acquisition of new rules and the refinement of earlier rules is based on mechanisms, such as increased memory capacity, which seem to underlie language competence (Menyuk, 1969).

Although there are no data to indicate that there is a one-to-one relationship between the number of transformations applied to a string and its resulting complexity or the difficulty with which it is generated by a child, there is evidence that, for intellectually-average children, increased use of transformations, as well as changes in the types used, seem to accompany gains in age and accuracy of utterances (Menyuk, 1969).

For the present group of retardates, Figure 1 shows the percentage of each subject's sentences that were produced without transformations and that were generated by the use of more than two transformations. As can be seen, the tendency is for the lower mental age (MA) subjects to produce a relatively large number of their sentences through the use of base string rules with no transformational rules being applied. On the other hand, the opposite tendency appears for the higher MA subjects. Over half of the sentences of two subjects (designated BK and RK) required

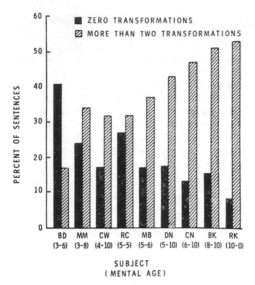

FIG. 1. Use of zero and of more than two transformations.

the use of three or more transformations, while a relatively small number were generated without transformational process. Subject BD stands by himself in being the only subject who used a greater percentage of no-transformation utterances than utterances derived through more than two transformations.

Even Subjects CW and MM used, for example, modifying constructions, questions, negatives, infinitives, and conjoinings in various combinations in over 30 percent of their sentences. The relationship between transformation usage and the MAs of subjects was analyzed by the Spearman rank-difference correlation coefficient (rho). For this analysis and all others, an alpha level of .01 was used. The correlation between MA and the percentage of sentences containing no transformations was .90, and the correlation between MA and the percentage of sentences containing three or more transformations was .95.

BD		RC MB MM CW DN		CN		BK RK

FIG. 2. Differences between mean transformations used per sentence. Subjects not under the same bar had significantly different mean scores (*p* < .01).

A Spearman rho was also computed for occurrences of a single transformation and for two transformations per sentence. These analyses yielded nonsignificant results.

The unique behavior of the subject designated BD is shown more clearly in Figure 2, which is based on each subject's average number of transformations per sentence. Subject BD formed his own "group" and differed from all other subjects. The group comprised of two subjects designated CN and BK was an interesting one. Subject CN's behavior was much more similar to that of Subject BK

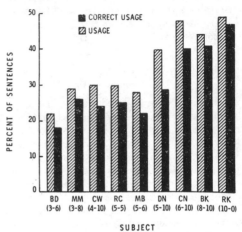

SUBJECT
(MENTAL AGE)

FIG. 3. Percentage of sentences in which generalized transformations were used and percentage in which generalized transformations were used correctly.

and, at times, that of Subject RK in most analyses than it was to his nearest counterpart in MA (Subject DN).

Product-moment correlational analysis of the MA and the average number of transformations used by a subject resulted in an *r* of .90. However, with the sample size, caution must be used in the interpretation of such a statistic, since it could be a chance (*p* = .05) deviation from a true correlation for these variables of between .58 and .97.

One may also compare the grammatical sophistication of these retardates by noting the type of transformations which they used.

248

Menyuk (1969) reported that children of nursery school through first-grade age tended to generate sentences from one underlyng string (by simple transformations) before they generated sentences by combining two or more underlying strings (by generalized transformations). Further, she noted that the older children used a greater number of generalized transformations.

Although theorists do not agree completely about what should be considered as the complete list of generalized transformations, such a list would include conjoining transformations, as well as infinitive and relative constructions. Figure 3 shows the usage of sentences generated by generalized transformations for each subject, as well as the percentage of sentences in which each used the constructions correctly. Again, the subjects arrange themselves in a rather orderly manner, with the higher MA subjects using more generalized transformations than the lower MA subjects (Spearman rho = .87). The same progression appears for the percent usage of correct constructions (Spearman rho = .85). As noted earlier, Subject CN, although closer to Subject DN in MA, tended toward Subjects BK and RK with respect to usage; however, the difference between Subject CN's usage and his correct usage was greater than for Subjects BK and RK. In other words, Subject CN was generating more of these constructions and with greater accuracy than was Subject DN, but with not quite the same accuracy as that achieved by Subjects BK and RK.

The simplest analysis of what is expressed at the surface structure level after the transformational process is to determine the relationship between the number of lexical items that appear in each sentence and the number of lexical items that the rules of the language require but which are not present. In counting lexical items, problems are encountered with certain compound words; e.g., the expression "fire truck" was counted as two units in "There is a fire truck," but as a single unit in "I like to play firetruck," since the latter use referred to a game which the subject played, and not to an object (*kind* of truck) with which he played. All contrac-

TABLE 2

CHARACTERISTICS OF OBSERVED SENTENCES

Subject (mental age in parenthesis)	Average sentence length	Deletion rate of required lexical items
BD (3–6)	3.8	11.5
MM (3–8)	5.6	7.2
CW (4–10)	4.8	8.2
RC (5–5)	4.8	10.1
MB (5–6)	4.7	10.7
DN (5–10)	5.1	11.6
CN (6–10)	5.6	11.5
BK (8–10)	7.7	2.7
RK (10–0)	8.0	4.0

tions were counted as single lexical units. The entries for the first column of Table 2 were derived from these counts. (Although it is generally accepted that mean sentence length is an inaccurate measure of language complexity, it is interesting to note, in this case, the orderly progression corresponding to MA appearing for these particular subjects.) The entries in the second column of Table 2 show, for a given subject over his complete language sample, the percent of the time that he deleted required lexical items from his utterances. Thus, the data in Table 2 indicate the relationships between each subject's accuracy and his amount of verbal output per utterance. In this case, Subject CN is clearly similar to Subject DN and does not approach the performance levels of Subjects BK and RK.

The relatively low error-rates for Subjects MM and CW as compared to those for Subject BD or Subjects RC and MB might perhaps be explained on the basis of some internal level of achievement. Perhaps Subjects MM and CW were at a stage at which they had achieved a degree of facility with their present rules and were getting ready to add more rules, or to add to the complexity and/or increase the range of their present ones. This, of course, can only be speculation. Although Subject BD was shown in Figure 1 to be producing the majority of his utterances through base-string rules without transformations, his deletion rate indicates that he was not very successful even at the elementary level.

In looking at the parts of speech involved in the lexical items deleted at the surface

249

structure level, all subjects (except Subject RC) demonstrated their greatest problem with verbal aspect. Such constructions as "I going," "They eating," "I been," "I got" (for "I've got"), as well as "Cindy's go home Saturday" and "She's eat," occurred for all subjects with considerable frequency. Although the omission of verb aspect was quite pervasive, there was not a general problem of auxiliary node expansion. All subjects, including Subject BD, used modal constructions appropriately for the most part and, although less frequently, generated appropriate question and negative constructions using modals.

Subject RC, unlike the other subjects, did not demonstrate his major problem in the expression of verbal aspect, although it was a problem for him too. His greatest deletion problem was one of pronouns in subject position. Utterances such as "Yeah, like school a lot" were quite common for him.

Discussion

The results of this study suggested certain tentative conclusions about the language behavior of institutionalized mentally retarded males between the CA of 10 and 20 years. It must be emphasized, however, that any conclusions stated at this time are, in reality, hypotheses offered for further evaluation, and that they are based on a small sample from a single institution.

The data suggest that there is an increase in the complexity of language behavior with a concomitant decrease in errors that is related to the MA of the retardate. At times, it appears that a trade between syntactic complexity and accuracy characterizes a given subject's behavior. In the case of Subjects BD and CN, for example, identical error rates of 11.5 percent were observed in deletion of required lexical items. The transformation data for these subjects in Figures 1 and 3, however, indicated the vast difference in the complexity of their utterances, with Subject CN demonstrating far more language sophistication. The converse may be observed, however, when Subject CN is compared to Subject BK on the same variables. In this case, it would seem that the sophistication in language

usage of these subjects matches until their error rates are compared.

Contrary to expectations about the language behavior of retardates with IQs in the 25 to 35 range, Subjects BD, MM, and CW demonstrated a considerable amount of verbalization which was obviously rule-governed. Although a detailed comparison between these three retardates and intellectually-average individuals of comparable MAs (3 years, 6 months, through 4 years, 10 months) was not undertaken in the present study, comparison to other reports (Menyuk, 1969) caused the authors to hypothesize that these two groups would be found to be operating in much the same manner.

As a group, the retardates discussed in this paper demonstrated a considerable amount of difficulty with expansions of verbal aspect. All, however, demonstrated a number of instances of correct usage, in addition to their instances of omission. Apparently, this portion of the verbal auxiliary rule still is in the process of being acquired by all of these retardates.

The data presented indicate that language facility for the retardate depends primarily on his MA. Furthermore, on the basis of the present study, it is tentatively hypothesized that nonmongoloid retardates such as those discussed here develop the rules of their language at a different rate, but in much the same way as do intellectually-average children.

References

Chomsky, N. *Syntactic structures.* The Hague: Mounton and Co., 1957.
Chomsky, N. Formal discussion. In U. Bellugi & R. Brown (Eds.), The acquisition of language. *Monographs of the Society for Research in Child Development,* 1964, No. 29.
Chomsky, N. *Aspects of the theory of syntax.* Cambridge, Mass.: The M.I.T. Press, 1965.
Goda, S., & Griffith, B. C. Spoken language of adolescent retardates and its relation to intelligence, age, and anxiety. *Child Development,* 1962, 33, 489–498.
Heber, R. *Manual on terminology and classification in mental retardation* (2nd edition). Washington,

D.C.: American Association on Mental Deficiency, 1961.

Jordan, T. E. Language and mental retardation: A review of the literature. In R. L. Schiefelbusch, R. H. Copeland, & J. O. Smith (Eds.), *Language and mental retardation.* New York: Holt, Rinehart and Winston, 1967.

Lenneberg, E. H., Nichols, I. A., & Rosenberger, E. F. Primitive stages of language development in mongolism. *Proceedings of the Association for Research in Nervous and Mental Disease,* 1964, 42, 119–137.

McNeill, D. Developmental psycholinguistics. In F. Smith & G. A. Miller (Eds.), *The genesis of language.* Cambridge, Mass.: The M.I.T. Press, 1966.

Menyuk, P. *Sentences children use.* Cambridge, Mass.: The M.I.T. Press, 1969.

Early Grammars

The "pivotal" grammars which emerged in the above studies were based on analysis of the texts obtained: extensive tape recorded samples of spontaneous language. It is important to understand that reference or contextual information accompanying the utterances were not considered. Rather, the utterances were analyzed in terms of the form and distribution of their elements and the elements were classified on the basis of their co-occurrence.

Since the publication of Chomsky's theory in 1957, there has been energetic and continuing evolution of the original theory reported, for example, in Postal (1964), Fodor and Katz (1964), and Chomsky (1965). One significant factor of the present theory is the emphasis on the distinction between the abstract *underlying* or *deep structure* (the semantic interpretation of the sentence), and the *superficial* or *surface structure* (the phonetic representation of the sentence), (Chomsky, 1965, P. 16). Semantically significant functional notions, the grammatical relations within a sentence, are directly represented in deep structure only (Chomsky, 1965, P. 117).

Developmental Sentence Types

By virtue of their exclusive reliance on analysis of surface structure the studies of Braine, Brown, and Miller and Ervin, do not take the above into account. Indeed, the research was done as the present theory has evolved. Therefore, the use of this data to induce such grammatical functions of the utterances as "designative," "predicative," "actor action," or "possessive," without benefit of knowing factors which contribute to or characterize the utterances, may be open to question. An isolated utterance "Mommy pigtail" can be interpreted out of context as:

1) "Mommy has a pigtail
2) Mommy's pigtail
3) Mommy make me a pigtail
4) Mommy is making a pigtail
5) That's Mommy's pigtail
6) Mommy made my pigtail"

Developmental Levels

What Lee has designated as levels are not necessarily distinctive for the purpose of measuring development, and the distinction be-

A COMMENT ON LEE'S "DEVELOPMENTAL SENTENCE TYPES: A METHOD FOR COMPARING NORMAL AND DEVIANT SYNTACTIC DEVELOPMENT"

Laura L. Lee (*JSHD*, **31,** 311-330, 1966) has applied findings obtained in several psycholinguistic studies of normal language acquisition to the appraisal and diagnosis of delayed language development. The studies which were cited (Braine, 1963; Brown and Fraser, 1964; Brown and Bellugi, 1964; Miller and Ervin, 1964) reported attempts to describe the system of grammatical rules used by the child to generate syntactic constructions. These investigators utilized the generative transformational linguistic theory of Chomsky (1957). The corpus provided by Weir (1962), consisting of her son's presleep soliloquies over a two month period, were also used as source material by Lee.

There are several points which need to be commented upon with respect to Lee's (1) utilization of this information to obtain a sequence of "developmental sentence types," and (2) methods for applying this sequence diagnostically in a comparison of speech samples from two children, one developing normally and the second a "language-delayed child."

JOURNAL OF SPEECH AND HEARING DISORDERS, August 1967, vol. 32, no. 3, pp. 294-296.

tween levels and the rationale presented for that distinction are questionable. First, "two-word combinations" and "noun phrases" are also "constructions," and utterances typical of Level I ("two-word combinations") and Level II ("noun phrases") occur concurrently in our data. The expansion of constructions into Level III type utterances, indicates further development. There is an increase in mean utterance length, but more significantly, such expansions are hierarchical with hierarchical constraints. In studying the underlying structure of sentences in our data, there appears to be a constraint on the number of syntactic nodes in the base structure which are ultimately expressed as formatives in terminal strings, a significant, structural constraint that underlies capacity for utterance length.

Our data contains such instances of consecutive utterances as:

1) buy more grocery store
2) raisins
3) buy more grocery store
4) grocery store
5) raisin grocery store

Rather than simply an inclusion of more elements in one member of a construction, as in Level III or the addition of the copula or verb form in Level IV, the process appears to be one of take as well as give. Elaboration of one member is often accompanied by a deletion of part or all of the opposite member. There is deletion of major categories, as well as deletion within major categories, when other major categories occur or are expanded.

The Rules Children Learn

With the advent of the theory of generative transformational grammar has come the idea that children may learn language by first learning phrase structure rules, and then, one by one, the transformational rules which generate more complex constructions from underlying kernel constructions. Although it's a neat idea, it has by no means been shown that such is the case. It is probably true that the phrase structure develops first, but the nature of the rules which operate at this level has barely been touched on, and it appears that certain transformational forms may be productive in child language before the base phrase structure is fully expanded. Two children in our study have used the question form with inversion of subject and modal auxiliary, productively, before modals were expressed in the auxiliary of the verb phrase in an active sentence.

It appears that the "construct" proposed by Lee, rather than tracing "the gradual emergence of phrase structure rules in children's grammar and the formulation of kernel sentences, from which transformational structures can be derived," (p. 329), is instead simply a pairing of traditional grammatical functions with groups of utterances reported in the literature, without regard to the functions of utterances as they occur.

Diagnostic Application

The principle objection to be raised with this section of the Lee paper has to do with the reported manner of obtaining the speech samples from the two children. The speech of the normal child was recorded as (1) he played with his mother, (2) read a book, and (3) engaged in conversation. The speech of the child who presented a language problem was recorded (1) in a clinical setting, and (2) as he and his clinician talked about a picture of a doctor attending a sick child. Further, (3) he "had to be prodded with questions to elicit speech at all." (p. 322).

It would seem that, since this "is not so much a test of the children as it is a test of the method of linguistic analysis" (p. 322), every attempt should have been made to equate the situations and stimuli for the two children. There are a number of factors which contribute to an utterance, not the least of which is the source of stimulus. There appear to be substantial qualitative differences between spontaneous and elicited utterances in our data. An utterance that has occurred spontaneously frequently does not occur when questions which might be expected to elicit the same utterance are presented. Comprehension of the question is only one factor. Moreover, certain elliptical adult utterances are considered grammatical in response to such questions as: *What have you got?—a book.* The fact that no "designative" or "predicative" constructions were found at any of the four levels with the child with a language problem, could be as much an artifact of the recording situation as it could be a "qualitative" difference in the speech samples of the two children.

REFERENCES

BRAINE, M. D. S., The ontogeny of English phrase structure: the first phase. *Language,* 39, 1-13 (1963).

BROWN, R., and BELLUGI, U., Three processes in the child's acquisition of syntax. *Harvard educ. Rev.,* 34, 133-151 (1964).

BROWN, R., and FRASER, C., The acquisition of syntax. *Child Dev. Monogr.*, **29**, 43-79 (1964).

CHOMSKY, N., *Syntactic Structures*. The Hague: Mouton (1957).

CHOMSKY, N., *Aspects of the Theory of Syntax*. Cambridge, Mass.: M.I.T. Press (1965).

FODOR, J. A., and KATZ, J. J. (Eds.), *The Structure of Language: Readings in the Philosophy of Language*. Englewood Cliffs, N.J.: Prentice-Hall (1964).

MILLER, W., and ERVIN, S., The development of grammar in child language. *Child Dev. Monogr.*, **29**, 9-34 (1964).

POSTAL, P., Underlying and superficial linguistic structure. *Harvard Educ. Rev.*, **34**, 246-266 (1964).

WEIR, R., *Language in the Crib*. The Hague: Mouton (1962).

Lois Masket Bloom

STATUS OF UTTERANCE

by

LEO ENGLER   and   ERNEST F. HADEN

This paper is an attempt to deal concretely with the problem of sentence types. While many linguists have been concerned with such matters, their attention has been focused upon what E. M. Uhlenbeck has referred to as "the phatic layer".[1]

By combining the intonation, or melodic layer, and the phatic layer, it is possible to define discrete entities and to draw up a useful inventory of them. The formal signals of syntactic arrangement form one constituent; the other essential[2] is the formal signals of the matching intonation contour.

To designate this construct we propose the term *Status of Utterance*. This term is somewhat parallel to "marital, or legal, status". It is intended to suggest also that the lexical, morphological, syntactic and phonological components are, as it were, latent until, at the moment of utterance, the addition of an intonation contour that fits, endows the potential sentence with the *Status* of a communication event.

Since, in English, such syntactic features occur mostly in the verb phrase, the term "status" (of verbs) has been used to identify certain syntactic or morphological characteristics of the verb phrase, but without achieving a clear inventory of discrete entities, because it referred only to elements in the phatic layer.[3]

---

[1] E. M. Uhlenbeck, "An Appraisal of Transformation Theory", *Lingua* XII, No. 4 (1963), p. 13: "In every sentence one has to distinguish two components: the intonation or melodic layer and the phatic layer, the layer that consists of discrete elements in linear succession." cf. Noam Chomsky, *Third Texas Conference on Problems of Linguistic Analysis in English* (Austin, Texas, 1962), p. 122 et passim.

[2] Richard Gunter, "Elliptical Sentences in American English", *Lingua* XII, No. 2 (1963), p. 137. In dealing with ellipsis, he is able to determine the expansion of his various elliptical utterances only by endowing each with an appropriate intonation contour. See particularly his footnote 14.

[3] George L. Trager and Henry Lee Smith Jr., *An Outline of English Structure* (Battenburg Press, Norman, Oklahoma, 1951): "...*Interrogative* ... *Negative*. These are the *Statuses*. (p. 79) ...interrogative status: does he see   did he see   negative status: he doesn't see he didn't see (p. 80)".—W. Nelson Francis, *The Structure of American English* (New York, 1940), p. 337: "English verbs have four statuses, the affirmative, the interrogative, the negative, and the negative interrogative..."—H. A. Gleason Jr., *Introduction to Descriptive Linguistics* (Holt, Rinehart and Winston, New York, 1961), p. 431: "... "sentences" are classified on the basis of whether they "state a fact", "ask a question", etc."

ACTA LINGUISTICA HAFNIENSIA, 1965, vol. 9, no. 1, pp. 25-36.

Status I $\quad$ /2 3ˊ1 ↓/

$$S + P$$

n vp (verb phrase)

wh-

The symbolization is based on the commonly accepted analysis of English which posits four degrees of stress / ˊ ˆ ˋ ˘ / (primary, secondary, tertiary and weak) to which we add /"/ overloud for our special purposes; four levels of pitch / 1 2 3 4 / (from low to high), and three terminal junctures /→ ↑↓/. The intonation contour, enclosed in phonemic slashes and limited to one primary stress, three pitch level digits and a terminal, is written above the line and the symbols for the syntactic arrangement below the line, to indicate the relationship between the supra-segmental and the segmental components of the *Status* of the utterance. The notation used here is intentionally broad in reference, i.e. to the syntax level rather than the phrase structure level. "S" stands for "Subject", "n" for nominal, including "who, what, which". (Elsewhere, "wh-" will stand for any one of the series "whom, who, what, which, when, where, why, how, whose", unless otherwise specified.) "P" stands for "Predicator", specifically the verb phrase, including at least a person/tense-marker carrier (finite verb form).

The label "Declarative" is obviously inappropriate, since this *Status I* covers both the declarative and some interrogative utterances within the limits of the formula.

On the other hand, there is no change of *Status* whether the utterance is affirmative or negative. We use the term "Polarity" to designate the affirmative and negative versions. Removing the negative from the ranks of the *Statuses* requires, however, the specification of the syntactic manipulation pertaining to the negative Polarity, i.e. the insertion of {not} after (a), the person/tense-marker carrier {be}, or (b), the first auxiliary, {do}, etc.[4] Thus,

He is going home. / ²hiy̆z gowiŋ³hówm¹↓ /
He isn't going home. / ²hiy izənt gowiŋ³hówm¹↓ /
He is not going home. / ²hiyz nat gowiŋ³hówm¹↓ /
He is going quickly. / ²hiyz gowiŋ³kwíkliy¹↓ /
He isn't going quickly. / ²hiy izənt gowiŋ³kwíkliy¹↓ /
He is not going quickly. / ²hiyz nat gowiŋ³kwíkliy¹↓ /
He is taking the elevator. / ²hiyz teykiŋ ðiy³éləveytər¹↓ /

---

4 First auxiliary may be *do, have, be,* or a modal.

256

He isn't taking the elevator. / ²hiy izənt teykiŋ ðiy³élɔveytər¹↓ /
He is not taking the elevator. / ²hiyz nat teykiŋ ðiy³élɔveytər¹↓ /
I do believe you're right. / ²ay duw biliyv yuhr³ráyt¹↓ /
I don't believe you're right. / ²ay downt biliyv yuhr³ráyt¹↓ /

These all conform to the formula for *Status I* in that the primary stress /´/ together with pitch level /3/ falls on the last word-stressed syllable:

/3   3   3   3   /
" hóme, quíckly, élevator, ríght."[5]

Each *Status,* then, admits of an affirmative and a negative Polarity possibility, each of which may occur in an accented[6] or in an unaccented[6] version, as represented diagramatically below:

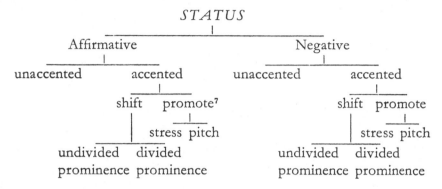

STATUS

The *Status* formula, with appropriate syntactic handling in the case of Negative Polarity, covers the unaccented version. But the accented version "depends on the intent of the speaker."[8] Often an unaccented utterance occurs without preceding context. On the other hand, the accented version has, typically, some previous context as in the following examples:

This little pig went to market. /³ðís litəl pig²→²went tə³márkit¹↓/
This little pig stayed home. /⁴ðís litəl pig²→²stêyd⁴hówm¹↓/

---

5 The rule is: adverbs of time, as opposed to other adverbs, are not available for /3´/ placement in the unaccented version, unless the adverb of time stands alone as complement: e.g. He'll go tomorrow /hiyl gôw təmárow ↓/ cf. He'll go home tomorrow. — cf. Robert P. Stockwell, "The Place of Intonation in a Generative Grammar of English", *Readings In Applied English Linguistics,* Rev. Ed. (Appleton Century Crofts, New York, 1964), p. 195.
6 We borrow these terms from Dwight L. Bolinger's article, "Around the Edge of Language: Intonation", *Harvard Educational Review,* Vol. XXXIV, No. 2 (Spring, 1964), pp. 282–296.
7 cf. Bolinger's use, in the article cited, of the term "separation".
8 Bolinger, *op. cit.*

In the first line, /³ðís/ receives undivided prominence i.e. both pitch and stress peak, as a result of "shift"; /pig/ is on pitch level /2/ and its "normal primary" is downgraded to /ˆ/. The phrase /²went tə³márkit¹↓/ conforms to the formula of *Status I,* unaccented.

The accent which shifts prominence to /³ðís/ conveys a contrastive meaning: "this, not the other four..."

In the second line (having preceding context) /⁴ðís/ receives the shifted undivided prominence, namely, primary stress and a promotion of pitch level /3/ to pitch level /4/ with the usual adjustments in the rest of the phrase; in /²stêyd⁴hówm¹↓/, we have an example of undivided prominence, resulting from the mere promotion of pitch level /3/ to pitch level /4/ without shift.

$$\textit{Status II} \quad \frac{/3ˆ\ 2\ 1↓/}{\varnothing \sim \text{you} + \text{P}}$$

In grammatical terms "P" is in the imperative, marked in English by absence of expressed subject (∅), and specification of the base form of the verb. A further possibility is an expressed subject, but limited to the morpheme {you}. Were it not for this limitation, i.e. if just any subject form were permissible, the syntax (formula below the line) would be the same as in *Status I.*

Example: Don't close the door. /³dównt²klôwz ðə²dôhr¹↓/

Some accented versions would be:

(a) /⁴dȫwnt²klôwz ðə¹dôhr↓/

with undivided prominence, as in the unaccented, but with promotion of stress or pitch or both;

(b) /²dôwnt klôwz ðə³dóhr²→/, (close the window)

with shift of pitch level /3/ and primary stress /ˊ/, with or without promotion to overloud /"/.

(c) Don't you do that again! /³dôwnt³yȗw dȗw ðæt əgén¹↓/

Note the obligatory placing of {you} after the negated auxiliary. Compare:

(d) You close the door! /³yúw²klôwz ðə dôhr¹↓/

There appears to be a built-in contrastive meaning: "you, not I", or "you,

X" not "you, Y", etc., as also in "I'll turn the pages, you just play your violin" or "You close the door, you lock the windows, and you go to bed", addressed to three separate members of the family.

Here again promotion of pitch level /3/ to pitch level /4/ with undivided prominence, or shift of stress (divided prominence) as well, serve to give accented versions:

(a) You close the door. /⁴yúw²klôwz ðə dôhr¹↓/

(b) Don't you do that again. /³dôwnt³yûw²dûw ðæt²əgén¹↓/

or again "Don't you dare!" /³dôwnt yûw⁴déhr¹↓/ showing undivided shifted prominence with promotion. Another variant is characterized by the use of specified {you}, but eliminating P, and maintaining the contour /3ˊ 1↓/, i.e. "You!" /³yúw¹↓/, as an ellipsis expandable to (a) above. The morpheme {you} may be replaced by any proper name, e.g. "Mary!" /³mériy¹↓/. As in many other cases, we consider any departure from the formula, either as to placement or degree of stress, or placement or height of pitch, as signalling *Accent*.

Zero P seems to preclude any possibility of negative Polarity, since Negative Polarity involves a syntactic mutation in the Predicator, but at least one possibility seems to belong here, i.e. "No no!" /³nów nôw¹↓/ to a baby, warning him.

$$\textit{Status III} \quad \frac{/2\ 3ˊ3\ \uparrow\ /}{P + S}$$

This is the *Status* of the so-called "yes-or-no" questions. In the Affirmative Polarity, the finite form of *be* or *have,* or the first auxiliary, (P), is in the first position followed immediately by the subject, (S).

e.g.   Is he going? /²iz iy³gówiŋ³↑/

Can he have been thinking of me?

/²kin iy əv bin θiŋkiŋ əv³míy³↑/

In the Negative Polarity, {not} /nat/, is inserted after the subject, e.g. /²iz iy nat³gówiŋ³↑/ or {not} in the reduced form /ənt/ is inserted after the (P) as defined above; e.g. /²izənt iy³gówiŋ³↑/.

N.B. /kæn/ + /ənt/→ /kænt/,
       /wil/ + /ənt/ → /wownt/,
       /æm/ + /ənt/ → /ahrnt/,
though many speakers may prefer /²æm ay nat ³.³↑ /.

The process of accenting involves the same devices as those previously detailed for *Statuses I* and *II* above.

The first portion(s) of the so-called "choice question" and many aphoristic examples are also in *Status III*:

e.g. Will you have tea, milk, (or coffee)?

/²wil yu hæv³tíy³↑³mílk³↑/

The more (the merrier). /²ðə³móhr³↑ ... /

This is also the *Status* of two of the four so-called "Tag Questions", one Affirmative in polarity, the other Negative,

e.g. (He's here,) isn't he? /²izənt³íy³↑/

(He isn't here,) is he? /²iz³íy³↑/

(We note here the co-occurrence restriction: The affirmative tag comes after a negative statement, the negative tag after an affirmative statement. But this is not germane to the *Status*.) The "tag", as described above, is often replaced by "Right?" /²ráyt³↑/ or "Okay?" /²ow³kéy³↑/,

e.g. (You're a linguist.) Right? /2 3˗ 3↑/

(The matter is settled.) Okay? /2 3˗ 3↑/

Note that the preceding context for these "tags" is typically in *Status I*, with the contour /2 3˗ 1↓/ varying with /2 3˗ 2→/. The replacement "Okay?", however, is often found following a context in *Status II*,

e.g. /3˗ 2   1↓/   /2 3˗ 3↑/
(Close the door.)   Okay?

Status IV	/2 3˗ 1↓/
	wh- + P + S
	non S

Typical utterances in this *Status* would be "What does she want?" /²hwət dəz šiy³wánt¹↓/ and "Why aren't you ready?" /²hway ahrnt yə ³rédiy¹↓/, commonly referred to as "information questions". The *accentuation* process is again the same as outlined in the diagram above.

One example of *accentuation,* among many, is of some interest because it is not exactly like the preceding case:

Red Skelton's "Why did you break my little nose?" is

/^{4}hwáy did^{2}yu breyk$^{2\to^2}$may witəl^{2}nówz$^{3\uparrow}$/

The unaccented version would be, possibly,

/^{2}hway did yu breyk may witəl^{3}nówz$^{1\downarrow}$/,

but the process of *accenting* is manifested by various devices:

1. A sustain juncture is introduced at "break". This is related to the following:

2. The primary /ˊ/ is shifted to "why" and the pitch level promoted to /4/,

3. The last syllable, "nose", bears the primary /ˊ/ in the unaccented version.

The *accent* here is conveyed entirely in the pitch signal and the associated terminal. We have here, then, a rather special case of "promote" from /1$^\downarrow$/ to /3$^\uparrow$/. This device seems to express a feeling rather than an intellectual contrast. It can easily be recognized as a whining utterance if there is any dragging of the last few syllables. If, on the other hand, ^{3}nówz$^{1\downarrow}$/ were replaced by /^{4}nówz$^{1\downarrow}$/ it would convey an "intellectual" notion: "nose, not head", or some such.

A parallel example is the childish:

Where are you going? /$^{4\sim3}$hwéhr ər yu^{2}gôwiŋ$^{3\uparrow}$/

Status V	/2	3ˊ	3$^\uparrow$/
	wh-	+ P	+ S
	non S		

We note that the syntactic arrangements of *Statuses IV* and *V* are very similar, but that in *Status V* we have an intonation contour like that in *Status III*, i.e. /2 3ˊ 3$^\uparrow$/. Here, then, the Combination in *V* is different from that in *III* or *IV*. Thus the "What did you say?" /2 3ˊ 1$^\downarrow$/ of *Status IV* contrasts with "What did you say?" /2 3ˊ 3$^\uparrow$/ of *Status V*, and both contrast with *Statuses I, II,* and *III*. In *I, II* and *III* we found differences, i.e. contrasts, "above and below the line"; but *IV* and *V* present something like a minimal pair. It is clear that there is an advantage in structuring such a contrast by making the "phatic layer" (the matter below the line) a constituent of *Status*.[9]

In the following dialogue, note the minimal pair /²hwɔ́t³↑/ vs. /²hwɔ́t¹↓/:

A. I have something for you.
B. What? /2 3ˊ 3↑/ (What did you say?)
A. I have something for you.
B. What? /2 3ˊ 1↓/ (What is it?)
A. I won't tell you.

The usual devices of accent, such as "shift" of stress (and/or pitch), are available, e.g. /²hwət did iy³dúw¹↓/; but with the "promote" device, we have an "echo" utterance as in the following exchange:

A. What did he do?   /2 3ˊ 3↑/
B. What did he do?   /2 4″ 4↑/ (He went home!)
A. Oh!

These "echo" utterances all have the following characteristics:

(a) obviously, some preceding context is required: but more significantly,
(b) the "echo" borrows the syntax of the preceding utterance (imperfectly heard, or surprising to hear) and combines this with the / 2 3ˊ 3↑/ contour (cf. *Status III*).

Thus, *Status V* with promote gives an "echo". *Statuses VI, VII* and *VIII* below are "echoes", but combine different elements.

Status VI   /2   3ˊ   3↑/ (cf. *Status I*)
‾‾‾‾‾‾‾‾‾‾‾‾
S (n~wh-) + P

He's going? /²hiyz³gówiŋ³↑/

Who's going? /²huwz³gówiŋ³↑/

This is perhaps the most common type of "echo question".

---

9 cf. Charles F. Hockett, *A Course in Modern Linguistics*, Third Ed. (Macmillan Company, New York, 1960), p. 199, par. 23.1: "If we lift the intonations from sentences in English... the remainder consists of a predicative constitute." Such a "constitute" is a constituent of the *Status* here proposed.

Status VII $\quad$ $|2 \quad 3^- \quad 3^\uparrow|$
$$\overline{\varnothing + \text{P}}$$

has the syntax of *Status II* as in "A" below:

A. Close the door, i.e. *Status II* $|^3\text{klówz ð}\text{ə}^2\text{dohr}^{1\downarrow}|$

B. Close the door? $|^2\text{klowz ð}\text{ə}^3\text{dóhr}^{3\uparrow}|$

The rejoinder of "B" here is an "echo" of "A"s' utterance, i.e. borrows "A"s' syntax, but combines it with $|2\ 3^-\ 3^\uparrow|$ intonation contour. Accenting by means of "promote" or "shift" generates a large number of possible utterances, such as "B"s' rejoinder in the following exchange:

A. Don't close the door. *(Status II)*

B. $|^3\text{dównt klowz ð}\text{ə}^3\text{dôhr}^{3\uparrow}|$

Status VIII $\quad$ $|2 \qquad 3^- \qquad 3^\uparrow|$
$$\overline{\text{S} + \text{P} + \text{wh-} \text{(non S)}}$$

You went where? $\quad$ $|^2\text{y}\text{ə went}^3\text{hwéhr}^{3\uparrow}|$

This occurs only unaccented, in the sense that the undivided prominence always falls on the "wh-" element in final position.

A variant form of this *Status* has the form {what} replacing P + wh- (non S):

You what? $\quad$ $|^2\text{y}\text{ə}^3\text{hwát}^{3\uparrow}|$

Status IX $\quad$ $|2\ 3^-\ 1^\downarrow|$
$$\overline{\text{P} + \text{S}}$$

This is the "20 questions" *Status*, e.g. Is it animal? Is it vegetable? Is it mineral? all with $|2\ 3^-\ 1^\downarrow|$ contour. Apart from that, it is reportedly quite common in some parts of the United States as a "yes or no question",

e.g. Is he going? $|^2\text{iz iy}^3\text{gówiŋ}^{1\downarrow}|$

Compare *Status III* $|^2\text{iz iy}^3\text{gówiŋ}^{3\uparrow}|$

In a previous paragraph, two of the tag questions were referred to, namely those with /2 3ˉ 3↑/ contour. The other tag questions, i.e. those with /2 3ˉ 1↓/, belong to *Status IX:*

(He's here), isn't he? /³ízənt iy¹↓/

(He isn't here), is he? /³íz iy¹↓/

Note that the "tag" /³ráyt³↑/ does not have a parallel here, and the form /³rayt¹↓/ belongs to *Status I* exclusively. The same can be said for the tag /²ow³kéy³↑/ in *Status III* vs /²ow³kéy¹↓/ in *Status I*, etc.

Without attempting to specify situations (semantic values) for all the *Statuses,* we must record the nature of the contrast between *Statuses III* and *IX* presented by these examples.

The majority of questions asked in playing "20 questions" and similar games are in *Status IX,* along with the "tags" just mentioned. All these utterances are requests for corroboration rather than for information. A peculiarity of English, as well as some other languages, is that corroboration is expressed in either the affirmative or negative Polarity:

A. Is he going? /²iz iy³gówiŋ¹↓/

B. Yes he is. /²yes iy³íz¹↓/

A. He isn't going, is he. /²hiy izənt³gówiŋ²↓³íz iy¹↓/

B. No, he isn't. /²nôw iy³ízənt¹↓/
Also:

A. He's going. /²hiyz³gówiŋ¹↓/

B. Oh, is he. /²ow³íz iy¹↓/

A. Yes. /³yés¹↓/

In the following examples, *Status I* and *Status IX* both with *Accent* are found:

A. (to C.) B is a linguist. /³bíy³iz¹ə liŋgwist¹↓/
A. (to B.) Aren't you a linguist? /³áhrnt¹yu ə liŋgwist¹↓/
B. Yes... /²yés³↑/

Also:

Five year old Peter to five year old Betty:

Peter to Betty: My daddy was in the war. /³máy²dæ²⁻̍diy²wəz in ðə ⁴wôhr¹↓/

Betty to Peter: He was not. /²hiy³wâz²nát²↓/

Peter to Daddy: Daddy, weren't you in the war? /²dǽ³diy²⁻̍³wɔ́rnt¹yuw in ðə wôhr¹↓/

Daddy: Yes /²yés²⁻̍/

In the first utterance (Peter to Betty) there is the now familiar "promote" from pitch level /3/ to pitch level /4/ with undivided prominence on "war"; undivided prominence also on "my" results from "shift" of pitch level /3/ to first position. The second utterance (Betty to Peter) shows divided prominence as a result of a shift of pitch level /3/ to "was", while the primary /ˊ/ remains on "not" with an automatic adjustment to pitch level /2/ but with a lengthening and a kind of "promote" /2ˉ1↓/ to /2ˉ2↓/.

These are both *Accented* versions of *Status I*.

Peter's utterance to Daddy is an example of *Status IX, Accented,* showing "shift" of undivided prominence on "were". But of particular interest, is the big interval resulting from the pitch drop on "you". Bolinger has called this separation.[10]

Peter's appeal to Daddy is clearly a request for corroboration.

Status X   /1ˉ1↓/
———————
S + P

(Oh, no,) she said.   /¹šiy séd¹↓/

This example is representative of a very restricted number of parenthetical clauses. The inverted order, "said she", which is obsolete, is a stylistic variant of *Status X,* not a contrastive form.

In a similar manner we consider the following to be stylistic variants:
a) simple inversion, P + S as a replacive of "if + S + P":
"Had I known that", "If I had known that..."
a variant *Status I;*

———————————————————————————————————

10 *Op. cit.*

b) stylistic inversion "Quoth the Raven: Nevermore."

c) stylistic device using *Accentuation*.

Accentuation, generally, is a stylistic device. Thus it is that it does not, in itself, give rise to separate statuses, but is found as a supplementary phenomenon to various *Statuses,* as has been indicated.

A limited number of (adverbs and other) forms placed in clause initial position, with a shifted primary stress, are followed by P + S:

Rarely (Seldom) have I seen such a mess.

/³réhrliy²hæv ày sîyn sâč ə¹mês¹↓/

I have rarely seen such a mess *(Status I).*

It has not been the aim of this paper to exhaust the inventory of the *Statuses* in English. Possibly others may be found beyond the ten presented here. But we believe that these are sufficient to illustrate the working out of the thesis we advance; of particular importance, we think, are the devices which we have included under the heading of *Accentuation,* and the relegating of the affirmative/negative opposition (which we designate as polarities) to a subordinate level adjunct to each *Status.*

Summary :

The sentence viewed as utterance comprises two constituents: a syntactic pattern and a matching suprasegmental pattern showing junctures, stresses and pitches. These constructs, called Statuses, serve to identify discrete entities in the inventory of sentence types.

Affirmative and negative in English are designated here as *polarities,* and not as statuses. The devices used for expressing these polarities are specified within the frame-work of the Status. Similarly emphasis (here called *accentuation*) is investigated as a system in some detail. Although transformational relationships are implied, this paper does not propound transforms or transformational rules as such.

266

LINGUISTIC ANALYSIS OF SPEECH SAMPLES:
A PRACTICAL GUIDE FOR CLINICIANS

Leo F. Engler, Elaine P. Hannah, and Thomas M. Longhurst

Linguistic procedures which allow the speech clinician to elicit, record, segment, and analyze the spontaneous speech of children in a relatively standardized test situation are described. The procedures are based on a combination of concepts borrowed from the three major approaches current in linguistics—slot and filler, immediate constituent, and elementary transformational grammar.

Speech clinicians presently have the technology for identifying and remediating articulatory dysfunction at the phonological level. However, they do not yet have the means to relate these deviations to the overall structure of the language. Neither do they have ways of identifying speech and language problems involving structural signals such as arrangement, intonation, grammatical inflection, concord and government, and function words. There is increasing professional recognition that the findings of linguistics may remove some of these inadequacies. Linguistics provides descriptions of English and techniques of analysis that could enable speech clinicians to describe the grammatical speech behavior of clients and compare the behavior with that of other speakers. By this objective means of describing linguistic behaviors beyond the phonological level, speech clinicians can add another dimension to the diagnostic process and the planning of therapeutic measures. This paper suggests some practical linguistic methods and techniques the clinician can apply with minimal formal training in linguistics. The procedure we suggest is adapted from one we developed and used to analyze the speech production of 150 "normal" children at the first-, third-, and fifth-grade levels, in a formal research project. Encouraged by our experience with the procedure, we modified it for everyday use in the Kansas State University Speech Clinic. We found it a useful diagnostic tool in evaluating speech and language development of children. This procedure is not designed for use with severely retarded, autistic, or essentially nonverbal children, but rather for children with some language performance. Typically these children have language, but have been singled out through impressionistic means by parents, physicians, or peers, as having speech or language problems. Ultimately, the speech clinician must face the question

JOURNAL OF SPEECH AND HEARING DISORDERS, May 1973, vol. 38, no. 2, pp. 192-204.

of whether clinical findings indicate a pathological state or "normal" inadequacy better left to be outgrown. The child's speech "problem" could be a matter of incompletely learned language structure, normal for the child's age group, which should be left to maturation and the educational system. On the other hand, it might constitute a deviation from the age norm, indicating a need for a program of language intervention. Other possibilities include foreign language or subdialect interference requiring the services of a specially trained teacher. Whatever the stated cause for referral, the speech clinician must first identify what gave rise to the impression of inadequacy and subsequently brought the child to the examination situation.

A SUGGESTED APPROACH

The central idea here is contrastive analysis. The child's speech is contrasted with that of the clinician or of other children of his own age or development. This requires eliciting a representative sample of the child's speech, transcribing the sample, segmenting it into manageable units, inspecting the constructions evaluated as inappropriate, and listing those which are conspicuous because of their absence. We will discuss each of these steps briefly, suggesting a procedure we hope is simple enough for everyday use in the examination situation and yet detailed enough to provide a better understanding of a child's language problem and some valuable insights into what ought to be done about it.

Eliciting and Recording the Sample

Recording a sample of a client's speech is more difficult than it might appear. The sample must be representative and free from the investigator's own biases. For example, a client's response to direct questioning can be unpredictable. A direct interview can miss significant parts of his speech usage. Also, a high frequency of "answer patterns" can lead to the exclusion of many other patterns. One method commonly used to elicit speech is to show the client pictures which he is to describe or discuss. Here, again, the subject of the picture may restrict or bias the sample of speech produced, so that care is required in selection.

We are studying a number of approaches, including experimental tape-recorded tests and the cloze procedure. However, we still do not have a standardized elicitation technique. After early experiments indicated that stimulus pictures may add yet another individually unpredictable variable to the testing situation, we used certain of the Adult TAT pictures (Murray, 1943)—specifically 9BM, 13G, 2, 12BG, 6GF, and 86F. Some experimentation indicated that these pictures stimulated verbalization representing a broad spectrum of structure while at the same time causing little discernible anxiety.

Realizing that known techniques have shortcomings and that one might want to elicit further samples as the analysis develops and inadequacies appear, one may begin by tape-recording five to 10 minutes of the client's speech, using optimum stimulus material. The clinician must exercise care in satisfying the clinical requirements of privacy, optimal rapport with the client, and appropriate environmental conditions. We cannot overemphasize the importance of taking precautions to get a good quality tape recording. The client is told he will be shown some pictures and he is to make up and tell a story based on each one, describe what he sees, or tell what is happening in the picture. (These instructions or promptings may produce different responses, and we are conducting research to investigate these variables.) For present purposes the client is told no more than this, lest the clinician impose biases on him. Then he is shown the pictures one by one and is allowed to talk freely about them, or about other subjects that may interest him at the moment. The clinician should allow him to talk freely if he wishes, and should avoid excessive participation, at the same time encouraging as much spontaneous speech as possible. The interview should last five or 10 minutes. We do not know how large the language sample must be to be representative of the client's behavior, but approximately 75 to 100 utterances should be sufficient to begin with.

Transcribing the Sample

The next step is to transcribe the tape-recorded sample. In the interest of saving time, the first transcription is usually in standard orthography but without capital letters or punctuation. (Siegel [1963] details some instructions that have proven helpful.) This is a verbatim transcription, including all "ums" and "ahs," lapses, word repetitions, and innovations. When there is a change in speaker, a new line is begun, although the previous line may not have been completely filled. The lines on the transcript are numbered and correlated with counter numbers on the tape recorder for ease in locating passages later. The transcription can be done reliably by any competent typist given the proper instructions and brief training.

Segmenting the Sample

After the transcription is completed, the tape-recorded sample is played back and compared with the transcript. Whenever a pause in the client's taped speech is perceived (Lieberman, 1967), a slash (/) is marked at the corresponding place on the transcript (Engler and Hannah, 1967). This helps to segment the sample into discrete units of manageable length, corresponding roughly to phrases, clauses, and sentences (Hockett, 1958). Often these slash marks will indicate bona fide grammatical signals (terminal junctures) marking the ends of syntactic units, but many of them will indicate so-called "hesitation phenomena" (Maclay and Osgood, 1959). Hesitation phenomena are poorly understood and there is great need of further study of them. In many cases they are manifestations of the client's problem. Even the best of spontaneous speech contains an incredible amount of material that would not appear in edited writing or edited speech. Apparently in the process of encoding and phonation a good deal of "noise" gets into the utterance; native speakers develop skills that enable them to listen to "noisy" utterances, discern the underlying well-formed constructions and comprehend them, and at the same time scan the culled material and make further judgments about the speaker. It is when this capacity is overloaded that communication breaks down, and it is in the amount and nature of this "noise" that the client's problem lies. Some of his noisy segments will be lapses, filled pauses, gibberish, and so on.

Analyzing the Segments

After segmenting the sample, one can begin the structural analysis by inspecting each of the segments. One procedure is to transfer the segments to preprinted cards so that they can be sorted. (A sample preprinted card may be obtained by writing to the authors.) Cards are numbered serially so that the context of any given segment can be readily ascertained and given the tape recorder counter number where the segment can be located on the tape and played back as often as necessary. One procedure is then to go through the cards while listening to the corresponding tape, and separate those segments that seem correct to the clinician from those that contain what seem to be inappropriate features of pronunciation, grammatical form, word choice, lapse, or other innovations unacceptable to the clinician. For each of these inappropriate features, note the functional (grammatical) relationship in which the deviation occurs, such as subject or object, and the phonological environment, such as initial, medial, final, intervocalic, consonant cluster or blend, stressed or unstressed syllable, and high or low pitch. These notes should be as detailed as is consistent with the sophistication of the clinician in linguistic description and with the time available. When these deviations are tabulated, a pattern should become apparent that will enable the clinician to predict their occurrences in terms of grammar or phonology. Any physical events in the environment or in the condition of the speaker that seem to coincide with deviations more often than by chance should also be noted.

The inventory of the client's linguistic patterns, appropriate or not, in comparison with those of his peers is also important. More normative data regarding grammatical development are desperately needed. These data could be used to determine the client's level of speech and language development and to identify his problem. Until appropriate normative data are available, it is necessary to devise a standard model as we have done, or an inventory of structural patterns, for comparison. No complete description yet exists for any language. However, the clinician can define patterns in her own speech as discrete entities and make a useful inventory of them. Current methods of linguistic analysis suggest ways of accomplishing this inventory. In the construction of the model, a number of approaches are available, each with its own strengths and weaknesses. The grammatical system sketched here was chosen for the convenience it offers in "prepackaged, prelabeled" patterns when the task is to identify and count constructions in speech samples of real clients rather than to ponder the competence of the "ideal speaker-hearer."

Sentence Types

Using a combination of concepts borrowed from slot and filler grammar and transformational-generative grammar, five basic simplex-sentence types are posited for English. All simple sentences are made up of a noun phrase used as subject, plus a verb phrase. However, sentences may be classified on the basis of what sort of construction the verb phrase contains in addition to the verb. Our categories are summarized, with examples of each, in the Appendix. Type I sentences are characterized as "equational" and use a copulative or linking verb such as *be*, with a nominal, adjectival, or adverbial in the postverbal slot (traditionally referred to as predicate nominative, adjective, or adverb, respectively). Type II sentences employ intransitive verbs with optional adverbials in the postverbal slot. Type III sentences use "object-taking" verbs and a nominal object or objects in the postverbal slot. Type IV sentences have a special verb, often one of those referred to as "transitive verb of the senses," and a construction resembling any one of the first three types in the postverbal slot. Passive sentences are considered by some to be transformations of Type III sentences, but we list them as a fifth type for frequency-counting purposes.

Each of these sentence types may be used alone as an independent utterance with either minimal or expanded fillers in the slots, and each is subject to conventions for features of arrangement, inflection (of grammatical forms), concord (agreement, such as that between third person singular subject and "present" tense verb form), government (such as use of object case form for pronoun in object slot), intonation (pitch, stress, and juncture), and the use of function words (such as articles with nouns or using *of* to indicate possession).

Each sentence type may be transformed in various ways (Engler and Haden, 1965) to form such versions as "yes or no" questions, information questions, and imperatives. Given the context, a part of a sentence type may be used as a minor sentence, such as "Home," in response to "Where are you going?" Further, two or more sentence types may be conjoined (strung together like beads), or one embedded inside another (as, for example, in a relative construction) (Campbell, 1965).

Theoretically, with the basic sentence types, expansion, conjoining, and transformation (Chomsky, 1965), one should be able to generate any sentence in English, given the vocabulary. Conversely, one should be able to reduce any sentence, no matter how rambling, to basically one or a combination of the five basic sentence types, a minor sentence, or a fragment. Our clinical trainees have demonstrated that speech clinicians with minimal linguistic training can follow the speech sample collection procedures, devise a simplified inventory, do a relatively quick analysis and tabulation, make a more accurate diagnosis of a client's language deviation than they could otherwise, and gain some valuable insights into planning a remedial program. More work is

271

needed in evaluating the utility of this procedure with extremely deviant speech.

Slots and Fillers

The examination of a segment begins with the determination of the slots. Those trained to do this have experienced little difficulty in identifying the subject and predicate and isolating the verb from the predicate, and it should offer few problems for most speech clinicians. It helps to underline the entire subject in one color, the verbal in a second color, the postverbal in a third color, and problematic material in a fourth color.

Subject Slot

The subject slot may contain a noun (in the traditional sense) or any of a number of words that can replace or function as a noun, from a single pronoun, a marked infinitive, or an "ing" form, to a phrase with a noun head and modifiers before and after it, to a complex construction containing whole clauses. A pronoun will be in a form inflected for person, number, sex, and case, and should be noted accordingly. If the head of the construction is a noun, then it should be noted for singular or plural, for mass or count noun characteristics, and for the type and order of all modifiers before and after it. Deviations from the convention followed by "normal" speakers in the order of modifiers with a noun and the number of modifiers used may be significant. Although our studies indicate that fifth-grade children seldom employ more than a determiner and one or two adjectives before a noun, the orders possible include those listed in Table 1. These include predeterminers (such as *all of, some of*); determiners *(the, a(n), this, that, my)*; ordinal and cardinal numerals;

TABLE 1. Categories of modifiers in usual order of appearance before a noun head.

Symbol		Example
Pr	Predeterminer	all of, some of, most of
D	Determiner	a, the, some, this, my
O	Ordinal	first, second
C	Cardinal	one, five
I	Intensifier	very, awfully, terribly
Q	Quality	good, bad, average
S	Size	big, little, short
A	Age	young, old
S_h	Shape	round, square
C_l	Color	red, pink
C_n	Condition	rundown, puny
O_n	Origin	Spanish, New York, Indian
M	Material	cloth, brick
S_t	Style	colonial, ranch-style
N	Nationality	Canadian, Icelandic
T	Type	two-wheel (bicycle), candy (apple)

intensifiers; adjectives of size, age, shape, color, material, style, and nationality before the noun head and group modifiers; and relatives after the noun head (Hsu, 1966).

Thus, such a construction as "All of those very first 10 big old square white brick colonial-style American houses on the main street that were sold last week" follows the convention and sounds right to a native speaker, while any change in the order without a concomitant change in the intonation sounds odd. Lees's (1960) work on the grammar of nominalization in English, Hill's (1958) treatment of orders, and that of Gleason (1961) and Fries (1972), among others, provide further discussion of this important aspect of English structure.

Verbal Slot

In the verbal slot the type of verb used is checked. This necessitates reference to the postverbal slot. At least 14 verb types are posited, depending on the filler in the postverbal slot. These types are summarized in Table 2.

It is also important to analyze the verb for "expansion," that is, compound verb constructions with auxiliaries plus main verbs. English has only two tenses—past and nonpast. Other temporal aspects, as well as the traditional mood and voice, are indicated by means of expansion, such as *be* plus "ing" for the continuous, or *have* plus past participle for the perfect. Modifying the analysis presented by Joos (1964), we posit 11 expansions derived from the typical transformational grammar rule "Aux→Tense (M) (have -en) (be -ing)," which translates something like "The verb expansions possible consist of an obligatory tense marker, plus an optional modal, plus optional *have* plus past participle, plus optional *be* plus 'ing.'" These expansions are summarized in Table 3.

In examining the verbal slot, one should note the concord between the subject and the person/tense marker on the verb or first auxiliary. In idealized adult speech this is /-s, -z, -əz/ in the present tense with third person singular subjects, and otherwise base form or past form, except in the case of *be*, which has a more extensive set of forms in both present and past.

Postverbal Slot

The postverbal slot may contain a complement, that is, nominal, adjectival, or adverbial (traditionally called predicate nominative, predicate adjective, and predicate adverb), an object which is always a nominal, or a zero (in the case of intransitive verbs, by definition). Every sentence has a fourth slot for optional adverbs of manner, place, and time. The orders of these adverbs are important, as are the co-occurrence restrictions on them and their individual mobilities. For example, an adverb of manner is not ordinarily used after *be;* and an adverb like *never* may occur after the verb but not at the end, and may occur in the first position, provided the order of subject and verb are inverted, as in "Never have I seen such complexity."

273

TABLE 2. A summary of verb types with examples.

Code	Type	Label	Example
	I.0	Copulative	
1.	.a	*be*	*be* (plus complement nominal, adjectival, or adverbial)
2.	.b	*get*	*get* (plus complement adjectival or adverbial)
3.	.c	*become*	*become, remain* (plus complement nominal or adjectival)
4.	.d	Vcomplement-taking	*look, seem* (plus complement nominal or adjectival)
5.	.e	Vsenses (intransitive)	*taste, sound* (plus complement adjectival)
6.	.f	Vmiddle	*weigh, mean* (plus complement nominal or adjectival)
	II.0	Intransitive	
7.		Vintransitive	*go, come* (plus optional adverbial)
	III.0	Object-Taking	
8.	.a	Vtransitive	*hit, write* (plus single direct object)
9.	.b	Vgerundive	*enjoy, like* (plus "ing")
10.	.c	Vindirect object	*give, sell* (plus two objects: [1] $object_1$ + to + $object_2$ [2] $object_2$ + $object_1$)
11.	.d	Vfacilitive	*call, elect* (plus two objects: $object_x$ is individual; $object_y$ is classificational)
12.	.e	Vcausative	*have, want* (plus object, plus verb in past participle form, plus optional *by* + agent and/or *with* + means)
	IV.0	Conjoining	
13.	.a	Vsenses (transitive)	*hear, see* (plus object, plus verb in base form or "-ing," plus object[s] or complement)
14.	.b	Vobject infinitive	*want, order* (plus object, plus marked infinitive, plus object[s] or complement)

Within the object slot, nominals will follow essentially the same lines as nominals in the subject slot, except that pronouns are usually in objective case form when used in the object slot.

Within the complement as outlined, adverbials may be true adverbs, which can be inflected for comparison and superlative and accompanied by intensifiers, or may be such constructions as prepositional phrases functioning as adverbs, for example, "He's *in the office*." Adjectivals may be true adjectives, which can also be inflected for comparison and superlative and accompanied by intensifiers, or may be various kinds of phrases functioning adjectivally.

274

TABLE 3. A summary of verbal expansions with examples.

Code	Label	Example Using "Go"
1.	FinV (finite form)	go, goes/went
2.	FinAux$_{do}$ + base-form V	do, does/did go
3.	FinAux$_{be}$ + "-ing"-form V	am, is, are/was, were going
4.	FinAux$_{have}$ + past participle V	have, has/had gone
5.	FinAux$_{have}$ + *been* + "-ing"-form V	have, has/had been going
6.	FinModal + base form V will shall can must may might dare need ought (to)	will go
7.	FinModal + *be* + "-ing"-form V	will/would be going
8.	FinModal + *have* + past participle V	will/would have gone
9.	FinModal + *have been* + "-ing"-form V	will/would have been going

10.	FinAux$_{quasi-aux}$ + base-form V
	Quasi-Aux: be to*
	            be able to
	            be made to
	            be going to
	            be about to
	            be supposed to
	            be in a position to
	            ask to† begin to
	            try to expect to
	            have to intend to
	            long to forget to
	            turn to attempt to
	            start to
		am, is, are/was, were to go
		seem to‡
		like to
		love to
		need to
		wish to
		appear to
		want to
		used to§
		have got to

11.	FinModal + base-form Quasi-Aux + base-form V	will be able to go
12.	FinModal + base-form Quasi-Aux + base-form Quasi-Aux + base form	will have to be able to go

* Take Expansions 1, 4, 6, 8, and, with certain restrictions, 10.
† Take Expansions 1–9 and some 10.
‡ Take Expansions 1, 2, 4, 6, 8, some 10, and some 11.
§ Take Expansion 1 only.

Conjoining

The possibilities for conjoining sentence types into what have been traditionally termed compound and complex sentences are astronomical. For practical purposes, however, they can be classified as juxtaposition, coordination, subordination, and embedding, for example, relative clauses. Since the amount and quality of conjoining practiced by the client is probably significant, conjoined occurrences should at least be classified and tabulated according to the sentence types linked together, and the arrangement and types of linkage.

The following symbols used to indicate discrete segments and relationships between segments are based on the procedures developed by Loban (1963) and Campbell (1965) and modified by Sadkin (1966):

$$Z = \text{Maze}$$
$$X = \text{Fillers, launchers}$$
$$+ = \text{Coordination}$$
$$\neq = \text{Subordination}$$
$$2\ 2 = \text{Compound predicate}$$
$$()\ () = \text{No pause between segments}$$
$$[\ ] = \text{Conjoining within a slot}$$
$$(\ ) = \text{Subject} + \text{verbal} + \text{postverbal slots}$$

Thus the utterance "Well, I would hit the ball/if I saw/that he could run over there and catch the ball/jump oh uh oh well . . ." would be written symbolically as follows: X (3a) $\neq$ (2 + 3a as object of 3a) Z

The following analysis of a response given by a third-grade boy illustrates the possibilities for using this system:

Response:
"When I tasted the sandwich/it tasted lakey/like it had/uh you know/dirty old lake water inside on the meat/."
Segment 1. *when* (subordinator) *I* (subject) *tasted* (verbal) *the sandwich* (postverbal)
Sentence Type IIIa—transitive verb + single object
Subject—pronoun (first person singular, subjective case form)
Verbal—transitive; Type 8; Expansion 1, past tense
Postverbal—object noun (singular, one modifier, a determiner)
Segment 2. *it* (subject) *tasted* (verbal) *lakey* (postverbal) matrix sentence
Sentence Type Ie—equational with postverbal adjectival
Subject—pronoun (third person, singular, neuter)
Verbal—intransitive verb of the senses, Type 5, Expansion 1, past tense
Postverbal—adjective (positive degree)
Segment 3. *like* (co-coordinator) *it* (subject) *had* (verbal) *dirty old lake water inside on the meat* (postverbal)
Sentence Type IIIa—transitive verb + single object
Subject—pronoun (third person, singular, neuter, case form not marked)
Verbal—transitive, Type 8; Expansion 1, past tense
Postverbal—nominal phrase, that is, noun head (singular, mass) with modifiers of quality and age before the head (note that the head itself is composed in traditional terms of a compound noun (noun + noun) with ´ + ` superfix).

In addition, /uh you know/ is obviously a hesitation phenomenon, while inside on the meat/ is a fourth slot adverbial, that is, an adverb that can be put in various places and whose addition has no effect on the classification of the sentence.

In terms of conjoining, number 2 is the matrix segment, preceded by number 1 and followed by number 3. The first segment is linked by means of subordination, introduced by *when,* and functions as an adverbial in relation to the matrix segment. The third segment is linked by means of coordination and introduced by *like*. According to the system for conjoining outlined previously, these three segments would be represented as $(\neq 3a)$ $(1e) + (3a\ Z)$

Tabulation

After all the segments have been analyzed to the degree of detail possible, tabulation is a matter of counting frequencies with which given items occur, making generalized statements about the results of the frequency counts, and drawing conclusions about the nature of the client's problem. To illustrate with a hypothetical example, let us assume that we have a preprinted card for each segment and that each card has a blank or Box 1 to be checked when the filler of the subject slot in that segment is a pronoun, a Box 2 to be checked when that pronoun is in subjective case form (I, we, they), and a Box 3 to be checked when that pronoun is in objective case form (me, us, them). Let us further assume that our frequency count revealed that in 100 segments our client's cards had Box 1 checked 50 times, Box 2 checked 10 times, and Box 3 checked 40 times. We might surmise then that the client is capable of using pronouns in the subject slot all right (we do not know if he does so significantly more or less often than his peers because we have no normative tables), but that he puts subject pronouns in objective case form four-fifths of the time, which might create a major part of the impression of inadequacy that brought him to the clinic. Let us assume now that each of the 10 appropriate segments had a simple pronoun in the subject slot, as "I did it yesterday," while all the 40 inappropriate segments had compound pronoun subjects as in "Me and him did it yesterday."

In this oversimplified hypothetical case, we have now identified and specified the nature of the client's problem in terms of grammar. He may have additional problems, and they will also be illuminated by further frequency counts in the same manner. When all the deviations have been specified, we will have a diagnostic profile that provides an intelligent basis for a therapy program.

ACKNOWLEDGMENT

Elaine P. Hannah is now affiliated with California State University, Northridge, California. Thomas M. Longhurst is affiliated with the University of Kansas, Lawrence, as well as Kansas State University. This work was supported in part by Grants HD-00870 and HD-02528 from the Department of Health, Education, and Welfare, Public Health Service, National Institute of Child Health and Human Development, and special grants from the Bureau of General Research, Kansas State University. Requests for reprints should be sent to Thomas M. Longhurst, Speech Pathology/Audiology, Kansas State University, Manhattan, Kansas 66506.

REFERENCES

CAMPBELL, S., Analysis of concatenations: The structures of nonminimal sentences in English. Master's thesis, Kansas State Univ. (1965).

CHOMSKY, N., *Syntactic Structures*. The Hague: Mouton (1965).

ENGLER, L., and HADEN, E., Status of utterance. *Acta linguist. Hafniens.*, **9**, 25-36 (1965).

ENGLER, L. F., and HANNAH, E. P., Juncture phenomena and the segmentation of a linguistic corpus. *Lang. Speech*, **10**, 228-233 (1967).

FRIES, P., *Tagmeme Sequences in the English Noun Phrase*. Santa Anna, Calif.: Summer Institute of Linguistics (1972).

GLEASON, H. A., JR., *An Introduction to Descriptive Linguistics*. (rev. ed.) New York: Holt, Rinehart, and Winston (1961).

HILL, A., *Introduction to Linguistic Structures*. New York: Harcourt, Brace, and World (1958).

HOCKETT, C. F., *A Course in Modern Linguistics*. New York: Macmillan (1958).

HSU, C. C., A descriptive study of noun phrases in the speech of fifth grade girls. Master's thesis, Kansas State Univ. (1966).

JOOS, M., *The English Verb: Form and Meanings*. Madison: Univ. Wis. (1964).

LEES, B., The grammar of English nominalization. *Int. J. appl. Linguist.*, **26**, 1-202 (1960).

LIEBERMAN, P., *Intonation, Perception and Language*. Cambridge: MIT (1967).

LOBAN, W. D., *The Language of Elementary School Children*. National Council of Teachers of English Research Report Number 1 (1963).

MACLAY, H., and OSGOOD, C. E., Hesitation phenomena in spontaneous English speech. *Word*, **15**, 19-44 (1959).

MURRAY, H. A., *Thematic Apperception Test*. Cambridge: Harvard Univ. (1943).

SADKIN, B., The development of complexity in the language of first, third, and fifth grade boys. Master's thesis, Kansas State Univ. (1966).

SIEGEL, G., Appendix H, prototypes of instructions to typists. *J. Speech Hearing Dis. Monogr. Supp. 10*, 100-102 (1963).

APPENDIX

Sentence Types

Type I. Subject + Verb   + Postverb
                    copulative   complement

   a. Subject + Verb   + Postverb
                    be   complement nominal
                                          adverbial
                                          adjectival

       The man is a professor.
                   here.
                   tall.

   b. Subject + Verb   + Postverb
                    get   complement nominal
                                          adverbial
       He gets angry.
              here.

   c. Subject + Verb   + Postverb
                    become   complement nominal
                                          adjectival
       He becomes a professor.
                   tall.

   d. Subject + Verb   + Postverb
             complement taking   complement nominal
                                               adjectival
       He looks a fright.
       He seems happy.

   e. Subject + Verb   + Postverb
                    senses   complement adjectival
                    intransitive
       Sugar tastes sweet.

   f. Subject + Verb   + Postverb
                    middle   complement nominal
                                          adjectival
       He weighs 200 pounds.
       Time weighs heavy.

278

Type II. Subject + Verb   + Postverb
                        intransitive   null
        He works.

Type III. Subject + Verb   + Postverb
                        object taking   object(s)

      a. Subject + Verb   + Postverb
                  transitive   object
        I see him.

      b. Subject + Verb   + Postverb
                  gerundive   "-ing" form + Q*
        I enjoy reading.
        I enjoy reading books.

      c. (1) Subject + Verb   + Postverb
                      indirect object   object$_1$ + to + object$_2$
        He gave a present to her.

        (2) Subject + Verb   + Postverb
                      indirect object   object$_2$ + object$_1$
        He gave her a present.

      d. Subject + Verb   + Postverb
                  factitive   object$_x$ + object$_y$
        They elected him president.
        She called him a liar.

      e. Subject + Verb   + Postverb
                  causative   object + past participle
        He had them cleaned.

Type IV. Subject + Verb   + Postverb
                    conjoining   object + verb + Q*

      a. Subject + Verb   + Postverb
                  senses   object + verb   + Q*
                  (transitive)   base form
                                    "-ing" form
        I observed him get/getting angry.
        I heard him sing/singing.
        I heard him sing/singing there.
        I watched him eat/eating his lunch.
        I saw him give/giving a present to his wife.
        I saw him give/giving his wife a present.
        I noticed them call/calling the boy John.
        I saw him have/having his hair cut.
        I heard him ask/asking her to go.

      b. Subject + Verb   + Postverb
                      object infinitive   nominal + infinitive
        He wants me to go.

Type V. Subject + Verb   + Postverb
                   passive†   optional (by agent/means)
        The window was broken (by him/with a stone).

Received July 13, 1972.
Accepted October 2, 1972.

---

*Q may be a complement, optional adverb, or object(s), depending on the type of verb underlying the preceding form.

†Verb$_{passive}$ consists of auxiliary *be* or *get* plus the past participle form of the verb. Often a problem here, when the auxiliary is *be*, and in the postverbal slot the optional (by agent/with means) is not present, is deciding whether the construction is a true passive or a Type I sentence with adjectival complement.

SCALE OF CHILDREN'S CLAUSAL DEVELOPMENT[1]

RICHARD B. DEVER

and

PATRICIA M. BAUMAN

INDIANA UNIVERSITY

In this paper we are presenting a scale which can be used to classify the spontaneous utterances of children who are CA 18-40 months of age. It is our hope that the scale will find a number of research applications among retarded children as well as among other children who have language development problems.

The scale is based on a tagmemic grammar, and was designed for use with linguistic _performance_ data; it is the result of over three years of developmental effort. Projected uses for the scale include the gathering of comparative data among groups of demographically - different children, the gathering of longitudinal data in the search for developmental milestones, and the establishment of baseline data against which the efficacy of intervention procedures can be compared. Originally, it was designed for use in our own studies of the language development of retarded children, but it appears to have application beyond this group: it should classify any utterance of any child who speaks a dialect of English as his native language. In the case of dialects such as those spoken by some blacks in which features such as the copula are often not present in utterances, judgment as to the rank of the utterance must be made by someone familiar with the dialect features.

---

1. The development of the scale contained herein was supported, in part, by NICHD Grant #03352 to the University of Wisconsin Center for Research in Mental Retardation during the period 1968-69; and by BEH Grant #OEG 9-242178-4149-032 the Research and Development Center in the Improvement of Teaching for Handicapped Children at Indiana University during the period 1969-71.

ORIGINAL MANUSCRIPT, 1974.

The scale was developed because of the paucity of adequate linguistic assessment devices available to us. Unfortunately, the sophistication of workers in the field of retardation relative to linguistics appears to be minimal, and as a consequence, much of the research in this area tends to be only tangentially related to the mainstream of language research. Rosenberg (1970) points out that the first task for researchers is to know what it is they are investigating when they do language research. We disagree strongly with Rosenberg's contention that transformational grammars are the only theoretical contenders for use in research on language development (Dever, in press), but his basic point cannot be denied: concepts of "language" in the research literature are weak and inefficient, and usually can be challenged on every point. Therefore, it is imperative for us to establish the subject-matter of the present tool as precisely as possible.

Definition of Language

Because we are mainly interested in performance data, i.e., what children say (as opposed to what they could say which is competence), we are following a structuralist definition of language:

> "Language is the arbitrary system of articulated
> sounds used by humans as a means of carrying
> on the affairs of their society" (Francis, 1958,
> p. 13)

As pointed out by Dever (1966) this definition separates "language" from the term, "communication" in the sense that a language is just one of the many tools available to humans for communicating information: "communication" is thus a superordinate term to the term "language". The specific tool considered here is that of American English. It is a social tool in the above definition, and as such, the degree to which it is learned will place the upper limits on the ability of a person to carry out the affairs of his society. Retarded children, the bulk of whom have difficulty with language, do not participate in the affairs of their society: in fact, they are often excluded from it in the form of institutionalization, placement in special classes, and simple exclusion from societal institutions such as the school. We are not hypothesizing a cause-and-effect relationship here, but it is clear to us that it is extremely important to begin to find out how well retarded children use American English in order that appropriate instruction might be given them. The scale presented in this paper is a step in this direction.

Given the above definition, it is possible to be more precise in the matter of language problems of childhood. Unfortunately, it has become quite apparent that there just is no easy way to identify the quantitative nor qualitative aspects of such linguistic problems. There are troublesome matters in the notion of testing language which have not been dealt with in any realistic way. These problems forced us into developing the present scale, and are discussed in the following section.

Problems in Testing Language

There are a few studies which show or purport to show deficiencies in the abilities of retarded children to use specific grammatical features of American English. One such set of studies, for example, has utilized the test paradigm first developed by Jean Berko (1958). This paradigm has been used in several places, e.g., Berko's Test of Morphology (Berko, 1958), Chappell's Picture Test of English Inflections (Chappell, 1968), and the Auditory-Vocal-Automatic (AVA) subtest of the Illinois Test of Psycholinguistic Abilities (ITPA, McCarthy & Kirk, 1961, 1970). This test paradigm first presents a picture to the child along with either a nonsense syllable or a real word stimulus, and then requires the child to inflect the stimulus "word" with the proper grammatical element, e.g., plurality, possession, verb past, etc. For example, one item in the AVA subtest of the ITPA presents a picture of a bed to a child. The tester then says, "Here is a bed." Then a picture of two beds are shown to the child and he is told, "Now there is another one. There are two of them. There are two _____." To get a score of "correct" the child must respond, "beds". Chappell's test also uses this form as does Berko's test except that the latter uses nonsense syllables as stimuli.

A number of studies have used this paradigm with the retarded or have reviewed "file data" of its use (Batemen & Wetherel, 1964; Dever & Gardner, 1970; Lovell & Bradbury, 1967; Mueller, 1967a, 1967b). All have reported retarded children to be less capable of using English inflections than normal children, even when the retardates and normals are matched on mental age. These studies are important as an illustration of the problems involved in testing language for two reasons: (1) the paradigm is seen as one of the best tests of linguistic proficiency available because of its simplicity (Slobin, 1967); and (2) it has been used as a diagnostic tool for the designing of programs of language remediation for the retarded (Blessing, 1964; Smith, 1962; and others).

Dever (1968) tested the ability of the test paradigm actually to predict errors made by retarded children while speaking. He found that while many children who scored 100% correct on the test also scored 100% correct in their speech, many other children scored 0% correct on the test and 100% correct in their speech. Correlations between test scores and free speech scores were quite low on every item, and for a number of items the correlations were actually negative. Dever interpreted these results as demonstrating that the basic test paradigm was not able to predict errors in the free speech of retarded children, and, therefore, could not be used as a basis for deciding what was to be taught in a language program. This held equally true for both the nonsense syllable form as used by Berko, and for the real word form as used in the ITPA, and by Chappell.

It is very important to note that the above test paradigm attempts to assess the development of a very minor aspect of English grammar: inflectional morphology. When considered in relation to the language system as a whole, inflectional morphology is relatively unimportant in the total grammar of English – yet it contains so much regularity that it should be very easy to test. The failure of a simple test of inflections to predict errors is indicative of the problems involved in the testing of the more complex features of English. We have made many informal attempts to test other features of English in retarded children with a singular lack of success. A good example of the kind of thing that happens in a test situation is found in one of the many attempts the senior author has made to find out what retarded children know about English. He tested one little mongoloid girl for her knowledge of certain prepositions. To do this a very nice set of overhead projector overlays were made so that a picture of a girl, a boy, a playground, trees, and a ball flying through the air could be projected; they were constructed so that each picture could be projected singly or combined in such a way that the boy was seen as throwing the ball to the girl who was standing under the tree in the playground. The picture of the girl was shown to the child being tested, and then, separately, the picture of a tree. When the two pictures were combined, of course, it should have been possible to elicit the phrase, "under the tree". Each time the child was asked, "where is the girl?", she pointed to the screen and answered, "up there". No matter what preposition he tried to get her to use, the same thing happened. Obviously, the little girl knew something about prepositions because she used one in her response, but we were unable to discover how much she knew. Evidently, extra-linguistic factors inherent in the testing procedure can preclude accurate assessment of the capabilities of retarded children to demonstrate their ability to handle American English on tests. We can tell what a child knows when he gives us the correct response, but when a child gives an incorrect response we know nothing. Retarded children give more incorrect responses than do normal children on tests of language (Dever & Gardner, 1970; Lovell & Bradbury, 1967, etc.) but we have no way of knowing whether these test results give us an accurate picture either of what the children know or do not know.

Unfortunately, problems like this may not be restricted to the testing of retarded children: it is likely to exist in the testing of language development in normal children as well. Another very simple test of linguistic development is the phoneme discrimination test (Templin, 1943, 1947; Wepman, 1958, 1960). The only thing phoneme discrimination tests attempt to do is to discover whether a child can tell the difference between two minimally different linguistically significant sounds, e.g., /p,b/. Presumably the assumption behind the use of these tests is that a child who can tell the difference is linguistically more sophisticated than one who cannot. Phoneme discrimination tests all use about the same paradigm, i.e., the examiner usually presents the child with two minimally different words or syllables, e.g., pan - ban, and is asked to tell if these words are "the same or different". Most of these tests produce error rates which are higher than would be expected on the basis of articulation tests (Rudegeair & Kamil, 1969), indicating that some sort of extra-linguistic task variable is likely to be operating

Rudegeair and Kamil (1969) explored the validity of these phoneme discrimination tests. They found that simply by presenting the tests on two successive days errors were markedly reduced. In addition, they found that a different presentation of the test stimuli also markedly reduced errors. This was done in the following way.

On a stereo tape recorder (which uses two-track tape, two microphones for recording, and two speakers for playback) one of the stimulus pairs to be discriminated was recorded on one track of the recording tape. After a short time interval, the other half of the pair was recorded on the other track. Then the question, "Who said (stimulus)?" was recorded on both tracks simultaneously. Speakers were placed 180° apart, one on either side of the child. When the tape was played, one speaker presented the child with one stimulus, e.g., pan, and the other speaker presented the child with the other stimulus, e.g., ban, and then simultaneously both speakers gave just one of the two stimuli, e.g., "Who said ban?" The child's task was to press a lever on the correct speaker. Errors were markedly reduced by this device. It is still unknown whether this method of testing will yield accurate assessments of a child's receptive phonemic inventory, however. Until the predictive validity of the method is explored by some method it must remain an open question.

The Dever (1968) and Rudegeair and Kamil (1969) studies present illustrations that much of the test data which has been recorded on the development of linguistic features of both retarded and intellectually normal children is likely to have limited utility in program development. If it could be possible to develop test paradigms for all aspects of language that are as clever as the stimulus presentation used by Rudegeair and Kamil (assuming that it has predictive validity), it might be possible to modify this statement. Unfortunately, however, such paradigms are not available, and the conclusion that testing of the development of a language lacks validity appears to be justified. This conclusion is further strengthened when one considers the minor nature of the features tested by the above tests. If testing these features of language is so difficult, what difficulties have to be faced when the attempt to test the more complex features of English is made? For example, what problems will be encountered when we try to test the development of the English verb modal system, or the intricacies of the noun phrase? Yet if we wish to develop remedial or developmental program of language teaching we must indeed be able to diagnose language problems and to assess the efficacy of any teaching problems which we institute.

Alternate Directions Available

If direct testing of language development appears to be so difficult, what are some of the options open to researchers in the field for the discovery of the linguistic status of retarded children? The following cannot in any way be considered an exhaustive list; it is simply one set of suggestions that has grown out of our experiences and biases. Others undoubtedly could extend the list much further and we hope that some would make the attempt.

One possibility is the use of traditional linguistic analysis. There are a number of drawbacks to this approach, however, which are likely to make this approach not feasible. In the first place, the training required to do this type of analysis is long and difficult, and not many workers in mental retardation have undertaken to obtain it. In the second place, once a trained person begins work, a great deal of time is needed to develop a small amount of data into meaningful results. Because of these factors, total reliance on traditional linguistic analysis may be unrealistic in the long run.

Another possibility is to train observers to gather data on specific features. However, this too presents problems. Even if persons in the field were to obtain training in the observation of relevant features, it is first necessary to have some notion of what features to look for during the observation. Unfortunately, most of the work done to date in developmental linguistics has been done on a very small number of children under 36 months simply because it has had to utilize the time-consuming traditional linguistic analysis methods. As a consequence, very little is known about the linguistic development of children of this age, and we have little idea as yet as to what to look for. The possibility of gathering data on very young retarded children with an eye to establishing programs which would prevent deficits from accumulating is not great. Even in the area of the language development of normal children over CA 3, the relevant information is somewhat sparse. In addition, the subjects used have been, for the most part, children of professionals and graduate students. Although these children are relatively accessible for study, they tend to be very bright, and the establishment of norms on the basis of the existing information is, at best, difficult.

Another possibility is to launch a concerted attack on the error factors in traditional testing. If we could find out what situational factors were operative in the actual testing of language, perhaps adjustments could be made to obtain results which would yield fairly accurate assessments of

286

the children's ability to use the language. This, however, would require much more sophistication than is presently available in the field.

Another possibility, and the point of this paper, is to develop a scale or scales which could be used to classify the spontaneous linguistic performance of very young children. A scale of this type would require the use of classification categories which would have to be in the form of abstractions of the possible utterances in child language in order that the scale might be compact enough for use. This must be done through the device of grammatical categories. It would not be possible to make up a list containing every utterance which could be produced by a child because children, like all users of a language, are capable of generating an infinite number of utterances. However, if rules for the utterances produced by children and adults were used in defining the categories, it would be possible to make a finite list against which utterances could be scaled according to the completeness of those rules. It would then be possible to gather data on the appearance of the rules by chronological age or any other indices of development. Lenneberg (1967), for example, ties language development to maturation. It is possible that maturational indices of motor development such as the ability to tiptoe might prove to be important concomitants of language development; a scale like the one described could find use in establishing these connections, if they exist.

Lee (1966) appeared to have developed such a scale, but we encountered certain serious difficulties in using the scale as it was published. We found a large number of utterances which could not be classified because of certain ambiguities in the scale or because use of the scale required information on the deep structure of the utterances which was impossible to ascertain. The result of the latter was that there were instances in which the same utterance could be classified in two categories. There were also a few instances in which provision had not been made for utterances which appeared. These are not major criticisms of Lee's work; in fact, because the basic idea behind her scale seemed eminently worthwhile, we decided to utilize it in our own attempt. Our debt to Lee cannot be overstated, and we here gratefully acknowledge it. However, we believe that she made a basic error in her attempt to utilize a transformational grammar as the base grammar for her scale (cf. Dever, in press). We have utilized, instead, a performance grammar. The resulting scale requires only that the child be understood – classification then becomes a matter of applying the rules in the scale.

The Tagmemic Base for the Scale

The Scale of Clause Development is couched in terms of tagmemics (Elson & Pickett, 1965), which is a highly developed structural grammar. Previous attempts to use transformational theory in categorizing children's utterances had not worked out to the present authors' satisfaction, largely because of the fact that classifying utterances meant that we were working with performance data. Because transformational grammars are grammars of competence, they find little use in situations such as the present one, wherein attempts are being made to impose some kind of order on actual utterances (Dever, in press). Tagmemic grammars, on the other hand, being structural grammars, were created specifically for the purpose of classifying and ordering obtained data. This makes them ideal for use in the present situation. There are other grammars of performance, but few are as well-developed as tagmemics.

Tagmemic theory considers a language to be made up of sets of functional relationships. These sets are "layered" and an analysis can be made of a language on any of the layers individually or on a layer as it interacts with the other layers. The following is an example of the kinds of layers one might expect to find in a language:

Figure 1

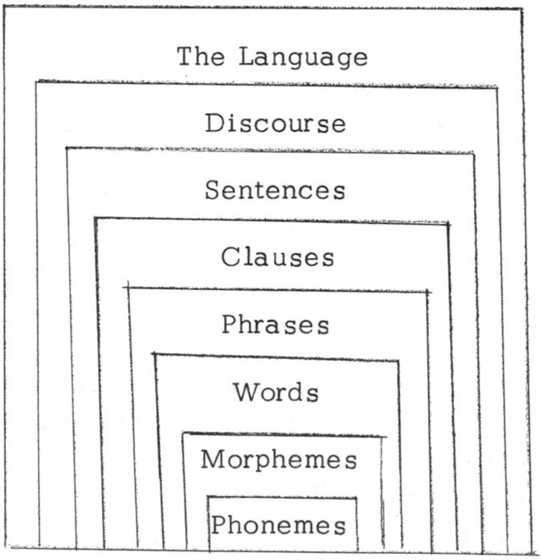

The Language
Discourse
Sentences
Clauses
Phrases
Words
Morphemes
Phonemes

In the above chart, which is by no means an exhaustive list of the types of analysis one might make of a language, each lower layer becomes part of the layer immediately above it when the upper layer is analyzed. A complete grammar of the language would analyze each layer in addition to the relationships between each layer and all of the other layers. There are few (if any) "complete" grammars in this sense.

Tagmemic grammars were developed in the structuralist tradition, i.e., a tagmemic grammar analysis only obtained data, and attempts to present a parsimonious accounting of that data much in the same fashion that a factor analysis of statistical data attempts to find the least number of factors which would account for all of the obtained data. Rarely are all possible layers of a language analyzed in a specific grammar simply because of the enormity of the task involved. Rather, a judgment is made as to which layer would yield the most information about the language in accordance with the purposes of the analysis, and the data are analyzed accordingly. The layer being analyzed is called the syntagmeme; for the purposes of creating the present scale the syntagmeme chosen was that of the clause. Any other unit of analysis could have been chosen -- for example, we might have chose the phrase or the sentence as the syntagmeme and scaled children's developmental utterances accordingly. Clause level analysis, however, seemed to have the greatest immediate potential payoff possibilities because our data appeared to consist largely of clauses or pre-clause utterances. The judgment appears to have been a good one to have made for the data from the children with whom we are concerned. Future work will concentrate on the syntagmemes on either side of the clause, i.e., the phrase (the next lower layer) and the sentence (the next higher layer). Phrase level analysis will allow finer discriminations between levels of development, and sentence level analysis will allow extension of the scale far beyond the ages now covered by the present scale. In relation to this last statement, several investigators (Hunt, 1970; Carol Chomsky, 1969; Kessel, 1970) have found that the development of language in humans continues far beyond the limit of CA 5 that many writers have assumed in the past (e.g., Brown & Bellugi, 1964). This higher-level development, in the present framework, seems to involve the combining of clauses into more and more complex sentences. Hence, a sentence level analysis eventually should provide us with the possibility for scaling utterances of children older than CA 4-5, the present limits of the scale.

A <u>syntagmeme</u> (unit of analysis) consists of <u>slots</u> and <u>fillers</u> of those slots. The relationships between the slots and fillers is the <u>tagmeme</u>. The slots are expressed as <u>functions</u> and are filled by classes of items. The relationship of a slot or function with its fillers is itself the tagmeme (Elson & Pickett, 1965). It is usually possible to express fillers as general classes of mutually substitutable items. A simple illustration of the above is presented in the following sample grammar:

Syntagmeme: Clause

Slots:	Subject	Predicate	Complement
Fillers:	The boy........hit.............the ball.		
	Mary..........quickly sees.....a little round object.		
	Some old men...never give up....their beer.		
Filler Classes:	Noun Phrase	Verb Phrase	Noun Phrase

The grammar could also be written as follows:

Cl = + Subj:Noun Phr + Pred:Verb Phr + Comp:Noun Phr

This formula is read: A clause consists of (=) an obligatory (+) subject slot filled (:) by a noun phrase; an obligatory predicate slot filled by a very phrase; and an obligatory complement slot filled by a noun phrase. That this is not a complete grammar of the American English clause is obvious, but it does indeed constitute a grammar of the data presented. Additional data might change the grammar considerably. For example, if we found the utterance:

(1) Birds fly.

we would find that the complement is optional rather than obligatory. We would then express this through the formula:

Cl = + Subj:Noun Phr + Pred:Verb Phr ± Comp:Noun Phr

The (±) here indicates that the complement tagmeme is optional rather than obligatory. The notation system used in tagmemics, while really rather simple, might need some introduction. Elson and Pickett (1965) have an excellent introductory test on the writing of tagmemic grammars, and we here recommend it to the attention of investigators who are interested in their use.

The Creation of the Scale

The Indiana Scale of Clause Development is an attempt to provide an instrument which will classify utterances made by children. The basic notion was to require as little judgmental input as possible on the part of the rater who would be using it. To this end we have attempted to provide written rules which would classify any single utterance of a child. The writing of the rules had two criteria: (1) that all English utterances in a transcript would be classified somewhere, and (2) that no utterance could be classified in two places. Insofar as our data allows evaluation of these aims, we seem to have accomplished both objectives.

The scale may be, but is not necessarily indicative of specific stages which children go through in their clausal development: our attempt to classify was made in terms of the language patterns which occur, not in terms of the development of children. Although it is possible to find fault with this view, it was the only way we were able to find to classify data consistently and accurately in all instances.

The scale is the final abstraction of the utterances made by children between the ages of 17 and 36 months. There were a total of 72 transcripts used in the work of developing the scale, broken down by CA in table 1.

TABLE I

CA (mos.)	# of Children	# of Transcripts
17–18	3	3
19–20	8	8
21–22	13	13
23–24	8	10*
25–26	12	13*
27–28	10	11*
29–30	5	6*
31–32	3	3
33–34	3	3
35–36	1	1
37–38	1	1
Total	67	72

* There were more transcripts than the number of children in these categories because some children were recorded twice in the two-month period.[2]

    The evolution of the scale went through several stages. The first stage was a generalized organization of the data which eventually resulted in a tagmemic grammar of those utterances. This grammar was presented in P.B.'s master's thesis (Bauman, 1971). This stage dealt with the data from 39 transcripts. The next step was the creation of definitions of classes of utterances holding commonalities, and a first attempt at scaling those utterances for complexities. Repeated attempts at scaling over a period of almost two years resulted in the final definition of the scale as a scaling of clausal development. The third stage was the refinement of the definitions of the developing clauses and clause types, with repeated attempts to use the evolving definitions in classifying the utterances found in 33 additional transcripts. When the present version of the scale finally evolved we found that we were able to classify every utterance in our data. The results of that classification attempt are presented at the end of this report.

---

2. We gratefully acknowledge the assistance of Dr. Rick Heber in providing us with the transcripts used in developing the scale.

The Indiana Scale of Clause Development

A pictorial overview of the scale is presented in Figure 2. Each utterance made by a child is classified by the scale as a vector point on several dimensions. The major dimensions are as follows:

A. Clauses. The clause is defined in the scale following Gleason (1965), i.e., as an utterance containing one predicate or predicate-like construction. Thus, the single most important defining feature of any clause is the presence or potential presence[3] of a verbal element as one of the nuclear tagmemes. Because of this, manifestations of the verbal element become the central notion underlying ranks, clause-types, and the classification of an utterance as a clause or as a sentence.

The breakdown of clauses into Declarative, Question, and Imperative is quite traditional, and presents some problems of definition. That is, there seems to be no efficient way to define these categories except to say that every native speaker of English knows when a clause is to be classified as one of the three. Traditionally, declarative clauses are defined as clauses which give information about something, yet both questions and imperatives can give information. For example, consider the following question and imperative clauses:

(2) Would you like some of this cake?

(3) Throw me that wrench over there.

Both give information under certain circumstances. For example, if the hearer of (2) did not know that there was any cake, the

---

3. We have to modify Gleason's definition slightly because young children's clauses often lack the verbal element where it would clearly be supplied in the adult grammar, e.g., "That my dog." All rules are stated in terms of adult English because the scale classifies degrees of approximation to adult English. In spite of the fact that we believe the grammar of a child to be a "complete" grammar for the child at any given point, it seems efficient, when classifying performance data, to do so in terms of a reference – in this case, the adult clause.

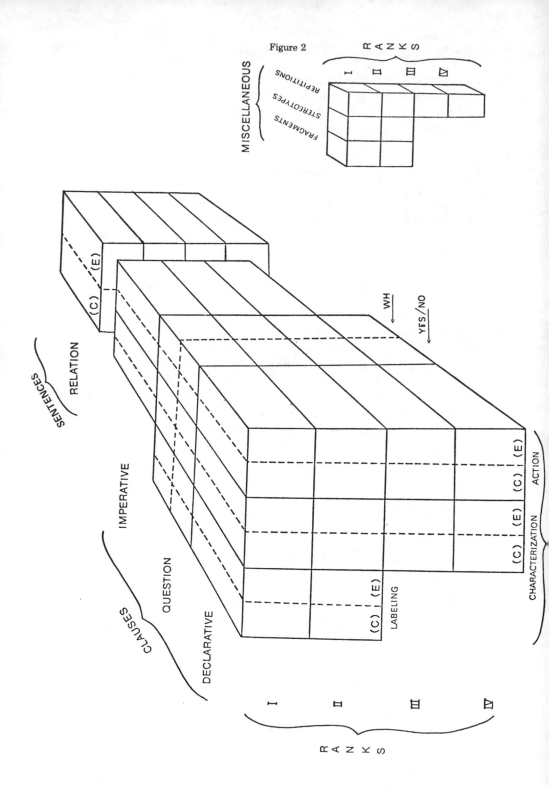

Figure 2

MISCELLANEOUS

FRAGMENTS STEREOTYPES REPITITIONS

RANKS

I II III IV

SENTENCES

RELATION

(C) (E)

WH

YES/NO

IMPERATIVE

CLAUSES

QUESTION

DECLARATIVE

CHARACTERIZATION ACTION

(C) (E) (C) (E)

LABELING

(C) (E)

RANKS

I II III IV

question would provide him with the information he needs; similarly, the command in (3) could differentiate between more than one wrench, or even provide the basic information that there was a wrench available. Questions, which are traditionally defined as asking for information, can give information as in the above example, as well as give commands. For example, every elementary school classroom abounds with questions such as:

(4) Would you like to come with me?

The child who hears this knows that he has little choice; the teacher (or principal, or whatever) is simply being polite. Similarly, the utterance:

(5) I don't know what I'm doing.

could under certain circumstances, be a request for help, or even a command. Thus, imperatives are also difficult to define in a traditional way: traditionally imperatives give commands, but so can questions as in (4) and declaratives as in (5). Imperatives can give information as in (3), and can ask for information as in:

(6) Tell me what's going on around here.

If it is difficult to define declarative, questions and imperatives in traditional terms, it is equally difficult to define them in terms of form and function. We have written rules for the developing clauses as part of the scale, but all of the rules, as stated, are remarkably similar to one another in many respects (varying only in the intonational envelope at times, a feature which is not formally expressed in the scale). In their abstract form any utterance rule could become confused with almost any other rule. Therefore, use of the scale relies very heavily on the knowledge that each native speaker has of his language for determining whether a clause is to be classified as being declarative, question or imperative. This will cause no trouble at all in practice simply because every adult native speaker knows far more about his language than can be expressed in a grammar.

B. Ranks. We have deliberately avoided the use of the term "levels" in the scale because it could give the impression that a rank within one clause is the equivalent of the same rank within another clause. This may not be the case at all. Consider, for example, the fact that the declarative clause:

(7) That is a dog.

is a Rank III Declarative, while the question:

(8) That is a dog?

is also classified as Rank III in the scale. The declarative in
(7) is a well-formed clause in the adult grammar (except in
special cases, as in the expression of incredulity). There
is a real problem in making the claim that the two utterances
are somehow "equal" because of this fact. Therefore, we
have conceived the scale as being a scale of development
within clauses and clause-types, and not as a scale which
indicates generalized development across clauses. In doing
so we expect to find that children will exhibit regular advances
within clauses, but irregular development across clauses. This
will certainly prove to be the case in relation to Clauses as
opposed to Sentences, and very likely the case in relation to
Ellipted as opposed to Complete utterances. We might
hypothesize that it would also be true for declarative in
relation to questions, etc.

The ranks within clauses are defined by the rules in
Table 2. Each of these rules is discussed below.

Rank I. This rank, with the exception of the category of
sentences, some miscellaneous utterances, most imperatives,
and some declaratives with intransitive verbs, consists solely
of one- or two-word utterances. That is, if a child produces a
one- or a two-word utterance, it is to be classified as Rank I.
The few exceptions to this rule are specified in the scale.
In the case of intransitive verbs, rules for the higher ranks
sometimes conflict with a rule for a lower rank; in this case,
the rule for the higher rank takes precedence. For example,
the utterance:

(9) He sees.

contains an intransitive verb, and fulfills all of the requirements
of a Rank III declarative in spite of the fact that it contains only
two words. It is to be classified as Rank III. In the case of
imperatives, there are certain optional clause subject (addressee)
rules which allow the general rules for Rank I to be violated.
For example, the imperative:

(10) Go!

Table 2

CLAUSE RULES

	Declarative Clause	Question Clause
Rank I =	Cl: + $\begin{bmatrix} \pm \leq \text{Two words} \\ + \text{Elipsis} \end{bmatrix}$	Cl: + $\begin{bmatrix} \pm \leq \text{Two words} \\ + \text{Ellipsis} \end{bmatrix}$
Rank II =	Cl: + $\begin{bmatrix} \pm \text{ Subj} + \text{Pred} \pm \text{Comp} + \text{Mod} \\ + \text{Elipsis} \end{bmatrix}$	Cl: + $\begin{bmatrix} \pm \text{ Subj} + \text{Pred} \pm \text{Comp} + \text{Mod} \\ + \text{Ellipsis} \end{bmatrix}$
Rank III =	Cl: + $\begin{bmatrix} + (+\text{Subj} + \text{Pred}_i) \pm \text{Mod} \\ + (+\text{Subj} + \text{Pred}_t + \text{Comp}) \pm \text{Mod} \\ + \text{Elipsis} \end{bmatrix}$	Cl: + $\begin{bmatrix} + (+\text{Subj} + \text{Pred}_i) \pm \text{Mod} \\ + (+\text{Subj} + \text{Pred}_t + \text{Comp}) \pm \text{Mod} \\ + \text{Ellipsis} \end{bmatrix}$
Rank IV =	Cl: + $\begin{bmatrix} + \text{Rank III} + \text{Pass T} \\ + \text{Elipsis} \end{bmatrix}$	+Cl: + $\begin{bmatrix} + \text{Rank III} + \text{Q T} \\ + \text{Ellipsis} \end{bmatrix}$

Table 2 (cont.)

Imperative Clause   Relation Sentences

Rank I

$$\text{S:} \quad + \begin{bmatrix} + \text{Cl}_\text{I} + \text{Cl}_\text{I} \\ + \text{Ellipsis} \end{bmatrix}$$

$$\text{Cl:} \quad \pm \text{Addr} + \text{Pred}_t$$

Rank II

$$\text{S:} \quad + \begin{bmatrix} + \text{Cl} \geqslant_\text{II} + \text{Cl}_\text{I} \\ + \text{Ellipsis} \end{bmatrix}$$

$$\text{Cl:} \quad + \begin{bmatrix} + (\pm \text{Addr} + \text{Pred}_t \pm \text{Comp}) \pm \text{Mod} \\ + \text{Ellipsis} \end{bmatrix}$$

Rank III

$$\text{S:} \quad + \begin{bmatrix} + \text{Cl} \geqslant_\text{III} + \text{Cl} \geqslant_\text{II} \\ + \text{Ellipsis} \end{bmatrix}$$

$$\text{Cl:} \quad + \begin{bmatrix} + (\pm \text{Addr} + \text{Pred}_i) \pm \text{Mod} \\ + (\pm \text{Addr} + \text{Pred}_t + \text{Comp}) \pm \text{Mod} \\ + \text{Ellipsis} \end{bmatrix}$$

Rank IV

$$\text{S:} \quad + \begin{bmatrix} + \text{Cl} \geqslant_\text{III} + \text{Cl} \geqslant_\text{III} \\ \pm \text{Ellipsis} \end{bmatrix}$$

would fulfill the Rank III requirements because it is an intransitive
verb. It is to be so classified. Again, when a higher-level rule
conflicts with a lower-level rule, the higher-level rule always
takes precedence. Sentences and the miscellaneous categories
have rules of their own (to be discussed below) which also allow
the generalized rule for Rank I to be violated in some instances.

Rank II. In general, this rank classifies utterances which, although
larger than two words, are incomplete in that they do not contain all
the nuclear obligatory tagmemes of Rank III. A nuclear obligatory
tagmeme is a tagmeme which is essential to the syntagmeme, and
is expressed in the rules as being obligatory (+). In relation to
declarative and question clauses these are:

$$+ \text{Subj} + \text{Pred}_t + \text{Comp}$$

in the case of predicates with transitive verbs, and:

$$+ \text{Subj} + \text{Pred}_i$$

in the case of predicates with intransitive verbs. In the case of
imperatives, however, only the predicate is obligatory: since the
subject of an imperative is always the person addressed (Addr),
the expression of the subject is optional and may or may not be
expressed at the option of the speaker.

The lines connecting nuclear tagmemes beneath the rules in
Rank II Declarative and Question Clauses indicate that at least
one of the nuclear obligatory tagmemes must be expressed. This
means that utterances which lack all three nuclear obligatory
tagmemes, as in:

(11) In the house.

cannot be classified in the main body of the scale -- hence one
of the reasons for provision of the category of "Miscellaneous"
utterances. Prepositional phrases occurring by themselves as in
(11) are to be classified as fragments (unless, of course, they
are Ellipted utterances).

Rank III. This rank classifies all utterances which contain all
of their nuclear obligatory tagmemes whether or not they are in
their correct sequence according to the adult grammar, and
whether or not other syntagmemes are completely expressed. That
is, in spite of the fact that a child may make an error on the
phase level, the morpheme level or the phoneme level, if he

presents an utterance which contains all of the nuclear
obligatory tagmemes on the clause level it should be classified
as Rank III. For example:

(12) I going home. (Rank III)

(13) I put down. (Rank II)

In (12) we find a subject, a predicate, and a object; the
utterance is classified as Rank III in spite of the fact that the
verb phrase lacks the proper form of "be". This is a phrase
level error which cannot affect clause level classification.
In (13), on the other hand, we find a subject and a predicate,
but not an object where one would be expected. Therefore, a
clause-level error has occurred, and the utterance is classified as Rank II. It is the occurrance of utterances of this
kind which causes us to believe that a scale of the syntagmeme
"Phrase" will be necessary.

Children sometimes reverse the order of tagmemes. Such
reversals are inconsequential to the scale. A child might say,
for example:

(14) I home go.

This would be classified as a Rank III Declarative Action
Clause, just as would:

(15) I go home.

Rank IV. For a clause to be classified as a Rank IV Clause,
all the nuclear obligatory tagmemes must be present, and a
reordering transformation must take place. There are only two
transformations to be considered: the passive transformation
on both the declarative and question clauses (and possibly
the imperative, though we have not found any in our data), and
the question transformation on the question clause. It is likely
that no Rank IV Imperatives will occur in children's speech.

In the passive transformation, the Comp is shifted to the
Subj position, the verb is inflected for passive, a form of
"be" appears, and the Subj is optionally included in a prepositional phrase. Thus:

(16) Mary sees John   John is seen (by Mary).

with the prepositional phrase (in Parentheses) being optional.

In the question transformation, several things may occur:

(a) in the yes/no question (questions that expect a response of "yes" or "no") the tense-carrying element in the verb phrase is shifted to the initial position in the clause:

(17) John is a boy   Is John a boy?

(18) John saw Bill   Did John see Bill?

(19) Dogs can swim   Can dogs swim?

(20) Frank has left   Has Frank left?

(21) John is going   Is John going?

(b) also in the yes/no question, the question part of the clause can be made negative and "tagged" to the end of the declarative form:

(22) Irene left Harry   Irene left Harry, didn't she?

(23) You don't like liver   You don't like liver, do you?

(c) in the wh-question a nuclear obligatory tagmeme or a modifier is replaced by a wh-word (who, what, where, when, why, how). The Wh-word appears in the initial clause position and the tense carrier is shifted to the clause position immediately following the wh-word:

(24) John left yesterday   Who left yesterday?

(25) Cats howl all night   What do cats do all night?

(26) Mary catches fish   What does Mary catch?

(27) Fish can smell terrible   How can fish smell?

(28) He goes because he likes it   Why does he go?

(29) Alfred lives at home   Where does Alfred live?

(30) He played cards as a young boy   When did he play cards?

(31) Some boys steal cars   What boys steal cars?

   Any question with a transitive verb can also be made passive.
Consider utterances (18), (22), (26) and (30):

(18) Was John seen by Bill?

(22) Harry was left by Irene, wasn't he?

(26) What is caught by Mary?

(30) When were cards played?

There are certain constraints on passivizing questions, however,
which are obvious to any native speaker. For example, utterances
(23) and (30) will probably sound strange to most native speakers
if they appear as:

(23) Liver isn't liked by you is it?

(30) When were cards played by him?

When, in the judgment of an adult native speaker of American
English, nonallowable transformations are made by a child,
the utterances should be classified as Rank III. All completed
transformations allowed by the language, however, will be
classified as Rank IV. Such transformations must be complete
in all respects. For example, if the tense-carrier element is
left out of one of the above transformations, the utterance would
be classified as Rank III:

(26) Mary catches fish   What Mary catch? (Rank III)

The Rank III classification is made because all nuclear obligatory
tagmemes for the clause are present, but the transformation that
defines Rank IV has not completely taken place. It will not be
complete until the tense has appeared in the position before the
subject. All transformations must be complete before an utterance
can be classified as Rank IV.

   No transformations of the reordering type can be made on the
imperative clause; therefore, there is no Rank IV for imperatives
(unless we should find a passive - see Table 3).

   C. Clause-Types. The Declarative, Question, and Imperative
clauses each have at least two clause-types: Characterization and
Action.

Characterization Clause-Types. These utterances are those which contain or potentially contain a form of "be". They are so named because the complement somehow "characterizes" the subject. Thus:

(32) He is John (Nominal Complement)

(33) That dog is over there (Adverbial Complement)

(34) The barn is red (Adjectival Complement)

Verbs other than "be" also have been called "linking verbs" traditionally, but the scale does not consider these in characterization clauses. Thus, utterances containing verbs such as "become", "weigh", etc., are classified under Action clause types.

Action Clause-Types. The name for this clause is potentially misleading because not all verbs other than "be" express an action. Simply for want of a better term, however, we chose "action". These clauses are those which have or potentially have verbs other than "be" as their predicate. Thus:

(35) Mary sees John

(36) Dogs prefer meat

(37) Mothers love their children

are all action clauses in spite of the fact that little overt "action" may be discernable.

Labeling Clause-Types. The labeling clause-type is not a true clause because it has no potential for a verbal element. Essentially it is an environmentally-conditioned (dependent on something in the environment other than on a linguistic utterance) noun phrase. It was built into the scale because it appears quite often in children's utterances. Linguistically conditioned (dependent on something in the linguistic environment) noun phrases would be classified as ellipses and are handled by the scale in a different manner from the labeling clause.

If a child utters a noun phrase with no indication in the linguistic environment that it has a reason to appear, it is to be classified as a Rank I or Rank II labeling clause-type. Thus:

(38) A dog (Rank I Labeling Clause-Type)

(39) Hey, my red ball. (Rank II Labeling Clause-Type)

There can be no Rank III or IV Labeling Clause-Type because of the
fact that, as soon as a verbal element appears or is potentially
available, the clause would be classified as either "Characterizati
or "Action".

D. <u>Complete and Ellipted Clauses</u>. The scale is actually
two scales in that any utterance may be a complete clause, with
the nuclear tagmemes being manifested with no reference to the
linguistic context in which they are uttered, or they may be
ellipted, that is, dependent, in some way, on the linguistic
context. Thus:

(40) Out!

may be a perfectly acceptable Rank III Imperative Action Clause.
But, in the context:

(41) <u>E</u>: Where did you go?

    <u>S</u>: Out.

we see instance of a Rank I Ellipted Declarative Action Clause.

All Ellipses are to be classified where they would have been
classified had they been complete clauses. To be classified as an
ellipsis, the utterance must be judged as being "grammatical"
by the rater. All "ungrammatical" elliptical utterances are to be
classified as being "complete". The clause <u>type</u> will often have
to be taken from the previous utterance. Thus, in (41), <u>S</u>'s
utterance will be classified as a Rank I Declarative Action Clause
and not as a fragment where it would have been classified, had
it occurred in isolation. Words such as "yeah", "uhuh", etc.
are classified as elliptical utterances where appropriate.

Labeling clause-types present a peculiar case. Many
elliptical utterances are similar to Labeling Clause-Types,
but are to be classified as ellipted labeling clauses <u>only</u> when
the previous linguistic context is itself a labeling clause-type
(see examples in Table 3).

We expect that ellipted utterances will begin to occur later
than complete utterances.

304

Wh and Yes/No Question Clauses. The one remaining classification in the clause scale is that of Wh- and Yes/No Questions. Some questions, when asked, expect an answer of "yes" or "no". Other questions expect some kind of information to be given when the answer is different from a simple "yes" or "no". These questions begin with words that typically, but not always, are spelled with a word beginning with "wh": who, what, when, where, why, and how. The yes/no and wh-questions are to be classified separately. The reason for this is speculative in that the two types of questions may prove to have different developmental sequences. This feature makes provision in the scale for discovering whether or not this will be true. If it proves not to be the case the category will be discarded in later versions of the scale.

E. Sentences. Children begin at a rather early age to make utterances which are combinations of clauses. That is, if an utterance occurs which contains two predicate or predicate-like constructions, it is to be classified as a sentence. This includes concatenation of clauses through the use of conjunctions and intonation, subordination of clauses as subjects or objects within a clause, and subordination through the use of infinitives functioning as subjects or objects within a clause. Any time two predicates appear (in reality or potentially), the utterance is to be classified as a sentence. Note that the following are not to be classified as Sentences:

(42) John and Bill ran home

(43) I saw the dog and cat.

The utterances in (42) and (43) each have only one predicate and cannot be classified as sentences. Although transformational theory would analyze them as being the result of the imbedding of deep structure rules for two separate sentences, our definition of "clause" prevents them from being analyzed this way in the present scale. The utterance in (42) simply has a complex subject, and (43) simply has a complex complement.

Sentences are to be ranked according to the complexity of the individual clauses combining to make the sentence. These rankings are specified in Table 2. Thus, in order for a sentence to be classified as Rank III, one of the clauses must be at least Rank III, and the other must be a Rank II.

305

The ordering of clauses in the rules is not mandatory, and either of the two combined clauses may be the Rank III clause. The highest rank that applies is the one in which the utterance is to be classified. Thus, a sentence containing two Rank II clauses will be ranked as Rank II sentence, as will a sentence containing a Rank III clause and a Rank I clause.

Miscellaneous Utterances

Not every utterance can be scaled. Children, like adults, sometimes say things that seem garbled or otherwise unclassifiable. The category of "Miscellaneous" was provided in order to be able to account for 100% of the utterances made by any one child. This category has three major sub-categories:

a. Repetitions. Children often repeat what an adult says. Since there is a possibility that children might be able to repeat a grammatical form at a different level than would be found in the same child's spontaneous productions, the decision was made to classify all repeated utterances in a separate category. This includes not only verbatim repetitions such as:

(44) E: That's a ball.

(45) S: That's a ball.

but also incomplete repetition such as:

(46) E: That's a ball.

(47) S: That ball

The category also classifies such things as nursery rhymes or songs produced by the child. Each clause of the rhymes or song receives one tally. Utterances which are somehow changed in the repetition are to be classified in the main body of the scale where they would ordinarily be classified. For example:

(48) E: What have you got there?

(49) S: What do I got there?

The utterance in (49) would be classified as a Rank IV Action Question.

Repeated utterances are classified in the same rank as they would have been classified had they been spontaneous utterances, e.g., (45) above would be a Rank III repetition, while (47) above would be a Rank I repetition.

b. <u>Fragments</u>. Children will sometimes say things that have no apparent clausal functioning, i.e., what is said is neither a subject, a predicate, nor a complement. It is <u>as</u> <u>if</u> they began and ended someplace within a clause. Such utterances cannot be classified according to the rules we have written, e.g.,

(50) <u>S</u>: In dog.

The utterance in (50) is evidently part of a prepositional phrase, and cannot be classified as either a labeling, characterization, or action clause type. It would be a Rank I Fragment. There can be only two ranks for fragments simply because as soon as a nuclear obligatory clause-tagmeme appears the utterance would be classified as a scaled utterance. Fragments are relatively rare in our data.

c. <u>Stereotypes</u>. Children will say things which could be analyzed as more than one word if an adult said them, but which seem to function as one word for the child, e.g.,

(51) Fall down and go boom!

(52) Go round and round.

These stereotypic utterances are classified separately when they occur unless they appear as part of a clause. At that point they become analyzable as they would be in the adult grammar, e.g.,

(53) Daddy fall down and go boom!

would be a Rank III Sentence. It should be noted that stereotyped utterances are all classified as Rank I unless <u>two</u> stereotypes occur in the same utterance, e.g.,

(54) S: Go round and round and fall down and go boom!

This would be classified as a Rank II Stereotype. There is no Rank III or IV Stereotype for the same reason that there is no Rank III or IV Fragment.

Examples

Table 3 presents examples of utterances found in our data and classified in their proper places on the scale. For some boxes we were unable to find actual utterances, but we knew that they were likely to occur. We invented utterances for illustrative purposes: these are marked with an asterisk (*). Some boxes in the scale appear to be impossible to fill, e.g., Rank IV Elipted Imperative Characterization Clauses. These have been left blank. We would appreciate hearing from users of the scale who have found actual utterances to take the place of our invented ones.

Table 3

Examples of Labeling Clause (Declarative)

Rank	Complete	Ellipted
I	a doo doo a cup two thing fuel truck hat	E: Daddy? S: <u>Yeah</u> E: Your fruit? S: <u>Yeah</u>
II	a pretty cracker my baby hat hello, a that a dishes a one, two, three cat	*E: My book? S: <u>No</u>, <u>my</u> <u>book</u> *E: A big dog S: <u>And</u> <u>a</u> <u>little</u> <u>on</u>

* Possible, but not found in our data.

Table 3 (cont.)

Examples of Characterization Clause (Declarative)

Rank	C	E
I	it door block there 's dishes here mine thatsa ball* itsa truck*	E: What's this? S: <u>a doll</u> E: Who's that? S: <u>my mommy</u> E: Is she wet? S: <u>Yeah</u> E: Where should the shoe hook be? S: <u>Right here</u> E: Is that John? S: <u>No</u>
II	it a this toy the baby here it a ball hi, 't me	E: What's this? S: <u>a coal truck</u> E: What's that? S: <u>a garbage</u> <u>truck</u> E: What's that part of the bus for? S: <u>For the suitcase</u>
III	the chicken is there baby is very cold baby cold is mom be home here's another bus	(probably no utterance possible)
IV	(probably no utterance possible)	(probably no utterance possible)

* "thatsa" and "itsa" seem to function as one word in very young children.

Table 3 (cont.)

Examples of Action Clause (Declarative)

Rank	C	E
I	help me want baby run	E: You hurt your what? S: <u>my ba</u> E: Who hung up? S: <u>My momma</u> E: Where you gonna put the duck S: <u>In here</u>. E: In where? S: <u>In here</u>.
II	feed my baby a have paper play with that can baby a hair	S: The blocks fell out. E: Fell out of what? S: <u>Out of here</u>. E: What are you going to do w your purse? S: <u>Hang it up</u>.
III	so take it off I love bake Walter go to bed I talk to you later I can't get out I don't see it	(probably no utterance possible)
IV	* The lady was seen (by the man) * The sound was heard (by the boy)	(probably no utterance possible)

* Possible, but not found in our data.

Table 3 (cont.)

Examples of Labeling Clause (Question)

Level	C	E
I	a doodoo? a lamp? my rabbit?	*E: Yours? S: <u>Mine</u>? *E: My doggy S: <u>Your doggy</u>?
II	a many turkey? oh, sombody baby?	*E: Johnny? S: <u>And Sally too</u>? *E: Lots of apples. S: <u>Apples and oranges</u>?

* Possible, but not found in our data

Characterization Clause–Question

Examples

Levels	C	E
I	what that? you hungry? that puppet?	E: What color is it? S: <u>That</u> <u>wagon</u>? E: What are these? S: <u>Cage</u>?
II	what your name? you hungry now? what that little thing... a doggie?	E: What's this? S: <u>A Cone</u> truck *E: Do you know where they are? S: <u>In the box</u>?
III	who the pencil is this? what is it is? where you are?	(probably no utterances possible)
IV	what's that? are you a baby? baby, what's wrong? where are you?	(probably no utterances possible)

* Possible, but not found in our data

Examples

Level

I   how doing?   S: Did Nelley break it? E: No

           call Lisa   S: <u>Who</u>? E: I don't know

           running?   S: The <u>boy</u>?

                                E: Will leave the parts on the Baby. S: On <u>it</u>?

                                E: Where'd it go? S: <u>Right</u> here?

                                E: You have to keep the books over here. S: <u>In here</u>?

II   Take off in the house? *E: Here it goes. S: <u>Fell</u> down

           Take off now?   <u>again</u>?

           Can you do?

III   we go?   (probably no utterances possible)

           what this car doin'?

           that's a rabbit?

IV   what's it doing?   (probably no utterances possible)

           can I keep this?

           It broke off there?

           Who broke it?

           Did Kelly break it?

* Possible, but not found in our data

Sentence

Examples

Levels	C	E
I	want take run, see	E: Who taught you how to make good coffee like this? S: My aunt E: Hmm? S: My mommy. E: Where did you say that was? S: In there. E: What makes the truck roll? S: The cow
II	Want you to play with me Wanna play piano That baby gone to sleep	E: Can you button it? S: I don't know E: What are the ducks saying? S: I dunno E: And then you can tell him "hi" and maybe shake his hand S: I don't wanna S: (I'm tired ...) don't feel good
III	* The book fell down and pick it up.	E: Selna, what is that? S: You know what. E: The dog is here and ... S: chicken is there E: You have to look through there S: Let me!
V	Let it be! Come look! Put her dress down, I say! I know how to sit her up I want to blow it I'm gon get ya, if ya'll don't give me my purse I wanna see this Let's go!	*E: What's that? S: A dog, and I see a cat, too.

314

* Possible, but not found in our data.

Imperative

Examples

Levels	C	E
I	Hey, wash! *Tear up!	(S: Get in this.) <u>The wagon</u>
II	give me! * throw over here now! put right down, there!	*E: You said, "Throw the ball". Who to? S: <u>To me</u>, <u>right</u> <u>here</u>.
III	put me up there! look at this baby! get up here! button this! Don't fall! Don't cry, baby! Shut up!	(probably no utterance possible)
IV	(probably no utterance possible)**	(probably no utterance possible)

* Possible, but no found in our data

** But: "never let it be said" is a passive imperative in
    the adult grammar – is it possible in a young child's
    grammar?

Repetitions

Examples

Levels

I   E: This is called the apple book. S: <u>Apple</u> <u>book</u>
     E: Say, "Hi, man". S: <u>Hi</u>, <u>man</u>.
     E: John Mack? S: <u>John</u> <u>Mack</u>.
     E: Are you a nice girl, Selena? S: <u>Nice</u> <u>girl</u>.

II   S: Pattycake, pattycake, baker man
     E: We gotta put the toys up first. S: <u>The</u> <u>toys</u> <u>first</u>.

III E: You're rocking her to sleep? S: <u>Rocking</u> <u>her</u> <u>to</u> <u>sleep</u>.
     E: See the boy fly the kite. S: <u>See</u> <u>the</u> <u>boy</u>.
     E: Let's turn. S: <u>Let's</u> <u>turn</u>.

IV   E: How are you? S: <u>How</u> <u>are</u> <u>you</u>?
     E: It's hard, that makes it bounce. S: <u>That</u> <u>makes</u> <u>it</u>
        <u>bounce</u>.
    *E: Let's turn it. S: <u>Let's</u> <u>turn</u> <u>it</u>.

*Possible, but not found in our data.

Stereotyped Utterances

Level

I   round 'n round
go boom
excuse me
I'm sorry

II   *round 'n round and go boom

Fragments

Level

I   quick over
in house

II   by the chair

*Possible, but not found in our data.

References

Batemen, D. & Wetherell, J. Psycholinguistic aspects of mental retardation. Mental Retardation, 1965, 3, 8-13.

Bauman, Patricia M. The clausal development of children aged 18-36 months, unpublished master's thesis, Indiana University, 1971.

Berko, J. The child's learning of English morphology. Word, 1958, 14, 150-177.

Blessing, K. An investigation of a psycholinguistic deficit in educable mentally retarded children: Detection, remediation, and related variables. Unpublished Ph.D. Dissertation, University of Wisconsin, 1964.

Brown, R. & Bellugi, Ursulla. Three processes in the child's acquisition of syntax, Harv. educ. Rev., 1964, 34, 133-151.

Chappell, G.E. A picture test of English inflection. Unpublished Doctoral Dissertation, University of Wisconsin, 1968.

Chomsky, Carol. The Acquisition of Syntax in Children from Five to Ten. Cambridge: The M.I.T. Press, 1969.

Dever, R. A new perspective for language research. Mental Retardation, 1966, 4, 20-23.

Dever, R. A comparison of the results of a revised version of Berko's Test of Morphology with the free speech of mentally retarded children. Unpublished Ph.D. dissertation, University of Wisconsin, 1968.

Dever, R. Before transformational grammars: the case for data-gathering. J. spec. Education, in press.

Dever, R. & Gardner, W. Performance of normals and retardates on Berko's test of morphology. Lang. & Speech, 1970, 13, 162-181.

Elson, B. & Pickett, Velma. An Introduction to Morphology and Syntax. Santa Ana, California: Summer Institute of Linguistics, 1965.

Francis, W.N. The Structure of American English. New York: The Ronald Press, 1958.

Gleason, H. Linguistics and English Grammar, New York: Holt, Rinhart & Winston, 1965.

Hunt, K. W. Syntactic maturity in school children and adults. Monogr. Soc. for Res. in child Devlpm., 1970, 35 (1).

Kessel, F. S. The role of syntax in children's comprehension from ages six to twelve. Monogr. Soc. Res. in child Devlpm., 1970, 35 (6).

Lee, L. Developmental sentence types: a method for comparing normal and deviant syntactic development. J. Speech hear. Dis., 1966, 31, 311-330.

Lovell, K. & Bradbury, B. The learning of English morphology in educationally subnormal special school children. Amer. J. ment. Def., 1967, 71, 609-615.

McCarthy, J. & Kirk, S. A. The Illinois Test of Psycholinguistic Abilities. Champaign, Illinois: The University of Illinois Press, 1961.

McCarthy, J. & Kirk, S. A. The Construction, Standardization, and Statistical Characteristics of the Illinois Test of Psycholinguistic Abilities. Madison: ITPA Inc., 1963.

Mueller, M. W. Comparison of psycholinguistic patterns of gifted and retarded children. Inspection and Introspection of Special Education. Washington, D.C.: Council for Exceptional Children, 1965 (a), 143-148.

Mueller, M. W. Language profiles of mentally retarded children. Inspection and Introspection of Special Education. Washington, D.C., Council for Exceptional Children, 1964 (b), 149-151.

Rosenberg, S. Problems of language development in children: a discussion of Olson's review. In Haywood, H.C. (Ed.), Social-Cultural Aspects of Mental Retardation. New York: Appleton-Century-Crofts, 1970.

Rudegeair, R. & Kamil, M. Assessment of phonological discrimination in children. Madison, Wisconsin: Technical Report (draft copy) of the Wisconsin Research and Development Center for Cognitive Learning, August, 1969.

Slobin, D. I. A Field Manual for Cross-Cultural Study of the
    Acquisition of Communicative Competence. Berkeley:
    University of California, 1967.

Smith, J. O. Effects of a Group Language Development Program
    Upon the Psycholinguistic Abilities of Educable Mental
    Retardates. Peabody College for Teachers, Nashville,
    Tennessee: Special Education Research Monograph
    Series, 1962.

Templin, M. A study of sound discrimination ability of
    elementary school pupils. J. speech Disord., 1943, 8,
    127-132.

Templin, M. Spontaneous versus imitated verbalization in testing
    articulation in school children. J. speech Disord., 1947,
    12, 293-300.

Wepman, J. Auditory discrimination test: Manual of directions.
    Chicago: Language Research Associates, 1958.

Wepman, J. Auditory discrimination, speech and reading.
    Elementary School J., 1960, 60, 325-333.

LINGUISTIC ANALYSIS OF CHILDREN'S SPEECH:
A COMPARISON OF FOUR PROCEDURES

Thomas M. Longhurst and Trudy A. M. Schrandt

The use of four current linguistic procedures for assessing the development of children's language was investigated. Clinicians need an accurate, reliable, and easily applied procedure to assess language performance that will enable them to prescribe treatment. Two subjects, one advanced and one delayed in language development, were chosen on the basis of their chronological age, mental age, and oral language skills. An examiner collected language samples from the two children and scored them according to instructions for the four procedures. The four procedures were then represented in similar tabular form to facilitate comparison. Each procedure was analyzed for its ease of application, interscorer reliability, ability to discriminate language differences between the two subjects, and ability to describe specifically the differences between the subjects. The procedures using a slot-filler (tagmemic) analysis appeared to handle the language samples most adequately. The authors believe that a renewed interest in basic structural linguistic concepts should prove valuable to the assessment of language development.

Oral language is frequently the most important single factor used to evaluate a child's growth and development. Therefore, it is vital that the clinician obtain as accurate a representation of the child's language performance as possible.

Recent clinical research has focused on measurement of the structural linguistic aspects of children's language performance (Lee, 1966; Lee and Canter, 1971; Engler, Hannah, and Longhurst, 1973; Dever and Bauman[1]). These procedures require that the speech clinician elicit, record, and segment; then analyze, classify, or score the speech of children. This report will compare and evaluate the efficiency of their procedures in assessing the language of children.

Lee (1966) applied findings obtained in several developmental psycholinguistic studies of normal language acquisition to develop a procedure for diagnosing delayed language development. Lee's purpose was to investigate whether the "language-delayed" child was slower in syntactic development or was proceeding in a bizarre manner. Speech samples from a "normally developing" child and a "clinic" child were collected and analyzed. Lee concluded,

---

[1]R. Dever and P. Bauman, unpublished work, Indiana University, 1971. Although unpublished, a copy of the Indiana Scale of Clausal Development may be obtained by writing to Richard Dever, Center for Innovation in Teaching the Handicapped, School of Education, Indiana University, Bloomington, Indiana 47401.

JOURNAL OF SPEECH AND HEARING DISORDERS, 1973, vol. 38, no. 2, pp. 240-249.

based on the comparison of the two children, that her developmental sentence types (DST) method of classifying sentences showed marked differences in her two samples. Her analysis demonstrated not only slower development in the "clinic" child but also failure to produce certain types of syntactic structures.

Engler, Hannah, and Longhurst (1973) presented a linguistic analysis of speech samples (LASS) procedure which allowed the speech clinician to analyze the spontaneous speech of children within a relatively standardized test situation. This approach utilized contrastive analysis and borrowed a combination of concepts from slot-filler (tagmemic), immediate constituent, and elementary transformational grammar approaches of current linguistic theory. The authors posited five basic sentence types for English, with the construction contained in the verb phrase as the criterion for classification. The categories were (1) sentences characterized as "equational" by using copulative or linking verbs, (2) sentences employing intransitive verbs, (3) sentences containing "object-taking" verbs, (4) sentences requiring a "transitive verb of the senses," and (5) passive sentences (although transformations of Type 3, they are listed separately for purposes of frequency count). Using Chomsky's (1965) theory, the authors posited that by applying the linguistic processes of expansion, conjoining, and transformation any English sentence can be generated, or reduced to one of or a combination of the five basic sentence types. They suggested that the LASS procedure provided a simplified inventory and a relatively quick analysis and gave valuable insights into the preparation of a clinical program.

Dever and Bauman based the Indiana Scale of Clausal Development (ISCD) on a slot-filler grammar and designed it to classify the spontaneous utterances of children whose chronological age was 18–40 months. The scale was not intended to indicate any specific stages within clausal development nor was it an attempt to describe clausal development in terms of the general development of children. It was an attempt at classifying language performance patterns. The scale was conceived of as being a scale of development within clauses and clause types (intraclause) and not as a scale which indicated generalized development across clauses (interclause). The expected outcome was that children would exhibit regular advances within clauses, but irregular development across clauses.

Lee and Canter (1971) developed a clinical procedure, developmental sentence scoring (DSS), intended to estimate the status and progress of children undergoing language training in a clinic. Lee and Canter predicted that by analyzing a child's spontaneous, tape-recorded speech sample, a clinician could estimate if a child had generalized rules sufficiently to use them in verbal performance. The DSS procedure gave weighted scores to a developmental order of different "parts of speech," specific morphological or syntactic constructions. Lee and Canter's objectives were to provide guidelines for planning lessons and estimating the status and rate of progress of children treated in a speech clinic.

Our purpose was to analyze these four techniques (DST, LASS, ISCD, DSS), to determine which procedures or parts of procedures best fulfilled the needs of the speech clinician.

METHOD

Subjects

Two females, Eve (CA 5.2) and Sara (CA 5.4), served as subjects. Subjects were chosen at the age of five, as it is with this age group that most clinicians first begin working with language-delayed clients.

Pretests

Eve was considered normal to advanced in language development by her parents, while Sara was undergoing therapy for delayed language. To describe further the differences between the two subjects a Peabody Picture Vocabulary Test (PPVT, Form A) (Dunn, 1965) was administered, and a 50-response speech sample was collected from each subject (Templin, 1957; Johnson, Darley, and Spriestersbach, 1963). From these samples a mean length of response (MLR) (Templin, 1957), type-token ratio (TTR) (Siegel, 1967), and a length-complexity index score (LCI) (Miner, 1969) were computed. Stimuli used to elicit the samples were multicolored action pictures (W 2, 4, 6, 7, 10, and 12) from the "I wonder" series of the Peabody Language Development Kit, Level #2 (Dunn and Smith, 1967). The results of these analyses appear in Table 1.

TABLE 1. Pretest differences between the two subjects.

Source	Eve (CA, 5.2)	Sara (CA, 5.4)	Difference
PPVT			
VIQ	116.0	90.0	26.0
MA	6.8	4.5	2.3
%-ile	89.0	23.0	66.0
MLR	5.96	3.00	2.96
TTR	0.772	0.546	0.226
LCI	5.80	3.40	2.40

Experimental Setting

The speech samples used to compare the four linguistic analysis procedures were collected in the Language Acquisition Laboratory at Kansas State University. The experimental room was free of distracting visual or auditory stimuli and the tape recorder (TEAC, TCA40) was housed in an adjacent room.

Testing Situation and Stimulus Materials

An additional set of "I wonder" pictures (W 1, 3, 5, 8, 9, and 11) from the Peabody Language Development Kit were used to elicit the samples during two sessions with each subject. Three pictures were used during each session.

Procedure

Each subject was brought individually to the experimental room and seated at a table. After rapport was gained, the examiner presented one of the elicitation pictures and said, "What is happening here?" The subject was then allowed to tell a story about or discuss the picture however she wished. The examiner attempted to encourage the child to talk by saying, "Yes," "Really," and nodding her head. Occasionally the examiner would say, "Is there more? Can you tell me more?"

Initial Protocol Preparation. After all sessions were completed, typewritten, verbatim transcripts were prepared from the tape recordings. The general procedures for preparing these protocols were similar to those used by Siegel (1963). A graduate student in speech pathology, experienced in protocol preparation, retyped a portion of the tape recording from each subject for reliability purposes. The interexaminer reliability coefficient for protocol preparation was 0.96 for Eve's sample and 0.94 for Sara's.

Segmentation. The corpora were segmented into manageable units following the procedures of Engler and Hannah (1967) after the general intent of Hockett (1958). For the present study, an utterance was defined as a unit of spoken language preceded and followed by a perceived pause (sustained pitch) or terminated by some change in inflection (rising or falling intonation). While listening to the tape recording the experimenter segmented the corpus into utterances by marking a slash (/) on the protocol corresponding with the pauses.

Final Protocol Preparation. The decision was made to use a corpus of 100 utterances for each subject in the analysis. An equal number of utterances was selected from each of the two sessions for both of the subjects. The middle 50 utterances spoken during each session were then retyped into a protocol containing one utterance per line, and the lines were numbered to expedite analysis.

Linguistic Analysis. The experimenter closely followed the specific method described by the authors of each of the four analysis procedures.

Because Lee and Canter used a highly readable table to present the method of scoring in their DSS procedure, the other three procedures were arranged in a similar tabular form, with the utterances from one to 100 presented on the vertical and the various classifications or categories appearing on the horizontal at the top of the page. (All of the data tables and a complete list of the subjects' utterances are available from ASIS/NAPS c/o Microfiche Publications, 305 East 46th Street, New York, New York 10017.)

Comparison Procedures. The four linguistic analyses were compared according to four criteria: ease of application, interscorer reliability, ability to discriminate language differences between the two children, and ability to describe specifically the differences between the two children.

Under the ease of application criterion we attempted to assess whether a great deal of background in linguistics or knowledge of specific terminology was needed to apply the procedure, also whether the written directions were sufficient to apply each procedure. This we assessed by seeing if another, equally skilled scorer would produce the same results given the same language samples and instructions. After the experimenter applied each procedure, a second scorer with similar training applied the four procedures. A percentage of agreement for each of the four procedures was computed from these recordings.

Since the primary linguistic data from each subject were categorized and classified in tabular form, visual assessment could be made as to whether the individual procedure seemed to discriminate between the two children. Also of interest was whether application of the procedure would describe specifically the differences between the two children.

RESULTS AND DISCUSSION

Developmental Sentence Types

Lee's (1966) DST procedure was a quasitransformational approach designed to classify utterances elicited from children. Lee apparently assumed the procedures used in eliciting the speech samples from the children were irrelevant to the results of her analysis, because she used different elicitation procedures for the two children she studied. Lee suggests that she designed her DST categories to mirror language development in normal children; however, DST appears to follow closely Chomsky's early (1957) description of adult grammar. Although Chomsky's transformational description of the grammar of English follows a specific order, there has been no evidence that this same order describes the development of language in children.

We observed, as did Bloom (1967) in her criticism of DST, that the scorers had to learn Lee's unique categories in order to analyze the utterances in terms of their form and distribution and then classify them on the basis of co-occurrence. It appeared to us that the only real developmental sequence in Lee's procedure was a repetition of terms at each hierarchical level. It was necessary for the scorer to classify according to the hierarchical progression of levels (for example, word, phrase, construction, sentence), because it was virtually impossible to follow the example type of instructions given by Lee. The interscorer agreement was 86% for Eve's and 84% for Sara's sample.

Different scatter was observed in the arrays of the two subjects. Eve scored almost exclusively at the sentence level and showed only a minimal amount of lower level (for example, word, phrase, construction) usage. Sara's array scattered a great deal more. A high percentage of Sara's utterances were classified at the construction level, while a number were also classified at the next lower level of phrase. Sara's remaining utterances scattered greatly from one-word naming responses up to the sentence level. Thus, DST discriminates between the two children. These results indicate that DST provided an accurate means of discriminating between the development of the two children's language samples. For describing the difference between the two samples the examiners felt that DST was no more informative than simply classifying the children's utterances by levels of development; for example, word, phrase, construction, sentence. DST was not, as Lee claimed, transformational. It simply followed the traditional, structural, hierarchical arrangement from sound to sentence. It appeared that Lee's DST procedure was simply a pairing of traditional (naming) and structural (levels) grammatical functions with groups of utterances without regard to the function of the utterance.

Indiana Scale of Clausal Development

Dever and Bauman's ISCD at first appeared to be a complicated procedure but proved to be easily applied. Although multiple ranks, classifications, and subclassifications were employed, they were easily understood through the excellent tagmemic descriptions given. Any ambiguity of rank, slot, or filler was avoided by the inclusion of sufficient rules to resolve discrepancies. ISCD clarified the definition of utterance by allowing contextual circumstances to indicate to what extent the utterance was accepted. For example, ISCD allowed questionable child utterances to be expanded to adult-like utterances which facilitated classification. Interscorer agreement of ISCD was 93% and 90% for Eve and Sara, respectively, which suggests that instructions for applying ISCD were relatively clear and sufficient.

The results of the ISCD showed different patterns of scatter for the two children. Overall, the array revealed Eve's clausal development was approximately one rank ahead of Sara's and her discourse was of the more developed narrative style rather than simply naming. Eve's performance within the declarative clause category revealed some evidence of Rank I ellipsed-constructions and an occasional completed utterance. Classification in Rank II was limited to only a few completed utterances under characterization and action. Rank III received a heavy concentration of completed characterization and action utterances with few ellipsed-action utterances and no question or imperative clause types. Eve's scoring at the sentence level showed small increases to Rank III, where a large number of utterances were classified as completed utterances.

Sara showed a small amount of declarative labeling but concentrated the majority of her declarative utterances under the completed characterization category. Sara's sample showed a heavy concentration of utterances classified in Rank II, while only a few occupied Ranks I and III. Some scoring appeared for the ellipsed action utterances of Rank II, while Rank III held a sizeable number of completed action utterances. As in Eve's sample, Sara uttered few question and imperative clauses and only one utterance under the sentence classification.

The ISCD procedure suggested areas where clause development between ranks could be enhanced for both subjects. Failure to score under certain clause type classifications probably did not show a failure of the ISCD procedure, but rather a lack of such utterances in the corpora. An isolated passive construction which occurred in Sara's sample was not enough to indicate the presence of such constructions in her overall speech. The ISCD adequately achieved its purpose in classification of utterances and certainly extends much further than the 17- to 40-month range indicated by Dever and Bauman.

Linguistic Analysis of Speech Samples

Engler, Hannah, and Longhurst's (1973) LASS was the most complex of the four procedures to apply and evaluate. This analysis presented an in-depth classification of possible verbs used by speakers of English. Extensive study of verb and verb forms was necessary for the scorer to use this procedure.

The elicitation method and instructions for segmenting the corpora in LASS were explicit and sufficient. This was the only procedure of the four that appeared to recognize the importance of the initial collection of the language samples to be analyzed. Elicitation and segmentation procedures followed well-established linguistic tradition.

Interscorer agreement of 80% for Eve and 78% for Sara was achieved, which reinforced the examiner's subjective judgments of the difficulty of applying this procedure.

As in the ISCD by Dever and Bauman, LASS allowed the context to be considered as an essential part of the utterance. This meant that utterances like "a bus" could be classified according to the corresponding adult-like utterance "This is a bus" instead of as a fragment.

Although different arrays were anticipated, both subjects showed essentially identical verb usage patterns. Both subjects' production was limited to the equational "be" verbs, intransitives, and object-taking transitives. Only Eve showed any evidence of verb development beyond these levels. It appeared the language of these two subjects was not advanced enough to be measured adequately by this procedure. We would predict from our experience with the measure that different arrays would appear as language development progressed.

The second part of this procedure deals with conventions for features of arrangement, or more specifically: word order; inflection (grammatical forms); concord (subject-verb agreement); government (case filler in correct case slot); the use of function words (such as the use of articles with nouns, the use of *of* to indicate possessive); and intonation (pitch, stress, and juncture).

The samples from both subjects showed development in features of inflection, concord, and government. Eve's sample provided only rare instances of ungrammatical form and it could be generally accepted that these features had been incorporated into her rule system for English production. On the other hand, Sara's sample provided frequent violations of the rules governing these features and it became apparent that she had not internalized these rules.

Eve's intonation patterns closely followed those of adult grammar. Sara's intonation appeared in an extremely exaggerated form. Stress was often misplaced, causing incomprehensibility of the utterance. Her pitch peaked or ebbed but seldom held a consistent form. Juncture was also a factor in utterance comprehensibility. Both subjects used function words, but the use of such words frequently enriched and expanded Eve's performance while Sara's grammar resembled more closely the Pivot-X type of construction (Braine, 1963).

While the LASS procedure of classifying utterances did not discriminate between the two subjects, the feature analysis proved to be particularly discriminative. None of the other procedures incorporated an observation of these features of arrangement in the detail used by LASS.

Developmental Sentence Scoring

Lee and Canter's (1971) DSS procedure was found to be the simplest of the four procedures to apply. Analysis was precast into tabular form and scoring instructions were relatively simple although sometimes incomplete. Interscorer agreement for DSS was 82% for Eve and 79% for Sara. In most instances these scoring discrepancies were due to arbitrary interpretation which allowed the scorers to score the utterance differently. No background information outside of the DSS instructions was found to be necessary to apply the procedure.

Some disagreement was found between Lee's "sentence" and the definition of utterance used in our study.

Of the 100 utterances collected from each child, only 69 of Eve's and 32 of Sara's were scorable using the DSS procedure. This may indicate that Sara's development was not sufficient for the DSS procedure to be used appropriately.

Seventy-seven percent of Eve's 69 scored utterances received sentence points. Average scores were: indefinite pronouns, 1.468; personal pronouns, 2.254; primary verbs, 2.407; secondary verbs, 3.058; negatives, 2.444; and conjunctions, 3.100. When Eve's DSS score of 9.080 was compared with the scores of Lee and Canter's normative group, she scored in the fiftieth percentile for her chronological age group. Of Sara's 32 scorable sentences, only 16% received sentence points. A DSS score was not computed for Sara because DSS must be computed on 50 utterances and thus her sample was unscorable.

Sara's array showed a heavy concentration toward the left-hand side (less developed) of the table while Eve's scoring scattered somewhat more, thus indicating more advanced development. A noticeable void was in Sara's secondary verb column, where she only scored once.

Throughout the use of DSS the breakdown in the categories of primary and secondary verbs bore remarkable resemblance to the Engler, Hannah, and Longhurst (1973) classification of verbs. Similarly, DSS application of "sentence point" echoes the LASS convention for features of arrangement. DSS does not extend the sentence point strategy far enough to hold the validity that the LASS method of describing features of arrangement does.

Overall, DSS tended to describe the subject's performance at a lower level than the other procedures or pretests indicated (for example, Eve ranked at the 89th percentile on the PPVT). It also failed to score the sample from Sara, whose Peabody language age was well within the defined age limits indicated by the procedure. Although certain utterances should have been classified in specific categories, DSS rules disallowed their classification, while there were other ambiguous instances where one entry could be classified in more than one way. These features probably lead to the lower interscorer agreement.

SUMMARY AND CONCLUSIONS

None of the four linguistic procedures investigated proved to be completely explicit and sufficient for analyzing the speech of children. All four, with the exception of DSS, would require some special training in linguistics, and each uses some unique terminology, particularly the ISCD by Dever and Bauman and the LASS by Engler, Hannah, and Longhurst (1973). These procedures, however, represent a much more detailed approach to the assessment of children's language performance than traditional methods (Kirk and Kirk, 1971; Mecham, Jex, and Jones, 1962; Johnson, Darley, and Spriestersbach, 1963).

Application of tagmemic analysis (ISCD, LASS) by slot-filler evaluation appeared to handle the two language samples in this study most adequately. Tagmemic analysis accounted for intraclause development in the ISCD and for verb development in the LASS procedures. Because of the detailed definition of a slot that must occur before a filler may be chosen, arbitrary categories are usually avoided with these procedures.

A renewed interest in basic structural linguistic concepts could prove valuable to the assessment of language development in children. This interest should be focused on such topics as analyzing how verbs develop at six-month intervals or how the various "features of arrangement" develop, much as the LASS procedure suggests. These data may then shed light on possible remedial techniques to alleviate verb deficiencies or arrangement difficulties in language-handicapped children. Dever and Bauman's ISCD should also be extended to include sentence and discourse development as well as normative data at various age levels.

Application of all four linguistic procedures emphasized the need for more complete and accurate normative data. Without appropriate normative data, it is difficult for a clinician to know whether a child she has examined exhibits normal development or whether the performance deviates far enough from the norm to raise concern.

In a real sense, success of the application of these linguistic procedures depends on the representativeness of the language sample that is obtained from the child. We know very little about the elicitation variables that may influence the quantity or quality of the language sample obtained. Variables, such as the examiner, stimulus materials, instructions, and elicitation situation need to be investigated. Eventually a standardized elicitation method must be evolved to make comparison with normative data meaningful and to allow interinvestigation comparisons of linguistic research findings.

ACKNOWLEDGMENT

This work was supported in part by grants HD-00870 and HD-02528 from the Department of Health, Education, and Welfare, Public Health Service, National Institute of Child Health and Human Development. The critical review of Leo F. Engler is gratefully acknowledged, and special grants from the Bureau of General Research, Kansas State University. The work reported in this paper was utilized by Schrandt as a master's report at Kansas State University, in 1972. She is currently affiliated with the University of Maryland, European Division.

REFERENCES

BLOOM, L. M., A comment on Lee's "Developmental sentence types: A method for comparing normal and deviant syntactic development." *J. Speech Hearing Dis.*, **32**, 294-296 (1967).

BRAINE, M. D., The ontogeny of English phrase structure: The first phase. *Language*, **39**, 1-13 (1963).

CHOMSKY, N., *Syntactic Structures*. The Hague: Mouton (1957).

CHOMSKY, N., *Aspects of the Theory of Syntax*. Cambridge: MIT (1965).

DUNN, L. M., *Peabody Picture Vocabulary Test*. Minneapolis: American Guidance Service (1965).

DUNN, L. M., and SMITH, J. O., *Peabody Language Development Kit*. Circle Pines, Minn.: American Guidance Service (1967).

ENGLER, L., and HANNAH, E., Juncture phenomena and the segmentation of a linguistic corpus. *Lang. Speech*, **10**, 228-233 (1967).

ENGLER, L. F., HANNAH, E. P., and LONGHURST, T. M., Linguistic analysis of speech samples: A practical guide for clinicians. *J. Speech Hearing Dis.*, **38**, 192-204 (1973).

HOCKETT, C. F., A course in modern linguistics. New York: MacMillan (1958).

JOHNSON, W., DARLEY, F. L., and SPRIESTERSBACH, D. C., *Diagnostic Methods in Speech Pathology*. New York: Harper, 160-187 (1963).

KIRK, S. A., and KIRK, W. D., *Phycolinguistic Learning Disabilities: Diagnosis and Remediation*. Chicago: Univ. of Ill. (1971).

LEE, L. Developmental sentence types. *J. Speech Hearing Dis.*, **31**, 311-330 (1966).

LEE, L. L., and CANTER, S. M., Developmental sentence scoring: A clinical procedure for estimating syntactic development in children's spontaneous speech. *J. Speech Hearing Dis.*, **36**, 315-340 (1971).

MECHAM, M. J., JEX, L. T., and JONES, J. D., *Utah Test of Language Development*. Salt Lake City, Utah: Woodruff Printing (1967).

MINER, L. E., Scoring procedures for the length-complexity index: A preliminary report. *J. commun. Dis.*, **2**, 224-240 (1969).

SIEGEL, G. M., Appendix H: Prototypes for instructions to typists. In *J. Speech Hearing Dis. Monogr. Supp. 10* (1963).

SIEGEL, G. M., Interpersonal approaches to the study of communication disorders. *J. Speech Hearing Dis.*, **32**, 112-120 (1967)

TEMPLIN, M., *Certain Language Skills in Children*. Minneapolis: Univ. of Minnesota (1957).

LANGUAGE ASSESSMENT: THE CO-OCCURRING AND RESTRICTED STRUCTURE PROCEDURE

John R. Muma

INTRODUCTION

Although generative grammars are not specifically addressed to pedagogical issues (Rosenbaum, 1969), several major pedagogical ramifications derive from concepts issuing from the literature on generative grammars. Among these ramifications are some conceptual and procedural issues concerning language assessment.

Consider, for the moment, the nature of the evidence about generative grammars, particularly the evidence on the emergence or acquisition of generative capacities. Concommitantly, consider the strategies for obtaining such evidence. Paraphrasing Menyuk (1971), the pursuit of generative grammars has formalized our inquiries concerning *what* is acquired and provided for more systematic inquiries into *why* and *how* language is acquired. Menyuk merely restated Chomsky's (1957, 1965) call for descriptive accounts of generative grammars which would hopefully lead to explanatory accounts.

Traditionally, language assessment has been in terms of products of a language, i.e. mean sentence length, inventory of word classes such as nouns, verbs, etc., sentence types, and so on. Operationally, these products were typically inventoried or scaled and related to either developmental or item-difficulty norms. The works on generative grammars, on the other hand, have virtually defined product-oriented approaches as superficial because they have not been addressed to grammatical mechanisms or capacities which produce language products. The first major ramification then, is that evidence on generative grammars indicates that it is more important to understand operations and functions of underlying grammatical mechanisms and systems than to inventory or otherwise assess in terms of language products. Language products. can be used to appreciate underlying mechanisms, but they should not be taken in their stead.

Second, recent works notably by Bloom (1970), but including **Brown**, Cazden, and Bellugi-Klima (1969), Lewis (1972), Lewis and Freedle (1972), and Bowerman (1971) among others, have clearly shown that language structure and

ACTA SYMBOLICA, 1973, vol. 4, pp. 12-29.

331

function are intimately related. Indeed, environmental referents are the primary determinants of structure; structure should be ascertained according to functional contexts. A corollary is the distinction between surface and deep structure. Surface structure is that which is manifest (visual code or auditory code). Deep structure pertains to underlying meaning. Surface structure merely acts as a tagging or mapping system for underlying concepts. Language structure pertains to these tagging and mapping operations whereas language function pertains to the underlying meaning of utterances. The distinction between surface and deep structure underscores the need for a priority for underlying mechanisms over products in language assessment. Underlying mechanisms permit one to convert his thoughts (deep structure) into a mutually coded form (surface structure). Inasmuch as one has innumerable ways of expressing a thought, the end-product − a specific form − is not as important as his mechanisms for producing the end-product.

The intimacy between form and function and their corollaries, surface and deep structure, has profound ramifications for language assessment. Specifically, it is imperative that assessment be undertaken in natural functional contexts rather than in formal tasks, because natural contexts provide an opportunity to more fully ascertain functional referents operating in the issuance of language products. This information offers an opportunity to describe the operations of underlying grammatical mechanisms and systems. This does not mean that formal tasks should be omitted from assessment. On the contrary, formal tasks may provide important *supplementary* information.

Third, and in extension of the second, language assessment should be focused on two important issues − grammatical context and referential context. Referential context defines the type of grammatical structures at hand whereas grammatical context reveals semantic-syntactic constraints and organization. It is these grammatical contexts − ascertained according to referential context − that offer an opportunity to appreciate underlying grammatical mechanisms.

Operationally, referential context is defined as apparent situational referents (Lewis and Freedle, 1972). These referents are very useful for ascertaining structure. Bloom (1970) showed that utterances that appear to be the same in surface structure actually vary in deep structure or underlying meaning. She showed, for example, that no less than five different interpretations could be made for "Mommy" in a series of child utterances. It was necessary to appeal to situational referents in order to ascertain meaning because form was superficially the same. And of course, there were occasions in which the situational referents were not always apparent. Grammatical contexts can be defined operationally in terms of co-occurrence with attendant orientation to restricted and adult forms.

Traditional assessment approaches contrast sharply with generative approaches. The primary motivation of traditional approaches seemed to be a resolution of language deviance (difference or pathology). Generative approaches strive to portray one's underlying mechanisms as they function in the issuance of products. Traditional approaches typically resolve language deviance through quantification of products which are referenced to developmental norms (Developmental Sentence Types, Lee, 1966; Developmental Sentence Scores, Lee and Canter, 1971; Koenigsknecht and Lee, 1971) and/or scaled item difficulty (ITPA; Kirk, McCarthy, and Kirk, 1968). Generative approaches achieve description of underlying mechanisms by ascertaining structure via function and by portraying structure in both referential and grammatical contexts. While quantitative-normative approaches presumably resolve issues concerning language deviance, they are relatively weak in predicating intervention. For example, a clinician who has just obtained an aberrant mean utterance length, complexity score (Frank and Osser, 1970), developmental sentence weight, ITPA subtest score is faced with a testing problem in trying to appreciate the relevance of these and other similar indices in intervention. These kinds of data are categorical. Their relevance to intervention is obscure and left essentially to intuition. On the other hand, descriptive approaches are weak in resolving deviance, but relatively strong in predicating intervention by virtue of the fact that they are addressed to an account of grammatical mechanisms and systems as they operate in one's functional environment.

Under the assumptions that a sufficiently representative language sample has been obtained (usually requiring several samples in varying situations) and that the situational referents were sufficiently documented to identify the semantic significance of structures at hand, a partial description of selected grammatical systems can be achieved. Evidence the works on negations and questions by Bellugi (1965); Klima (1965); Klima and Bellugi-Klima (1969); Brown, Cazden, and Bellugi-Klima, (1969) and Leach (1972). And of course, evidence the works by Bloom (1970, 1972), McNeill (1966, 1970), Menyuk (1969, 1971) and others which provide descriptive evidence on the acquisition of grammatical systems. Descriptive evidence such as this is potentially valuable for investing intervention efforts. This evidence merely suggests in which dimensions or systems of grammar to invest one's efforts, but not necessarily *how*. Remember descriptive evidence is provided, *not explanatory evidence*.

I have indicated that co-occurring and restricted structures when ascertained in a functional context offer an assessment approach that is rich in descriptive power. Moreover, the assumption is made that a sufficiently representative spontaneous language sample is available for evaluation. Let us proceed by discussing the concepts of target structures, co-occurrence, restricted structure, and the operational procedure in which these concepts are employed.

TARGET STRUCTURE

Ideally clinicians should write a complete grammar for their clients. Then clinicians could appreciate the various grammatical systems in the context of other systems and their functions with a variety of situational referents. Such an enterprise is much too time consuming and undoubtedly beyond our present appreciation of grammatical systems and their interface with cognitive systems and situational referents.

Clinicians are severely limited in the amount of time they have for each client. Yet, descriptive evidence is potentially very useful for appreciating underlying grammatical systems and subsequently for increasing one's efficiency and effectiveness in intervention. The co-occurring and restricted structures procedure represents a compromise in which clinicians can obtain descriptive evidence for selected underlying grammatical mechanisms and systems, thereby affording an opportunity to utilize such evidence in intervention. The compromise is an obtainment of descriptive evidence for selected dimensions of grammar rather than a complete grammar. Under this compromise, clinicians run the risk of obtaining descriptive evidence for grammatical systems that are somewhat peripheral to a client's needs. The selection of target structures or systems becomes a major issue because of this risk. There is, however, a twofold strategy which increases the likelihood that an appropriate target is selected. First, any grammatical structure or system can be chosen. That is to say, there is no *a priori* list of structures that should be target structures. Second, a client's language performance is the determinant of target structures. That is, clinicians should select a target structure on the basis of a preliminary perusal of representative language samples. Such a perusal will direct one's focus to those grammatical systems in which a client apparently has difficulty. As an indication of the range of systems, the following is merely a brief list of possible targets: nominal systems, adverbial systems, auxiliary systems, predicate systems, interrogative systems, negation systems, pronoun systems, etc.

Upon perusal, clinicians will realize several important things. First, 'errors' are not always limited to the same grammatical systems. Second, within any given grammatical system a variety of 'errors' occurs. Third, within any given grammatical system a specific structure may be found in an adult form and also in 'error' forms. Fourth, on repeated samples a given grammatical system may appear 'errorless' in some samples, but laden with 'errors' in other samples. There are legitimate reasons for these variations. Not incidentally, such variations are virtually obscured in quantitative-normative procedures, but become evident in generative description. These variations reflect dynamic operations. They reflect contextual learning, partial learning, operantly determined loci of learning and switching of loci of learning (Menyuk, 1963a, b, 1964a, b, c, 1969, 1971; Brown, Cazden, and Bellugi-Klima, 1969; Bloom, 1970, 1972; Nelson, 1970, 1971; McNeill 1966, 1970). The co-occurring and restricted structures procedure partially parcels out these operations on a descriptive level, thereby affording a clinician an opportunity to selectively deal with them. Co-occurrence clearly reveals contextual constraints, loci of learning and switching of loci. Restricted structures portray partial learning. Collectively, these concepts provide new insight for a phenomenon such as a 'dampened oscillatory function' in the progressive reduction of errors and error types reported by Menyuk (1963a, 1964b). Marked increases in errors could easily result from a child's venture into new grammatical systems, whereas marked reductions could be due to his selective utilization of relatively familiar systems. And even with familiar systems, variations in co-occurring structures could result in alterations in adult and restricted forms.

With these potentially significant variations in language samples, the selection of target structures becomes important. What assurance does a clinician have that he will select relevant target structures? There is no absolute assurance, only relative assurance. And, it is only after descriptive evidence is obtained and employed in intervention and effectiveness of intervention determined that relevance can be ascertained either through estimation or quantification. Nevertheless, the probabilities of appropriate selection can be significantly increased in this procedure, because we are dealing with a highly integrated and dynamic system. That is to say, virtually any given grammatical system is relevant to one degree or another simply by virtue of the fact that the systems are integrated with each other. Operationally, the selection of one target will, at some point, be relevant to other potential targets because the underlying systems are integrated. Because this holds for all potential targets, generalization from one target to another is to be expected in intervention.

Thus, the first point concerning relevance of a target structure is that a target structure must be a grammatical system rather than a product of grammar. Therefore, even if the particular system that was initially selected may not be immediately germane to a client's needs, it will at some point be pertinent to another system with which it integrates.

This leads to the second point: an initial target selection can serve to direct assessment and intervention to other specific grammatical systems by virtue of emerging patterns of co-occurring and restricted structures. For example, an initial target might be the auxiliary system. Upon obtainment and perusal of co-occurring and restricted structures for the auxiliary system, it may be apparent that another system has richer descriptive evidence and therefore affords greater opportunity for selecting alternatives in intervention. 'Richness' in this sense refers to an increased range of co-occurrences and patterns of adult and restricted structures.

Third, clinicians have the prerogative of choosing as many target structures as needed for directing the nature and course of intervention. Said differently, the purpose of descriptive evidence is to account for the operations of various grammatical systems as they function in the context of each other and in various situations. Such accounts provide numerous hypotheses about these mechanisms which are directly relevant to intervention. Alternative target structures have the potential of reducing the number of hypotheses because they provide descriptive evidence on mechanisms from differing perspectives. This serves as a convergent methodology in narrowing down assessment (McCaffrey, 1969).

Notice that the selection of target structures is open. They are not limited to a set of a priori structures. Determination of targets can be as many as a clinician deems useful. Moreover, the levels of description for any given target structure are open. In some instances, a very elaborate portrayal of co-occurring structures may be sought whereas in other instances only a relatively few co-occurrences may be sought. The determining factor is the nature of available evidence rather than an *a priori* set of structures preferred by a clinician or contained in norms.

Operationally, I have found it useful to select target structures in the following way. First, scan representative language samples for an initial identification of potential systems with which a client (adult aphasic, child with delayed language, deaf child, retarded child, etc.) has some difficulty. Second, initially select a grammatical system in which there are adult structures as well as restricted structures. Third, select a system in which there are many instances thereby affording an opportunity to obtain rich patterns of co-occurrences and restrictions. Fourth, set aside for the moment those instances in which there is some suspicion that they were produced on a rote basis rather than generative basis. Fifth, look at sentence types before examining specific systems. Sentence types can be viewed as grammatical matrices in which various systems operate. Muma (1971) showed that at the four year level children have a decided preference for certain transformational operations on certain sentence types. Harris (1957), Thomas (1965), Muma (1971) outlined basic sentence types of English. By following these five steps, clinicians will come up with a list of two to four systems that appear to be relevant.

Clinicians should, for motivational reasons, select target systems that show a moderate degree of difficulty. Such systems could encourage the client because there are some instances in which he does well (produces adult structures). These systems would also show the need for intervention because of the instances in which he produces 'errors' (restricted structures). And, systems with moderate difficulty should be expected to generalize to other systems as one obtains increased capacity or knowledge.

Harris (1957) provided a formal description of co-occurrence in syntax. Indeed, his original work also included transformational operations. The concept of co-occurrence pertains to semantic systems (Hutchins, 1971, Fodor and Katz, 1965), syntactic systems (Chomsky, 1957, 1965) and phonology (Halle, 1965a, b; Chomsky and Halle, 1968). And, it should be stressed that co-occurrence is a salient dimension among semantics, syntax, and phonology. In recent years, the evidence on language acquisition has been strongly influenced by the principle of co-occurrence. In the developmental literature, co-occurrence is dealt with in terms of grammatical contexts and referential contexts. In grammatical contexts, the emergence of certain target structures is described as a function of other grammatical structures. Bellugi (1965), Brown, Cazden, and Bellugi-Klima (1969), and Klima and Bellugi-Klima (1965) have described the emergence of the negation and interrogative systems in terms of stages in which co-occurring structures were given. In referential contexts, contingencies and referents for grammatical events are given (Bloom, 1970; Lewis and Freedle, 1972).

As stated previously, the present discussion of co-occurrence is in terms of grammatical co-occurrence. Moreover, it is assumed that situational referents were used to resolve structural forms under consideration. Grammatical co-occurrence pertains to those structures that co-exist in structural relationships to each other. A crude, but nonetheless instructive, example will illustrate co-occurrence. Given the sentence, *The boy opened the big box*, some co-occurrences for the common noun in the subject (target) can be readily shown.

Target	boy
Co-occurrence	*the* boy
Co-occurrence	*the* boy *open(ed)* *((the) box)*
Co-occurrences	*the* boy *open(ed)* *((the (big)) box)*

Because we are primarily interested in underlying grammatical systems rather than products, the above example should be converted into a schematic of underlying grammatical systems which (in concert) issued these structures.

Target	N					
	subject-					
	animate					
	definite					
Co-occurrences:	article	"				
Co-occurrences:	"	"past transitive	NP			
		tense verb	object-modified			
			inanimate			
Co-occurrences:	"	" " "	definite	adjective	N	
			article		Object	
					inanimate	

We can see that co-occurring structures are any that have a contextual relationship to a target structure. While we intuitively feel that adjacent structures probably affect a target structure, it turns out that certain non-adjacent structures also appear to affect a target structure. These data appear below in Tables 1 and 2. Accordingly, it behooves us to consider several patterns of co-occurrences for target structures of interest. Over a language sample, or indeed several samples, one could obtain a very rich pattern of co-occurrences for a target structure. Such a pattern would indicate the contextual effects of certain adjacent structures, sentence frame types, levels and types of modification or lack of modification, etc.

RESTRICTED STRUCTURES

Children do not possess a full knowledge of adult language. Accordingly, their utterances are sometimes the same as those of adults and sometimes different. Moreover, a child's utterances may have some parts that are the same as adult forms and some parts that are different. A number of studies have been made on children's utterances. The evidence is clear that the differences between adult and child utterances are not attributable to mistakes by children because the differences follow certain highly predictable patterns. Mistakes are errors; they are the result of incorrect applications of rules. But child utterances typically do not contain errors; they are simply the result of grammatical rules that are not as fully defined as adult rules. A child has limited or restricted knowledge in comparison to an adult. Accordingly, children's utterances are restricted structures rather than 'errors'.

Children do not learn adult language directly. They move through a series of stages in progressive approximation of adult grammatical knowledge. The studies on emergence of negations and questions show that there are at least three major stages. Studies on the acquisition of inflections reveal three developmental stages: vocabulary, discrimination and overgeneralization of rules, and appropriate rule generalization (Cazden, 1968; Palermo and Eberhart, 1968). Studies on concept developmental reveal stages: perceptual classes, idiosyncratic functional classes, appropriate functional classes (Bruner, 1964). Studies on word associations show that children shift from syntagmatic to paradigmatic responses (Brown and Berko, 1960; Entwisle, Forsyth, and Muuss, 1964). In grammatical structure, progressive approximations from restricted to adult structures have been described in terms of types of restricted structures. Menyuk (1964a, b; 1964b, c) showed that children progress from omissions to substitutions to redundancies to adult forms. The following are examples of these restricted structures:

Omission	This green
Substitution	He took me at the circus
Redundancy	That's mines

The following examples show restricted structures for the auxiliary, i.e. progressive and tense.

Omission	He be running yesterday
Substitution	He is running yesterday
Redundancy	He ranned yesterday
Adult	He was running yesterday

Patterns of restricted structures appear to index the locus of learning for grammatical systems. That is, restricted structures identify which systems and particular dimensions of systems in which mastery is in progress. Moreover, the type of restricted structure identifies the status of progress.

Notice that the criterion for determining a restricted structure is whether or not a given structure appears in an adult form for a particular language or dialect. This is a very important matter because it raises the distinction between language differences and language deficits in assessment. Traditionally, any language differences between adult structures of a prestigious dialect and either a child's restricted utterances or utterances by non-prestigious speakers were regarded as errors. Subsequently, these 'errors' became targets for compensatory intervention. The fallacy of this traditional policy was a failure to make the distinction between language differences that indexed development ('restricted structures') and dialect variation. 'They runned home' contains a restricted structure. However, the following two sentences do not contain restricted structures, but dialect variations from Standard English. (a) I bes here. (b) We got fifteen cent. Their respective Standard English counterparts are (a) I am here. and (b) We got fifteen cents. Notice that the underlying or deep structure is the same between the dialect and Standard English sentences, but the surface structure is different. The implication is that before a judgment is made about restricted structures, it is imperative that the structure in question is not a dialect variant.

CORS: OPERATIONAL PROCEDURE

CORS is simply an acronym for the co-occurring and restricted structures procedure. It is when observations on co-occurring and restricted structures are made in concert that the descriptive power becomes apparent.

Once a target structure is chosen, the procedure becomes a relatively simple straightforward matter. All utterances containing the target are separated out for study. These utterances should be grouped by sentence type. Within these types, systematic portrayals of co-occurrences can be made.

And, the patterns of restricted and adult structures for these co-occurrences describe the level of attainment. Notice that clinicians can portray restricted and adult forms for both the target structure and co-occurring structures. It is operationally convenient to set up an array of restricted and adult forms of the target structure for each sentence type. An examination of these arrays usually reveals significant co-occurrences. Usually, it turns out that restricted structures occur in the context of certain co-occurring structures whereas adult forms of the same dimension of a system occur in different contexts. Evidence of this type can lead to direct and specific intervention alternatives.

The CORS procedure is very flexible because there are no *a priori* structures of interest. This flexibility means that the assessment procedure is adaptive to a client's performance. Under the assumption that his performance is representative, the descriptive evidence obtained in CORS is relevant. CORS is flexible in both scope and level of description. It is flexible in scope because it extends, at least in principle, across any and all structures and systems available. It is flexible in level because it admits various types of restricted and adult structures.

The following is a brief example of the application of CORS on a few sentences that were constructed for this purpose.

(a) The boy was riding a bicycle.
(b) Some girl who were walking by stopped to watch.
(c) The big boys (singular) turned too fast and fell.
(d) Him bicycle was scratched but it was O.K.
(e) They giggled at he as him rode away.

Considering only the subject noun phrases as targets, let us describe them and classify them as adult or restricted.

	Adult	Restricted	Type
(a) The boy	X		
(b) Some girl who were walking by		X	Omission
(c) The big boys (singular)		X	Substitution
(d) *Him* bicycle		X	Substitution
(e) They	X		

Now the value of observations on co-occurrence can be shown. The first prominent observation for this series of sentences is that restricted structures co-occurred with various types of modifications on noun phrases. Moreover, nominal replacements such as 'for him to ride,' 'riding,' 'to ride,' etc. were not evidenced. Let us look within the co-occurrences for both adult and restricted structures in the hope of obtaining a definition of grammatical knowledge for noun phrases. Co-occurring structures for adult targets were also in the adult form. Moreover, they evidenced an expanded auxiliary in (a) and complement in (e). However, restricted structures in the target co-occurred with various types of noun phrase modifications (non-deleted relative clause) in (b), prenoun adjective modifier in (c), and possessive prenoun marker in (d). Obviously, it is necessary to obtain many sentences in order to fully appreciate the descriptive power, i.e. a descriptive definition of the grammatical contexts which influence the occurrence of adult or restricted forms of a target structure. Nonetheless, the above example provides suggestive evidence. Tentatively, it could be said that in this example adult forms of the subject noun phrase occur when the noun phrase is unmodified even though restricted structure occurred elsewhere in the utterances. Restricted structures occurred in co-occurrence with various types of modification on the subject noun phrase. Moreover, substitution-type restricted structures occurred when prenoun modification co-occurred, i.e. adjective+noun and possessive+noun. This particular example did not survey co-occurrences and restricted structures in reference to sentence types as suggested above because the distribution of sentence types was too limited (parenthetically, the sentence types for sentences a-e, respectively were: VT, VI comp, VI, VI, and VI comp).

Another illustration of CORS is provided by the data summaries in Tables 1 & 2. The target system in Table 1 is the auxiliary-progressive (be + ing) as underlined in 'The snails *are* dry*ing* up.' The target system in Table 2 is the auxiliary-perfect (have + participle) as underlined in 'The zebra *had spooked*.' These data are summaries of the types of co-occurrences and restricted structures that appeared in spoken language for four and five year old children.

Notice the patterns within each table and between the two tables. We see that restricted structures for both progressive and perfect occur as a function of co-occurring negation and interrogative transformations. Notice that when complex utterances are made, as in the last sentence for perfect and other expansions within the auxiliary and as in the last sentence for progressive, the pattern of restricted structure changes considerably. Notice also that the most prevalent site of restriction is the tense marker for both progressive and perfect. These tables contain only a meager sample and some suggestive evidence. A CORS assessment task entails 'filling-out' such suggestive evidence with more elaborate descriptive evidence so a clinician can make

342

Table 1. Some co-occurrences and restricted structures for some selected utterances containing the 'progressive.'

Target: progressive (be + ing)

Utterance	Co-occurrences	Restrictions
I going	Personal pronoun + tense + VI	(be) + ing
I going to da beach	Personal pronoun + tense + VI + Adverb-place	(be) + ing
What you reading	Personal pronoun + tense + VI + Wh transformation	(be) + ing
I not going	Personal pronoun + tense + VI + NOT transformation	(be) + ing and NOT for be
It always making me mad	Pronoun + tense + VI + personal pronoun + adjective complement + adverbial + adverbial shift	(be) + ing
He has been sleep	Personal pronoun + present + perfect + VI	be + (ing)

( ) = omission

Table 2. Some co-occurrences and restricted structures for some selected utterances containing the 'perfect.'

Utterance	Co-occurrences	Restrictions
He has get one	Personal pronoun + present + VT + indefinite pronoun	have + (participle)
I been to a party	Personal pronoun + tense + BE + adverbial-place	(have) + participle
That never been done	Relative pronoun + tense + BE + adverbial + negation transformation + adverbial shift	(have) + participle and NOT for have
You seen it?	Personal pronoun + tense + VT + pronoun + Yes/No transformation	(have) + participle
Teacher has just ask	Ø + common animate noun + past + VT + adverbial-time + VT deletion transformation + adverbial shift	have + participle

( ) = omission

intelligent choices about which dimensions of language to focus on in intervention.

SUMMARY

The CORS assessment procedure identifies and describes which grammatical systems a person is in the process of acquiring. This identification and description is in terms of co-occurring and restricted structures. Evidence of this sort offers a clinician an opportunity to selectively invest his efforts on specific systems in specific contexts rather than products of language.

REFERENCES

Bellugi, U., The development of questions and negatives in the speech of three children. Unpublished paper, Harvard University (1965).

Bloom, L., *Language Development: Form and Function in Emerging Grammars.* Cambridge: M.I.T. Press (1970).

Bloom, L., *One Word at a Time: The Use of Single-word Utterances Before Syntax.* The Hague: Mouton (1972).

Bowerman, M., Structural relationships in children's utterances: Syntactic or semantic? Research Training Paper No. 66. *Bureau of Child Research*, University of Kansas. Presented at the University of New York at Buffalo Summer Linguistic Institute (1971).

Brown, R. and Berko, J., Word association and the acquisition of grammar. *Child Development*, 31, 1-14 (1960).

Brown, R., Cazden, C. and Bellugi-Klima, U., The child's grammar from I to III. In Hill, J. (ed.), *Minnesota Symposia on Child Psychology*. Vol. 2. Minneapolis: University of Minnesota Press (1969).

Bruner, J., The course of cognitive growth. *American Psychologist*, 19, 1-15 (1964).

Cazden, C., The acquisition of noun and verb inflections. *Child Development*, 39, 433-448 (1968).

Chomsky, N., *Aspects of the Theory of Syntax*. Cambridge, Mass.: M.I.T. Press (1965).

Chomsky, N., and Halle, M., *The Sound Patterns of English*. New York: Harper and Row (1968).

Entwisle, D., Forsyth, D., and Muuss, R., The syntactic-paradigmatic shift in children's word associations. *J. Verbal Learning Verbal Behavior*, 3, 19-29 (1964).

Frank, S., and Osser, H., A psycholinguistic model of syntactic complexity. *Language and Speech*, 13, 38-53 (1970).

Halle, M., On the bases of phonology. In Fodor, J., and Katz, J. (Eds.), *The Structure of Language*. Englewood Cliffs, N.J.: Prentice Hall (1965).

Halle, M., Phonology in generative grammar. *Word*, 18, 54-72 (1962). Reproduced in Fodor, J. and Katz, J. (Eds.), *The Structure of Language*. Englewood Cliffs, N.J.: Prentice Hall (1965).

Harris, Z., Co-occurrence and transformation in linguistic structure. *Language*, 33, 283-340 (1957).

Hutchins, W., *The Generation of Syntactic Structures from a Semantic Base*. New York: Humanities Press (1971).

Katz, J., and Fodor, J., The structure of a semantic theory. In Fodor, J. and Katz, J. (Eds.), *The Structure of Language*. Englewood Cliffs, N.J.: Prentice Hall (1965).

Kirk, S., McCarthy, J., and Kirk, W., *The Illinois Test of Psycholinguistic Abilities* (revised edition). Urbana, Ill.: University of Illinois Press (1968).

Klima, E., Negation in English. In Fodor, J. and Katz, J. (Eds.), *The Structure of Language*. Englewood Cliffs, N.J.: Prentice Hall (1965).

Klima, E., and Bellugi-Klima, U., Syntactic regularities in the speech of children. In Reibel, D. and Schane, S. (Eds.), *Modern Studies in English*. Englewood Cliffs, N.J.: Prentice Hall, Inc. (1969).

Koenigsknecht, R., and Lee, L., Validity and reliability of developmental sentence scoring: a method for measuring syntactic development in children's spontaneous speech. Presented at *Am. Speech Hearing Association Annual Convention*, Chicago, Illinois (1971).

Lee, L., Developmental sentence types: a method for comparing normal and deviant syntactic development. *J. Speech Hearing Disorders*, 31, 311-320 (1966).

Lee, L., and Canter, S., Developmental sentence scoring: a clinical procedure for estimating syntactic development in children's spontaneous speech. *J. Speech Hearing Disorders*, 36, 315-340 (1971).

Lewis, M., State as an infant-environment interaction: An analysis of mother-infant behavior as a function of sex. *Merrill-Palmer Quarterly of Behavior and Development*, 18, 95-121 (1972).

Lewis, M., and Freedle, R., Mother-infant dyad: The cradle of meaning. Paper presented at a symposium on *Language and Thought*, University of Toronto (1972).

McCaffrey, A., Convergent methodologies and the study of language usage by children from differing sub-cultural environments. Paper presented at the *Society for Research in Child Development* (1969).

McNeill, D., Developmental psycholinguistics. In Smith, F., and Miller (Eds.), *The Genesis of Language*, Cambridge, Mass.: M.I.T. Press (1966).

McNeill, D., *The Acquisition of Language: The Study of Developmental Psycholinguistics*. New York: Harper & Row Publishers (1970).

Menyuk, P., A preliminary evaluation of grammatical capacity in children. *J. Verbal Learning Verbal Behavior*. 2, 429-439 (1963a).

Menyuk, P., Syntactic structures in the language of children. *Child Development*. 34, 407-422 (1963b).

Menyuk, P., Syntactic rules used by children from preschool through first grade. *Child Development*. 35, 533-546 (1964a).

Menyuk, P., Alternation of rules in children's grammar. *J. Verbal Learning Verbal Behavior*. 3, 480-488 (1964b).

Menyuk, P., Comparison of grammar of children with functionally deviant and normal speech. *J. Speech Hearing Research*. 7, 109-121 (1964c).

Menyuk, P., *The Acquisition and Development of Language*. Englewood Cliff, N.J.: Prentice-Hall (1971).

Menyuk, P., *Sentences Children Use*. Cambridge, Mass.: M.I.T. Press (1969).

Muma, J., Syntax of preschool fluent and dysfluent speech: A transformational analysis. *J. Speech Hearing Research*. 14, 428-441 (1971).

Nelson, K., Word and phrase learning strategies in early language acquisition. Unpublished paper, Yale University (1970).

Nelson, K., Pre-syntactic strategies for learning to talk. Paper presented to the Biennial Meeting of *SRCD*, Minneapolis (1971).

Palermo, D., and Eberhart, V., On the learning of morphological rules: An experimental analogy. *J. Verbal Learning Verbal Behavior*. 7, 337-344 (1968).

Rosenbaum, P., On the role of linguistics in the teaching of English. In Reibel, D., and Schane, S., *Modern Studies in English*. Englewood Cliffs, N.J.: Prentice-Hall (1969).

Thomas, O., *Transformational Grammar and the Teacher of English*. New York: Holt, Rinehart, & Winston (1965).